Hartwick

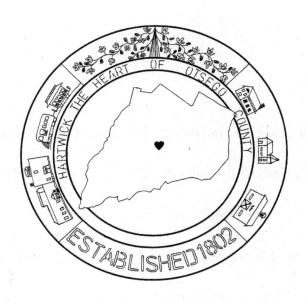

The Heart of
Otsego County, NY

Syl·la·bles Press

Hartwick, NY

Copyright 2002 by the Town of Hartwick Historical Society

Published by Syllables Press, Hartwick, NY

ISBN 0-9709433-0-X

Library of Congress Control Number: 2001098201

PRINTED IN THE UNITED STATES OF AMERICA

Dedication

This book is dedicated to Kenneth and Hilda Augur, Madge R. Hughes, Archie Ainslie and Ermagarde Gardner whose financial endowment made publication possible and to all the Hartwick Historical Society members, past and present, whose photography, research and writings are included in these pages.

Acknowledgments

This volume is the result of many people's dedication and hard work. The Hartwick Historical Society owes a debt of gratitude and many thanks to Faith Chase whose computer skills converted our manuscripts into the form necessary to submit to the publisher and to Barbara Potter who acted as "general chairman."

An equal debt is owed to the folks at Syllables in South Hartwick, who volunteered their publishing facilities and considerable knowledge to turn our submissions into a finished product.

Mary Bergen offered her services in proofreading and editing.

John Mott has to his credit the Historical Society's extensive photo collection which was added to by contributions from many community members during the production of this book.

From the beginning of the groups' existence Hartwick Historical Society members have researched various topics and devoted a part of their energies to collecting information on all aspects of Hartwick history. These researchers and authors are given recognition in these pages.

We cannot pretend this is the definitive work on our township's history. It represents what could be completed in time to get something printed for our bicentennial. More topics remain to be covered. History continues to be made and we look forward to future publications.

Town of Hartwick Historical Society

President:	Anita Harrison
Vice President:	David Petrie
Secretary:	Barbara Potter
Treasurer:	Nadine Phillips
Board of Directors:	William Powers
	Homer Martin
	Eva Chamberlin
	Dan Conklin
	Andrea Conklin
	Orrin Higgins

Table of Contents

Dedication 3
Acknowledgements 4
Table of Contents 5
Autographs 7
Native Americans 9
John Christopher Hartwick 12
Early Settlers and Purchasers 28
Hamlets
    Hartwick Seminary 52
    Toddsville 56
    Clintonville 61
    Recollections from Hyde Park 66
    South Hartwick 70
    Hinman Hollow 87
    Arnold's Lake 91
    Christian Hill 93
    Notes from Roy Butterfield 99
Holden Inn - Trials and Results 104
Churches
    Congregational (Presbyterian) Church 109
    First Baptist Church 113
    Reverend Fisher 117
    Christian Hill Church 118
    Christian Church of Hartwick Village 120
    Bowe Hill Camp Meetings 126
    Hartwick United Methodist Church 128
    Hyde Park Churches 131
    Evangelical Lutheran Church 134
    The Manuscript Found 141
Education
    Common Schools 143
    Schoolhouse John 157
    Select Schools 160
    Brookwood School 163
    ARC Otsego Treatment Centers 167
Agriculture
    Farming 170
    Hartwick Dairy Industry 179
    Hartwick Hatchery 184
    Sheep 186
    Hops 191
Business and Industries
    Notes on Village Commerce 194
    Hartwick National Bank 205
    The Trolley 209
    Polish Beds 219

The Grist and Saw Mills 222
Maple Industry 227
Meat Markets and Delivery Routes 229
Milliners 233
Blacksmiths 235
Leather Workers 239
Garages, Gas Stations and Farm Machinery .. 242
Funeral Homes 248
Printing and Publishing 250
Country Kitchen 253
Laura's Restaurant 256
Public Services
    Post Offices 260
    Rural Electrification 266
    Telephone 271
    Hartwick Town Insurance Company 274
    Fire Departments 276
    The Hartwick Water Works Company 286
    The Stage 288
    Town of Hartwick Highways 291
Professions
    Physicians, Dentists and Veterinarians 302
    Lawyers 314
Elections 316
Entertainments and Amusements 319
4th of July and Memorial Day 331
Crime 336
Organizations
    4-H 343
    Boy Scouts 352
    GAR 358
    Independent Order of the Good Templar 362
    Rebekahs 364
    Maccabees 366
    Women's Village Improvement Society 367
    WCTU 369
    Independent Order of the Odd Fellows 374
    Order of the Eastern Star 376
    Hartwick Rod and Gun Club 378
    Kinney Memorial Library and
        Hartwick Historical Society 379
    Other Organizations 384
Cemeteries 387
Weather 389
Morrell Smith 397
Tidbits 401

Autographs

Native Americans

It's impossible to say who was the first white man to visit this area and encounter the Native people who lived here. More than likely it was a Dutch trader or a Frenchman made captive by the Iroquois.

In 1614, a Dutch trader named Kleynties and a comrade, journeyed from Fort Orange (present-day Albany) up the Mohawk River and traveled the Indian paths that lead to Otsego Lake. These two travelers were the first white men to record their passing, which was noted in Kleynties' journal.

Over a century later another white man recorded his impressions of the area. This man was William Johnson. Johnson was a young man when he arrived from Ireland to manage his uncle's estate on the Mohawk River. In a very short time Johnson made friends with the local Iroquois and began to make his living as a trader. Johnson, seeking to expand his influence in the fur trade, made a trip to the Iroquois village of Oquaga. The village was on the site of the present day village of Windsor, NY. On his trip Johnson kept a journal of his travels. On June 30th 1739 he writes as follows "The lake the Natives call Otsego is a bright gem set in the dark forest…around the lake mountains swell up its sides and give way to valleys and rolling hills. At the foot of the lake there is an ancient apple orchard, and it is alive with the singing of birds. As I walked this place I crushed a clay pipe bowl underfoot….A turfy square of broken rampart told of an indian village lost to history beyond recall. Here we met some Onieda people, their faces were streaked with vermilion, lampblack and white lead, the present village consisted of 3 wigwams and about 30 souls."

In his journal, Johnson speaks of an ancient apple orchard and of a village lost beyond recall. In Johnson's day the Mohawk, Oneida, and Tuscarora people inhabited the lands around the shore of Lake Otsego and the Susquehanna River below. These three nations were part of a larger confederation of Native peoples called themselves the "Haudenosaunee" or People of the longhouse. Their enemies referred to them as the "real snakes" and the French gave them the name Iroquois. Long before the Iroquois nations claimed the land as their own, other peoples had lived here. Their names and the location of their villages are long forgotten, but all throughout Otsego county and the Town of Hartwick, remains of their culture can still be found. In recent years large mortars and pestles made of stone have been found on the hillsides surrounding the village. Net stones, arrowheads and tools for making dugout canoes have come to light along the creek. These tools were not made by the Natives that William Johnson or John Christopher Hartwick met, but by peoples who lived over a thousand years ago. On the hillsides surrounding the village have been found Otter Creek, Genesee, Meadowood, Susquehanna and Levanna arrowhead and projectile points. The earliest points – the Otter Creek and Genesee – date between 8000 BC to 1000 BC. These points usually were used to hunt small game. The people using them did not plant crops but depended on plant gathering and moved their camps with the seasons.

The Susquehanna and Meadowood points were developed around 1500 BC to 1000 BC, the same time that Native peoples began to use soapstone for cooking pots. This period is commonly considered a transitional period, from a nomadic way of life to an agricultural village life. Levanna points are the last type of point made before European contact. These points were made around 1000 AD and continued in use until they were replaced by copper and iron points produced for the Indian trade by European artisans. The Levanna point is associated with the woodland period. During this time Native people developed pottery, began to cultivate crops and began to establish semi-permanent villages.

Although no village site has yet to be discovered here in the town of Hartwick, all indications are that a village may have existed here. Villages were spaced at or about 10 miles apart. Settlements have been found up and down the route 205 corridor. This pathway was a trail that led from Canadarago Lake to Oneonta.

In 1754 John Christopher Hartwick purchased from the Mohawks 24,000 acres of land

for the price of 100 pounds York currency. At the time of the purchase the Mohawks were living in three villages along the river that bears their name. The eight signers of the land exchange were from the Upper Mohawk Castle and

Hendrik, sachem of the Mohawk, sold Hartwick his first parcel of land in 1750, but the transaction was invalid due to Hartwick's failure to obtain a permit.

Photo courtesy of the Paul F. Cooper, Jr. Archives, Hartwick College, Oneonta, New York

is located east of the city of Little Falls.

The Mohawks had long used the Otsego Lake as a seasonal hunting and fishing area. Since the lake is the source of the Susquehanna River, every spring fish would run up the river in great abundance. Shad and herring would come on to the lake and spawn in the creeks and streams. The Iroquois would use nets to catch upwards of a thousand fish a day, which they later smoked for use in the winter.

John Christopher Hartwick had the idea of starting up a school for the education and conversion of the Native peoples found in this area. As early as 1764 there was a mission school for Mohawk Indian children at the foot of Lake Otsego. This school was under the instruction of a Mohawk named Moses who had been educated at the Wheelock Indian School in Lebanon, Connecticut. This is about the time George Croghan, a land speculator and officer of the British Indian department, had his cabin on the lake, near the present grounds of the Baseball Hall of Fame. Reverend J. C. Smith, writing from Croghan's house, records the following: " I am everyday diverted and pleased with a view of Moses and his students, as I sit in the study and see him and all his scholars at any time, the school being nothing but an open barrack."

Susan Cooper was the last person to record the fact of Native people in our area. In her reflection *Rural Hours*, she records the presence of Oneida people making baskets on Mill Island, a small landmass in the Susquehanna River, which is now the location of the Bassett Hospital parking lot. She also described the Native women selling their wares to the citizens of the area. These are the last words that were written about Otsego's Indians.

The Iroquois may be gone from the shores of Lake Otsego, and Indian nets and sinkers no longer catch fish in the streams and creeks of Hartwick. But with every spring rain new artifacts are revealed along the hillsides and streambeds of the village. Anyone who finds such treasures is urged not to keep these items to themselves, but to share their finds with the village. In this way over time we might more fully understand those who were here before us and how they lived.

Dave Rickard NYS Historical Association
Director of Native American Programs

John Christopher Hartwick

PREFACE

The reader of the following article will soon conclude that I have covered only the main facts in the life of John Christopher Hartwick and have touched only briefly on the formation of the Hartwick Township and the creation of the Seminary. My purpose is to show the relationship of the residents of the Township to the actual location and existence of the Seminary for well over a century. I have listed only the original lot owners and have left, for more capable hands, the story of each individual settler as he came to the Hartwick lands.

Perhaps you may ask why I undertook such a task and I will say only that I claim a deep and twofold love for the Hartwick tradition. First, as a resident of the Township, with my roots going back to the year 1794 when my great, great grandfather, Martin Luther Comstock settled in the eastern end of Great Lot 26 in the Hartwick patent - and since that date a member of the family has always occupied the farm (perhaps the only farm in Hartwick's 8/11th division whose property lines are the same today as when surveyed by William Allison in 1794). Secondly, I attended and graduated from Hartwick Seminary and as most of my spiritual life has been associated with the Evangelical Lutheran Church of Hartwick Seminary and its wonderful Chris-

tian leaders of the past, you see I claim a deep and loving heritage of the Hartwick Tradition.

It is very fitting in this Bicentennial Year, when we are celebrating the 200th birthday of our great nation, that we pay tribute to the Rev. John Christopher Hartwick and to the pioneers who settled here, and the part they played in having the Seminary located within the Patent, and last, but by no means least, the contribution of the Seminary to our cultural, spiritual and economic life for well over one hundred and seventy-five years.

To unfold this bit of history as it should be told is a task far beyond my humble and limited ability, but perhaps a few interesting facts about Hartwick, his Patent and his school can be brought out in a little different light than that used by other writers of the Hartwick story. Each of the former writers has done outstanding work which I am sure we could never hope to improve, although there are a few well established facts which they either overlooked, or felt unimportant - but to us they seem essential in getting a true picture of the Hartwick story.

According to Henry Hardy Heins in his book "Throughout All The Years" John Christopher Hartwick was born January 6, 1714 in Molschleben, duch of Saxe-Gotha, province of Thuringia. Very little is known of his early life but we do know that his father was Andreas Hartwig (German Spelling) and that he had younger twin brothers: Sebastion and Conrad, and an older sister, Anna Barbara Brigitta. He also had a brother Christian Hartwick who lived on No. 34 of the 'reserved lots' of the Hartwick patent (which I shall bring out more fully later).

He received a very fine education and was ordained a Lutheran Minister by Dr. Krauter in the German Trinity Church of London November 24, 1745 and in the spring of 1746 he arrived in America.

Soon he was actively preaching in churches in the Hudson Valley, at Rhinebeck, East Camp, Tar Bush, Ancram, and Staatsburg. He was a very peculiar person - very strict with his congregations, preaching up to two hours or more (even after arriving an hour or more late). He never showed any compassion for his flock, frequently leaving his congregations unattended for long periods of time while he traveled to New York or Philadelphia. Quite often he was sadly in need of clean clothing.

During all his wanderings he became acquainted with the Mohawk Indians. He was attracted to them and they apparently liked him. From this association he got the idea of a school where he might not only teach them the white man's ways, but more importantly, convert them to Christianity and eventually prepare some for the ministry.

Being encouraged by the wonderful work of Samuel Kirkland who founded Hamilton College and that of Eleazer Wheelock of Dartmouth, Hartwick was more convinced than ever of the soundness of this idea. He had learned a great deal from his associations with Robert Livingston's family and the Muhlenburgs in regard to financial and business matters and realized that to build and promote a college of theology would require an enormous amount of money, which he certainly did not have. He decided the best course

for him was to buy huge tracts of land from the Indians and thereby acquire the funds with which to put his dream into effect.

He wasted no time and began immediate negotiations for four separate tracts. In 1750 he bought 250 acres in the Beaver Dam Patent which was really a part of a 500 acre southerly extension of the Cherry Valley Patent. He sold this to Peter Martin, an Albany innkeeper in 1760. In 1752 a deed was prepared for Hartwick for 4000 acres in Ulster County, but this transaction was never completed. In 1750 he purchased the Indian rights to a 9 mile long and 4 mile wide tract south of the Mohawk River, and 12 miles west of Schoharie. Having failed to secure a license to deal with the Indians for land he had to start all over again. Now with a license from the proper authority and a new group of petitioners he negotiated for a far larger tract including all the land bounded by Springfield, Cherry Valley, and the Long Patents east of Otsego Lake and the Susquehanna River. This is what is now the Town of Middlefield. It was granted April 16, 1761 to 15 proprietors, Hartwick's name not appearing. On July 14th the same year 14 of the 15 proprietors transferred their rights to Hartwick for 5 shillings each -the remaining share to Peter Martin. It is doubtful if Hartwick ever realized any financial profit from these dealings. They are mentioned here only to point out that the township of Hartwick was not the only venture of our hero in land holdings.

Now let us pass along to the fourth tract - what is now Hartwick Township. On November 16, 1752 the Governor issued Hartwick a license to purchase 24,000 acres of the Indians for 100 pounds with the proviso that he act within one year. There was a slight misunderstanding as to what the property lines were to include, so the parties concerned met about November 1, 1753 at the home of William Johnson, Superintendent of Indian Affairs, and came to an agreement. It was nearing the deadline and winter was approaching. There was no time to make the necessary surveys. Hartwick had to wait until spring and make a new start. On March 5, 1754 he received his new license and on the 29th of May the same year he received his deed from the Indians describing his land as beginning on the west bank of the Susquehanna River at a point where the north line of the Long (Othoudt) Patent crosses the river and extending six miles up the river and six miles into the woods. Johnson certified that the Indians were paid on the same date, and the next day the Surveyer General also certified that Peter Van Dreisen had surveyed the tract in the presence of the subscribing Indians. It was nearly a year later that Hartwick and his ten associates applied (April 5, 1754) for letters of patent. This required another survey which was returned July 27th. Thus two surveys were required - one arranged by the petitioners to locate, with the approval of the Indians, the desired tract; the second by the King's surveyor for the use of the Attorney General in drafting the patent instrument. This survey, of course, used the same starting point but stated the line going west 480 chains, north 480, east 480 to the Susquehanna River, thence south along the west bank of said river to the place of beginning. It called for 21,000 acres with usual allowance for highways. Of course, the patent overran the survey due to the fact that the river-for nearly four miles after issuing from Otsego Lake flows southwest, not due south as supposed. This lengthened the north-line nearly two miles. This was fortunate, for the recipients paid quitrent only on net acreage.

Now everything was in order for Hartwick to apply for the letters patent, giving the right to bring in settlers, but this was not the case. It was nearly six years before Hartwick made an effort to obtain his letter patent, and during that time we find him actively serving churches in New York City, Reading, Pennsylvania, and Hackensack, New Jersey. But early in March of 1761 he petitioned for a new patent which was issued him on April 22, 1761.

Due to the size of the patent it was necessary that there be 11 petitioners and those named were: - John Christopher Hartwick, John Maurice Goetschius (a prominent Lutheran minister), Derk Brinckerhoff (a Dutch merchant of New York City) and eight German residents of Philadelphia. The eight were merely trustees to make up the necessary number called for by the patent. In order for Hartwick to secure his patent it was necessary that he raise about $1700.00 to cover the fees of the Governor, Secretary, Surveyor-General, as well as the Indian purchase prices. There was also a perpetual quitrent of two shillings and six pence on every 100 acres to be paid the Crown.

Through Goldsborough Banyar, Deputy Secretary of New York Colony, who through his land dealings of this nature had become a very wealthy man, Hartwick was able to finance his patent. On July 18, 1761 he transferred his 1/11th of the patent to Banyar, and in September the eight residents of Philadelphia released their interest to Hartwick for a small consideration. On November 12, 1761 Hartwick paid 200 pounds on the fees and costs and at the same time gave Banyar his mortgage for 127 pounds, three shillings — the small amount still due. This mortgage ran for 30 years with interest added every 10 years and, of course, grew into a sizable amount. On May 2, 1765 Brinckerhoff sold his 1/11th share to Dirck Lefferts, a New York City merchant, leaving the title of the patent in the hands of four individuals: - Hartwick with 8/11ths, Banyar, Lefferts, and Goetschius with 1/11th each.

Another long period of inactivity followed. Hartwick did visit his patent on several occasions but had little success in attracting settlers. Several historians have stated that in 1765 Hartwick made a clearing near the foot of Otsego Lake but, realizing his patent didn't extend that far north, abandoned the work. The actual source of this story cannot be found, but (according to Roy Butterfield, the very noted and competent historian) the Banyar papers do contain some information to substantiate the incident. Whether or not this is true, it is a well known fact that Hartwick preceded George Croghan (trader with the Indians) by at least 10 years and William Cooper by about 30 years. There is no doubt that Hartwick was the first white man to make any attempt at colonization in or around the present site of Cooperstown.

Croghan was connected with the Indian Department under the Crown and he, with 99 other secured 100,000 acres north of Hartwick's land. This was in three plots and was disposed of in a few years through mortgage sales, etc. In the autumn of 1785 William Cooper first came to the area to survey that portion of the Croghan Patent that he and Andrew Craig had secured in May 1785 from the Sheriff of Montgomery County. I might add that both Cooper and Craig were from Burlington, New Jersey.

The Cooper-Craig Patent consisted of lands in both the present towns of Burlington and Otsego and a narrow strip along Hartwick's north line. Craig was only an investor but Cooper immediately went to work and divided their patent into nine large lots which he soon sold or leased. He had made one mistake.

He assumed that Hartwick's north line was correct and it wasn't. Consequently some of the land he sold was within the Hartwick Patent. It was several years before he was able to rectify his error, as it was not noted until Hartwick had a survey run north and south through the center of his patent in 1791 for the purpose of dividing the patent into the 11 divisions that the patent instrument called for. This showed the true line to be over 1/2 mile to the north.

Hartwick, noting Cooper's great success in attracting buyers, made an effort in 1788 and 89 to dispose of some of his patent but it is doubtful if he met with much success. After all Cooper was a businessman, knowing what kind of deal would attract settlers and giving them every opportunity to make good. Hartwick was greatly lacking in this ability. Cooper's ability was soon recognized and his services sought by a number of landowners in other areas.

I have previously mentioned that Hartwick had had David Cully of Milford run a north-south line through the center of his patent in 1791 to determine the 11 divisions. This I now explain more fully. A tree was marked every 43 chains, 72 links to show each division in the patent. It was divided thus: - Lefferts was given the first, Banyar the second, Hartwick the third through tenth and Goetschius the eleventh which Cooper purchased in 1792. With the purchase of the 11th division Cooper was in a position to rectify the encroachment on the Hartwick lands. I might add that Hartwick's portion amounted to about 16, 000 acres.

Noting the great success of Cooper in land sales, Lefferts in 1790 empowered him to lease his portion, when divided, for a period of 10 years at an annual rate of one shilling per acre. The paid-up tenants at the end of the period were offered the privilege of purchasing for 14 shillings per acre. Cooper was to receive a commission of 5% and he was to pay the surveying, conveying and recording fees.

In the spring of 1791 Hartwick made a couple of important decisions: - First, he retired from preaching and second, at a meeting in Albany (May 13th) he appointed Jeremiah Van Rennsalaer, a very important Albany businessman, politician, and banker, as his attorney for his entire estate. At the same time he empowered him to employ William Cooper as his land agent on the same terms as those of Lefferts. Hartwick immediately had his eight divisions divided into six lots per division giving him a total of 48 lots. Cooper took over the mortgage that Banyar held on the Hartwick division, which now with interest amounted to 525 pounds. Of course, as sales were made the mortgage was taken care of. Now Cooper had charge of all the sales except Banyar's. No doubt Hartwick and Cooper had a verbal agreement for we find that Cooper made no sales in the Hartwick's nine "Reserved Lots" although in June of 1792 in a letter to Van Rennsalaer Hartwick did have the nine lots reserved. Cooper lost no time and within a month had leased 39 of the Hartwick divisions. Many of the first sales were to speculators who had no thought of ever living on the patent and were soon to be subleased and broken up into smaller farms the size determined by the settler. Most of the original lots were of 300 and more acres.

Assuming that former surveys were correct, Cooper had gone ahead with sales, no doubt using those made for the Sauther's Patent Map of 1779 and the Surveyor General Simeon DeWitt's Map of 1790. Both of these maps showed a separation, about the width of Cooper's encroachment, between the Long and Cherry Valley Patents. The official description of the Long Patent adjoins the Cherry Valley Patent with a common boundary. The Hartwick Patent began at a point where the Long Patent crosses the Susquehanna River and, as all surveys up until then were incorrect, the settlers found they were paying for more land than they actually had. So let me quote from the Hartwick College Archives, Document #11, October the 22nd A.D. 1793:

"Reverend Sir:
We, whose names are hereunto subscribed having taken Leases upon your patent for a certain number of acres of land specified in our leases, find when the lots come to be tried by the chain that the lots that specified three hundred and forty acres fall short thirty or forty acres. The land was valued at 14 shillings per acre and interest cast upon the whole number specified in said leases so that as it now stands your petitioners pay for a considerable more land than what they really have to the great damage of your petitioners we desire that the lots of land may be surveyed that is marked and bounded to each of us without altering the lines and to give us new leases so that we may not pay for more land than is within our lines. We hope that it will be in our power to fulfill on our part our leases.

The Reverend Mr. Hartwick has had a desire that there might be upon his patent a house for the worship of God and a house for the Education of Youth your petitioners join with you in your desire that there might be as soon as may be a house for the worship of God that created us and that gives us all things that we enjoy that he may bless us with spiritual and temporal blessing. If Mr. Hartwick should think it convenient to come and reside amongst us we should think ourselves happy and would provide accomodations for him.

To the Reverend John Christopher Hartwick:

Signed by -William Baker, Abraham Lippitt, Nathaniel Averill, Josiah Brigham, Issac Barns, Thomas Robinson, Hezekiah Tiffany, Nathan Payne, Joseph Lippitt, William Cummings, James Cummings, Daniel Cummings, John Newland, Ziba Newland,

William Baker Jun., Silvanus Douglas, Benjamin Fuller, Abner Alger, Michiah Robinson, and Stephen Smith."

As you can see the settlers had every right to complain for no one wished to pay for 30 or 40 acres of land that he didn't have. Early in the spring of 1794 William Ellison of Cooperstown was employed and a new survey made. The old leases were returned to Cooper and new ones issued giving the actual acreage as found by the new survey. The settlers were then content as this was all they wanted. The Ellison survey was the most accurate of any yet made and brought to light errors of former surveys (and I would refer you, for a more detailed study, to Mr. Roy Butterfield's study of the Hartwick Patent which clearly explains how the north line of the Patent was finally determined).

I would like to tell you of some of the activities of John Christopher Hartwick during the last year or so prior to his death. Of course, he had always had the dream of a "new Jerusalem" on his patent, ever since the letters patent were issued him and his petitioners in 1761, but lady luck was never to be his companion. After he had commissioned William Cooper, his land agent, he found his patent disposed of so rapidly that, I imagine, it made his head swim. He attempted a few sales only to find the land already leased, though he did have his nine reserved lots where he made a few sales himself.

As you will recall, in their petition for a new survey the residents had invited Hartwick to come and live among them and to build his church and school. According to his diary (which is Document #21 in the Hartwick College Archives) we find that on April 17, 1795 he arrived on his patent and immediately set about to find some unleased land in the middle of the patent on which to build a church and also a house. First he went to the carpenter, William Cummings, who at one time had been his agent. Then he went to the shoemaker, Sam Craft and I quote: "his wife was put to bed mit a young boy" — end quote. He was told it would be best for him to go and talk about his business with Mr. Davison. Here he was told that all the land was leased and that he (Hartwick) would have to build on his (Davison) land. Hartwick writes "I did not listen." I can well realize his discouragement, for each place he went thinking to find available land, he found that the land was leased and settlers established. He complained to Cooper but, as usual, he had waited too long before acting.

In Vol. 1 #51 of Hartwick Seminary Journal at Hartwick College Archives we find an interesting letter written by Van Rennselaer to Cooper:

"Dear Sir:

The bearer hereof, Simon Laible, who claims merit of having been the first settler at the place now called Cooperstown has by adversity or misfortune in his life been reduced once more to seek asylum in your quarter, he therefore comes forward with Mr. Hartwick's request that you place him on that angular piece or point of land between the Susquehanna River and the Oaks Creek, on which was or now is a forced possession of one Shipman which he wished may be removed and the bearer aided in forwarding the Improvement which Mr. Hartwick intends to occupy himself and to fell timber proper for building a house."

It would be interesting to know if this could have been the Shipman that tradition says was the character that James Fenimore Cooper portrayed in his famous Leatherstocking Tales. It would also be very interesting to know which of the two gentlemen Jonathan Newman found occupying the point lot later the same year, for we also find in Hartwick College Archives Document #62 dated August 20, 1792 a memorandum of Agreement between Van Rennselaer, Attorney for Hartwick and Jonathan Newman for the same property at an annual rent of five shillings, if demanded. Newman was authorized and named Hartwick's true and lawful attorney to remove any persons as now are or may be in possession thereof and the same to keep, hold, enjoy, etc.

We find that the point lot was leased to Newman and in 1795 this lease was exchanged for one in Lot #14. To me this is interesting due to the fact that in Lot #14 Hartwick had 30 acres reserved as a "school lot", which was not sold until many years following Hartwick's death. Could it be that Hartwick wanted the noted Methodist circuit rider as instructor or preacher in his "new Jerusalem?" In passing I might note that the "school lot" was high on the hills east of Hartwick Village and the point lot was in that portion of Great Lot #47 which is north of the Oaks Creek and west of the Susquehanna River and now in the township of Otsego.

On April 8, 1795 Mr. Hartwick employed one, Carl Henrick Huner, to go immediately to the Hartwick Patent where he was instructed to build a house for him on that point of land where the Oaks Creek and the Susquehanna river meet, and also make necessary improvements on the land. The year before Hartwick had had his friend, Mr. Davison, clear the land

of trees where he wished his house to be built.

Hartwick gave Huner explicit directions on how to find the site. He was to turn left when he came to the main road and by Stacy's Tavern "but you must not stop there" but to pass him and two houses more passing blacksmith shop and on to Mr. Davison where he was to receive further instructions. Huner was to (quote) "try my tenants, whether they will help you upon a reasonable wage, if they are extravagant, then go with my mare to German Flats (Herkimer) to William DeLeny and give him intelligence, ask his advice, about hiring Germans, and where you may leave my mare, and act accordingly." (end quote) Just what type of house Huner built we do not know. It could have been of logs or framed. We do know that he was given three months and no longer to finish the construction. In his diary, on May 14, 1795, Hartwick says, "I have made a garden where the house stands." Evidently he had had some land cleared and. plowed and some improvements made, but it is doubtful that he ever lived there; for on the 15th of May the same year we find he paid Davison for board and also left his saddle and bridle with him.

Hartwick made his home with John Andrews in Albany, but being very uneasy by nature, we find him on the move much of the time. When on his patent he would sometimes stay with his friend, David Cully of Milford, or William Cummings; but Stacy's Tavery was his usual abode. We find several accounts where he paid board, purchased candles, paid the barber and bought three 1/2 pints of wine every other day. On a few occasions he bought a gallon just to tide himself over.

Of course, by now (1795) he was getting old and perhaps a little feeble and we find where he hires John Baker, Abraham Lippitt, and others to carry him to Albany with horse and wagon.

It seems that during this period Mr. Hartwick was employing Richard Edwards Attorney of Cherry Valley, to do some legal work for him. There is evidence that Edwards prepared ejection papers for him, as Hartwick gave instructions to Huner to stop at Cherry Valley and pick up the papers and at the same time to receive instructions about serving them. It would appear that it was getting increasingly hard for Hartwick to get along with people as we find he is threatening certain tenants with court actions. There is no doubt that by now he is tired and very much discouraged. He is sick, not only in body but in mind. He has spent nearly a half century trying to build his "new Jerusalem" and school, nor can he understand how, in so short a time, his patent has been sold or leased and he has only his "reserved lots" left.

Before passing along to the death of Hartwick and the settling of his estate, I would like to say that all writers of the John Christopher Hartwick story have stated that there were two - the one a Lutheran Missionary and minister, the other a poverty stricken resident of Cooperstown. This is entirely incorrect, as I will point out. The poverty stricken gentleman did not live in Cooperstown, but was a brother of John Christopher Hartwick living where the dominie had put him - in the west end of Great Lot #34 in the "reserved lots" of Hartwick Patent on 100 acres. His name was Christian. His neighbors and friends nicknamed him "Chris John (from the sound of his given name). The tenants referred to the clergyman as John Christopher and to the brother as Chris John. Christian's nearest neighbor, across the valley, was Martin Luther Comstock (my great-great grandfather) who came to Hartwick Patent and settled on the

eastern end of Great Lot #26 in. the year 1794. Living less than a 1/4 mile from Christian, he of course, knew him well. The story that was handed down to me through the years is that the two were brothers. John Christopher would come and visit Christian but never stayed with him. Both were very peculiar and never agreed with one another for very long at a time - not long enough to live together. Hartwick must have felt very much responsible for him for we find several places in the Hartwick accounts where Christian was extended charity, and on February 11, 1795 John Christopher directs Van Rennselaer to lend Christian two dollars on his account and to take his receipt for the same. I have a copy of this receipt bearing Christian's signature. This charity was an annual grant and was carried on after the death of John Christopher and up until the death of Christian in 1800. Besides the annual charity Christian was given money for bread, and on another occasion money for blankets.

In a letter dated March 18, 1792 to Van Rennselaer, William Ellison, surveyor, seeks instruction in regard to a certain survey that he was asked to make and suggests to Van Rennselaer that the two chainmen be paid in land saying; "the dominie can find no fault with this, as he may make his own bargain with his own Christian." To me this establishs a pretty close family relationship, specially when added to the fact that Hartwick's will left Christian 100 acres "upon which he hath made an improvement," and the fact that the claim was allowed.

At the thirteenth Annual Meeting of the Board of Trustees of Hartwick Seminary, August 26, 1828, "It was also ordered that the agent quit-claim one hundred acres of the Hartwick estate to Charles F. Scidel as the agent and representative of Christianus Hartwick. He was a descendant of Andreas Hartwick, and whose claim under the will was allowed by the Board." (The land agent mentioned was William C. Bouck of Schoharie.) If John Christopher and Christian were both descendants of Andreas Hartwick it should make their relationship quite close, don't you think?

As the story was told me, Christian was not right mentally, and following the death of John Christopher, he became worse and more depressed until on June 22, 1800 he slashed his own throat with a razor. He lived until July 2nd. A very vivid account of this incident appeared in the July 10, 1800 issue of the Otsego Herald. The editor of the paper did the interview, thinking it to be John Christopher Hartwick, who had died of asthma four years before at the home of Robert Livingston. One thing I am sure of - I know the site of Christian's cabin and the site of his unmarked grave. That is more than can be claimed for John Christopher who, even after his death, was kept on the move for many years. The above facts together with the fact that on the 9th of January 1799 Van Rennselaer was given power of attorney for Christian make it evident to me that Christian was more than a cousin or just another man bearing the Hartwick name.

A moment ago I mentioned the death of John Christopher Hartwick. He was making a return trip from New York City to Albany by boat and became ill, so stopped at Clermont with his friends, the Livingstons, who cared for him until his death July 17, 1796. He was buried in the Lutheran Churchyard at Germantown but, as the will stated he was to be buried beneath the pulpit in the Ebenezar Church in Albany, two years later his wish was carried out. His remains were buried in the chancel and a marble slab laid over his coffin. The marble slab is now at Hartwick College. His rest at Ebenezar was not long, for in 1816

the church was remodeled and the body removed to a cemetery in the city. There it remained until 1868 when the cemetery became a part of Washington Park, but there is no record of Hartwick's body having been moved.

His will was, no doubt, the most unusual ever probated, making Jesus Christ his chief heir. He left instructions for the formation of his new Jerusalem, legacies to several of his friends such as Van Rennselaer and the John Andrews family, and to relatives, if any ever qualified. He named Dr. John Christopher Kunze and Dr. Justus Helmuth as curators and, shortly before his death, appointed Frederick August Muhlenburg one of his Executors, Administer, and Curator for his estate.

Muhlenburg, a Lutheran clergyman actively engaged in Pennsylvania politics, having been speaker of both the Second and Fourth United States Congresses, twice a candidate for governor, and finally Receiver-General of Pennsylvania Land Office, would seem a fine choice; as would Dr. Kunze, a son-in-law of Muhlenburg's, who for several years had been very active in religious education in both Pennsylvania and New York City. Both had made endeavors to promote schools of Theology but were unsuccessful. True, both Muhlenburg and Dr. Kunze would love to start a Lutheran Theological Seminary in Pennsylvania or in the New York City area, but certainly not among the woodchoppers on the Hartwick Patent who were made up of Baptists and Methodists from Connecticut and Rhode Island.

Meanwhile, back on the Patent, the residents were expecting the "new Jerusalem" of Hartwick's dream to take form, but no moves were made in that direction. On September 14, 1797 Cooper and 16 others invited the Executors to join with them in an academy which they had established within one mile of the Hartwick Patent. Their petition arrived two days too late as Muhlenburg, Van Rennselaer and Dr. Kunze had met September .15, 1797 in New York City and Founded Hartwick Seminary. (Note - little did the Cooperstown residents realize then that during the next 130 years they would come forth several more times with offers two days too late.) This meeting of the founders lasted five days. They postponed the final location of the school but appointed Dr. Kunze Director of the Institution with a salary of Five Hundred Dollars per year, to remain with his New York City congregation and to teach Theology at his home. The Rev. Anthony Braum was selected as Professor of the Institute at a salary of $250.00 per year. He was to teach college level sciences and languages at Albany. The Reverend Frederick Ernst at $250.00 per year was to give spiritual instructions and teach on an elementary school level back at the Hartwick Patent. Rev. Braum was the pastor of Ebenezar Church and operated from there. The Reverend Ernst was to go to the Patent as soon as a call was extended him. He received the call from the Hartwick residents and about two years later we find him and his family located in Cooperstown (not on the Hartwick Patent). No doubt he devoted some time on the Patent but it certainly was not a convenient or satisfactory arrangement either for him or for the residents of the Patent. He gave up in 1802, returning to Pennsylvania, but certain members of his family remained in Cooperstown and were active in the Episcopal Church for many years.

The Executors of the Hartwick Estate felt some obligation to the residents of the Patent so we find they were granted $150.00 per year in 1799-1800-1801 toward the support of two schools. One on the east side was taught by

Avery Averill and John Guller, and one on the west side of the Patent was taught by Seth Ransom and Daniel Gardner. The monies were paid to Micaiah Robinson, Treasurer, for both schools and were divided equally between the two schools.

During the years following Hartwick's death the Executors of the estate considered several locations for the Seminary:- New York City, Schoharie, Rhinebeck, Albany, and lastly, but not enthusiastically, the Hartwick Patent. Of course, they were under pressure from the New York Ministerium and strong Lutheran communities to locate elsewhere. To me, even though they were men of fine character and high religious morals, they grossly failed their obligation and responsibility in not carrying out the will of Hartwick.

Certainly they knew his wishes.

To complicate things more, Muhlenburg died in 1801 in bankruptcy and, as Judge Cooper had for several years paid him the rents from the Hartwick Estate, half of the estate was lost forever. The financial condition of the estate had so greatly deteriorated that, as a last straw, the Trustees accepted Albany's bid for the Seminary and on October 27, 1801 signed ten articles of agreement with the Ebenezar Church for the Seminary to be built in Albany, and transferred the funds of the Hartwick Estate to the Church.

Things lagged for several years but the construction was finally started in 1804 on what is now Park Street, on the old Lutheran Cemetery site. With the selection of the Albany site Dr. Kunze terminated the annual donation of $150.00 toward the support of the schools on the Hartwick Patent. This decision, of course, touched off a bees nest with the residents on the Patent, and justly so. Hartwick became a township March 6, 1802 at the home of Joseph Lippitt, but the final location of its north line was not determined until 1803 (see Butterfield for detailed account). At their first meeting town officers were elected: Rufus Steere, Town Clerk, and Philip Wells, Supervisor. This was more or less an organizational meeting. At the First Annual Meeting, held at Holden's Inn March 5, 1805, the same officers voted to raise $150.00 toward the prosecuting and obtaining a donation from the Executors and Curators of the late Rev. John Christopher Hartwick, deceased. To carry this into effect the following committee was appointed: Micaiah Robinson, Stukey Ellsworth, and Thomas Loomis. The residents meant business as the town records show. A special meeting was called on the 17th day of August the same year at which time an additional $150.00 was voted for carrying these resolutions into effect. In 1806 the committee was to continue its efforts and to prosecute by law, if they saw fit. Another committee of Nathan Davison, Williams Cummings, and Eliphalat Dewey was appointed to help and advise the existing committee. We find in the town records that the committee continued active through 1807 and 1808, resolved that all funds be conveyed back to Van Rennselaer. This was done and the materials on Park Street sold. The contruction at Park Street was over, as were the possibilities of Albany ever having the Seminary again. Van Rennselaer died in 1810 leaving Dr. John G. Knauff, an Albany physician, the official Executor of the Hartwick Estate. He had previously been named by Van Rennselaer as his successor.

Due to Muhlenburg's bankruptcy and the cost of maintaining a school of Theology in New York City, a preparatory school in Albany, an elementary school in Cooperstown, and other current expenses, such as building an unused foundation for the Seminary in Albany, the Estate had now dwindled to less than eigh-

teen thousand dollars. Of course, this situation was promptly blamed on Judge Cooper, certainly not on faithful Van Rennselaer or good old Muhlenburg.

In a word of defense for Judge Cooper, I would like to quote from the noted Roy Butterfield who, during the last years of his life, made a most detailed and comprehensive study of the Hartwick Patent through sources of material at Hartwick College Archives, "Throughout all the Years" by Henry Hardy Heins, land papers at the office of the Secretary of State at Albany, Surrogate's and County Clerk's records of Albany, Tryon, Montgomery, and Otsego Counties, as well as the Banyar papers at Albany. Mr. Butterfield says, "Statements have frequently been made that the latter's estate received but a fraction of the amount justly due. With such a position the present writer, after a long and close study of the documentary evidence, cannot agree."

Dr. Knauff began to set the wheels turning. On October 11, 1811 he purchased five acres of land from Elisha Eldred on which to build the Seminary. It was located on the east side of the Patent as the residents there had done better than those of the west side in their efforts to raise funds. It had been decided that the side which raised more money for the school would have it on their side of town. The east won.

The November 2, 1811 issue of the Otsego Herald carried the following ad:- "Proposals will be received by the subscriber until the 20th of November next for the erection by contract of a brick building in 'the Town of Hartwick, County of Otsego, near the dwelling house of Elisha Eldred, on the Susquehanna Road, intended for the Seminary of the Rev. John Christopher Hartwick, deceased, as directed by his will.

For particulars inquire of Farrand Stranahan,

Esq., of the Village of Cooperstown, or of the subscribed in the city of Albany. Albany 18th October 1811.

Signed John G. Knauff,

Executor Sec."

Three bids were submitted - Cyrus & Cyrenus Clark $5,000.00; Lorenzo Bates $5,200.00, and Robert Wilson and Enoch Sill $3,925.00. In passing I might note that C & C Clark had built the Cooperstown Academy and the Presbyterian Church, and that Bates was the builder of the three stone cotton mills at Index, Toddsville, and Phoenix.

On February 24, 1812 Knauff signed the contract with Wilson & Sill for $3,500.00 - not the $3,925.00 named in the bid. The architect was P. Hooker (Note - contract and plans are Vol. 4, pp 80-85 Hartwick College Archives).

The building was to be brick construction, 48 feet by 36 feet, with a center cupola on top of the second story. The basement was to contain a kitchen, dairy, and root cellar. There were to be three classrooms on the first floor and four on the second. On the 2nd of April, 1812 Mr. Samuel Craft wrote to Knauff accepting his offer as overseer of the construction.

On August 11, 1815 Dr. Knauff wrote to Mr. Craft giving him instructions for building a good board fence in front of the building with a gateway with two wings. The front and exposed ends of the fence were to be painted a color of Mr. Craft's choosing. He was also to build a barn large enough for one or two cows and one or two horses, with sufficient room for fodder. Included in the instructions were provisions for a driveway, a fence in the rear and a necessary with two parts, two seats, and two doors with a partition through the middle. The principal's necessary, some distance to the east, near the woodhouse was to have a lock on the door. Most of these details in regard to the barn, woodhouse, garden, etc. were left to Mr. Craft's good judgement.

Work seemed to drag, as it usually does, but by the last of November 1815 the building was ready, as well as a thirteen room brick house for the Principal, together with aqueduct to serve both buildings with water. A call had been extended, August 24, 1815, to the Rev. Ernest Lewis Hazelius, a Lutheran Minister of Prussian birth. He accepted the call and became the first principal of Hartwick Seminary officially opening the school December 5, 1815 with 19 scholars enrolled. The opening ceremonies were attended by a large number of the local residents and friends.

The course of study covered everything from the three R's to Latin and Greek as well as Bible instructions. The scholars came mostly from the local area. Anyone from a distance had to seek living quarters with the neighboring families. Arnold Lippitt didn't seem to be impressed with school, as we find him absent more than present in those first few months.

From the School Journal of the Rev. Hazelius, at the Hartwick College Archives, dated January 23, 1816 "Reuben T. Comstock entered the Seminary today - found it difficult by the increase of scholars to have charge of all the classes alone. I agreed with Comstock to take charge of the arithmetical class, and likewise to keep every Wednesday and Saturday p.m. a writing class for which I promised him tuition gratis." In his book "Throughout All the Years" Henry Hardy Heins has Adam Comstock as the first assistant teacher. That is, of course, incorrect, as Dr. Hazelius' Journal points out. I might add that Reuben Taylor Comstock was a great-great Uncle of mine, being the son of Martin Luther Comstock whom I cited as being a very near neighbor of Christian Hartwick.

It was very fitting that the first assistant teacher at the Seminary be a resident of the Hartwick Township. Mr. Comstock devoted his life to teaching. For several years he had his own Academy in Cooperstown but in 1831 he moved his family to Chautauqua County where he continued teaching for the remainder of his active life. There are several other references to Comstock in the Journal. I mention one dated Saturday, July 3, 1816; "disagreeable circumstance took place today with Horatio Averill to his brother. I reprimanded him severely for such conduct."

The Seminary was incorporated April 17, 1816 by a special act of the State Legislature and received its charter on August the 13th the same year. Under the Act of Incorporation there were to be twelve trustees, a majority of whom were to be Lutheran clergymen. For many years some of these men were selected from the local area. Father Nash, and Supreme Court Judge, the Honorable Samuel Nelson (both of Cooperstown) served on the Board for many years. The Hartwick Seminary area furnished such men as Husbands, Craft, Loomis, Swartout, and several others.

Dr. Hazelius carried on very faithfully and capably as Principal and Professor for a period of fifteen years. He was, of course, relieved of some of the teaching with help in the lower grades from his assistant teachers, such as John Quitman and others. An interesting ad ran in the local papers September 1, 1817 telling the public of the three school terms and giving the cost of the several courses of study. Children of Hartwick residents were given a reduced rate in each course that was offered.

Dr. Hazelius struggled along, with the help of the students until 1827 when George B. Miller came to the Seminary as an assistant professor, greatly relieving the duties of Dr. Hazelius. Dr. Miller was to remain at the Seminary for 42 years, the last 25 of which he served as Professor of Theology. To give an account of the many fine professors and principals who served in the Seminary would take a great deal of time. To those wishing an accurate and detailed account, I would refer you to the splendid work of Henry Hardy Heins - "Throughout All the Years."

During the first half century of Hartwick's history it had its ups and downs. In 1839 the enrollment dropped to 17 but that was soon to change. During the same year the Seminary Church was built and gave the school a great boost and the community as well. Now it would seem that the dreams of John Christopher Hartwick were coming true. His Seminary and Church were both realities. Professors from the Seminary acted as Pastors for nearly a century.

Realizing their existing facilities were not adequate for the successful operation of the institution, the Trustees added two stone wings to the original building in 1841. The students were then housed at the Seminary and not among the residents of the neighborhood.

Another forward step was taken in 1851 when Hartwick became one of the first to become co-educational. With the addition of 27 young ladies in the fall the Hartwick student body numbered 89. Still another forward step in 1853 was the addition of a normal course of study. This was to prepare young men and young women as teachers on the grade school level and preceded the State Normal at Oneonta by 35 years.

It seems that every few years from 1833 until about 1870 there would be movements, promoted by synod, to move the Seminary to a new location such as Cobleskill or Schoharie where there were large Lutheran communities, as compared to Hartwick. In 1833 Cooperstown again put in a bid for the Seminary and an amusing item appeared in the local paper stating that an old lady declared it could not be done as they couldn't get the Seminary over Hope Factory Bridge. Each time there was an attempt made toward the removal of the Seminary the residents voiced their feelings. The Trustees of the Seminary realized they could do nothing without the consent of the residents of Hartwick Township for one of the Trustees, the Honorable Samuel Nelson, Supreme Court Judge, had concurred with the Bar Association that under the will of John Christopher Hartwick, deceased, the inhabitants of the locality had acquired certain "vestal rights" in the institution of which they could not be deprived, and that the Trustees could be stopped by an injunction, if they made the attempt. The above ruling appeared in the July 14, 1875 issue of the Republican-Democrat when, once again, the Seminary was about to be moved to Cooperstown. (This ruling was handed down many years before - probably in 1839 - and mentioned by one of the Trustees in 1875. Fifty years later the ruling was forgotten or ignored when the Seminary was moved to Brooklyn, New York. Judge Nelson served as a Trustee for 38 years — until his death - 1835—1873.) During the mid 1860's the Trustees carried on a fund raising campaign for the expansion and remodeling of the then existing building. About the same time they were offered by the Lutherans of Warrensville, Schoharie County, their building, etc. if the Seminary would come to them. So the Trustees of the Seminary went to the Hartwick Town Board and told them that unless they were willing to help out financially they would move the Seminary to Schoharie County. The Town Board agreed to raise $5,000.00 if the Trustees would match their offer. So the Seminary remained.

The work of removing the stone wings proceeded nicely. New and larger brick wings, replaced them. A third story was added and a new tower adorned the front. They also decided to renovate the Principal's house at the same time. The cost of these improvements amounted to around $23,000.00. The Trustees became slightly perturbed when the Hartwick residents insisted on paying their $5,000.00 in labor rather than cash. I am of the opinion that the residents may have had a fast one pulled on them, for other building improvements were not included in the agreement.

The new building was completed in 1869 and it added greatly to the teaching and living facility of the institution. During the construction period the Seminary had to close its doors for two years. The Seminary was at a low ebb. Most of the endowment funds were used to pay for the new building, and within a four year period four of Hartwick's beloved leaders were called to their Eternal Home. Before the new building could be opened Dr. Miller died. In 1870 Dr. Scholl died and was followed by the Reverend Titus in 1873.

In that same period the long-talked-of railroad entered the Susquehanna Valley. In July 1869 the first train ran to Cooperstown and the Oneonta—Cooperstown stage stopped operations on the same day. This was a great thing for the students from distant places.

In 1872 the Reverend James Pitcher came to the Seminary as principal and thus began a period of half a century or more which, I believe, were the golden years of Hartwick.

In 1912 Mr. Andrew B. Yetter, an alumnus of the Seminary, gave a new gymnasium which would, through the next 25 years, add so much to the facilities of Hartwick. Besides the basketball court, bowling alleys and other equipment were made available. The stage was the scene of many plays and other school activities. These facilities were also used during many Summer Assemblies which were an important part of Hartwick Seminary history.

It would not be fitting to leave unmentioned the two Literary Societies of the Seminary. Philo - for young men, and Zeta - for the young ladies. Rensaelear Williams founded the Philophronian Society during the first year of Hartwick's existence, and the Zetasophian was organized shortly following the admission of girls in 1851. Both groups were of outstanding service to the Seminary by helping young men and women to better prepare themselves in debating, public speaking, and learning to work with one another in the preparation and presentation of literary programs. Several times a year joint programs were held.

In passing I might mention the fact that during the many years of the Seminary many of the young Theologians gained a great deal of confidence and ability by preaching on Sunday afternoons at the County Home, at several of the cotton mills and the district schools in the area. For many years the Seminary provided Sunday afternoon services in my home district of Hinman Hollow. If a Theologian was not available for the service one of the professors would come. What a wonderful service of love. The giver as well as the receiver was blessed. Something that I shall always remember.

Several of the local youths, having received academic training at the Seminary, went on to become fine doctors, lawyers, architects, etc. Several also became very fine ministers:- Amos Traver, Philip Luther, Erwin Tucker, Dorr Fritts, and Clifford Bound come to mind. No doubt there were others. These were some of the fine men I was privileged to know who came from the immediate area.

To give credit to all the wonderful Professors, Teachers, and Instructors throughout the history of the Seminary would be a task far beyond my limited ability. But none of us who attended "The Good Old Sem" could ever forget the wonderful Christian influence of such men as Daddy Kistler, Dr. Hiller, Dr. John Gideon Traver, Dr. Frank Wolford, Dr. Carney, and Rev. Joseph C. McLain; to mention a few of the ones we learned to love and respect. The influence that the Seminary had, for well over a hundred years, not only on the immediate area but throughout the world, could never be measured. The influence, not only of the ministers but also those of other professions who received wonderful Christian training at Hartwick, has had a great impact on the cultural and moral life in the many communities where they served. With the passing of Hartwick Seminary our area here at Hartwick suffered a tremendous loss. Something vital to the character and culture of our town was lost. Although we are not predominantly Lutheran in Hartwick, we felt a sense of pride in claiming the Seminary as part of our heritage. Today we rejoice that Hartwick College has grown into one of the country's outstanding small colleges, and are especially happy that the good old spirit of Hartwick still exists, not only in the student body but in the faculty as well.

I doubt if any historian, attempting to write a true and complete history of John Christopher Hartwick will ever be absolutely sure of doing so for the following reason, and I quote from the minutes of the August 26, 1828, meeting of the Board of Trustees of Hartwick Seminary: "Thirteenth Annual Meeting, Messrs. Husbands, Medcalf, together with the Principal, Rev. Dr. Hazelius were appointed a committee to examine the papers of John Christopher Hartwick and authorized to destroy such as were useless." We will never know, if any of the papers were destroyed or not. What might have seemed unimportant to them at the time, might have been of great importance to us today.

Just a word in behalf of poor old John Christopher. When you think that the poor soul labored more than forty years, traveling through a wilderness, infested with Indians, while the country was fighting the French-Indian War, as well as the Revolutionary, it is little wonder he became tired and dejected, in body and spirit. Evidently, the last few years he trusted few people, but remained steadfast in his Faith in God. He is to be pitied, rather than criticized. His dream of a new Jerusalem he could never see materialize.

By: Kenneth Augur 1976
Sources of Material:

I am greatly indebted to Hartwick College for their splendid cooperation in allowing me the use of their Hartwick Archives.
To the wonderful research done by the late Roy Butterfield, without whose extensive research I would have been at great loss.
To Henry Hardy Heins for the splendid volume "Throughout All the Years," which portrays such a vivid picture of the Hartwick story.
To the Town of Hartwick Town Clerk's Book.
To the tales my father told me.
To Hilda, my wife, for her untiring research in the local newspapers.

Tombstone of John Christopher Hartwick.

Hartwick Seminary recovered the tombstone in 1913 and it was transferred to Hartwick College in 1934. For some years it was stored in the boiler room of Bresee Hall and became the subject of occasional student pranks until it was finally embedded in the wall of Arnold Hall on the Hartwick College campus in the 1960's.

Photo Courtesy of the Paul F. Cooper, Jr.
Archives, Hartwick College, Oneonta, New York

Translation of German verse by Henry N. Pohlman, 1866:

> Man's life in its appointed limit
> Is seventy, is eighty years;
> But care and grief and anguish dim it
> However joyous it appears.
> The winged moments swiftly flee
> And bear us to eternity.

Early Settlers and Purchasers

Settlement

The distribution of the town lands, already acquired by large owners, occurred in stages and covered a considerable period of time. Repeated subdivisions, leases, and frequent transfers of title all were made before a settled population of resident owners. Most of the transactions can be traced but to do so the ground must be gone over several times. It seems essential also for full comprehension to include all the territory either in the Hartwick Patent or in the present town. It should be kept in mind that nothing east of Oaks Creek is now in the town, but that it was not always so.

The Otsego Patent

The Otsego Patent portion was ready five years before the Hartwick Patent was partitioned and so will be presented first. Some settlements had been made before the Revolution on parts of Croghan's previous possessions, but none that affected this town. With the land in hand Cooper and Craig advertised for settlers, saying that application might be made at Burlington, N. J. until the 26ᵗʰ of April, 1786 and that "thereafter attendance would be given on the spot." This item appearing in the "Pennsylvania Gazette" brought a warning from Croghan's executors and creditors that a secure title could not be given. Cooper and Craig answered and the differences aired in succeeding issues are of great help in reconstructing the previous history of the Otsego

Patent. Cooper made the final and telling point. His parting shot was that fifty families were waiting to purchase at Otsego by the time he arrived on the ground. In the ensuing transactions Cooper followed a pattern which was to be repeated many times as he expanded his operations. He was dealing with men of little means but who were eager to secure land and were willing to take some risks. He sold in as large parcels as applicants would accept. For a small down payment - as little as 10¢ - he gave a deed and accepted a mortgage for the rest. The mortgages he readily assigned to ready takers among his Burlington friends. Then his own capital was kept liquid for continuing developments. When no down payment could he obtained he made conditional sales, receiving interest but title not passing at the time. Many of the purchasers were speculators like himself but on a smaller scale. Some continued to be Cooper customers in later ventures.

As before stated, Cooper and Craig's purchase bordered on the Hartwick Patent. Cooper mistook the location of the dividing line, supposing it to be two-thirds of a mile too far south. It is a fact that the sheriff's deed describes the parcel as beginning near the mouth of Oaks Creek but it would seem that some evidence of the true line would have remained from earlier surveys, which had been made for Hartwick in 1754 and for Crogan in 1769 and in 1774. The correct line would have begun at the west near the Potter school house, passed Oaks Creek near the upper bridge at Toddsville, and met the river between the Susquehanna Avenue bridge and the mouth of Red Creek. At any rate Cooper believed he was right and at the time others interested seem to have agreed. David Cully who was a neighborhood resident and employed by the State Surveyor's office, was present at the sheriff's sale and soon bought some of this land. In selling it he located the line precisely where Cooper conceived it to be. Later he did surveying for Hartwick and seems never to have raised a question. Hence Cooper encroached to the extent given and not until eight years later did a new survey uncover what had happened. Meanwhile farm boundaries had become too well established to be disturbed and nothing could be done except to compensate the losers by the encroachment through adjustments in other ways.

Because of this error all published maps showing surveys within the town are misleading. These show the divisions, as they should have been, not as they were actually occupied. A new map has been drawn to accompany this volume in order to depict settlement clearly, and is so attached at the end of this article, that reference may be made to it while reading the text. The lot numbers in the Hartwick Patent are found on actual surveys; for the Otsego Patent arbitrary numbers 1 to 48 have been assigned for convenience.

Cooper divided this particular section into nine large lots. These and their subdivisions are now discussed in order, beginning at the west. The date for these transactions as listed below is in all cases 1786. In a few cases the original contract has not been located, but doubtless the whole was disposed of by one method or another in that year.

1st	1 – 7	900 acres	Ebenezer Walbridge and others	deed
2nd	8 – 9	187	not found	
	10	295	James Butterfield and Johnathan Runyan	deed
	11 – 13	260	John Tunnicliff (sold by Cooper to Gerritt Boon-1792)	
3rd	14 – 15	380	David Cully	deed
	16 – 17	250	Robert Riddle	
4th	18 – 23	625	William Abbott	deed
5th	24 – 27	627	Labuh Meacham	
6th	28 – 33	625	Abiel Lyon	
7th	34 – 39	625	— Moffatt	
8th	40 – 47	1501	Samuel Tubbs	deed
9th	48 – 51	500 approx.	not found	

A deed is noted above when one is known to have been given. The others were probably leases or conditional sales. These last are referred to by Cooper as "the Meacham lot," "the Moffatt lot" and so forth. All these and some of the others came back into Cooper's hands and he sold them later in smaller parcels. There are instances in which he allocated the same farm for the third time before a buyer wished, or was able to stay put. The Walbridge lot was one of four, totaling 5702 acres, bought by a group of six persons. This one included an additional 108 acres, now in the Town of Burlington, and marked "A" on the map. Some of the contracting parties here bought of Cooper elsewhere some already owned other local lands. Lyon transferred his interest to Elijah Hawkins. Samuel Tubbs returned all but 480 acres of his large purchase. Of course these first lots, as sold, were entirely too large for actual farming operations in that day. This confirms the speculative factor that was involved.

Going back again to the beginning point, the next step in settlement is now reviewed. Names in parentheses indicate the seller unless this was Cooper himself.

1	500	Phineas Potter	1790
2	50	Spencer Weaver	1800
3	100	Roger Thrall	1793
4	50	Ariel Coe	1794
5	65	Samuel Cooper, by will sold to Andrew Brown	1811
6	85	Joel Elmer	1800
7	50	Asael Whipple	1795
8	80	Phineas Potter	1793
9	107	Rufus Thrall	1793
10		see preceding list	
11	59	Rufus Thrall	1797(Boon)
12	105	William Bradley	1797(Boon)
13	102	Benjamin Weaver	1797(Boon)
14	130	Rufus Hawkins	1789(Cully)
15	250	John Runyan	1787(Cully)
16	125	Philip Wells	1793
17	125	Rhodes Fry	1793
18	50	Jacob Pratt	1788(Abbott)
19	175	Reuben Irons	1794
20	50	Royal Crosby	1794
21	50	Hanan Hawkins	1794
22	25 ½	Asa Irons	1794
23	224 ½	William Field	1794
24	100	Zatter Andrews	1796
25	175	Nicholas Steere	1794
26	127 ½	George Pearce	1794
27	214	Amos Winsor	1794
28	100	Joseph Winsor	1794
29	100	David Fisk	1794
30	100	Stephen Cook	1794
31	50	Josiah Jones	1794
32	100	Edward Eddy	1794
33	125	Noah Eddy	1794
34	100	Samuel Morris	1794
35	100	Stephen Babbitt	1794
36	100	James Aplin	1794
37	100	Josiah Jones	1794
38	100	Joel Holbrook	1794
39	125	Alpheus Wentworth	1794
40	125	David Matthewson	1796
41	125	James Aplin	1796
42	200	William Eddy	1796
43	100	Simeon Ingalls	1796
44	200	Robert Carr	1796
45	95	Daniel Carr	1796
46	480	Samuel Tubbs	1796
47	150	Daniel Kenyon	1796
48	300	William Abbott	1786
49	154	Joseph Strong	1800
50	159	John Howard	1790
51	100	Jonathan Potter	1800

Many of these pioneers, having leased the lands, were here earlier than the date of their purchases. About a dozen of such names are on the 1790 census list for the area. As might be expected either then or now, a mortgage lay on every parcel. Cooper's mortgages for this period fill many solid pages in the county clerk's index.

The many entries for 1794 above should be especially noted. That was the year when the encroachment on the Hartwick Patent became clearly evident and when Cooper made the adjustments and compensations so necessitated.

A portion of the Abbott purchase was evidently lost track of when the surrounding farms were sold. There in 1801 Cooper deeded to Aaron

Rice 30 acres.

Several parcels listed above still were larger than the owners wished to retain and further subdivisions were soon made. Phineas Potter (#1) in 1797 sold to his son David 50 acres, to Jonathan Runyan 80 and to Simeon Randall 100. The rest was returned to Cooper who sold 85 acres to Benjamin Camp in 1805 and 100 to Daniel Potter in 1806. There was also a lease of 45 acres to Leaman Potter, which came by will to Samuel Cooper and was sold to Russell Fay. Phineas Potter did not retain his second purchase (#8) either. This was leased to Freedom Potter, willed to Samuel, and eventually purchased in two parcels by Nathaniel Gott and Joseph Whaley. James Butterfield (#10) sold farms to Robert Coe, Samuel Wilson and Jonas Parker and house lots to Doctors Gott and David Hatch. He still had left for himself 90 ½ acres.

As an inducement to settlers to make prompt payments, the following item of interest may well be introduced here. Cooper and Craig in 1786 promised each of their first purchasers a free lot in the chief village, soon to be laid out, if their land was fully paid for within the specified ten years. Butterfield seems to be the only Hartwick resident who qualified for this premium. His mortgage was discharged in eight years and in 1796 he received the Cooperstown village lot, 35 by 150 feet, at the southeast corner of Water (now River) and Fourth (Elk) Streets. Actually Elk Street was never extended east to the river. Butterfield sold this in 1809 to Richard Cooper, whose homestead (Apple Hill) it adjoined.

Rufus Thrall sold his second farm (#11) to George Norton, John Runyan (#15) sold 50 acres to Spencer Weaver in 1796 and the remaining 100 to Stephen Bolles in 1803. The manner in which Rhodes Fry and his brother-in-law Philip Wells divided the square 250-acre plot (# 16-17) is interesting. A good water supply, access to a highway or an equable division of the more tillable lands, may have been reasons. Fry is known to have been on his site as early as 1787. He was unable to keep up his payments after his purchase in 1793. At Cooper's suggestion he exchanged his deed for a lease in 1801. James Cooper was willed this farm and in 1812 Fry was able to retain the title. He became a substantial citizen who reared a notable family. This is an excellent illustration of Cooper's way with the settlers, looking after his own interests, and at the same time assisting the pioneers to solve the difficult problems of frontier life and maintain their self respect.

Jacob Pratt became insolvent and his 50 acres (#18) came into the possession of Samuel Wilson and Reuben Root who sold it to Daniel Green in 1797. Samuel Tubbs also disposed of some of his 480 acres (#46) but there was still 310 acres in this lot when it was bought by Jehiel Todd in 1806. The northern part of #48 lay out of the area here considered.

It will be perceived then that nearly all of this portion of the town was owned under deed and in manageable parcels, within a decade after settlement began. Here it will be left for now.

The Hartwick Patent

Meanwhile matters were at a standstill on the Hartwick Patent. It had been obtained, as already noted, in 1761. In the thirty years following no successful moves were made to bring settlers on those lands. In 1764 Hartwick gave it a try. On the 27th of July in that year the four current proprietors-Elizabeth Roosevelt, widow, Brinkerhoff, Banyar and Hartwick signed an agreement that each would furnish a proportionate share of 640 acres of such shape and location as Hartwick might select, part for a minister, part for a schoolmaster, two-acre home sites for mechanics, up to 200 acres each for farmers, to be paid for at eight shillings an acre, plus quit-rents and one-tenth the produce. Further allotments would be made as needed. James Fenimore Cooper writing his "Chronicles of Cooperstown" about 1838, has this to say about the site Hartwick chose, "Mr. Hartwick, being under the impression that his grants extended to the shore of the lake, caused a clearing to be commenced not far from its outlet. Becoming satisfied that he had passed the boundaries of his estate this gentleman soon relinquished his possession, and altogether abandoned the spot." This statement has been quoted many times but its ultimate source is unknown. There is nothing that bears upon it in the Hartwick papers. If entirely true it further illustrates the confusion in regard to the Hartwick Patent north line. Hartwick could have located at just about that "spot" and have been right. There are other tales of persons on the patent at various times, but none can be substantiated. It is said that Nathan Davison, then a soldier stationed at Albany, came to the site of his later home in 1779, bought 200 acres of Hartwick, cut logs for a cabin, returned to Monson, Mass., came back in the spring of 1780 with his wife and made a thousand pounds of maple sugar. His own son has stated that Nathan came in 1785. It will be shown further on that he did not lease on this patent until 1791. There might be some truth in the sugar episode. The patriot garrisons were low on this article and there is at least one well-documented instance of detachments of soldiers making sugar not far away that spring.

It is also alleged that Hartwick tried again in 1783. Then there is the story that Samuel Benjamin visited the patent in 1784 returned to Connecticut and came back the next year with sixteen families, who settled in the White House area. This is extremely doubtful, not to say incredible. The location would indicate the Otsego patent, if in this town, and these persons were certainly not there when Cooper and his surveyors traversed the country that year. This party may have gone to southern Burlington where Benjamins did arrive early and which was outside Cooper's limits. Furthermore there is William Cooper's affidavit "that this affirment is well acquainted with the whole premises and that in the year of our Lord 1784 no house, shed, or building of any kind whatever was erected on or within the boundaries of a Patent granted to the late, John Christopher Hartwick and others." Hints of a change were in the air. Cooper had his eye upon every nearby tract awaiting development. His reputation for attracting settlers and for putting idle acres to work was growing rapidly. This would not have escaped the attention of the astute Banyar, who likely thought it time something was paid on that mortgage. He may have exerted some pressure on Hartwick. It would not be strange if the other proprietors had a like attitude. At any rate Hartwick spent considerable time on the scene in 1788 and 1789, and in 1791 retired from the pulpit and had no excuse for further delay. And now from every angle was the time appointed.

On the 20th of August 1788 Mr. Bliss of Massachusetts, and a Mr. Brekinridge, of Connecticut, offered to buy out Hartwick's entire interest at eight shillings an acre. This may have been Jacob Bliss, who in 1791 bought 500 acres in the 12,000-acre tract. Banyar gave his consent as mortgagee. The deal did not go through. Had it done so, Hartwick would have received very much less than he eventually realized.

On the 22nd of September 1790 Lefferts empowered Cooper to lease his portion (when divided) for a period of ten years at the annual rate of one shilling an acre, with the privilege to paid-up tenants of purchasing at the end of that time at fourteen shillings an acre plus interest. On the 27th of September in the same year Cooper purchased a one-half interest in the original Goetschius share, now in the possession of William Lupton, husband of the former Mrs. Frelinghuysen.

In the spring of 1791 Hartwick employed David Cully, of Milford Center, to run a north and south line through the middle of the tract, marking a tree at every 43 chains and 73 links to indicate the eleven parts into which the patent directed the land should be divided. A meeting at Albany was then arranged for the 13th of May to partition the patent among the several owners. This partition must have been by agreement, as Lefferts was assigned the first, or southern division, Banyar the second, Hartwick the third to the tenth inclusive, and Lupton and Cooper the eleventh, or northernmost. Thus Hartwick's portion lay all together and Cooper's was adjacent to his Otsego Patent lands. This turned to be fortunate for Cooper when the encroachment matter had to be remedied. Hartwick had had a map made, which appears, on the back of the patent instrument. It is worthwhile to record here that this shows the Susquehanna flowing directly south the whole length of the Hartwick Patent. It doesn't and this made a difference. The map also denotes the breadth of each division as 43 chains and 72 links. Eleven divisions each of that breadth would cover more than six miles. It is curious that the parties concerned, all familiar with land affairs, let this error pass. Did they think the patent was actually more than six miles wide? Actually as first surveyed it was slightly short. A later surveyor immediately detected this mistake. The whole patent was now ready for individual sales with Cooper in the saddle except for Banyar's division. Beginning at the south these for the several proprietors will be taken up in order. It had been understood that division would be divided into six lots, each one mile wide, except for the two tiers at the west where the Otsego Creek was used as a boundary, making irregularities. Thus Hartwick's eight divisions would contains 48 lots. Here

again the basis of sales was articles of agreement. Now reference to the map will again be useful.

At the Albany meeting Hartwick also made Jeremiah Van Rennselaer attorney for his entire estate and empowered him to employ Cooper as land agent on exactly the same terms as obtained for the Lefferts division. It would thus appear that those terms had been suggested by Cooper himself. The commission in both cases was to be five cents, out of which Cooper was to pay surveying, conveying and recording costs. Cooper also took over Banyar's mortgage, now amounting to over 524 pounds, for the payment of which he was to withhold the first rents collected.

The First Division - Lefferts

Within a month after the date of the partition Cooper had leased the entire Lefferts share as follows:

1	330 acres	Jonas Perry
2	340 acres	Peter Millington
3	335 acres	Zachariah Cheney
4	344 acres	Ebenezer Carley
5	532 acres	Moses Richards
6	156 acres	Samuel Huntington

Perry was the only one of these men who settled down to farming there. Richards, Millington, and Huntington were Cooper customers elsewhere, and the last named kept a store and a tavern at Cooperstown.

There was some uncertainty about the size of #5 and both Cooper's commissions and later sales call for a larger acreage. The whole division evidently contained just under 2100 acres. The leases soon increased in number and decreased in size to form fifteen farms. Lefferts did not live to the end of the lease period. His executors in February of 1802 extended Cooper's authority so he might give deeds to the tenants who had qualified for them. This he did in 1803 and thereafter his agency ceased. The unredeemed farms went to John R. Beekman of New York

Acres Leases 1803 Ownership Later Sales

Acres	Leases	1803 Ownership	Later Sales	
166	Jonas Perry	Jonas Perry		
118	William Jewell	William Jewell		
107½	Jeremiah Hopkins	Jeremiah Hopkins		
220	Benjamin Bissell	(Beekman)	Samuel Brownell	1844
235	Isaac Stacy	(Beekman)	Jacob Stout	1808
111¾	William Barnard	Nathan Thorp	Josiah Arnold	1809
111¾	Reuben Barnard	Reuben Barnard		
130	Timothy Griswold	(Beekman)	Alpheus Bissell	1844
64	Peter Goodsell	Peter Goodsell	Alfred Haselip	1805
100	Holden Stone	(Beekman)		
100	Peter Goodsell	Peter Goodsell	James Morgan	1816
100	Charles Morgan	Charles Morgan		
100	Edward Bowe	Edward Bowe		
282	Samuel Sumner	Samuel Crafts	Seth Wright	1805
156			Job Harrington	141 acres

City, who was one of the executors, and later part of them to his heirs. The table below shows the situation, the farms being given in order from east to west.

All the persons named in the column of leases, except Stacy and Sumner were living there when the 1800 census was taken. It will be noted that the Beekman estate held on to some of the farms until long-term farm leases became extremely unpopular. Captain Jacob Stout of New York City, was a considerable investor in upstate lands. Other men known to have been either owners or tenants in this division for an appreciable time during the pioneer period are Joseph Dexter, Stephen Jorden, Samuel Baker and Isaac Bissell.

Second Division (Banyar)

Here were about 2025 acres, but as Arnold Lake is almost entirely within it, the equivalent of an average farm was under water. Banyar owned an immense amount of New York real estate, much in this county. Rather than sell, he preferred to rent and on the manorial plan used by the great Hudson Valley landlords. His descendants felt the same way. Some Banyar family history will help to make later developments more clear. When Goldsbrow Banyar died he left a daughter Martha, whose married name was Leroy and who was his executrix. She had a son Goldsborough (note change in spelling) who legally took the name Banyar in accordance with his grandfather's wish. Both mother and son shared in the estate. Martha died in 1829, leaving her share to be divided equally among her daughters Cornelia (Mrs. Robert H. Ludlow), Harriet (Mrs. Campbell P. White) and John Campbell White, son of daughter, Mary deceased (Mrs. Henry White). Hartwick property came to all these.

Banyar in his lifetime did sell about 800 acres here. The remainder lay in nine farms which were numbered consecutively from the east and were leased "for three lives," whereon tenants could hold the land until the death of third living person named in the lease. There were plenty of willing, even insistent purchasers for these farms. One such advised him in 1801 that he "could sell faster than rent." Dr. Thomas Fuller, of Cooperstown, in 1805 offered to buy 300 acres west of Arnold Lake, and pay for it with Western Turnpike Stock of the First Company. He stated that this land was "entirely in a state of nature, no squatters." Frequently Banyar was informed of thefts of timber on unoccupied land. All this indicates that this division was occupied later than the rest of the patent.

Since leases are not necessarily publicly recorded and since varying acreages are at times given for the same parcel, it is difficult to present an accurate account of settlement here, but wills and estate papers allow a fairly satisfactory reconstruction.

	Leases			Bequests		Sales	
Lot 1	Aaron Jewell					Jeremiah Hopkins	1798
	93½ acres	Jeremiah Hopkins	1800	Martha Leroy		Joseph D. Husbands	1818
	73½ acres	Samuel Thomas		Martha Leroy		Joseph D. Husbands	1818
	81½ acres	Nehemiah Tower	1796	Martha Leroy		Joseph D. Husbands	1818
Farm 2	130 acres	James Angel		Cornelia Ludlow		Warner Brownell	1844
Farm 3	130 acres	John Bowington		Harriet White		Leonard Brownell	
						Peter Mickel	1849
Farm 4	117¾ acres			John C. White		Andrew Salisbury	1848
Farm 5				G. Leroy Banyar			
Farm 6	98 acres	Nehemiah Howe	1814	Cornelia Ludlow		Nehemiah Howe	1841
Farm 7	100 aces	Adolphus Downer	1809	G. Leroy Banyar		Hiram and Samuel	
						Harrison	1853
Farm 8	100 acres	Elihu Ackley		Harriet White		Stephen Hoose (lease)	1870
Farm 9	100 acres	James Lane		G. Leroy Banyar		Henry Shove (lease)	1870
Lot 5	498 acres	Joseph Clark	1793			Joseph Clark	1810
Lot 6	206 acres	Joseph Clark	1793			Joseph Clark	1810

It may be that Aaron Jewell had rented all of Lot #1. It also seems that Husbands' purchase comprised Farm #1. This was made before Martha Leroy's heirs divided the estate in 1833. Joseph Clark sold seven parcels, totaling 403 acres, from his large purchase in the period 1810 - 1823 the buyers being John W. Clark, Thomas Clark, Erastus Wright, Thomas Johnson, Jr., William Andrews, and Oliver Bowe. Of the leasees Tower, Thomas, Hopkins, Jewell and Clark were living there at the 1800 census. Elijah and Josiah Mason were also residing somewhere between Clark and Arnold Lake.

Hartwick's Eight Divisions, 3rd to 10th

Hartwick had always yearned to handle his land himself and he had hoped to settle families of his own denomination. He had visions of a central town with a church and school. He had failed because he did not give the project the prompt and close attention it required. He lacked the qualities requisite in a successful colonizer anyhow. Nevertheless much pressure must have been exerted before he yielded the management to other hands. Almost from the first he appears to have regretted that he did so. On 22 June 1791 he wrote Cooper that he was now revoking "the power given to Mr. Rentzelaer and your Honour" because of a protest by the guardian of Frelinghuysen heirs against proceeding without a further hearing. This was only five weeks after Cooper had accepted the agency, but already 34 lots had been contracted. Hartwick did not record a revocation so legally one did not exist.

In fact, Cooper testified that his power of attorney had never been revoked. Neither he nor Van Rensselaer gave this matter any serious attention. On 10 September Cooper disposed of the last one of the 39 lots under his control. Hartwick continued to be unhappy about the arrangement, and was embittered toward his land agent. He also entered into direct negotiations with some tenants of his own choosing to occupy the reserved lots, sometimes informing Van Rensselaer, sometimes not. By this time Hartwick's mental powers had clearly and greatly declined. Van Rensselaer bore the consequent trials patiently, keeping affairs in as good order as he could, but naturally there was confusion later. To this period belongs the frequently quoted lease to Jerome Bates, wherein is the stipulation that the "tenant shall join Hartwick's congregation and help build church and school houses." Following Hartwick's death, a number of statements supported by witnesses, were filed with the executors, citing special conditions promised them in obtaining land.

It has already been inferred that Cooper lost no time in distributing the Dominies acres. Actually he moved too fast. He did not wait for the tract to be surveyed into the 48 proposed lots. He knew that the patent conveyed 21,500 acres, with an additional highway allowance. He estimated 22,000 acres for it all, so 2,000 to a division, and therefore 16,000 acres for Hartwick. This would work out to about 333 acres per lot. The Otego creek was taken as the boundary between the two tiers of lots at the west. There would be irregularities and these were surveyed. They varied greatly in area but were thought to average 344 acres. Some deduction was made in two divisions because of bends in the Susquehanna. Otherwise he proceeded, as he said "on the face of the division made." That is he accepted the preliminary work already done by Hartwick. Six miles was still taken to be the length of the northern boundary. On these bases the articles of agreement were executed. They included no measurements and only the briefest of descriptions, For examples, for lot #21, "the fourth lot from the Susquehanna in the seventh division, containing 330 acres," or for lot #6, "bounded north by the ninth division, east by the Otego Creek, south by the seventh division and west by the west bounds of the patent." Hereon could be based an excellent commentary on the man and the times; Cooper, the land colonizer, restive at the sight of unworked fields; prospective purchasers, willing to take conveyances without exact "metes and bounds" so long as they could get in there first. Today no one in his right mind would accept a land conveyance so loosely described, but such transactions were frequently recorded at the period; "fifty acres off the west end of the farm, later to be surveyed," or "by a line parallel to the north boundary so as to include 103 acres." Such methods invited (even insured) difficulties to come and so it was in these cases.

Speculation was the motive behind many of the first leases in this area. Most of them were for entire lots or even more, too large for a farming operation at the time. Several leasees conducting well-established businesses outside the area. The connection of many with this enterprise was of brief duration. Even those who intended to remain as residents took more land than they wished for their own use. All these classes must have counted upon the increase in land values, which would accompany the arrival of more pioneers.

Meanwhile they were secure in their possessions for ten years, if the low rent (or interest) was kept paid, and legally they could transfer their leases or sublet parts of them. In fact these large holdings were very soon split up. There were 39 lessees on Cooper's agency in 1791 and about 100 in 1794.

When actual farmers began to clear the land during the next year or two, they found the lots deficient in breadth. The explanation of course is that Cooper's sales in 1786 had included some of the Hartwick Patent. This shortage naturally disturbed the minds not only of the tenants, but those of Hartwick, Van Rensselaer, Banyar and Cooper as well. A resurvey was ordered, which was completed early in 1794. The encroachment of eight years before was now, for the first time clear to all. Cooper took measures to correct the situation. On 8 December 1792 be had purchased from William Lupton the remaining one-half of the eleventh division, thus canceling any further claim of the Frelinghuysen heirs. With this acquisition, he was now able to solve a difficult problem.

On 10 May 1794 all the tenants on the agency reconveyed their leases to Cooper.

He then issued to them new ones in his own name with the acreages reduced to fit the recent survey. These tenants were satisfied. Their holdings were still large enough and the rents were correct for the land occupied. Critics of Cooper then and since have regarded those transactions as a scheme of Cooper's to seize the Dominie's land. Actually they were forced upon him and

he was fortunate to have found a solution. Cooper was now tenant under Hartwick for the whole tract and responsible for the quit rent and the one shilling per acre annually on it all, whether completely subleased or not. But under the original terms he was also privileged to buy it all at the expiration of ten years at a guaranteed price. This he did, as will later appear.

Of course the shortage extended also to Hartwick's reserved lots. To atone for this and the land lost to Hartwick by the encroachment, Cooper released one more lot (#28) to be added to the reservations. A glebe lot of 120 acres had been reserved in lot #38. This was interfered with by the shortage, but lot #48 had an excess of 122 acres due to the westward flow of the river, which circumstance, seems now to have been recognized for the first time. The glebe lot was transferred there. Cooper also continued himself to make up the rents to the total of the original leases. This was no more than just.

Cooper also made adjustments in the area of encroachment. Although a few deeds had already been given there and all that land was well occupied, the most of it was being held under articles of agreement and title had not passed. Several such tenants exchanged with Cooper for land elsewhere in the county. In 1794 Cooper sold the lands here concerned in farm-sized portions to new purchasers in fee simple. These deeds include the phrase, "formerly thought to be in Croghan's, found to be in Hartwick's."

Also in 1794 Hartwick's mortgage was due, so in that year Cooper and Van Rensselaer had an accounting. Cooper paid three years rent and received payment for the mortgage, its interest and for his commissions. After Hartwick's death in 1796, Cooper divided his payments equally between the two executors, Van Rensselaer and Muhlenberg. From time to time, beginning in 1799, the executors deeded a considerable number of the lots to Cooper, who made some immediate sales in them. The year 1801 brought to an end the ten-year lease period. In that year Muhlenberg also died and Van Rensselaer, now as sole executor, sold to Cooper all the remaining lots in the agency. It was stated in the deed that Cooper had already paid all principal and interest, so the final consideration was a nominal ten dollars.

The parties did not easily arrive at a meeting of minds for this final deed. Van Rensselaer wished to sell "by length of chain," that is, by an actual survey. Cooper would buy only on the basis of the original leases. They agreed to refer the question to Philip Schuyler and Simeon DeWitt, both highly competent men. Schuyler was the first State Surveyor-General, DeWitt was currently holding that office. Each side presented a brief. On the same day that the matter was submitted to them, the referees returned a decision upholding Cooper. He paid for 13,030 acres. The reserved lots totaled 2926 ½ acres. This is but slightly short of the estimated 16,000 acres of 1791, and is consistent with the leases and the survey of the reserved lots made in 1794.

Again in these last acquired lots Cooper issued deeds to all the tenants who were able to buy and wished to do so. Many of them either preferred, or felt obliged, to continue on lease. For those new agreements were made whereby purchase could be consummated on any anniversary date at a price whose interest would yield the rent. The rents could be paid in beef, pork, corn, or wheat. At Cooper's death in 1809, 73 farms in his purchase here were still being held by lease.

Some settlement began under Hartwick's own eye in the reserved lots in 1792. Manifestly it was to the advantage of his project to have improvements undertaken, quit-rents and taxes transferred to others and rental revenues coming in. However he set conditions that were a deterrent. He advanced the purchase price over the arrangement made for Cooper the year before from 14 shillings to 20 shillings an acre. He specified that any who settled on portions he himself might wish "by and by" would be allowed what they had paid to be applied on a new location. This was not an attractive situation for the most desirable type of pioneer. There were frequent changes in occupancy and the records are too scanty for a full account. William Cumming, a tenant secured by Hartwick, acted for a time as local agent.

Hartwick died in 1796. His will imposed further restrictions on the land. Farms were bequeathed to several named persons. Provision was also made for further gifts to an unspecified number of Hartwick relatives in Germany, should they ever migrate to America. Land had to be set aside against this contingency. No one ever qualified in this way, although a number of attempts were made and the problems thus presented were a source of trouble for many years.

In 1798 ten persons were found willing to take leases for 21 years on land totaling 1154 acres at the former rate of one shilling annually per acre. Most of these parties were already occupants. The executors also proposed at this time to lease in perpetuity to Cooper all Hartwick lands except a glebe, the bequeathed farms and the 1154 acres here mentioned for $2,000 a year. This would have continued the rental rate at just about the old figure, but would have precluded Cooper's later purchase. Neither of these plans took effect. In 1799 advantage was taken of the statute permitting commutation of quit-rents through payment of a lump sum. That drain on the assets of the estate was now terminated. In 1801 occurred a flurry of real activity in the disposal of reserved land. Muhlenberg had died. Van Rensselaer was now sole executor. He was anxious to get the Hartwick affair off his hands. He made a real effort but did not succeed while he lived. New articles of agreement, again running for ten years, were executed for most of the unencumbered land. Several farms were sold outright and at higher prices, $4.50 to $5.00 an acre. Suits were instituted against tenants much in arrears and the whole matter assumed a more business like aspect. In 1811 the new leases expired. By now John G. Knauff had become trustee for the Hartwick estate. He disposed of much of the unsold land and resorted to stern measures to collect all accounts, both from the tenants and from other sources where the funds had been invested. His object was to get that Seminary into operation. He saw to it that a building was erected. Its doors opened in 1815, and charter obtained in the following year. Thereupon he turned over to the trustees the assets of the estate, shown by his accounts to be then $26,870. In 1817 the trustees were empowered by the Legislature to sell real estate on condition that the proceeds be treated as an endowment and the interest only be expended. William C. Bouck, one of the trustees was appointed financial and land agent. Under his wise management the remainder of the reserved lots was soon converted into cash with the exception of a single 100 acre farm in #33, which was held until 1838 in case a Hartwick relative should present a valid claim.

The following tables show the progress of settlement in detail. Reserved lots are indicated by "R." The year 1791 for columns 2 and 3 is taken because then the land was first distributed, 1794 for columns 4, 5 and 6 because a map showing tenants for that year exists and 1800-1801 because outright sales could then first be made. The acreage in column 2 is according to the first survey, in column 4 as reduced in Ellison's findings. (This is especially marked in Lots 1, 9, 17, 25, and 33). Fractional acres have been given to the nearest one-half. Lot lines were disregarded in some instances. For example, in #2 and 10, separated by Otego Creek, the mill site required possession of both banks.

On several lots changes in occupancy were common before a sale in fee transpired.

Many tenancies were of brief duration. Some residents during the period, but not at the years selected above, were Orange Spencer, Abner Bruce, Daniel Griffiths, William Dillingham, Whittington Sayre, Peter Davison, Josiah Platt, Elisha Taylor, Luther Gaines, John Scott.

1 Lot	2 Acres	3 Leases 1791	4 Acres	5 Leases 1794	6 Notes
1	240	Samuel Huntington	142	Hezekiah Tiffany	
2	254	Samuel Sleeper	92	Ziba Newland	See further infor mation
		also in #10	88	John Newland	in text following table
			5	Samuel Sleeper	Total 185
3	292	Preserved and	70	Wm. Baker, Jr.	
		Charles Alger	97	Wm. Baker, sr.	
			83	Thomas Green	Total 250
4	341	Cyrus Rowland	999	John Webb	
			50	Isaac Hedges	
			74	Jesse Bostwick	

			74 ½	Nijah Griffiths	Total 297 ½
5	374	Hubbard Fuller	50	Caleb Wells	
			101	Benjamin Fuller	
			82	Hubbard Fuller	
			82	Edward Doud	Total 301 ½
6	374	Phillip Howard	47	Lodowick Hotchkiss	
			37	Lodowick Hotchkiss	
			110	Abner Alger	
			59	Azariah Bradley	
			59	Henry Wright	Total 314
7	385	Israel Foster	120	Israel Foster	
			97	Samuel Bates	
			100	Not given	Total 317
8	448	James Gray	92	James Gray	
		Stephen Skiff	101	Stephen Skiff	
		Robert Coe	50	Joshua Wells	
		James Bacon	20	Peter Cook	
			39	— Wentworth	Total 417
9	448	Asher Bergen – 276　288		Asher Bergen – 77	some unrented
		Abiel Lyon – 172		Jacob Bunn - 60	
				Stukeley Elsworth - 103	
10	434	William Bergen – 212469		Samuel Sleeper – 150	some unrented
		Samuel Sleeper – 222		Asa Pride - 100	
				William Bergen - 58	
11	396	Nijah Griffiths	369	Nijah Griffiths – 80	some unrented
				William Joiner &	
				Thomas Lee - 39	
				Josiah Brigham - 125	
				Isaac Farwell - 132	
12	346	Ephraim Andrews	336	Ephraim Andrews - 150	
				Stephen Smith,Sr. - 150	
				Not leased - 36	
13	313	Samuel Rice	314	Samuel Ward – 78 ½	
				Cyrus Ransom – 78 ½	
				John Hughes - 78 ½	
				Aaron Adams - 78 ½	
14R	313	"Parish of the Patent of Hartwick"	308	No leases made here until 1795 a 30 acre school lot at N. E. corner	
15	303	Lot Crosby	307	Samuel Mudge – 40	some unrented
				Samuel Smith – 50	

				Seth Shippy - 100
16	240	Comfort Cook and Lot Crosby	245	Comfort Cook - 115
				Lot Crosby - 120
17	340	Joseph Wilbur	232	John R. Place – 100
				Thomas Fuller - 132
18	340	Daniel Howe	321	Preserved Alger – 100
				Ezekiel Jacobs - 150
19	330	Nathan Payne	320	William Kane - 70
				Squire Luther – 150
				William Johnson - 100
20	330	Nathaniel Johnson	323	Ignatius Wilson – 80
				Elisha Fullam – 143
				Chandler Robinon - 50
				Jared Robinson - 50
21	330	Reuben Closs	322	Reuben Closs – 150
				Eliakim Robinson – 86
				Chandler Robinson – 34
				Not leased – 52
22	330	William Waggoner	315	Abner Adams, Jr. – 60
				Micaiah Robinson - 100
				Jesse Robinson - 105
				Silas Robinson - 50
23	330	Preserved and Charles Alger	314	Adam Ballard - 50
				Charles Alger – 55
				Abner Adams, Jr. - 39
				Micaiah Robinson - 39
				Jonathan Thurber - 80
24	330	Josiah Alger	315	Josiah Alger - 115
				Josiah Alger, Jr. - 50
				Joseph Burgess - 100
				Not leased – 50
25	340	Samuel Blanchard	226	Cyrenus Clark - 113
				Cyrus Clark - 113
26	340	John Ransom	313	John Ransom - 150
				Luther Comstock – 150
				Not leased - 13
27R	350		322	William Cumming - 125
				Ebenezor Trusdel - 100
28	340	John Nichols	313	Abraham Lippitt - 163
				Abraham Lippitt, Jr. - 150

29	—	Nathan and John Davidson (See #37 & 45)	310	Salmon Comstock - 150 Joseph Lippitt - 150 Not leased - 10
30	—	Elisha Fullam and Jonas Hodgkins (See #38 & 46)	309	Stephen Holden -103 Daniel Birchard - 103 Solomon and Brewster Jewett - 103
31	—	Isaac Stacy (See #39 & 47)	298	Hopkins Burlingham - 100 Rowland Cotton – 100 Not leased - 98
32	—	James Averell and John Howard (Se #40 & 48)	312	Anson Sessions - 150 Solomon Clark - 150 Not leased - 12
33R	—		226	Christopher Hartwick - 100 Little Pond here
34R	—		319	Christopher Hartwick - 100 Little Pond here
35R	—		325	William Cumnings - 25
36R	—		338	
37	—	Nathan and John Davison (See #45)	322	Nathan Davison - 89 John Davison - 20 Asaph Potter - 107 Not leased - 105
38	—	Elisha Pullam and Jonas Hodgkins (See #46)	330	Elisha Fullam - 50 Matthew Derbyshire - 110 Benson Aldridge - 50 Glebe lot - 120
39	—	Isaac Stacy (See #47)	303	Isaac Wren - 101 Thomas Nichols - 100 MatthewDerbyshire - 100
40	—	James Averell and John Howard (See #48)	333	Eliphalet Williams - 96 John Howard - 100 Moses Wheeler - 100. Not leased - 37
41R	—	Lots No, 41, 42 and 43 became in 1794 the nine lesser lots.		
42R		These totalled 623 ½ acres.		
43R		No Leases or sales were made there before 1800. Not well known.		
44	330	Nathaniel Pierson and Joseph Ford	280	Nathan Pierson – 107 Noah Ford - 83 Moses Richards – 89

45	—	Nathan and John Davison	240	Nathan Davison - 154 John Davison - 88	The Davison three leased lots (29, 37, 45) were in 1791 computed to total 960 acres
46	—	Ellisha Fullham and James Hodgkins	327	Jonas Hodgkins – 63 Bille Williams – 150 Not leased – 114	The three Fullam& Hodgkins leased lots (30, 38, 46) were in 1791 computed to total 970 acres.
47	—	Isaac Stacy	353	Samuel Hartshorn -104 Isaac Stacy – 150 Jared Clark –11 "The Point Lot" – 33 Not leased - 55	Stacy's three leased lots (31, 39, 47) were in 1791 computed to contain 1,000 acres.
48	—	James Averell and John Howard	474	Isaac Carr – 111 Ambrose Clark – 102 Jared Clark – 51 East of Oaks Creek, (not reported) - 210	Averill & Howard's three leased lots (32, 40, 48) were in 1791 computed to total 1,000 acres.

The Eleventh Division

Detailed information concerning the eleventh division is not shown in early surveys. Later transactions fix the breadth at 30 chains, the length at very nearly seven miles and the consequent extent at about 1680 acres.

The southern one-half (the Philadelphia lot) was the last land parcel in the town to be made available to settlers. The dates of many of the first conveyances there have not been ascertained. Doubtless all was largely leased very soon after Cooper concluded its purchase in 1792. A few deeds were given before 1800.

The northern one-half (Elizabeth Cooper's) was all leased in 1791 as follow.:

Lot 1 —   Samuel Preston
      2 —   Thomas Kellogg
      3 —   Ezek Beverly
      4 —   Samuel Bissell
      5 —   Lebuh Meacham
      6 —   Joel Coe

A number of changes in occupancy occured before 1800, for example, Benjamin Weaver and Abraham West had followed Coe in #6 by 1794.

The development of these lands (divisions 3 – 11) will now be carried forward as well as may be to the period when the Cooper family interests had ceased and bona fide resident owners had secured title. Some parcels have eluded search. In the table following these plots are marked with interrogation points. In column 3 only persons taking up leases in the years 1800and 1801, when Cooper secured title, are named. Many were on the ground earlier but some at unascertained dates. In column 4 the bequests of William Cooper, Sr. were all effective in 1809, those of Hartwick in 1796. The Christian names only of Cooper heirs are given. Column 5 names those nonresidents who succeeded the heirs on the breakup of the Cooper estate. Continuity of transactions may be traced from the preceding table.

Lot	Acres	Leases 1800-1801	Bequests	Successor	Acres	Settler's Sales
1	71	Thomas Booth	Isaac		71	
	71	Ichabod Perkins	Samuel	W. H. Averi	71	?
2	92	Ziba Newland	Samuel	W. H. Averell	98	?
	89 ½	————			89 ½	Job Cole 1801
	16 ½	————			16 ½	Abraham Lippitt 1801
3	70	————			70	Randall Wells 1801
	97	William Baker	Isaac	George Clarke	97	Lyman Green 1837
	83				83	Thomas Green 1801
4	99	————			99	John Webb 1801
	50		————		50	Isaac Hedges 1801
	74	Jesse Bostwick	Richard	George Clarke	63	Joseph Brownell 1837
					11	Charles Dillingham 1813
	74 ½	Nijah Griffiths	Estate	Executors	74 ½	John Webb 1813
5	55	Jeremiah Rumsay	Samuel	W. H. Averell	55	Silas Robinson 1827
	101	————			101	Benj. Fuller,Jr. 1800
	82	————			82	Joshua Munroe1800
	82	————			82	Edward Doud 1800

6	47	William Schooly			47	?
	147	———————			147	Abner Alger 1802
	59	Azariah Bradley	Isaac		59	Azariah Bradley 1813
	59	Israel Dwight	James	Thomas Ward	59	?
7	92	Ambrose Fostor	James		92	Levi Beebe 1819
	94	Samuel Bates	Richard	George Clarke	94	Truman Head 1824
	130				130	Isaac Babbitt 1801
8	92	———————			92	James Gray 1801
	10	James Gray	Ann		10	Gardner Cook 1813
	101	———————			101	Stephen Skiff 1802
	42	Stephen Skiff	William		42	?
	40	James Young	William		40	Christopher Hall
	59	Christopher Hall	Samuel	W. H. Averell	59	Christopher Hall
	48	———————			48	Jonathan Thurber 1801
9	51 ½	Asher Bergen	Isaac	George Clarke	51 ½	Jacob Bunn 1837
	26 ½	———————			26 ½	Thomas Johnson 1801
	60	Jacob Bunn	Issac	George Clarke	60	Jacob Bunn 1837
	103		———————		103	Stukely Elsworth 1801
	47	Henry Baker	Isaac	Executor	47	Stukely Elsworth 1821
10	97	———————			97	Abraham Lippitt 1801
	100	M. & E. Pride	Ann		100	Micajah Pride 1830
	105	Henry Baker	Isaac	Executor	105	Stukely Elsworth 1821
	50	Perry Ellsworth			50	Joseph Moss 1802
	57	Ebenezer Hubbard	Ann		10	Paris Pray 1816
					47	Clark Smith 1834
11	124	Josiah Maples			124	Josiah Maples 1800
	123	Josiah Brigham	Isaac	W. H. Averell	120	Henry Field 1840
	41	Thomas Green	Richard	George Clarke	41	Stephen Holden 1823
	62	Benjmin Green	James	Thomas Ward	62	?
	20	Sylvanus Campbell	Isaac	W. H. Averell	20	Clark Smith 1834
12	168	———————			168	Solomon Owens
	84	Stephen Smith	Samuel	Executor	168	Stephen Smith 1820
	84	Stephen Smith, Jr				
13	79	Samuel Ward	William	George Clarke	79	David Ward 1837
	79	William Alworth	William	George Clarke	79	?
	157	Jonathan Ashcraft	Richard	George Clarke	157	?
14R	100	Jonathan Newman-1795	Hartwick Estate		100	Jonathan Newman 1817
	100	Ezekial Newman-1795	Hartwick Estate		100	Philo West, Jr.
	75	Jonathan Newman	Hartwick Estate		78	Robert Van Schaick 1811
	30	School Lot	Hartwick Estate		30	Harris Winsor 1817
15	40	Elnathan Mudge	Isaac	W. H. Averell	43	Paris Pray 1884

Lot	Acres	Name			Acres	Owner / Year
	50	Elnathan Mudge	Isaac	W. H. Averell	57	Levi and Isaac Beebe 1824
	60	Seth Shippy	Samuel	W. H. Averell	60	Renesselaer Cook 1824
	40	Nathan Shippy	Samuel	W. H. Averell	40	Holden
	50	Silvanus Douglas	Ann		50	Swift
	67	Alexander Chilson	Isaac		67	Amasa Peters
16	115	Comfort Cook			115	Comfort Cook 1802
	72	Lot Crosby	Isaac	Executor	72	Harris Winsor 1820
	50	Heman Comstook	Isaac	Sheriff	50	Paris Pray 1824
17	100	———			100	Joseph Moss 1801
	132	———			132	Thomas Fuller 1801
18	100				100	Abner Adams 1800
	100	Ezekiel Jacobs	Ann		100	Jacobs heirs 1849
	50	William Kelly	Ann		50	Henry and Charles Adams 1844
	70	Abner Adams, Jr.			70	Abner Adams, Jr. 1811
19	78	Hezekiah Smith	Samuel	W. H. Averell	78	?
	———				90	Squire Luther 1801
	60	Amasa Wade	William		60	?
	———				100	William Johnson 1801
20	80	Ezra Loomis	Samuel	W. H. Averell	80	Henry Field 1824
	———				143	Micaiah Robinson 1801
					50	Joshua Luther 1801
	———				50	Bille Williams 1801
21	100	Ziba Robinson	Samuel	W. H. Averell	100	?
	120	———			120	Joshua Luther 1801
	97 ½	Ichabod Woodworth	William	George Clarke	97 ½	Silas Marlette 1837
22	60	———			60	Abner Adams, Jr. 1801
	100	——			100	David Maples 1801
	105	Jesse Robinson	Estate	Executors	105	David Maples 1810
	50	———			50	Silas Robinson 1801
23	50	Adam Ballard	Richard	George Clarke	50	?
	55	Charles Alger	Richard	George Clarke	55	David Cook 1837
	40	———			40	Abner Adams, Jr. 1801
	119	———			119	David Maples 1801
	50	———			50	Parshall Wheeler 1801
24	166	Josiah Alger	Richard	George Clarke	166	?
	37	Adam Ballard	Richard	George Clarke	37	?
	62 ½	Benoni Pearce	Ann		62 ½	Harris Winsor 1830

	50	———				50	Parshall Wheeler 1801		
25	226	Cyrus and Cyrenus Clark				226	Cyrus and Cyrenus Clark 1805		
26	163	Moses Barnes and Stoddard Bowen	Estate	Executors		56 ½	Moses Brown 1807		
						106 ½	Nathan Davison 1810		
	150	Martin L. Comstock	Isaac	Wm. H. Averell		150	Edward B. Augur 1840		
27R	125	William Cummings				125	William Cummings 1803		
	100	John M. Hughes				100	Salmon Comstock		
	98	?				98	Samuel Mallery 1817		
28	313	Abraham Lippitt (reserved after 1798)				313	Abraham Lippitt, Sr. 1805		
29	182	———				182	Salmon Comstock 1800		
	128	Joseph Lippitt				188	Joseph Lippitt		
30	103	Stephen Holden				103	Stephen Holden		
	103	———				103	Hopkins Burlingham 1800		
	103	David Cole	Isaac		George Clarke	103	Peter Augur 1837		
31	100	———				100	Serile Adams 1801		
	100	———				100	Asaph Adams 1801		
	75	Daniel Lee	Ann			75	Peter Augur 1840		
	25	Asaph Adams	Richard		George Clarke	25	George Murdock 1837		
32	50	———				50	Joseph Porter 1801		
	50	Elisha Field	James		Thomas Ward	50	Elisha Robinson 1840		
	50	Amos Winsor	William		George Clarke	25	Ira Tucker 1837		
						25	Comfort Chase 1837		
	131	George Murdock 1810	Ann (part in #40)			131	George Murdock 1819		
	65	Solomon Clark	(part in #40)			65	Comfort Chase 1805		
33R	100	Isaac Barnes				100	P. & E. B. Auger 1811		
	127	Hugh Rogers (did not appear)				27	Joseph Crafts 1811		
	100	Held for possible claimants under will				100	John Rich 1838		
34R	120	Thomas Robinson	Christopher Hartwick			120	Thomas Robinson 1797		
	80	Christopher Hartwick				80	Marmaduke Aldrich 1806		
	100	———	John Andrews			100	Joseph Potter 1810		
	100	Thomas Cully	Little Pond here			50	Earnest Hazelius 1819		
						50	(under water)		
	19	not leased				19	Joseph Crafts 1817		
35R	25	William Cummings				25	William Cummings 1803		
	100	Thomas Robinson	Jeremiah Van Rensselaer			70	William Cummings 1806		
						30			
	84	Thomas Cully				84	Thomas Cully 1811		

	57	Eliphalet Dewey				57	Eliphalet Dewey 1811
	34	Joseph Crafts 1811				34	Joseph Craft 1811
	49	not leased				49	Elijah Lattin 1828
36R	49 ½	John Davison, Jr.				49 ½	James Averell, Jr. 1811
	50	Joseph Crafts				50	Joseph Crafts 1811
	239	John, Archibald &				50	Eliphalet Stickney 1811
		James Cummings				189	Simeon Parker 1823
37	89	John M. Hughes	James	Thomas Ward	89		Wm. G. Northrup and Hopkins Burlingham 1844
	20	———————			20		John Davison 1800
	107 ½	Miles Comstock	Samuel	W. H. Averell	107½		Miles Comstock & Peter Augur 1824
	105 ½	Joshua Hinman	James		110		Jabez Pendleton 1817
38	60	———————			60		Bille Williams 1800
	110	Matthew Derbyshire	James	Thomas Ward	110		Geo. H. Derbyshire 1824
	50	Clark Cummings	Isaac		50		Jerome Clark 1812
	116½	Joshua Hinman			116½		Joshua Hinman 1817
39	104	Joshua Burke	Richard	George Clarke	104		?
	100	Wm. Burke	Isaac	Sheriff	61		Jerome Clark, Jr. 1823
			Isaac	Executors	39		Silas Williams 1825
	100	Matthew Derbyshire	James	Thomas Ward	100		Geo. Derbyshire 1824
40	50	Solomon Clark			50		John Bissell 1802
	100	———————			100		Samuel Bissell 1801
	100	———————			100		Moses Wheeler 1801
	60	Noah Adams	Ann		60		Alexander Murdock
					1840		
				See #32 for			Comfort Chase 1805
Lesser 1	72	Asanath Jewel			72		Joseph Crafts 1812
2	73 ½	Asanath Jewel			73 ½		Joseph Crafts 1812
3	75	Samuel and			75		Strong Hayden
4	58	Amasa Short			58		Strong Hayden
5	52 ½	Amasa Short			52½		Spaulding Wheeler 1812
6	53 ½	Nathan Pierson			53 ½		Eliphant Dewey 1817
7	66	———————			107		Eliphant Dewey 1800
8	81	———————					
9	92	———————			132 ½		Thomas Cully 1800
44	173	———————			173		Elisha Eldred 1801
	107	———————			107		Samuel Craft s 1805
45	154	———————			154		Nathan Davison 1800
	88	———————			88		John Davison 1800

Lot	Acres	Leases			Acres	Settler's Sale
46	63	———			63	Jerome Clark 1800
	150	——			150	Bille Williams 1800
	114	———			114	Salmon Rich 1801
47	105	———			105	Thomas Loomis 1801
	205	———			205	Salmon Rich 1801
	11	Jared Clark			11	John Hurd 1808
	33	———			33	Abel Hyde 1801
48	88	———			88	
	22	———			22	Thomas Loomis 1801
	102 ½	———			102 ½	Thomas Loomis 1801
	51	Jared Clark			51	
	88	James Averill			88	James Averill 1805
	122	"Glebe" 1798 Restored to hartwick estate			122	William Stowell 1811

Eleventh Division – Philadelphia Lot

Lot	Acres	Leases 1800-1801	Bequests	Successor	Acres	Settler's Sale
1					22	Jonathon Potter 1804
			Richard	Executor	23	William Stowell 1814
					68	William Stowell 1799
					120	Ashbel Armstrong 1794
2	60	Samuel Bissell	Isaac	W. H. Averell	10	Samuel Bissell 1825
					50	Comfort Chase 1839
	60	———			60	Simeon Ingalls 1801
3	40	Comfort Chase			40	Comfort Chase 1823
	50	Duty Hawkins	Ann		25	Comfort Chase 1820
					25	Stephen Holden 1820
4	55	Stephen Reynolds	Richard	George Clarke	55	?
	65	Joshua Wells	William	George Clarke	65	Elisha Steere 1837
5	71	Zephaniah Hough	Estate	Executors	71	Philip Wells 1812
6	14	Abraham West			14	Christopher Hall 1801
	18	Stephen Skiff	William		18	?
	52	Jonathon Thurber	William		52	?
	85	Jehiel Rowley	William (40 ½)		40 ½	?
			Ann (44 ½)		44 ½	Henry Chapman 1819

Eleventh Division – Elizabeth Cooper's

Lot	Acres	Leases 1800-1801	Bequests	Successor	Acres	Settler's Sale	
1	43	?			43	Jonathon Potter	1804
	30	Jacob Preston	Elizabeth		30	Jacob Preston	
	100	Nicholas Denise			100	Jonathon Sprague	1809
	120	William Compton	Elizabeth		120	Thomas Fuller	1812
2	64 ½				64 ½	John Hubbard	1801
	61 ½				61 ½	William Ross, Jr.	1802
3	120				120	Laban Ross	1801
4	55	————			55	Aaron Norton	1801
	65	————			65	John Wells	1801
5	74	————			74	Philip Wells	1801
6	75	Solomon Dwight	Elizabeth		75	Joseph Winsor	1813
	50	Jehiel Rowley			50	Jehiel Rowley	1802
	40	Abraham West	Estate	Sheriff	40	David Weeks	1824

By: Roy L. Butterfield

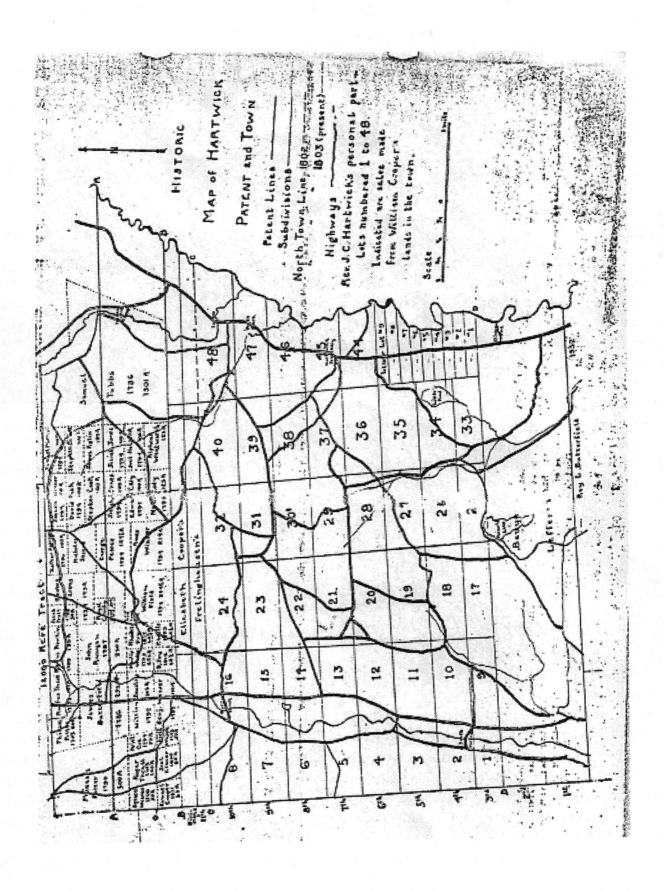

Hartwick Seminary

Hartwick Seminary has changed more in the past ten years than it had in the 50 years prior. Today this mile-long stretch of Route 28 is experiencing a surge in commercial development, with The Commons paving the way on a field that had once borne the fruits of farming. New ventures have been proposed to the Hartwick Town Board that would impact even more of the landscape.

Hartwick Seminary was once alive with activity, a busy site of commerce relative to the day. It was not only home to the Lutheran Seminary which later evolved into Hartwick College, but also the site of an active hops industry.

Kinne Hop Yard

From 1869 to 1903 a train station welcomed Seminary students and their families and seasonal laborers from nearby cities in search of farm work. A trolley was accessible a relatively short walk away in Index, which would take one toward Cooperstown or to Hartwick and points beyond.

Train Station in Hartwick Seminary

Aside from the activity the Seminary generated, this area wasn't much different than other rural communities of the day. Social events usually centered around the church or the farm. Husking bees were popular at harvest time, and neighbors collaborated in many ways to tackle the more formidable tasks associated with farming. Laborers were either imported from nearby cities or came on their own looking for work. Hobos could be seen wandering the area, scavenging from local gardens while seeking jobs.

Perhaps because of the lack of technology we know today, the community itself was more intimate in times past. People knew their neighbors and forms of entertainment necessarily involved gatherings of people. The Seminary offered its own brand of entertainment, including religious and academic speeches and other educational programs. In 1912 alumnus Andrew Yetter donated the funds for a gymnasium, which offered greater opportunity for recreation.

Across the road from the Seminary football

A. B. Yetter Gymnasium

games with other schools were staged. (Hops were also grown on this site, which was level with the road, and a hops kiln was situated behind this field). The Seminary housed a secondary school, known as 'The Academy." which local youth attended. A traditional one-room primary school was at the opposite end of the hamlet. Many Seminary students boarded with local residents, even after the building was expanded to provide student housing in 1861. Professors and administrators for the school lived in homes in the immediate vicinity. Thus Seminary life and community life intermingled.

Student life included many recreational activi-

Group of Teachers and Students, 1916

ties, though hardly what today's youth would consider entertaining. Debate societies were active throughout the early years of the seminary, covering a wide range of "provocative" dis-

cussion. Social gatherings included Sunday walks to "The Jams," regardless of the season. While it's very casually described in historical accounts, by today's standards this "picnic/walk" would seem nearly impossible to most. From the Seminary students would walk two miles south to what was then (and still is to some) Clintonville, where a road went over a bridge crossing the Susquehanna. They would continue their journey to this picturesque gorge with cascading waterfalls another few miles beyond. The Seminary became known as "The Match Factory," as many romantic relationships blossomed from friendships formed on the campus. No doubt these walks to "The Jams" provided ample opportunity for couples to get to know one another better.

One campus based event that influenced the community as a whole was the Student Strike of 1924. An unruly student whom fellow students disliked finally pushed the limits of well-respected principal/professor John Dudde. The student was asked to leave the seminary but, because of his family's political ties, a decidedly biased disciplinary committee overturned the young man's expulsion. In response, Mr. Dudde submitted his resignation. Seminary students supported Dudde's course of action (they had previously dumped the student in the river then tarred and feathered him in the middle of winter). The students staged a strike and refused to return to classes until, among other things, Principal Dudde's position was restored. The President of the Seminary, M. G. L. Reitz, solicited the assistance of Sheriff Converse and three of his deputies to evict the students the following Monday. These events were sensationalized by local newspapers. Residents of the community housed the displaced students until matters were resolved a few days later. Principal Dudde was eventually reinstated, but he and three other teachers resigned at the end of the year. It has been speculated that this was the beginning of the end of the Seminary.

The school's enrollment waxed and waned during its existence. During the first 20 years the school averaged between 60 and 70 students. Enrollment dropped nearly in half in the late 1830's and 1840's. Women were admitted for the first time in 1851, bringing the student population to 89. In the 1880's over 100 students attended.

In 1926 the Seminary launched the "Greater

Hartwick Seminary 1909

Hartwick" campaign, with the end in mind to establish the school as a bona fide four-year college. This initiative sparked generous support from the citizens of nearby Oneonta, who eventually offered money and land to relocate the college to the "City of Hills." In 1927 the school expanded to a 4-year college and was moved to Oneonta. Classes began on September 26, 1928 in temporary quarters at Walling Mansion. Faith Perkins Buechner, a life-long resident of Hartwick Seminary whose family boasted a number of Seminarians, was in this first group of students. The Lutheran Seminary remained in Hartwick Seminary until 1930, when it moved to Brooklyn. It went out of business in 1947. The Academy stayed in its original location until 1934 when classes were discontinued.

This community subsequently transformed to a more remote agricultural lifestyle. The Seminary building was used as a Resident Work Center under Franklin Roosevelt's New Deal. Poultry and cheese were among the commodities processed here, and a visit to the site by Eleanor Roosevelt was a highlight of its existence.

The property was conveyed by the Lutheran

Eleanor Roosevelt visiting Hartwick seminary

Synod to Hartwick College in 1944. The college then sold the building to an area farmer who used it for some community gatherings but mostly for agricultural purposes. It eventually became a chicken coop, age and weather deteriorating its once majestic presence until it was finally (mercifully) torn down.

Hartwick Seminary was primarily an agricul-

Hartwick Seminary Lutheran Church

tural community in the years that followed the college's move, with most non-farming residents commuting to jobs in Cooperstown or Oneonta. Cooperstown was the closest venue for the area's children to find part-time or summer work; most had to settle for farm work closer to home. Ingalls' Farm still employ seasonal help, of which many local kids have taken advantage. As is the case today, the youth of the community found each other and formed bonds between neighbors. Hartwick Pines and another trailer park on the other end of the hamlet became home to many young, growing families, and their presence contributed to the overall fabric of the community. The number of homes in these parks dwindled gradually in the 1980s. This and other indicators of low population density led to the closing of Hartwick Seminary's Post Office, (zip code 13349) located in Fields' Store.

The Cooperstown and Milford post offices

Post Office and store in Hartwick Seminary operated by Bill and Dorothy Fields

now jointly serve this community.

Today many residents rent out their homes to families of the 600-some campers who come to the Dreams Park each week during the summer. Pizza Hut and McDonalds, who for years fought to position their businesses in Cooperstown, now greet visitors traveling northward into the village. The Cooperstown Dreams Park, a little league baseball camp has brought with it a host of new commerce, primarily in tourism and housing businesses. Bed and breakfasts are increasing in numbers throughout the area. The Best Western, which boasts both traditional rooms and suites, will soon be joined by a Holiday Inn Express. A train station is to be built behind the baseball camp and a water park is scheduled to appear in Hyde Park in the near future. Summer and year-round part-time jobs abound, not only for the youth of Hartwick Seminary but also for kids from surrounding communities.

The environmental impact of recent development in Hartwick Seminary has sparked tremendous controversy. It is important however, to remember that this once sleepy hamlet has seen change before.

By: Susan Knight

Toddsville

In January of 1786, William Cooper and Andrew Craig purchased at auction the Otsego lands. The auction took place at Albert Mabie's Tavern in Canajoharie.

Roy Butterfield says of these times in his 'History of Hartwick Patent and Settlement,' found in the Hartwick Sesqui-Centennial edition of the Otego Valley News, Friday October 10, 1952, "In 1785 (86) William Cooper with his silent partner, Andrew Craig, acquired that part of Croghan's patent bordering the Hartwick Patent on the north, and began his spectacular career as a colonizer. He was ambitious, energetic, and far-sighted. He was always mindful of his tenants' interests. He fitted his policies to their conditions. His success was so great that other landowners eagerly sought his services as their own agents did. Soon he entered the Hartwick scene."

About this same time, Samuel Tubbs came to Otsego and purchased of Cooper 1565 acres on both sides of Oaks Creek (including the present village of Toddsville), and extending east to the Susquehanna river.

However, a few years later it was discovered that the surveyors hastily ran sloppy lines that pressed too far south to include 3000 acres from the northern tier of the Hartwick Patent. Much of Tubbs lands were within this area.

After some time and at great expense to William Cooper, the boundaries were resurveyed, and the present village of Toddsville lies partly on the west side of Oaks Creek in the town of Hartwick and partly on the east side of Oaks Creek in the Town of Otsego.

Tubb's House

Tubbs built a log house, a sawmill and a gristmill on the west side of Oaks Creek near the present upper bridge. In about 1794, he built the first frame house on the knoll west of his mills.

The house still stands, and is owned and occupied by William and Betsey Hayes. Tubbs called his settlement 'Tubbs Mills'. However, he died soon after, and this part of his property reverted back to Cooper.

About 1796 Jehiel Todd and his family migrated from Connecticut and purchased from William Cooper the southern part of the Tubbs property. The Todds were millwrights, and were interested in the waterpower from Oaks creek. They developed the water power and built, in addition to the sawmill, a gristmill, a papermill

Paper Mill

on the east side creek of the creek, and a woolen knitting mill on the west side of the creek. He called his settlement Toddsville.

On March 27,1809 a company was incorporated bearing the name 'Union Cotton Manufacturing Co.,' Toddsville, by Rufus Steere, Thomas Fuller, James Averill, Jr. and Jehiel and Lemuel Todd. And on August 22, 1809 Richard F. Cooper gave a 'grant of privilege', to erect a dam.

A wooden building for the manufacture of cotton cloth had been constructed a year earlier by Charles Smith. This building burned a short time later, and was rebuilt of stone from a local

Union Cotton Mill

quarry. This cotton manufactory was one and the same. In its "heyday," it employed over one hundred people.

Ed Moore, in the Oneonta Star in 1973 tells of the Otsego Paper Mill located at Toddsville. He says that the Otsego Paper Mill started in the first decade of the 19th century by Jehiel Todd. In 1835 the annual output of the company was valued at less than $10,000, but in 1853, after the mill had been rebuilt after a destructive fire, the output amounted to about a ton a day with a great increase in the concern's revenue.

The mill operated sporadically until about the close of the century. There was still some market for the writing paper which it made but its days of manufacturing newsprint were long over.

Since Toddsville was built entirely as a mill town, it lost its importance after 1900 when the last of the mills closed. The cotton mill, as was the papermill, was torn down to secure the valuable stone for important new building in Cooperstown.

Toddsville became a community for residential living.

Even the last doctor had gone, that being Dr. Clappsaddle, who having come here in 1889, was no longer practicing by 1910.

The earliest doctor was Walter Almy Jr., who came to Toddsville in the early 1800's. He practiced for many years here, and his son Dr. Ed

Dr. Almy, Jr.

Almy, practiced here after his father's death.

Also gone were the large millponds that were actually a part of Oaks Creek, and served both the papermill and the cottonmill with the help of dams. The dams broke during high water and rotted away, while the mill-race was partially filled in, and only a trace of it is visible today.

Although Toddsville is by no means noted for its architecture, there are a few fine examples of period architecture remaining. The Tubbs house or "oldest house in Toddsville," has good federal lines, though the porches are a later addition. The Andrew Todd house built in 1848 on the east side of Oaks Creek displays a nice gingerbread look with Gothic overtones.

The hotel, now empty, was operating well into the 1920's, and has survived to the

Wasontha Hotel

present. It is now being restored by its new owners, Mr. and Mrs. William Hayes, who plan to make apartments of it.

The stone store declined in business along

with the mills, but was run as a private store well into the 1930's when it was finally closed, and in 1944 moved to the Farmers Museum in Cooperstown. Other small stores did take over however, the last one being one run by Reginald and Pearl Higgins in the brick basement of the home built by Lemuel Todd in 1812 on the corner opposite the hotel.

Bert and Flora Jackson conducted a small grocery store and post office in their home on the main street in 1915. Bert also worked as a gardener at the Walter Flanders estate at 'Westridge' in Cooperstown. He was an amateur photographer as well. Following are some

scenes of Toddsville about 1915 that reflect his interest in the camera.

The first school was probably a log school, though the first known frame school was located on the east side of the main street just a few buildings down from the corner. It was a typical one-room school that served that end of the village, while a second one room school served the southern part near the cottonmill.

The two schools were consolidated in 1874, and the lower school building was sold, moved, and made into a residence.

A new and larger school building was in use from about 1914 until 1950, located on County Highway 26 on the Otsego side of Oaks Creek. After that the children were bused to Cooperstown Central School.

A recent independent school came to Toddsville in 1982, a vision of Ann Wienke, who started the Christian Hill Montessori School. Ann retired in 1995, and the school was sold to the current owner, The Brookwood School. They continue her tradition of educational excellence and special learning atmosphere. It is located on the edge of Toddsville village on county route 59.

Although a church building did not exist until 1875 or so, church services were being held in the schoolhouse, probably right from the beginning. In 1867 a group met and decided to build a church building to be used by five different denominations. It was called the Union Church, and the first worship service was held January 29, 1876.

In 1961, after being closed for a number of years, this church was reorganized and reopened as Toddsville Baptist Church, first under the leadership of Franklin Harmon, and the 'American mission for the opening Closed Churches' and in 1982, under 'Village Missions', with Stephen Holmes as Pastor. Now known as Community

Union Church in Toddsville

Bible Chapel, it is still a "Village Mission

Church" proclaiming God's Word, and pastored by John Klosheim.

The Methodist Society built in 1901 an attractive church building on the west side of the main street opposite the Rufus Steere house. Prior to this the Methodists were meeting at the Union Church, and holding their service Sunday evening. In an 1882 issue of 'The Pastoral Visitor', published monthly at Fly Creek, we read, "Preaching at Toddsville each alternate Sunday at 6:30 PM." A ministry continued here until 1951 when the congregation was transferred to the Cooperstown parish. The church was closed, and sold to an individual who made it into a dwelling.

Across the street from the Methodist Church stood the Rufus Steere house built about 1830. It still stands as one of the finer houses of Toddsville, and is owned and occupied by Deborah Geurtze and Richard Bird.

Deborah left her teaching job in 1980 to pursue her artist career. She uses a four hundred-year-old process to create etchings that are rich in color and detail, through a technique called 'overprinting.' Her prints are mostly of upstate New York, especially of the Adirondacks and Otsego Lake areas.

Much of the history that we have about Toddsville comes from a man who lived and attended school here around the turn of the century. Cuyler Carr lived in the stone house built by his grandfather in 1825 located on the road to Oaksville.

Later he inherited the old house; lived there and in Milford, NY, as his work dictated. He was a fine looking man, bright and gifted, owning a coal business in Milford at one time. Later he worked for the telephone company.

We are indebted to him for preserving the memory of this early mill town.

For further reading about the early life in Toddsville, see 'Recollections of an Early Mill Town, Toddsville' published in 1974 by the writer.

By: Lawrence Gardner

Carr Homestead

Clintonville

The west has many ghost towns but the Town of Hartwick has one too. It is called Clintonville located on the Susquehanna River near Milford town line. Now there are only two homes on the West Side of the river and two on the east. I chose it for my topic because I lived there for many years, was courted and married from there.

Samuel Crafts was given permission by the state in 1813 to build a dam at this location. The Susquehanna cotton and Woolen Manufactory Co. bought land from him for a mill. From 1815 to 1819 it was managed by Joseph Phelon with Samuel Budlong as agent. David Fairchild owned the mill for a short period and sold it to John Cockett when the settlement was named Cockettville. In 1840 William Clinton bought the mill and from then on it was known as Clintonville.

Clintonville Cotton Mill

Clintonville was a thriving community with homes, two boarding houses, a store the upstairs of which was used for a church, a community hall, school, blacksmith shop, cooper shop and sawmill. The Clinton Cotton Mill hired 35 to 40 people turning out 624,000 yards of cloth per year. The cotton mill became the Clinton Power Company and furnished Cooperstown with their first electricity. The dam washed out in 1914 and the power plant closed.

Clinton's Cotton Factory at Clintonville, Town of Hartwick, NY

Otsego Herald July 20, 1815:
Just received and for sale by the Susquehanna Manufactory Co. at their store in Hartwick a general assortment of dry goods, groceries, crockery, glass, hardware with a good assortment of cotton goods of their own manufacture which they offer for sale. Lumber and most kinds of country produce. Cash or a short approved credit. Samuel Budlong, agent.

Freeman's Journal Jan., 1834:
Wanted: Throttle spinners, card drawing and speed tenders. Also power loom weaver and dresser hands. Either families or single hands will find constant employment and liberal wages by applying down at the cotton factory of Mssrs. John Cockett & Co. about two miles south of Hartwick Seminary. Some learners will also be employed.

From the 1855 census:
Clinton and Leonard — cotton factory
Capital invested - $10,000 real estate
$10,000 machinery and tools
Raw materials- 60 tons cotton value $13,500
Annual output - 624,000 yards printed cloth value $24,960
Kind of motive power — water
Persons employed — 6 men, 18 women, 6 boys, 6 girls under 18
Wages exclusive of board -
Average monthly wage of men $20
Average monthly wage of women $8

Freeman's Journal July 10, 1879:
Myron V. Stupplebeen, a student from Hartwick Seminary, preached for us the last time until after vacation on the 22nd ult. It was a feeling farewell discourse tho he promised to return if God willing.

Diphtheria has again made its unwelcome appearance among us. Charles Dinger, a bright little fellow of seven summers, died a few days ago and at this time, July 1st, Nettie, youngest daughter of Oscar and Sarah Bradley, lies a corpse while three other are sick in the family. One of the three is partially convalescent.

From a letter written by Mary Perkins of Hartwick Seminary to Charles Perkins in Dakota April, 1879:
Ted and I went to a nite society at Clintonville held for the benefit of the I.O.G.T. There were a great many there. They only had about $1.60. There is to be an open Lodge next week or week after, admittance fee 10¢. Went to hear Stupplebeen preach a week ago Sunday night. I think he can talk splendid.

West side of River showing Store. Upstairs was a community center and church services were held there.

Freeman's Journal Feb. 26, 1880:

Death of Wm. M. Clinton - This well-known gentleman died at his home in Hartwick township on Sat, evening last of typhoid pneumonia. He was in New York on the 9th when he froze his feet but did not know it until he took his stockings off at night. He also took a cold at the same time. He had previously expressed the belief to one or two of his children that he should not survive the winter as he had for some time suffered from diabetes. He was in the 58th year of his age. Mr. Clinton was a native of this town, having been born in Fly Creek. For a time he was in business in South Adams, Mass. where he resided for ten years. For about thirty-three years he engaged in manufacturing cotton goods at Clinton Mills. At times he dealt largely in hops and during the war he made a large amount of money buying cotton in the South....

He owned factories at Clintonville, Laurens, New Berlin and South Adams, Mass. and also had an interest in Ross Mills at Sherburne.

Hartwick Seminary Monthly Oct., 1881:

Miss Nellie Clinton has recently placed in her factory at Clintonville a new turbine water wheel, which gives more power than the two formerly in use.

Hartwick Seminary Monthly Jan., 1882

John E. Luther is teaching the school at Clintonville.

Otsego Farmer Jan. 21, 1887:

Clinton Mills. The new proprietors, Short and Luther, are getting their property in better shape. They have rebuilt the dam and are repairing the saw, grist and shingle mills. The yard is well filled with logs and looks like business again on the Middlefield side. Some talk of starting the factory.

Mrs. Lucy Lowell is succeeding finely with our school awakening an interest on the part of the scholars and shows the best average attendance we have had for years.

Sidney Smith has completed his blacksmith shop. Bring in your work.

Stephen Eldred has moved in the Cyrus Clinton house and will open a cooper shop.

Saw Mill, Clintonville

Otsego Farmer Mar. 1, 1889:

Miss Cora Lattin closed a very successful term of school at Clintonville last Friday.

1893 - The Clinton factory situated about five miles south of Cooperstown and which had been lying idle for several years was leased of Short and Luther by Rufus Steere for the manufacture of cotton yarn.

In 1896, the Village of Cooperstown considered purchasing the Clintonville property for the purpose of providing electric power to the village.

The papers printed the following description of the property. " There are eighteen acres of land embraced in the purchase. Fifteen are on the West Side of the river and three on the East Side. There are five dwelling houses, three of them occupied, also a hop house, the old store and a number of other buildings in more or less dilapidated condition. The purchase includes the old knitting mill in remarkably good condition, a gristmill, shingle mill and sawmill. An orchard containing over 100 apple and pear trees cover a portion of the tract...."

On west side of River, old dwelling house with boarding house in the rear.

The water above the dam backs up a distance of two miles and the right to overflow on low-lying lands has been litigated and settled. The flume or raceway from the dam to the wheel-house is covered by a stone archway about 18 feet wide and 12 feet deep. There are three turbine wheels. The one on the west side of the river is a Lefel wheel bought by Miss Clinton a few years ago at a cost of $3000 and capable of developing 150 horsepower. The two on the east side of the river develop 75 horsepower each. All three are in good condition.

A public vote on the acquisition of the Clintonville plant resulted in the village of Cooperstown turning down the opportunity to purchase the plant. It remained the property of Mr. George Brooks.

Clinton Mills, Power Company and Dam

Otsego Farmer Oct. 30, 1896:
Work at Clintonville Mills. The workmen finished the dam at Clintonville Mills this week. At present a force are at work tearing down a portion of the old knitting mill. Only the basement walls will be left and roofed over for a power house in which will be placed the dynamos. Preparatory to tearing down the structure all machinery, costing thousands of dollars is being pitched out of the windows.

The Clinton Mills Power Co. finished its plant at Clintonville and began furnishing power to Cooperstown in 1897. There were 2,500 incandescent lamps in use the first year.

Feb. 3, 1897:
The county has contracted with the Clinton Mills Power Co. to light the county buildings and the County House at Phoenix Mills for three years at an annual cost of $1,050.

Oneonta Herald Dec. 21, 1911:
Russell Warren stated Tues. that the Clinton Mills Power Co. and the Cooperstown Gas Company had been taken over by New York City interests and that the properties will eventually be merged with

the Hartwick Power Co. which latter named company owns the water power plant at Colliers. The Hartwick Power Company now operates the lighting system for the villages of Richfield Springs and Hartwick. The Clinton Mills Power Co. recently acquired the franchise for Milford and, it is assumed, that village, as well as Cooperstown, will eventually be lighted by the Hartwick company.

Storm Damage

Damage done by storm

Freeman's Journal Apr. 2, 1913:
The high water of the river lifted the big iron bridge at Clintonville from its foundations and dropped it in the river, with the piers apparently intact.

Otsego Farmer Oct. 27, 1916:
A veritable hurricane visited Otsego County Friday night of last week and at several places, which seemed in line of its maximum force, wrought damage which in the aggregate will mean many thousands of dollars of loss... .

Practically all of the houses about the Clinton Mills site were more or less damaged.

————

By: Hilda Augur

Interior of Clintonville power house which supplied electricity to the area.

Recollections of Hyde Park

Hyde Park is a quaint little settlement nestled in the Susquehanna valley. It was named for Abel Hyde, a tanner, and settled in 1801. It has also been known as Pluck City or Pluck. I have memories of this little hamlet from 1909 -10. I was three years old then. My parents and I were living with my paternal grandparents at the time, Clarence and Helen (Quackenbush) Baker.

Photo of the Losee Farm and the intersection of County Route 11 at Index with State Route 28 looking south on 28. December 12, 1931

Same house as above. Owned later by Clarence Hoose and made into a one family dwelling.

I think it's best to start just south of the Hope Bridge, better known now as the Index Bridge, which spans Oaks Creek. The bridge separates Hyde Park and Index. The first house from the bridge was a two family dwelling. The Index post office was in the north side and my grandparents occupied the south side. The Postmaster and mistress, Mr. and Mrs. Patrick Connor, an elderly couple were much loved by all. The post office was established in 1903 (when the electric railway passed through the Hope Factory district) and discontinued in 1916. Fred Winsor and his mother owned the next house. Fred had the first automobile around and it sure was a novelty. Of course this automotive wonder frightened the horses and once in awhile a horse would become so frightened that it equaled the speed of the car and sometimes exceeded it. The occupants of the buggy or lumber wagon were jostled around a bit until the horse or team could be brought under control.

The Irv Petrie family owned the next house. Their daughter, Lena Doyle, maintained this old homestead for many years. At the right of this house is the road leading to the Hartwick village.

Continuing on down what is the present Route 28, the next place is the Losee farm. My parents, Earl and Maude Baker, lived there for a number of years. My dad rented the farm. Getting along down the road now starts a thicker settlement, Hyde Park proper. Our Deputy Sheriff, Daniel

Chapman, and his family lived in the next house; then the Bliss home. Across the road from Bliss' was the Andrew Murdock home on the corner of the main road and Compton Road. Right across from Murdocks was our blacksmith shop operated by Jim Mercer. This was on the opposite corner of the main road

Hotel at Hyde Park, July 12, 1903 taken by Merton Petrie

and Compton Road.

Next to the Bliss home was Hyde Park hotel. A news item dated Jan. 14, 1909 stated "The Hyde Park property was bid in at foreclosure sale last week and has been sold by Elmer Sergent to Mrs. George Groat. Mr. and Mrs. Groat have conducted the hotel for some time." I remember this hotel when it was owned by Nate and Winnie Jackson. When

The bar at Hyde Park Hotel

Prohibition started around 1917-18, Mr. Jackson sold the property. The hotel was later razed and the Parshalls built a beautiful home on the site. Across the road from the hotel was the Benjamin home. Their daughter, Clarissa, became a RN and married and moved away.

Next to the Parshall home (old hotel site) was the home of Sarah Teachout, a maiden lady, highly esteemed by everyone for her mild manner and kindness. My parents later bought this home. It was a quaint little house with a sunken kitchen. My parents lived there a few years while they worked at the County Farm. When we moved back to the Fisk farm they rented it to a maiden lady, Mae Tarbox. Mae did baking for a livelihood. During election time the people sitting on the election board were favored by Mae's hot meals. This was her contribution to civic affairs. The Hellers now own this little place.

The next house was the one occupied by John Duffy and his two maiden sisters. Then came our little Methodist church. The church was dedicated Oct. 13, 1859 in a service conducted by Rev. J. Shank, presiding elder of the district. About 50 persons joined the church on that occasion. The minister I remember the most is Rev. Charles Adams. The same minister officiated in both Hartwick and Hyde Park churches. Rev. Adams loved horses and had a nice horse and buggy, which he drove from Hartwick to Hyde Park for our services. When the weather was bad he came on the Southern New York trolley. Next to the church was the General store. It was owned by Loie and Hubert Wayman. They sold everything for the home, clothing for all members of the family and foodstuffs. The Waymans took orders and delivered a day or so later. Their routes were to Toddsville, Beaver Meadow and Clintonville. The store was a gathering place for elderly retired men and many a problem was solved around the pot bellied old stove that heated the place. The Waymans lived above the store for quite a few years then

they built a nice home below the store. Their daughter, Ruth, still lives there.

Next is the "old Wilson Jarvis" farm. The farmland has been cut into building lots. Where the barn once stood is a garage owned by Ron Streek. Between the garage and the Wayman home is Hartwick Fire Department #2. The Jarvis home is also still there. Below the farm is a little house once owned by Mrs. Jones and her daughter, Lucy. This house has had many owners.

We have to go across the road now to Charles Teachout's wagon shop. It stood right across the road from the store and church. Any part of a wagon or a complete wagon could be made in this shop. The Teachout home was next to the shop to the south. North of this was the home of Sam Petrie, his mother and brother. Sam was a silversmith and his little shop stood next to the wagon shop. He did replating and made all sorts of things from silver. He melted down my great-grandfather Quackenbush's silver watchcase and made my grandmother Baker six silver teaspoons, which I still have in my possession.

On the same side of the road was the Ben-jamin home, then the Mercer home on the corner of Compton road. Let's take a stroll down this road away. On the right side is the Wykoff home. Claud Whitbeck owns the home now. Across the road is the Louden home as we get closer to the Compton Bridge span-

"The King Home" Home of Dr James Greenough

ning the Susquehanna River. Years later Andrew Murdock had his slaughterhouse on the flats near the bridge.

Going back to the Hartwick-Index road, at the top of the hill is the farm once owned by Patrick King. He grew hops along with his other farm crops and had a large dairy. In late years this farm has had two owners. One was Dr. Greenough, a prominent surgeon affiliated with Fox Hospital. After his death his widow sold to Mr. and Mrs. Hansen from Oneonta. Leaving this home, next is the Hugh Hall farm. Mr. Hall had a milk route at one time. His daughter, Alexandria (Queenie) Hall Schultz, is residing there still. These two places are part and parcel of Hyde Park. These two farms had their own water supply from wells and springs. Hyde Park proper had a water problem in the early 1900's. Its drinking water was nil. The old hotel and the Jarvis farm had deep wells with hand pumps. All the residents of Hyde Park were granted permission to get their drinking water from these two places. Each house had a cistern of rainwater for bathing, laundry and cleaning. There were no inside toilets at this time.

By: Elsa Baker Schneider

The Hyde Park Diner started as a drive up ice cream stand and expanded from there. First owned by Francis Ryan, it was sold to Charles Drake and Jack Hussey in 1969. Sandra Renwick Chase, who had worked in the diner as a waitress during high school, leased the business from 1985 until 1990. Deborah Rawliegh and Anthony Anzolone both ran it for periods. The diner then became a pizza place and was burned down.

Hyde Park General Store ca. 1900—L to R: Susie Thayer Renwick, Mary Thayer, Pearl Thayer, Claude Talbot, Lizzie Thayer Talbot. On wagon: Harlow Thayer

Route 28, Hyde Park, NY—Building on the right was once a business run by Harlow and Mary Thayer. Harlow and Mary were the parents of Susie Thayer who married Charles Renwick on March 2, 1904 at Westford, NY.

The former Pat King farm and house. It was sold to Dr. Greenough, then to W. D. Hansen. Now the 1819 House Restaurant.

South Hartwick

From the hilly summit of Glen Myer's hill, we can see all of South Hartwick: from Jone's Crossing in the north to the hills bounding Marlette's Flat in the south. In back of us is the New Lisbon Town Line, the western boundary of the Hartwick Patent. As we look to the east, Bilderbeck Mountain (Pine Hill) and Bunn Hill separate us from Pleasant Valley. Down in South Hartwick, parted by the Otego Creek, we can hear the traffic on State Route 205 and County Route 11. If we look closely, there is Everett Kane's tractor going up Bunn Hill. We can see some cows on the four remaining dairy farms. We look at the many fields of crops and pasture and wonder "What was it like when those early settlers cleared their land and built homes in South Hartwick?"

Most of South Hartwick was in the Hartwick Patent purchased from the Indians in 1752.[1] The southern part was in Patent Divisions claimed by Banyer and Leffert.[2] In 1792, Zeba Newland (b.1769, d. 1/16/1845) came from Norton, Massachusetts with his brother. They followed a trail, secured a tract of land in South Hartwick, and cleared a small part of it. They built a cabin and returned back east to Massachusetts. There, Zeba married Lucy Henry. In early spring, the young couple drove an ox team through the trails to South Hartwick. Here, Zeba built a blacksmith shop and forge, where he made nails, iron shoes for horses & oxen and other metal tools.[3] His shop was near the site of Baggio Cardone's home on Co. Route 11D.[4]

Seth Wright came with his family to South Hartwick from Sharon, Connecticut in the late 1700's. They came by sleigh in the snowy cold of mid-winter. Seth and his wife had 11 children, 4 girls and 7 boys. Henry Clark Wright was the tenth child. (He was only 4 when they made that long trip.) When they arrived they found about 80 acres of their land was in stump lots; the other 80 acres was woods. Seth was a farmer and a builder. He made a dam in Pleasant Brook and built a sawmill near it. His neighbors were a quarter of a mile to a mile away in any direction. Probably his first home, like others at that time, was built of logs with a stone chimney and fireplace (worth $40—$50). One of their early crops was Indian corn. During a time of scarcity, a neighbor came to Seth to buy a bushel. Seth measured and bagged the corn, but would only take half price for it ($1.25). Seth said that he couldn't thrive on the misfortunes of others.[5]

In 1801 there were only a few cabins scattered in South Hartwick. Abraham Lippitt had built Lippitt's Mills on the west side of Otego Creek (near the beginning of the New Lisbon road to Harrington's Mills [on McIntyre's farm]). Remington Kenyon was the miller for both mills and ran them night and day. Arbor Inn was said to have been built by Lippit as a rival for Harrington's "Pochuck" in New Lisbon.[6]

The Arbor House, which used to occupy the

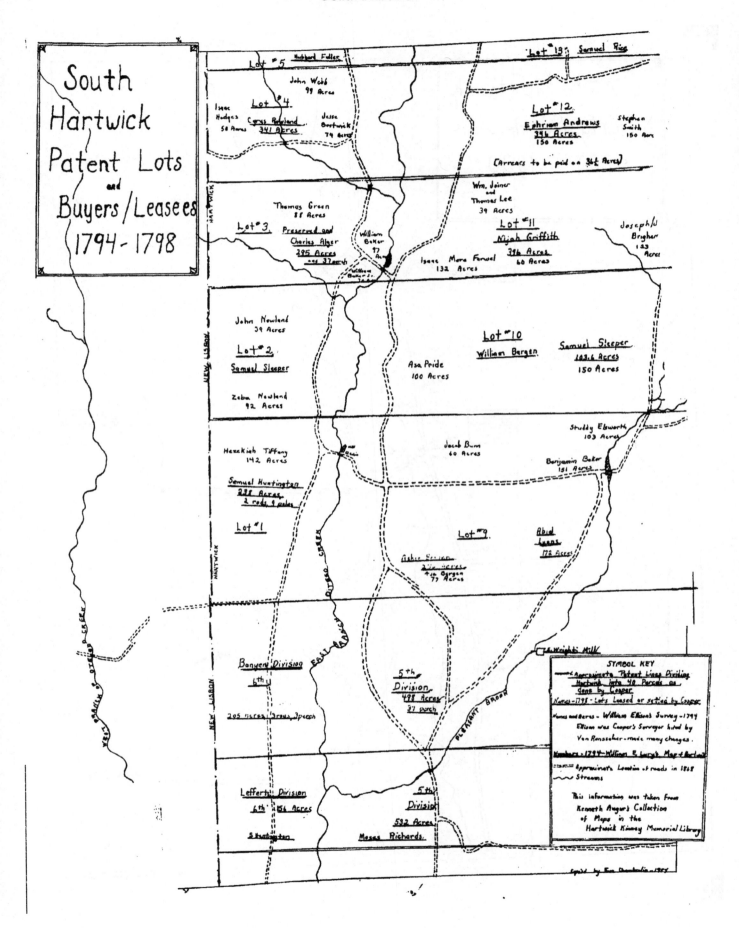

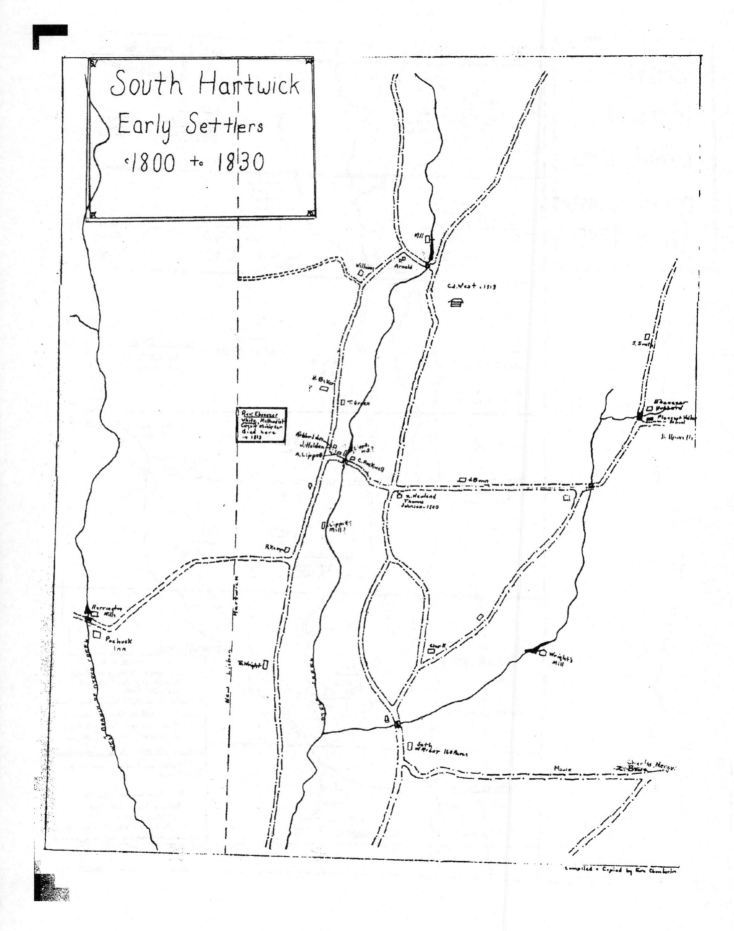

northeast corner of the intersection of Rt. 11 and 11D, was a busy, attractive tavern in the early 1800's. It was a large colonial style building surrounded with flower gardens, a grape arbor, and a well curb. [7]

At the Arbor house, the weary traveler would find welcome rest for himself and his animals. A farmer walking to market even found trees for roosting his flock of turkeys! There would be a hearty meal cooked in the kitchen fireplace and many stories told as neighbors gathered for an evening's gossip. [7] Even though the inn has been replaced by a modern home, each spring, north of the site, crocus blossoms still bloom a visual memorial to Arbor House. [8]

Jacob Bunn was one of the early settlers, who purchased his farm in the late 1790's from Judge William Cooper (the agent for Rev. John C. Hartwick). Jacob Bunn and his wife, Jane, had a farm that began with 60 acres but increased it to over 100 acres. "It was one of the best farms in Otego Valley." [9]

Another early settler, Thomas Johnson, had a small farm next to the Bunn farm. We don't know how long he farmed it after his purchase from Judge Cooper in 1801. The next farmers that we could find that owned the farm were Josiah and Almira Brown in 1842 and 1855. They sold it to Mary Wilcox in 1864. From then on, eleven different families lived here until the Chamberlins bought it in 1951. One of those families, Uriah and Emma Balcom, have great grandchildren farming in South Hartwick and Mount Vision (William Balcom and Margaret VanDuesen). [10]

Some other early settlers were Thomas Booth, Thomas Green, Orrin King, Joseph Holden, Randall Wells, Thomas Clark, Samuel Holman, Henry Baker, and Chester Rockwell. [11,12]

After the death of Abraham Lippitt, Chester Rockwell purchased the mill and sawmill in 1813. Then he built a mile-long dyke to use for waterpower for his woolen mill, which he built about this time. In this mill, the wool was carded, spun into yarn. The yarn was dyed, color-fixed with salt and carried to the drying yard. Then it was woven into beautiful warm cloth. His mill employed about 35 workers (I am told that some of the workers lived in small cottages along the nearby roads. Today there are a few of these buildings that have been moved to local farms for storage sheds.) In addition to his mills, Chester Rockwell built his home east of the Otego Creek. At that time, his home had a kitchen fireplace with a brick oven, a cheese room, a buttery, a loom room and a woodhouse. It has since been owned by the Bilderbecks, the Skubitz brothers and Keith Skubitz.

Chester Rockwell House[13]

Chester Rockwell also built the home west of the creek (the Derr home). Erastus Rockwell built the home across the road for his bride in 1843

Erastus Rockwell House[13]

(now Denis and Pat Hennessy's home). Rockwell Mills continued to run until they were destroyed by fire in 1861 [14, 15] (there will be more about the mills later in this account). We wondered about the workers in the mill: Was there a postal service? Did they have a store? Were there other businesses in South Hartwick?

Before 1832, the first store in South Hartwick was managed by Joseph Holden and Thomas Wilcox. Since this store was held in Arbor Inn / House, where Joseph Holden also ran a tavern, probably that was where Joseph set up house-keeping with his bride, Nancy Brown, after their wedding in 1828. In 1834, an old store journal listed a Dr. Thomas Pine's purchases: 2 gal. wine; 2 gal. gin and 1 gallon of brandy for a total cost of $5.00. It was said that the whiskey was dipped from pails behind the counter. [16] Later on, there was a store across the road from Arbor Inn that was kept by Channing R. Fitch. He sold grocer-ies and woolen goods. This was advertised in the *Otsego County Gazeteer.* [17]

In 1835, Hezekiah Watkins carried the mail from Oneonta to Cooperstown through Laurens, Jacksonville, and South Hartwick. He rode on horseback in all kinds of weather. [18] Chester Rockwell was the first postmaster in South Hartwick. We are not sure of the location of the Post Office. [19]

Erastus Wright, who lived on the road to Laurens, south of the New Lisbon road was an-other early farmer. He died in 1834. Erastus was born in 1778. His wife, Phebe Davenport, was 3 years younger and lived until 1853. They had at least two children: Cordelia and Miles. These four Wrights were all buried in the South Hartwick Cemetery. [20]

Dr. J.M. Peak, Physic & Surgery, moved here in 1832. He lived north of J. Holden's store. He was also a surgeon Dentist. His advertise-ment in "The Hartwick Reporter" read: "Those afflicted with diseases of the teeth, inflamma-tion & scurvy of the gums will find impor-tant relief from using his remediate means." [21]

The old Dist. #10 schoolhouse was built in the early 1800's. By 1842, there were 42 schol-ars in the South Hartwick School. It was called the Sodum Point School. Old records show that in 1845, there were 35 scholars here. [22] In March 1847, the school meeting voted to build a new school. On March 30, 1847, the trustees resolved to sell the old school building to the highest bid-der. The bids were due by September 1 and the building was to be removed by the 10th. This school building stood north of the present school (between the barn and the road on the

South Hartwick School House

Kent Myers farm).

It was sold to Chester Wilson for $11.77. The School Meeting resolved that 20' x 30' was to be the size of the new school. They decided to adopt the specifications of the trust-ees on April 6, 1847. The trustees met and resolved to raise $147.00 with taxes to cover the cost. The school must have been built be-cause their next meeting in September 1948 was held in it. In 1949, they voted to raise a tax of $14.95 to pay for a new stove and pipe. In 2001 this building still stands. [22]

Leonard Matteson, when he was 39, bought a farm in South Hartwick in 1841. His wife was Clotilda Winton. Their children were:

Leonard, Jerome, Amos, Henry, and Martha. Amos (b. 3/14/1835) taught school for two terms while he lived in South Hartwick. In 1863 Amos's daughter married Fred Field. [23]

Joseph Holden sold his store to Thomas Wilcox and the tavern to Peter Kendall. Joseph moved to a new home he built on the east side of the road to Mount Vision about ½ mile south of South Hartwick. He probably took his store journals with him. After six years, in 1852, Joseph Holden moved to Virginia. He left his journal with his sister, Phebe Wells, who lived on East Hill in Joseph's birthplace (there it was used as a scrapbook). It probably took the Holden's a week or more to drive their emigrant wagon to Virginia. [24, 23]

In a letter from Phebe Holden written in 1856, she wrote "Arver is keeping Tavern across the creek at the Johnson Place. He and Sargents and Rockwell have bought the Johnson farm and divided it among them." [25] On the 1855 map of South Hartwick, Thomas Johnson is listed as the owner. But that same year, Josiah and Almira Brown are listed in the census. (Josiah Brown was a carpenter) In 1864, Josiah and Almira sold their 13 acres to Mary Wilcox. On the 1868 map, this part of the Johnson farm was named Thomas Wilcox. Today, in 2001, the Chamberlins have lived here for 50 years. [26]

In 1854, a son, Elmer L., was born. His parents were Leroy and Louise (Wright) Sergent. Elmer later married Nellie Goodrich. [24]

In 1855 on October 1, there was an ad in the "Oneonta Herald" that read:

Thomas Tiffany offers a $5.00 reward for the return of a pocketbook containing $28.00 plus valuable papers; Lost between Oneonta and South Hartwick.
Address: South Hartwick, N.Y.

(All Otsego money) [27]

In 1857, Rockwell Mills ran the following ad in the Herald:

ROCKWELL'S MILLS
WOOLEN MANUFACTORY
South Hartwick, Otsego County, N.Y.
C. ROCKWELL & SON

We continue to manufacture Cassimeres, satinette, plain cloth, flannel, and yarn. So, which for durability and finish are not surpassed by any establishment of the kind. Cloth and yarn on hand for sale. For wool customers coming from a distance can have their wool brought and their cloth returned by informing us by mail or otherwise.

Homemade cloth dressed as usual. Owing to our increasing patronage, we have made large improvements in our establishment and have introduced a TWELVE HORSEPOWER STEAM ENGINE, which will run the machinery in times of low water, and secure to the Patrons a sure and much earlier completion of their work. We intend our work as heretofor shall give satisfaction. Wool intrusted to the care of Wm. A. Comstock of Cooperstown; Ford A. Cope of Oneonta, or Darius Henderson of Otego will be promptly attended to and the cloth returned to the same place. [27]

The Otego Creek had been shrinking and losing its force, so even with the dyke, Chester Rockwell had to use steam power to run his machinery. This was also true in his other mills, both the grist and saw mills. The Rockwell Woolen Mill continued to prosper until the night of August 27, 1861, when fire destroyed it.

Pearl Weeks gives this account:

"Phoebe Rockwell was an eye witness of this disaster. One night she looked out of her window and saw a fire in the woolen mill. The girl ran to alert her parents. Everyone came to fight the fire, but their efforts were in vain. There were no phones, no cars or trucks, no mechanical fire equipment. So the Rockwell Woolen Mill burned to the ground." [28]

Erastus Rockwell, who had been running a mill in Mt. Upton, sold this mill to Chester Rockwell in 1862. Chester's daughter Phoebe married Henry Bilderbeck and they lived in the homestead.

In 1862, on June 18, the following advertisement appeared in the Oneonta Herald:

An ad for C.W. Rockwell's Mt. Upton Mills was followed by this message.

"Grateful for the liberal patronage conferred while at the old stand in South Hartwick. Also for the consideration and sympathy I received on account of my heavy losses by fire, the undersigned takes pleasure in announcing to my former patrons and 'the rest of mankind' that I am now carrying on the business of making GOOD and DURABLE CLOTH" - C.W. Rockwell.

"J.R.FITCH of South Hartwick has constantly on hand for sale a general assortment of our cloths. He will exchange cloth for wool or take wool to be manufactured."[29]

In 1865, the Potashery run by Job Card was still active. He collected ashes from nearby farms and brought them to his potashery north of his farmhouse. He took the potash in barrels to Albany on horsedrawn lumber wagons. [30]

On February 4,1865, Phoebe (Rockwell) Bilderbeck and Henry were blessed with the birth of a daughter, Ida S. Bilderbeck. [29]

In that same year, in November, the School Meeting moved to sell the old school stove to the highest bidder. It was sold to Henry Bilderbeck for $.95! Then they moved that the trustees be authorized to buy a new stove. [22]

About that time, there were a few weddings in South Hartwick. Henry C.Bunn married Clarissa Bissel on Jan.12, 1866. Oscar Maples married Mary E. Carr on Dec.25, 1866. E.W. Murdock of South Hartwick married Denora Fritts of Davenport on October 27,1868. [33]

Our local law enforcer, Amos Matteson, was appointed Deputy in South Hartwick on March 6, 1867. [34]

In 1870, Henry C. Bunn was postmaster in South Hartwick. In February of that year, M.H. Bissell of South Hartwick bought a home on Grand Street in Oneonta for $3000. He continued his egg trade, which had been so successful. In March Bissell's had a large sale of cows and farm utensils. At that time, Asa Pride was a Blacksmith here. His shop was located between the old store and Menzo Balcom's farm. [24]

In 1872, South Hartwick had a gristmill, sawmill, 2 stores, a shoeshop, a blacksmith shop, a potash kiln and a brick kiln. There were about a dozen homes and more than 20 farms. Some of these were listed in the Otsego County directory:

Abijah Munson – Farmer - 60A.
Amos Mattison - Farmer -75A.
Anson Vars - Farmer - 60A.
Arnold Carr - Farmer-80A.
Chad Alger - Farmer -15A.
Chandler Taylor - Farmer - 4A.
Channing Fitch -woolen goods, grocery store
Chester Jacobs - Farmer -114 A.
Daniel Cook - Carpenter & Farmer -1 3/4 A.

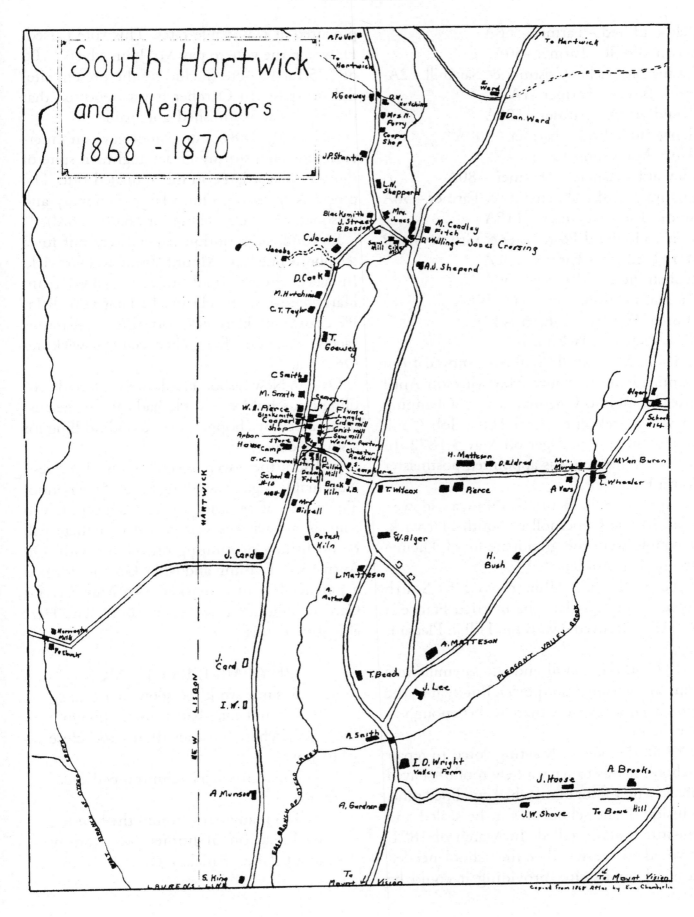

Deloss Eldred - Farmer - 66A
Enoch Bissell - Farmer -50A.
Erastus Brownell - Gristmill & Sawmill - 2A.
Frank Beach - Farmer -1A.
Gerald Smith - Farmer - 100A
Henry Bilderbeck - Farmer - 108A
Henry Matteson - Farmer - 72A
Job Card – Ashery & Farmer – 80A
Jonathon Card – Shoemaker & Farmer – 36A
Landin King – Farmer – 118A
LaSalle Hubbard-Postmaster & Grocery here?
Morrell Smith – Farmer – 92A
Reuben Pierce – Farmer – 50A
Thomas Goewey – Farmer – 108A
Thomas Wilcox – Farmer – 13A
W.H. Pierce – Blacksmith [31]

In 1871, Mr. LaSalle Hubbard moved from Oneonta Plains to South Hartwick on April 20,after he sold his Oneonta farm. [24] Channing Fitch was storekeeper until 1882. Job Cook married Minervaette Alger on May 5,1872. In 1874 P.C. Vanburen was appointed postmaster of South Hartwick. [32]

On April 5,1874, Henry C. Bunn, a widower, married Fannie Copernoll of South Hartwick. This couple were the grandparents of Thelma Bunn and her brothers. [24, 32]

In 1876, Ira C. Allen moved to South Hartwick. Ten years later he married Francelia Vars. (Her folks lived over Bunn Hill in Pleasant Valley).

In 1877, the gristmill and the sawmill were still operating using waterpower. But by July, the Otego Creek was so low there wasn't enough to power the mill. [33]

In 1880, the School Meeting voted to repair the school. It was to have a new roof of shaved hemlock, a new floor of matched and lined pine. The inside of the school was to be sealed and Patent-iron seats installed. In March of 1881, they voted to see whether the school needed more land for its site, providing it could be procured at reasonable rates. This vote passed. However, the vote to pay Mr. John Myers $100 or $75 for ¼ Acre (including the present site) did not pass. In October it was reported that the repairs were finished and paid.

In January 1881, our school gave an entertainment on a stormy Friday night. In spite of the weather, a large number turned out. The proceeds were to go for a large dictionary and seasoned firewood (selling for $6.00 a cord). [22]

In 1882, subscription papers were out for a telephone line from Mount Vision to Hartwick. In May, the railroad survey pushed from Hartwick to South Hartwick. That year, R.H. Pierce of South Hartwick made three regular trips each week hauling freight between Hartwick and Oneonta. [34]

Over in New Lisbon Frank Bresee started peddling household wares. He had earned the cost of his stock by chopping wood and fiddling for a square dance. [35]

In 1883, there were several items of interest. New maple sugar was selling for $1.56 a pound. The best coffee sold for 12¢ a pound. On Aug. 3, a town law was passed that there will be no fishing or hunting on the Sabbath. On April 13, C.E. Bunn and Mike Gregory formed a partnership in a market. On May 11, Ed Card is building a new farm home. The Herald printed this:

WHY FARMERS GET SICK
1) Resume work too soon after eating.
2) Do not take baths often enough.
3) Kitchen & other drains too close to house.
4) Unclean cellars & untrapped cellar drains.
5) Too many trees around the house.
6) Location of homes on swampy ground. (site of malaria)[36]

A temperance meeting was held in 1889 at the schoolhouse in South Hartwick. In 1886, I.P. Coates exhibited his Gospel Temperance Panorama on Feb.1, in the Hartwick Methodist Church. Then he showed his sterioptican views on the various schoolhouses here about, closing Sunday night with a free (collection) Panorama at the South Hartwick School. [37]

In 1889, H.A. Holbrook was storekeeper here until 1915. [36] The map shows him living in the Arbor House. About 1890, Frank Bresee started a mercantile store in the old building that still stands west of Co. Rt. 11. Later he moved to Hartwick Village in a store in the corner block. From there, he moved to Oneonta and developed Bresee's Department Store, a great shopping center for many years, famous statewide.

Bresees Store [38]

In 1891, our school opened with Samuel Pashley the schoolteacher for the winter term. He was a graduate of Hartwick Seminary. Two local women, Anna Fitch and Lovina Munson, will teach at Gilbert's Lake and the Maple's District. Local sports: —Amos Matteson killed a very large fox with birdshot. [23]

During the 1890's the Johnson Farm (Chamberlins) changed owners five times: F. Wilcox, H. Bilderbeck, E. Robinson, H. Bilderbeck, and William Tuller. William Tuller

was a carpenter who made many improvements to the house and barn. They lived here for 30 years. In 1893, a January prayer meeting of the South Hartwick Young People was held at Jesse Card's home.

There were three weddings of importance, Ida Bilderbeck married Clelland G. Eldred on Dec.20, 1894. In 1891, Thomas Mills married Francelia Bird on Nov.10. In 1895, Albert Straight of Laurens married Lottie Ada Lee of South Hartwick. [39]

In 1895, the School Meeting voted not to

Chamberlin's House

spend more than $3.00 for a new flag and staff. It was passed. [22] Mr. and Mrs. John Myers, in 1896, were surprised by a company of their friends on their 25th wedding anniversary. [23]

A newspaper social was held in 1898 at the home of Mr. and Mrs. Eldred Pratt. They had a supper and charged 10¢ a couple. A tragedy in South Hartwick: Dean, the second son of John Myers died after a brief illness. He had acute inflammation of the kidneys. Dean was only 17 years old. His funeral was held at the Christian Church in Hartwick. The Hartwick Union School attended as a group. [23]

Another wedding-Abijah Munson married Carrie Mae Cobb of South Hartwick in February, 1899. Later in the year, the Literary Society

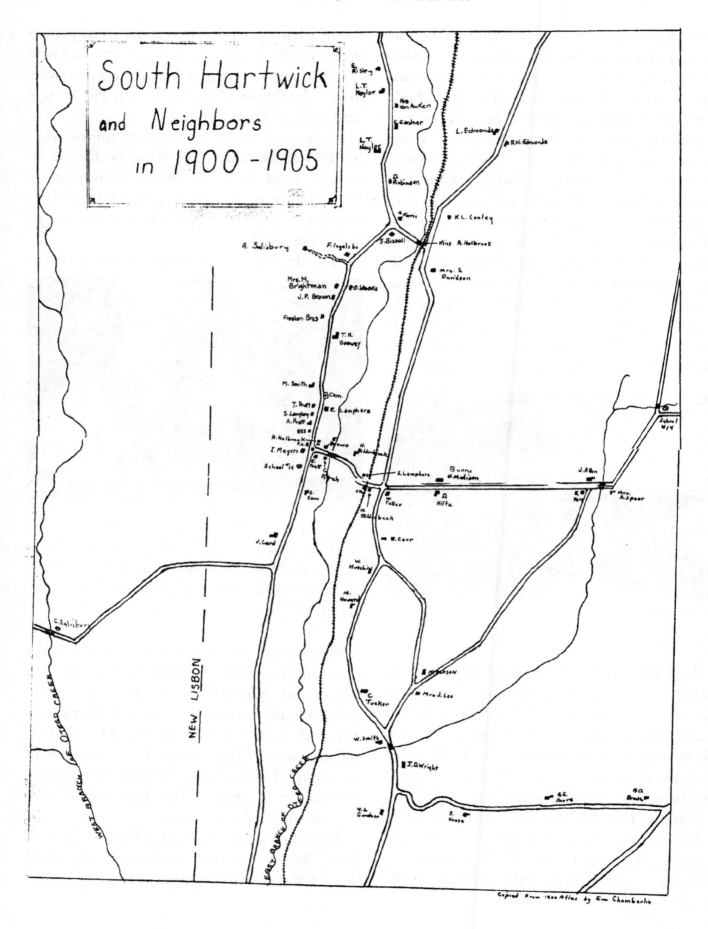

South Hartwick and Neighbors in 1900-1905

Copied from 1900 Atlas by Eva Chamberlin

met at Whitemans. The following officers were elected: President; T.L. Pratt; Vice-President, Henry Matteson; Secretary, Grace Pride; Treasurer, T.H. Allen; organist, Mae Pratt; Chorister, Mrs. Will Tuller. The next meeting will be at Amos Matteson's.

Henry Bilderbeck is getting out a quantity of lumber from his VanSchoick lot for the rebuilding of his large barn, which had burned in August 1898. [23]

In 1901, Mr. & Mrs. VanHolbrook had a son.

Mr. Dexter, the organ & piano tuner, made a business trip through South Hartwick in 1901. If anyone wanted work done by him, they sent word to Mrs. Frederick Field for a time.

A neighborhood picnic was held at Arnold's Lake. All that attended had a fine time. [40]

In February 1903, Henry Bilderbeck died. He left five children: Mrs. Clelland Eldred, Frederick, Rockwell, George, and Henry. [41]

Another wedding- Jennie Estes, daughter of Lewis Estes, married Harold Whitmore on June 29,1904. [41]

In 1905 on February 17, Mrs. Joseph Pashley died at the age of 74. Her children were: Mrs. Frank Lake, Mrs. Arthur Wart, and Mrs. Adelbert Lamphere. [42] In August 1905, Albert Wilcox died. He was the son of Thomas and Mary Wilcox. Albert's wife was Sarah Salisbury. He also left a son, Carl Wilcox. [40]

In August 1907, Iva Myers married Miles Hall.[23]

The pupils here have received the announcement of the marriage of their teacher, Miss Elizabeth Fields to Mr. Gilbert Marlette of Mount Vision. The wedding took place on December 19,1908 at the home of her parents. Her school students here in 1908 were: Gerald Hughes, Grant Robinson, Seymore Robinson, Chauncey Robinson, Fenimore Tilyou, Kenneth Bunn, Mac Bresee, Milton Bunn, Bernice Robinson, Helen Barney, Hazel Card, Ira Robinson, Pearl Fitch, and Lynn Barney.[24]

In 1910, we see that Miss Anna Lane of Mount Vision will be the teacher. She will board with Chester Brownell. [23]

In 1913, at the School Meeting, Austin Barney was elected trustee, and Charles Tucker, collector. Miss Celia Sherman of Mt. Vision has taken the South Hartwick School for the next term. A medicine show was given at the schoolhouse for 2 nights. It was advertised as well recommended. [24]

In 1913, some of the young men that went to work as section hands on the trolley road did not seem to like their work. Now Seymore Robinson is working for Arthur Eldred and Julian Markel for Andrew Salisbury at Schuyler Lake. [43]

In 1913, many of the local farmers will have their spring plowing hurried along by using the tractor operated by Gilbert Marlette. The tractor is certainly a great saver of time, labor, and horseflesh. Gerald Hughes has hired out to George Luce to work on the farm occupied by Frank Robinson for this season. Mr. William Wart from Fly Creek has purchased the store property in South Hartwick from H.R. Holbrook. Mr. Holbrook has been in the store for 26 years. Paul Robinson will run the peddling cart for Mr. Wart.[44] William Wart was storekeeper until 1917. [24]

In 1912, the Christian Aid Society had a Social at the home of Mrs. William Tuller. In May 1913,the afternoon Social Club met with Mrs. Fred German in South Hartwick. [45] In April 1918, several ladies attended the Home Economics Club meeting held at Mrs. A.L. Straight. In April, the Red Cross branch organized here with 12 members. They have completed and sent to headquarters the following articles: 3 pajama suits, 3 pair socks, 24 triangular bandages, 30 sculttes bandages, 2 refugee dresses, 2 skirts, and 2 chemises. They met at Mrs. Belle Fitch's home. [45]

During the spring of 1918, several people were

ill with the Liberty measles. Among them, Clifford Salisbury and Mrs. William Tuller as well as Susie and Willie Munson. [45]

In 1918, Ray Jenks and Andy Salisbury were working on the highway with their teams. In 1920, Adolph Hanson moved to South Hartwick. Jesse Card was building a new barn in 1921. Carleton Irons is attending school in South Hartwick and helping his grandparents with the chores. Mr. Wart had been very ill. [45]

The automobile encouraged road improvement. In 1920 & 1921 the East and West Main streets in Hartwick village had been reworked and topped with a hard macadam surface. In the next year it had reached Jones' Crossing. By 1923, South Hartwick was at last connected to Hartwick with a hard surfaced road. [46]

During the early 1900's the citizens of South Hartwick had another major means of transportation, THE TROLLEY. The tracks bisected our valley, lying east of the Otego Creek. The South Hartwick Trolley Station was located north of Rt. 11D on Baggio Cardonne's farm. The farmers now had a nearby place to send their milk, cream, and other produce. There were 14 passenger round trips a day between Oneonta and Mohawk, giving folks a rare traveling opportunity. The trolley was a great improvement to life in South Hartwick until the automobile became more usable and convenient. When the car barns burned in Hartwick in l925, they were not rebuilt. Passenger service ended in 1933 soon followed by the end of freight service.

After 1926, Gerald Hughes sold his farm to Albert Hanson. In May, Gilbert Marlette was elected trustee at the School Meeting. Our postmaster was complimented about the new post office, which was installed in the 1930's. There were social evenings spent at various homes: about 60 friends gathered at Charles Holbrook's. They had a great evening with dancing and refreshments. In the winter, several sleigh loads went over the hill to Harry Sergent's home in Gardnertown, not coming home until early morning. They all had a fine time in spite of the stormy weather. [47]

In 1928, Uriah Balcom bought the Tuller Farm at the foot of Bunn Hill on Rt.205. He and Emma lived there 18 years. The next year, their son, Menzo, married Nellie Weeks, the sister of Pearl and Ralph. The Balcoms had some cows and chickens. They also had a beloved dog, Pal (his gravestone was in the eastern lawn when the Chamberlins moved here in 1951). Uriah and Emma had a son, William in 1931. [26]

In 1925, an improved road was built from Hartwick to Index but there was still a dirt road south from Hartwick east of the Otego Creek. During 1928-1930, Route 205 had been built as far as Laurens. Then in the spring of 1931, the Keller Corp. of Massachusetts began work on the Hartwick-Laurens section. Since much of the work was done by men, the road took all

Roadwork

Spreading Macadam on Route 205

that summer to build. There hadn't been so much excitement since the construction of the trolley line. This would be much safer for automobile traffic than the narrow, muddy and dusty road laid out years earlier by the early pioneers. The road was completed in October. It became the main highway for the valley after the Hartwick-Oaksville section was done in the fall of 1933. [46]

By 1933, Hartwick was again having a safe, smooth way to travel by automobile to points north or south. Now, 80 years later, those folks would be amazed at the traffic on 205.

In the summer of 1933, Arthur Bennington of South Hartwick gave some musical selections on a musical saw at the Christian Church in Hartwick. He was accompanied by his mother, Mrs. Hobart Bennington. The Benningtons lived on Bunn hill (across from Elizabeth Bunn's). Two years later, Hobart Bennington died in July. He had farmed it there for twenty years. [24]

In 1937, Elizabeth Schneider married Kenneth Bunn. Later in the summer, a surprise shower was given to the newlyweds at the home of Clarence Bunn. More than a hundred guests joined in the celebration. Later in August, Harry Bilderbeck married Naomi Burch in Schenectady. The friends of Henry and Eva Murdock gave them an informal reception and shower in honor of their recent marriage. (Romance was busy in South Hartwick!)

Later in August more than a hundred past & present residents of South Hartwick enjoyed a community picnic at the Pine Woods.

At this picnic, Frank Bresee was the main speaker. He gave a most interesting talk. After owning small stores here in Hartwick, New Lisbon, Fly Creek, Schenevus, and Sidney, he went to Oneonta and started a small store in the Baird block. From this small business, with a staff of only six, he increased in size to the Oneonta Department Store with a staff of 147 by 1962. [48]

In 1938, we see that Frederica Potter has been attending Cobleskill State College. Dorothy Manley has graduated from the Utica School of Commerce. Later, Frederica was to marry Everett Hornbeck and Dorothy was to marry Ralph Weeks. Both of these women have been active community workers.

Later in 1938, there were 75 relatives at the annual Eldred Reunion held at Bunn's Grove. Burton Eldred of Laurens was chosen President; Clarence Bunn, Vice-President, and Norris Eldred, Secretary-Treasurer. That year too, a marker honoring Ebenezer White, the Methodist Circuit Rider, was erected beside the South Hartwick Cemetery. [24]

1939 was an important year in South Hartwick. The houses here were finally being wired for electricity. The store, school, and post office would also be wired. The right of way has been secured and the line was built[49].

We were glad to see another wedding: Lillian Johnson of Forkshop and Lyle Jones, son of William Jones, were married (today their son, Lyle, is Otsego County Emergency Dispatcher). The Jones lived on the Jones Homestead on Rt.11.

In the 1940's South Hartwick was a busy farming community. Many of the farmers were young couples with small children. They worked hard from dawn to after dark. During the 40's, there were more than a dozen dairy farmers in South Hartwick. There was an active Dairymen's League and some belonged to the Grange. The women of the community hosted an annual oyster supper for the Dairymen's League. This was a truly delicious meal given in the schoolhouse.

A map of South Hartwick showing its residents would have listed at least the following names: Howard Marlette, Munsons (?), Kenneth Bunn, Kendall Marlette, Arthur Lawrence, John Sihoven, Emmett Robertson, Irwin McIntyre (Carrs), Bagio Cardone, George Grass, H.

Bilderbeck, John George, Eric Holmes, Glenn Myers, Gilbert Bunn/ Robert Derr, E. Rowe & A. Rowe, Irving Doyle, G. Hughes, George Bookout, P. Hetzler, H. Smith, Silas Robinson, Earl Grisby, Clesson Pashley, Menzo Balcom, Egbert Scott, Uriah Balcom, H. Young , T. Nichols, K. VanWarner & H. Greulich.

In 1945,the women of South Hartwick met at the home of Mrs. Lawrence to organize a Home Demonstration Unit here. This was a state organization based in Cornell, to enrich and instruct women whose lives often seem overworked and without much enjoyment. The women elected the following officers: President, Nellie Balcom, Vice-President, Mrs Arthur Lawrence; Secretary, Lillian Jones; Treasurer, Dorothy Weeks; Project Leader, Viola Smith; Clothes, Betty Bunn; Household Management, Elsie Bennett; Family Life, Henrietta Hetzler; Food & Nutrition, Alice Barney. This club was active for many years. They held regular instructional work meetings, usually at the school with a lunch. The women hosted Holiday Community dinners and parties at the school, They also organized annual homecoming picnics at various places. [50]

The South Hartwick Home Bureau had its first meeting on October 31, 1945 Hilda Augur helped organize it. The members were given permission to use the schoolhouse for meetings and activities. They agreed to provide wood for fuel, pay for the electricity, and maintain the building. The group chose their projects for the year. Members volunteered to lead each project. The secretary had to send reports to the County Office. The leaders had to participate in workshops before they could instruct the members about the projects.

From 1945 to 1950's the membership grew to include women from the other parts of Hartwick. Most of those are listed here:

Aluffo, Madeline	Gilette, Lena	Mead, Ora
Andrews, Ethel	Gras, Thelma	Miles, Lulah
Augur, Hilda	Greulich, Louise	Munson, Pauline
Balcom, Nellie	Grigsby, Edith	Murdock, Eva
Barney, Alice	Grigsby, Millicent	Neal, Ruth
Beach, Grace	Heiter, Gertude	Pashley, Olive
Bennett, Elsie	Hetzler, Henrietta	Phillips, Nadine
Block,Dorothy	Hetzler, Yvonne	Potter, Emily
Bunn ,Betty	Holmes, Helen	Potter, Susie
Bunn,Jennie	Hornbeck, Frederica	Powers, Doris
Bunn, Susie	Hughes,Madge	Reynolds, Nellie
Bunn, Thelm	Jacobsen, Nelda	Schallert, Violet
Burkhart, Fannie,	Jones, Lillian	Schneider, Elizabeth
Burns, Florence	Jones, Maude	Scott, Virginia
Bush, Ella	Kellogg, Margaret	Shafer, Alice
Cady, Margaret	Kohinke, Marion	Smith, Viola
Carvin, Azalia	Kimmey, Katherine	Stanton,Berthe
Chamberlin, Eva	Lawrence, Annie	Telfer, Mildred
Christensen, Ida	Lawrence, Emma	Thering, Mrs.
Clark, Lolita	Luffler, Delia	VanRiper, Sophie
Conklin, Ruby	Luffler, Doris	VanWarner, Jean
Derr, Elizabeth	Lyons, Janette	Weeks, Dorothy
Dibble,Frances	Mack, Roberta	Wilsey, Alice
Doyle, Helen	Manley, Catherine	Wilsey, Gertude
Fashay, Frances	Marlette, Bernice	Wright, Esther
Gerst, Gertrude	Marlette, Diana	Wright, Lillie Mae
Gillette, Eleanor	Martin, Leila[51]	

Of course, many of these people were not members all of the time, but they were all listed at least for one year. It was a valuable club. It held the community together, the women became a close, caring group. They discussed national concerns as well as local ones. Their influence makes us still a caring community in which to live.

Hay Harvester

As we move on through the 50's toward the present, we find that some of the farmers have changed. Mitchel and Anton Skubitz bought the Bilderbeck farm. Everett Kane bought Irving Doyle farm. The Chamberlin's bought the Balcom place on the corner.

Round Hay Bales

The farmers, having changed to tractors were using more laborsaving, time wise machinery.

Most of the barns were equipped with milking machines. Strict sanitary laws had made some changes in milk collecting. Farmers worked together, sharing machinery and labor.

Some of the residents here now worked away from home instead of farming. Some of their land was farmed by neighbors, which was good for the land as well as adding crop acreage. Our children were now all bussed to Hartwick High School. Later on, Hartwick (including our district) would belong to the Cooperstown school. This change had many conflicts that have been slow to smooth. It also had great advantages for the children, many of whom were scholarship recipients

Here in South Hartwick, The Home Demonstration Club changed to the Community Club. They met at the school and were responsible for it for many years.

During these Years there were many changes in South Hartwick. Some farmers retired, some could not continue farming, families and young couples moved in. One couple, John Williams and his wife, Gertude, purchased a small acreage, built a small cabin and barn, raised sheep, chickens, and rabbits. He was a stonemason, so after they got the animals sheltered and a large garden growing, he began to dig the cellar for their home. As he dug, he saved all of the usable stones and put them in the cellar wall. That cellar was seven feet deep! Then he proceeded to build his stone house. Most of the wooden parts were from lumber that others had discarded. He traveled around the country doing stone work and digging graves. When he saw stones, he would pick up ones that were "good", bring them home for his house. Today, his house is beside Rt. 205, a fitting memorial for John, who loved animals, stone, and hard work. In fifty years,

fourteen new homes have been built in South Hartwick as well as nine mobile homes. It is a great place to live.

Bridge over Otego Creek

Logging Truck

The schoolhouse still stands. Now it is really town property. The Hartwick Historical Society has it as a preservation project. The store and Post Office no longer exist. The trolley bed is the only reminder of that once busy electric trolley. However we have had some improvements in transportation. The Bunn Hill road was paved. A new bridge was built over the Otego Creek in 1993. It was started March 10, and was finished June 16. It is sturdy enough for milk trucks or buses, or even log trucks.

In the last few years, many of the landowners of the lands around South Hartwick have been harvesting their trees. Log trucks are a daily sight.

Today, and for the past 50 years, we have really enjoyed life in South Hartwick. It is a wonderful place for a family. Our people are great. They are hard working, caring, reliable friends. We are probably prejudiced, but we think this is one of the most beautiful valleys in the country. We hope that it will be a farming community for many years.

————

By: Eva Chamberlin

1. OTSEGO COUNTY: by Edwin F. Bacon, Ph.D., pub. Oneonta Herald, 1902, p.45
2. LAND PATENTS OF OTSEGO COUNTY: by Roy Butterfield, pub. Freeman's Journal
3. BIOGRAPHICAL REVIEW OF OTSEGO COUNTY: by Biographical Review, pub.1893
4. PIONEER INDUSTRIES: By Pearl Weeks, Pg. 7
5. OLD TIME NOTES: by Willard Huntington, Pub. 1915, Vol.4
6. OLD TIME NOTES: by Willard Huntington, Pub. 1915, Vol.2
7. HISTORY OF HARTWICK VILLAGE & TOWN: By Pearl Weeks, Reprint, 1981,Heritage Press pg. 35
8. OBSERVATIONS BY THE AUTHOR, E. Chamberlin
9. RECORDS OF THE BUNN FAMILY: by Thelma Bunn
10. RECORDS OF THE CHAMBERLIN FARM -Researched by E. Chamberlin
11. HISTORY OF HARTWICK VILLAGE & TOWN: By Pearl Weeks, Reprint, 1981,Heritage Press
12. CENSUS RECORDS- County Clerk's office.
13. PHOTO— by E. Chamberlin —1975
14. HISTORY OF HARTWICK VILLAGE & TOWN: By Pearl Weeks, Reprint, 1981,Heritage Press pg. 34,32
15. PIONEER INDUSTRIES: By Pearl Weeks, pg. 34, 2
16. HISTORY OF HARTWICK VILLAGE & TOWN: By Pearl Weeks, Reprint, 1981,Heritage Press pg. 33,34
17. PIONEER INDUSTRIES: By Pearl Weeks, pg. 32
18. OLD TIME NOTES: by Willard Huntington, Pub. 1915, Vol.9
19. PIONEER INDUSTRIES: By Pearl Weeks, pg. 38
20. SOUTH HARTWICK CEMETERY: Observed & recorded by E. Chamberlin & Nellie Balcom
21. HARTWICK REPORTER-: 1832, Spring
22.NOTES FROM DISTRICT # 10 SCHOOL MEETINGS: by Nellie Balcom & Thelma Bunn
23.ITEMS FROM EVA MURDOCK'S SCRAPBOOK-by Eva Murdock
24.ITEMS FROM NELLIE BALCOM'S SCRAPBOOK: by Nellie Balcom
25. HISTORY OF HARTWICK VILLAGE & TOWN: By Pearl Weeks, Reprint, 1981,Heritage Press pg. 33
26.RESEARCH IN DEED BOOKS IN COUNTY OFFICE- E. Chamberlin
27.ITEMS FROM THE ONEONTA HERALD: 1857,1855
28. PIONEER INDUSTRIES: By Pearl Weeks, pg. 38
29. ITEMS FROM THE ONEONTA HERALD: 1862
30.PIONEER INDUSTRIES: By Pearl Weeks, pg. 19
31 GAZATEER & BUSINESS DIRECTORY OF OTSEGO COUNTY: by Hamilton Child, Pub.187
32. ITEMS FROM THE ONEONTA HERALD: 1872, 1874
33. CHARLOTTE' STEER'S JOURNAL: kept by Pearl Weeks
34. ITEMS FROM THE ONEONTA HERALD: 1882
35.HISTORY OF HARTWICK VILLAGE & TOWN: By Pearl Weeks, Reprint, 1981, Heritage Press, pg. 68
36.ITEMS FROM THE ONEONTA HERALD: 1886
37.RICHFIELD SPRINGS MERCURY—1886
38.HISTORY OF HARTWICK VILLAGE & TOWN: By Pearl Weeks, Reprint, 1981, Heritage Press, pg. 69
39. ITEMS FROM THE ONEONTA HERALD: 1894, 1891, 1893
40. ITEMS FROM MRS.DEAN'S SCRAPBOOK, the N.Y. Room, Huntington Library
41.ITEMS FROM THE ONEONTA HERALD: 1904
42.ITEMS FROM THE ONEONTA HERALD: 1907
43.HARTWICK PAPER-1913
44. GRANDMA CURRY'S SCRAPBOOK
45.OTSEGO FARMER: Jan. 1918
46.HISTORY OF HARTWICK VILLAGE & TOWN: By Pearl Weeks, Reprint, 1981, Heritage Press, pg. 88
47.OTSEGO FARMER: Jan.1925,
48.IN OLD ONEONTA: By Edwin R. Moore, Reprint, 1986-vol. 1, pg. 54
49.HARTWICK REPORTER-: 1939
50.PHONE CONVERSATIONS-E. Chamberlin with Dorothy Weeks
51. Meeting notes of The SOUTH HARTWICK HOME BUREAU; now in The Hartwick Museum (from Dorothy Weeks) .

Hinman Hollow

View of the Hollow

Early history calls it "The Hollow," located in the center of the Town of Hartwick with District 12 School House as a center. The Hollow is formed by seven small tributaries that terminate in a large beaver swamp.

Early settlers moved to the area after the Revolutionary War, coming from Connecticut and Newport, R.I. about 1789 or later. Some of the early settlers were Joseph Lippitt, George Latin, Wm. Tinkham, Dexter Fisher, Soloman Comstock Augur, Stephen Holden, and Hopkins

Brickyard

Burlingham.

The early settlers were an industrious people, and soon many industries were at work.

Burlingham's brickyard, north of the schoolhouse, used the blue clay found in the Beaver Swamp. Many chimneys made with this brick are still in use. The Burlinghams also made whiskey in their distillery. Whiskey was a by-product of rye that could be shipped much easier.

The schoolhouse, originally built on the west side of the road was moved to its present location and added onto in 1875.

Schoolhouse

The land ¼ acre was bought from Morell Burlingham for $25.00. The school was the center of the community. Besides school programs, weddings, funerals, Church services and other public meetings were held there. At one rowdy school meeting, a barrel of Burlingham's whiskey was rolled into the swamp and sunk. It has never been found. The last teacher at the school was Adelia Kiley. The school closed in June 1928 due to a shortage of pupils.

Just above the new house in the left-hand corner was the "Hinman" house, formerly the Burlingham house. At one time it was the Hinman Hollow Post Office. Hinman is the family that the Hollow got its name from. Fire destroyed the house in 1924.

Opposite the schoolhouse was the Hinman Hollow Cheese factory, built about 1906. It was a Cooperative. They stopped making cheese when they could ship the fluid milk by railroad to New York City. It was more profitable.

YOUR MILK 4738 lbs.	Hinman Hollow Cheese Factory
Ratio 2 cent $1.06	DIVIDEND TO John Brose.
	Sale No. 2 and 3 No. Cheese sold 76 Price sold for 12 3/4 cts.
	Whole amount of Cheese sold 2787 lbs. Milk 37686 lbs.
	Comprising Cheese from April 28 to May 13 Both Days Included
	Pounds of Milk Required for lb. Cheese 10 3/5 Dividend $ 50.22
	For Making and Furnishing $1.25 per cwt. Amount of Cash received
	W. A. KILEY, Manager.
	C. R. Willard

Hinman Hollow Cheese Factory Receipt

Before this cheese factory was built, the Phillips family had a shop on the same spot. Their house was across the road (The Dick Duke house). They made pack baskets and other baskets, also violins. The violins were of excellent quality, but they were made on a (Baroque) form. They were made with a straight neck played down in the arm and not up at the chin. The Historical Association has one. It was donated by Willard

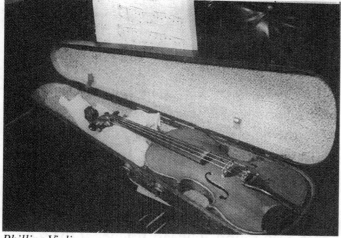

Phillips Violin

Wells. Bill Powers has one, formerly owned by the Sherman family. There are many others in the area.

The Phillips family also ran a sawmill, which was just above the Grange Hall. The mill was built by Ike Kenyon. It used an up and down saw, and was slow. Ike sold it to George Latin and moved to Maryland to set up a faster mill. There were other water-powered mills down the valleys including a gristmill at the Augur farm and a broom factory (undershot) at Esther Henleys. Farther down by the town line was another sawmill. A heavy rain washed all the dams out at one time.

While we are on the subject of water, we must note that Hinman Hollow is flanked by two beautiful lakes. One is Goey Pond, a privately owned water source for the Village of Milford. The other is Arnolds Lake, completely surrounded by private cottages.

Among one of the first residents of the Hollow was "Christian Hartwick", brother of John Christopher Hartwick. He lived in the southern part of the Hollow on the Bill Boyle

farm. As the story goes, he dug his own grave on a knoll on that hill. He then made a mess of cutting his throat. It took him three days to die. He was buried in the grave he dug. Two hundred years later, the Hartwick Historical Association, with the help of the town highway crew, put a large stone and plaque, marking his grave on that high knoll.

Another notable person was Marcus Wells. He wrote the hymn "Holy Spirit Faithful Guide" and many other hymns while he was living on the farm opposite the Grange Hall. He also made wooden forks.

Hinman Hollow Grange

The grange hall was built by the Knights Templars as a Temple Hall. It was later used as a private home.

The Grange bought the building in 1914 from George Smith. The first Master was S.J. Winslow, the present Master is Dorothy LaGasse. In 1928 the Grange became dormant, but due to the effort of F. Lynn Augur, the Charter was left in the hall. On Dec. 13, 1933 the Grange was reorganized. Since then it has been a very active Grange, with membership at over a hundred at one time. Today it has about 30 members. The first Rural Life Sunday service was held in this Hall in June of 1946. The Otsego County Fair was organized as a Grange Fair in this Hall on Oct. 10, 1945.

In 1994 the Hartwick Grange merged with Hinman Hollow Grange, leaving only one Grange in the Town of Hartwick.

To the East of the Hollow was the Lippitt house, now at the Farmers Museum. It was at this house that the first Town Meeting was planned. Abraham Lippitt was one of the Methodist Ministers who preached at Bowe Hill and Methodist Hill camp meetings, in the 1800 to 1840. In 1807 Joseph and Rose Lippitt sold adjoining property to Dexter Fisher. His house was opposite the Powers road where it meets Route 45. The Lippitt house was moved to the Farmers Museum in 1950. The Lippitt family still owns the original farm.

Holden's Inn

Due north on the high ground, Stephen Holden built an Inn.

It was on the Maples Road near the Junction with Chase Road. The first Hartwick Town meeting was held there in 1802. It was a stopping place for travelers going westward in the county. The house was of plank construction, with a large 6-hearth chimney. The house burned

Lippitt Homestead

Maples Homestead

in 1986. A new house has replaced it.

To the west was the Maples Homestead.

It was said, the Maples came from Connecticut with money and were our capitalists. They were very prosperous .In January 1924 the house, barn and cattle were all destroyed by fire. The family descendants are just now, in 2000, building a new house.

The William Timken house, built of oak plank and pine rafters some time in the early 1800's, is one of the oldest houses in the Hollow. William Timken also had a wagon factory just below the stone quarry. A blacksmith shop was down on the corner of Bill Powers Road and Route 45. It was gone after 1860.

According to old maps, an early cheese factory was just opposite the large Comstock house. It was on the same 5 acres owned by Dexter Fisher and also had a very good spring. I think they were all connected.

George Hinds came to the Hollow in 1860. By 1863 he had bought land from Lippitt, Comstock, Burlinghouse and Burlingame, Wm. Timken and Dexter Fisher for a total of 300 acres. He created a large hop farm. By 1890 he was bankrupt. The farm was bought by the Cross family of East Springfield. They drove their cows down in one day. The large red dairy barn built by Hinds, blew down in 1923. This is the farm Bill Powers has lived on for the last 65 years.

A few of the outstanding citizens of Hinman Hollow were: Marcus Wells who made organs, wooden tools and wrote hymns; the Phillips family who made violins and pack baskets; and the Lippitt family who today operate a fine jewelry store in Cooperstown. Also notable was the Augur family, who lived where Beaver Valley Campground is, and moved to Cooperstown and founded Augurs Bookstore. A local boy who did well was Tom Cross, who got his primary schooling in Hinman Hollow.

He trapped muskrats in the swamp and peddled "Larkin" products all over Hinman Hollow in order to get a "Larkin" desk. He enlisted in the Calvary when he was sixteen, in World War 1. He rose to the rank of Captain. His rank in World War II was Colonel, and in the Korean conflict he was a Brigadier General. He retired as a Three Star General. He made

many trips back to the Hollow. He retired about 1955 after two heart attacks. His grave is in Arlington Cemetery, about 30 feet from President Kennedy's.

There are many who got their start in Hinman Hollow and went out in life to make a place for themselves. There are doctors, nurses, lawyers, judges, and engineers. The list goes on and on, so does Hinman Hollow.

By: Bill Powers

Information for this article was gotten from the following:
Old Deeds and Maps
School Records
80 years of Personal Experiences and Memories

Arnold's Lake

Captain Josiah Arnold, born in 1773 the son of David and Waity (Lippitt) Arnold, came to the area from Warwick, Rhode Island in 1793. On November 15, 1809 he purchased 111 3/4 acres in the town of Hartwick from Nathan Thorp [Liber L, p.265]. This acreage is located at the southern end of Arnold Lake and is now forested state land.

Steve and Laura Child are in possession of Arnold Lake historical materials which includes ownership records of individual camp properties and recollections of some of the earlier residents. The following are excerpts from recollections of Barbara Laird and Nancy Launt.

"Fanny Scatchard came up to Arnold Lake in the early 1900's taking the trolley from Oneonta to Mt. Vision where the farmer at the lake would meet them with his horses and wagon. ....The mailman drove a cute "doctor's" buggy with a one seater, leather top and a beautiful white horse to pull it. He came from Milford up the back way (using Chlorinator Road) up Sutter's Hill around to the north end of the lake to the outlet and then back again.

"Peaman" Squires, who lived near the cross-roads where the old schoolhouse was, would come up Sutter's Hill in his wagon with nice fresh veggies. We had milk delivered from a farm a mile and a half from the lake.

Kerosene lamps were our only light source. How I hated cleaning the chimneys. We had no telephones, but did have a radio with headphones. Mother had a wooden washing machine on the porch. Everything was rinsed in the lake. We got our water from a spring located at the end of the driveway by Carvin's camp. We would drive over and fill up our bucket."

Stanley Sherman contributed the following memories of life at Arnold Lake.

"My grandfather, William Stutts, had an early camp, which is now Dean's camp. He was a minister who graduated from Hartwick Seminary.

Without running water you had an outhouse. Ours was up on the hill. Our garbage was different back then also. It was buried for years in a field behind the camp because by the time you burned everything that could be burned, you had very little garbage left. One of my jobs at camp was to dig a hole up in the field about 2 feet deep and 3 feet wide. It would hold all our summers garbage. Today you could fill that hole in one day.

Before I went into the Merchant Marine we still had oil lamps up here at the lake. Electricity was put in while I was away. There were one or two telephones in Mt. Vision. If you wanted to call someone you went down to Glenn Tilley's store."

With population growth at the lake and more boat usage occurring, several men including Donald Sutter, Frank Austin, Orbie Jones, Spencer Feldmann, Sr. Bud Launt, Nellis Bronner , Bob Armstrong, Jim Champlin Sr. and Ken Collier, had a meeting to establish a lake association. The Arnold Lake Association was incorporated August 26, 1966. The purposes for which it was formed include protecting and preserving the natural beauty of the lake and surrounding woodlands and encouraging good conservation practices. Over one hundred lake residents signed on as charter members.

Two Arnold Lake Camps

Over the years a number of the camps have become converted to year round residences. Arnold Lake is no longer just a summer vacation spot.

Excerpts from Scrapbook of Laura and Steve Childs

Christian Hill

Our topic for this article is Christian Hill, probably so-called because of the Christian Church there in 1813. Records from 1813 to 1869 listed several first settlers and the ancestors of many of the present residents.

The first church was located on what is the Shepherd place and was built of stone.

According to a 'Watchtower' magazine of January 26, 1824, the church and an adjoining schoolhouse were destroyed by fire which originated in the meeting house and was believed set by design.

Some minutes show that pioneer churches were a substitute for many departments of our present government – for instance- complaints of intoxication, not telling the truth and fencing off a road.

During the late 1800's the church was abandoned and many of the members united with the Christian church in Hartwick.

It has been said that the last clerk's book was used to paste in articles, etc. as a scrapbook. The church was torn down about 1904 – 5. Mrs. Bush and her mother and the minister were the only ones at the last meeting so decided to give up.

The boundaries of Christian hill as on the map are Chase on the south, Toddsville on the east, Fly Creek on the North, and Hartwick to the west. It is situated in both Hartwick and Otsego townships.

There are only three farms on the hill still in the possession of the original families – Green's, Well's, and Hackley's. I should like to tell some of the Green history, which includes the Edgar Jones family. I am indebted to Marion Green for these items.

"The Greens:
Oct. 12, 1965
Flora Green, age 94, June 4, 1965
To my Grandson, Lynn E. Green, Jr.

On my mother's side Mary (Holbrook) Jones we are descendants of John Holbrook, your Great, Great, Great, Great Grandfather born Sept. 5, 1721 died May 12, 1780 his wife Paturnia B. June 19, 1726 died Dec. 15, 1784. Their son Joel Holbrook Born Apr. 26, 1766 Died Oct. 5, 1844 married Polly Carr born June 24, 1771 died May 14, 1855.

The Joel Holbrook family lived and owned the farm where Alex Forster lives now also the George Salthouse residence and the Engelman place.

Polly Carr came with her brother from Conn. to the town of Hartwick by ox team to settle here. They built a shack down the road from our home toward Toddsville about a mile and a half near a big rock off the left side of the road on the farm owned by the Shultz family now.

The Carr family owned then the Shultz farm, Clifford Balcolm farm and both sides of the road toward Fly Creek including the Stone House farm. I remember when a member of the Carr family lived on every place mentioned.

The first winter Polly stayed on in the shake (shack) alone, then a wilderness, while her brother went back to Conn. for more of their family. Martha Hollister has visited the old home in Conn.

Now my grandfather Holbrook, son of Joel Holbrook married Ceylina B. Winthrop. I suppose she was born and brought up near the little graveyard as you leave the hard road going up to Dorr Kinney's.

My grandmother Ceylina Holbrook's great uncle was the Shipman called Leatherstocking, the great hunter you read about in James Fenimore Cooper's novels. He died with relatives living at Toddsville near the bridge connecting the towns of Hartwick and Otsego. He was buried in the cemetery at Fork Shop with no marker for his grave although relatives knew he was buried there.

Years ago I went to Leatherstocking's grave, or where it was supposed to be- it was near the fence to the left back halfway or more near a white stone, with big mark clear across it (as I remember it).

Edgar Jones House

My father Edgar Jones, your Great Grandfather, married Mary Holbrook, daughter of Harvey and Ceylina Holbrook. The Holbrook family owned at that time the Forster farm, the Salthouse residence, also the Engelmann place. My father Edgar Jones was born and brought up on the next farm now known as the Foag place.

On the stream of water at the north was a flax mill also further up a tannery and other mills I have heard the family talk about near Konchar Bros.

William Clark Green, one of eight children of Allen H. Green and Demarcas (Cook) Green was born, March 20, 1851 and was brought up on a farm in West Oneonta.

When he was about 20 years old he came to the farm of Edgar Jones as a hired man.

Edgar Jones had purchased this farm on March 26, 1862 from Susan Wheeler. His family owned the old Foag place on which he was born and reared. He was 24 years old at the time. He had married Mary Holbrook four years before.

Jones had set out a hop farm and also raised and trained horses. He was a co-author of a book on training horses. They had one child, Flora Estelle, born on June 4, 1871.

William Green and Flora Jones were married on March 2, 1898 and lived at home with her parents. By this time Edgar Jones was 60 and was slowing down. The hop business was prosperous until shortly after the turn of the century. At that time the blue mold fungus set in and destroyed the crop.

The Greens turned to poultry, apples, potatoes, and milk as their cash crops.

The farm took the name Orchardside Poultry farm and registered the name which Lynn Green, Sr. maintains.

The Greens had 2 children, Lynn Edward Green and Marie Emma (Green) Bishop, having married Homer Bishop in 1940.

Lynn Green married Marion De Angelo in 1944 and moved a mile away on the old Windsor homestead road.

In 1951 William Green died and the young Greens moved to the home farm with their only child, Lynn E. Green, Jr. They have carried on a dairy farm and during the 1950-67 years had chickens and sold eggs.

Flora Green lived with them for 14 years after which she moved to Syracuse to live with her daughter and family. Emma had one daughter Carol Ann. Flora visited here summers until she died in 1969.

Lynn Green, Jr. attended school in Cooperstown and showed great interest in dairy cattle, especially Brown Swiss. He owned several and showed them in the 4-H shows. He attended law school, practiced law in Watertown, NY for 4 years, and returned to Cooperstown in July 1974 to practice with Van Horne, Fleury, & Gozigan law firm.

He has built a home up the road from the Green Homestead and has named it Woodside (the name of Ira Green's home – the Foag place). He resides with his wife Judith Lynne (Johnson) Green (married August 7, 1971) and his son, William Clark Green II, born January 29, 1975.

The following was taken from an article on Hops by John Mott to be found in the book "Pioneer Industries" by Pearl Weeks.

"We (meaning the Greens) lodged all pickers. The migrant helpers were lodged in bunkrooms in the big barn; the native pickers were kept in the twenty-room house, one room being large enough for seven beds. The house was made larger to accommodate hop-pickers.

She mentioned the cooking process with a sigh. They baked thirty loaves of bread daily. Molasses and sugar cookies were made in advance, they being about the only things, which could be kept any length of time. When hobos called for food, her father always invited them to stay for a meal. One evening there were thirty people for supper because a number of these "guests" dropped in. The cooks were so tired that they thought they would die, she said."

I do not have much information on the Well's family. Olney Wells is noted on the 1856 map as residing on the Well's farm now occupied by Jesse Wells.

Next the Hackley family:

About 1795 Joseph Winsor came to Otsego County from Rhode Island. He had planned to settle in the Susquehanna Valley but thinking it too damp to be healthy; he came on to Christian hill and to this place where Abiel Lyon then lived in a log house. According to history, Mr. Lyon was one of the roving kind and couldn't stay put in any one place very long. He was anxious to sell and sold to Mr. Winsor for a pair of shoes, a loaf of bread, and for having his goods moved as far toward Unadilla as one could go and back in one day. Mr. Winsor took him as far as he could, unloaded his goods under a tree, and returned home. Mr. Lyon never did get to Unadilla – he stayed where he was unloaded.

Mr. Winsor built the original part of the house about 1800. The place passed on to the Hackley's, Aaron, Samuel, and John Hackley, the grandfather of Gerald Bush, who resides there now.

Schools:

There was a school on the four corners near the Christian Church. In about 1841 it was changed to the next corner north because the people in the district wanted it in the center of the district.

Following is a copy of the deed to the second place:

"Made this 5 day of March 1841 between Edward Lewis of Town of Otsego and Alexander Taylor, Gaylord Pierce, and Ira Steere Trustees of school district No. 4 formed partly of Towns of Otsego and Hartwick for the sum of $10.00 situated in the Town of Otsego beginning at stake standing on west side of highway leading to the Steere meeting house six feet from the fence. Thence south 28 ft., thence west twenty ft., north 28 ft., east 20 ft., to place of beginning to have and to hold as long as it is a schoolhouse and no longer and to pay one farthing each and every year on demand and to return to farm when no longer used as a schoolhouse.

Sealed and delivered in presence of
Chester Jarvis Apr. 8, 1841
Signed   Edward Lewis
                Alexander Taylor
                Gaylord Pierce
Recorded March 23, 1846"

This schoolhouse was abandoned and sold at auction to Jim Jarvis who moved it and made a residence.

Eddy schoolhouse:

This school (near the grange hall) was named for Noah Eddy who came to Hartwick before 1790. He built the sawmill later purchased by the Winsor's.

The land (1/4-acre) was purchased from Jesse Well's grandfather. Oliver Weeks brought trees over from his place and set them out. It was used to be in the corner of the fork of the road, but was later moved.

The teacher in the old days boarded around. Some teachers here were Ed Lindsey (he taught one term when Jesse Wells was 16 years old), Flora Jones, Laura Bowmaker, Neva Kane, Emma Green (Flora Jones daughter).

Hartwick Grange:

The grange was organized March 23,1891 at a meeting held in the Eddy Schoolhouse. Twenty-seven signed as Charter members. Officers were elected.

Meetings were held at the schoolhouse for awhile but more space was needed so they rented John Winsor's house and barns. Later they bought the Ezra Bolton property for $500 – where the present hall stands. On April 10,1922 all the buildings were destroyed by fire. Within a year a new hall was built by members who furnished trees, lumber, and labor. Meetings have been here since and we hope they will continue for many more years. Flora Green joined at the second meeting in 1891 and was a loyal member for over 75 years. Jesse Wells is our oldest member at the present time.

The Morris family

In 1790 Samuel Morris came from Connecticut to the town of Hartwick and purchased property (now Konchar Bros. Farm). He returned to Connecticut. In 1793 he married Betsey Bradford who was a great great-granddaughter of Gov. Wm. Bradford of the Plymouth Colony. She was also the grandmother of Marcus Wells and Great-great-grandmother of Ramon Chase. They came to this place to live and built a log cabin in which Mrs. Morris opened a private school, one of the first schools in the town of Hartwick. They lived here only a few years, then sold the house, now occupied by Stanley Konchar, in 1800. The date is carved in a stone of the foundation wall. His son, Jerome Steere, sold to Burlingham, who sold to Konchar's.

Industries

Hops were grown mainly on the Jones, Carr (Schultz), Lewis, and the now Victor Williams farms.

Dairying was mainly for butter and cheese.

There were two flax-beating mills and also itinerant sawmills.

On Winsor Creek, now called Chase Creek there were several mills. Near Perkins Crossing was the Eddy sawmill, later bought by Winsor. Next below was the flax-beating mill owned by Nehemiah Burch. In the gorge was Ingalls sawmill. At the foot of the gorge was a Cooper shop. There was a brick kiln beside the creek opposite the corner at the junction of the Kinney and Brunner roads run by Samuel Bissell. He also ran a pottery factory on the corner between the Kinney and Main road. Some pottery remnants have been found on this site. Next on the sharp bend was a sawmill, first operated by Comfort Chase and later by his son, Nathan Chase. On the crossroads by Schultz was a sawmill on the upper side of the road (Murdock mill). On the lower side of the road was a crate factory.

Chase Gorge

Cemeteries

The Eddy cemetery is on the Perkins place.

The Wheeler cemetery is on the Green farm.

The Burlingham cemetery is on the same side of the road and between the Kane and Konchar houses.

The Steere cemetery is back of the James Jarvis residence.

Back of the Hackley place where Gerald Bush lives was the Winsor Babbitt cemetery. Following are some stone inscriptions:

"In memory of
Samuel Whaley who died
July 14,1841 age 52 yrs. 8 mo.
Samuel Whaley here he lies
Called by a mandate from the skies
The messenger was lightning red
The electric fluid shot him dead."

"Yet again we hope to meet there
When the day of life is fled
Then in heaven with joy to greet thee
There no farewell tear is shed."

"James Smith
A revolutionary soldier
Died August 2, 1827
Age 63 yrs."

"Joseph Winsor died
May 11, 1850 in
84th year of his age."

"Harris Winsor born on
this farm Apr. 7, 1798
Died Feb. 12, 1880
Last one to be buried in cemetery.
This is son of Joseph Winsor."

An interesting lady named Mrs. Cass used to live where Lamberson's live now. She gathered roots, herbs, and plants and made cordials, wines, and medicines. When she had a good supply on hand she delivered them with a horse and wagon to Cooperstown. She fought with her husband a lot and wouldn't let him in the house sometimes. (She lived during Mrs. Bush's lifetime).

There are two old roads on the hill – a crossroads above the Petkewec farm used to have three families on it – Anson Cook's where neighborhood sings (sometimes called camp meetings) used to be held. Two other families were named Bunn and Tucker. No houses remain and the road is used to reach the farm fields.

Another road going east of the church had a house and barn on the right where Eliza and Nancy Field lived. Another house a short distance away was where Abigail Irons lived, mother of Emmett Irons. Farther on at the four corners was the cheese factory operated by Wm. Sponenburg – he had 5 or 6 children who went to the Christian Hill School.

Mail for some parts of the hill was left at Chase where someone picked it up. Sometimes whoever got it left some in a box at Forsters' to be gotten later. There was another abandoned road from Chase to Green's.

By: Emma Chase, written for a Historical Society program, late 1970's.

Material Sources:
    Gerald Bush
    Marion Green
    Hilda Augur
    History of Hartwick by Pearl Weeks
    Pioneer Industries by pearl Weeks

House at "Cooks Summet" lately owned by J. Paul Jones. Built by George Pierce in 1805 and operated as a tavern. Long the home of Mordington Cook, grandson of Pearce and of Comfort Cook, the pioneer of Hartwick village. Now the home of John Briggs.

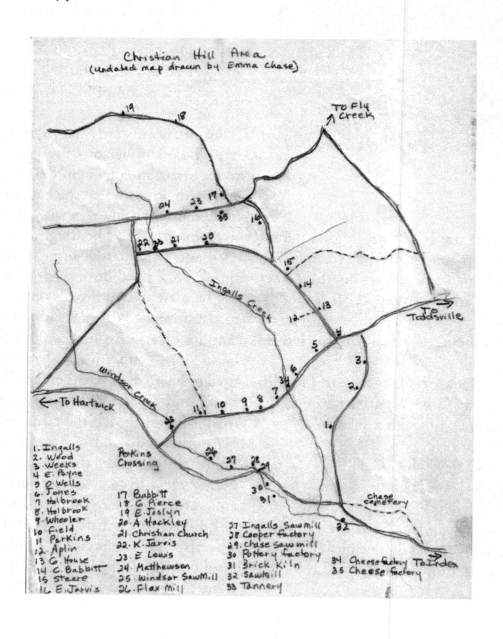

Christian Hill Area
(undated map drawn by Emma Chase)

1. Ingalls
2. Wood
3. Weeks
4. E. Payne
5. O. Wells
6. Jones
7. Holbrook
8. Holbrook
9. Wheeler
10. Field
11. Perkins
12. Aplin
13. G. House
14. C. Babbitt
15. Steere
16. E. Jarvis
17. Babbitt
18. G. Pierce
19. E. Joslyn
20. A. Hackley
21. Christian Church
22. K. Jarvis
23. E. Lewis
24. Matthewson
25. Windsor Saw Mill
26. Flax Mill
27. Ingalls Saw Mill
28. Cooper Factory
29. Chase Saw Mill
30. Pottery Factory
31. Brick Kiln
32. Sawmill
33. Tannery
34. Cheese Factory
35. Cheese Factory

Perkins Crossing

Notes from Roy Butterfield

The first road to "Peth" (Hartwick Village) was over the hill from the East from Cooperstown to Toddsville, over Christian Hill along the Town's north line and then by Domion farm to White house road to the Brooklyn side of the Village. The Domion house represents one of the styles of early frame houses first constructed in this area. The places I shall mention were first purchased from their owner Mr. Cooper at an early date.

This first tract by:
Rufus Hawkins 1789 built house about 1800
    John Dunbar1854
    Henry Jarvis 1861
    Edward Card1865
    Austin Moran
    August Domion
    Joseph Domion

Tuller House on Kallan Road

Top of hill on Kallan Road (East of Otego Creek)

House built on corner of Hawkins place in 1820 by Jacob Dunbar, son of Rufus Weeks 1868

R. D. Lamb 1903 our cheese maker at White House factory for years
    Clifford Stoller
    Gerald Tuller
    Webber
    Bishop Farm
    John Runyan Sr. 1787

Greeley Bishop farm
    Stephan Bolles 1803
    Abel Caulkins 1840
    Robert L. Ainslie
    Greely Bishop
    August Domion
Located in woods in an extreme portion of this tract near the Mott boundary is a stone memorial where Merton Green was killed while

cutting wood December 18,1878. Due to the great esteem for which he was held in the community a memorial was placed here in his memory.

Moran farm North of White House on 205
    Rufus Thrall 1793
    Son Rufus Thrall

Moran Place built by Ed Card

    John Roman Jr.
    John Murdock 1828
    James Barton
    Joseph Cone 1847
    Perry Barton
Edward Card 1881 Built house and barn one year later
    Austin Moran 1919
Tannery- on South side of Otego Creek owned for a while by John Moon and was in hands of various owners from time to time.

White house

WHITE HOUSE _ said to be first White House west of Albany. Cheese factory stood across road East of White house; water supplied by spring across road West of White House.

Dunnigan place now Dibble house

Russell farm North of Butterfield family cemetery:

    James Butterfield war veteran 1786
    Cap. JONANAS Parker 1808
    Caleb Camp
    Serile Adams 1829
    Franklin Eastin
    Charles Russel
    Albert Field 1903 (our country fiddler)
    Merton Beckley
    Leslie Day
    John A. Mott
    Marsiak
    Dunnigan
    Dibble

Robert Ainslie home burned in the late 1920's on the site where Corcoran's are now

Butterfield homestead
James Butterfield 1786 son of John Butterfield
Isiah Blood 1821
John Harris
Henry Caulkins 1847
Hiram Bush 1848
Charles Russel
Simon Willis
Robert L. Ainslie 1900 House burned in late 20,s & rebuilt
Thurlow Sargent
Claud Bliss
John A. Mott
Walter Haldenwang

Pope, Yauger house

Robert and Louise Mott Curry

Robert Curry farm (Carol & John Niedzialkowski)
James Butterfield 1786
Robert Coe 1794
Anasa Peters 1801
Hubbard Fuller
Edmund Skiff 1812
Richmond Rowley 1813
Aron Baldwin 1816
Darius and Eli Popple 1834
Robert Curry 1903
Otis D. Mott   - Mary Ginegaw
John A. Mott
Jensen
Niedzialkowski

Rodolph (adjoining Low Schneider to North)
This represents an early basement house
    Gerritt Boon 1792
    William Bradley 1797
    H. Fuller 1799
    E. Bliss Jr.
    Anasa West 1808
    Heat Semour 1834
    Nathenial Caulkins 1868
    Everett Pope
    Charles Baker
    Yauger
    Rodolph
    Low Schneider

Gerrit Boon, a Dutch sugar refiner by trade, used this place as an experimental venture to supply the nation and the world with maple sugar. The publicity from this enterprise and others like it greatly helped Cooper in promoting sale of land and resulted in populating this new settlement.

This all came about at a time when the struggling group of colonies of a new nation were trying to achieve self-sufficiency in its industries.

Cady house on State Route 205

Benjamin Weaver 1797 first cheese house

    Benjamin Richards
    Samuel Waley 1822
    Simon Willis 1855
    Martin Williams 1868
    George Lough Sr.
    George Lough Jr.
    Alfred Schneider
    Kenneth Cady

Pierce Mott house

Pierce-Mott
    David Cully l786 (Milford Center)
    John Runyan Sr. 1787 (part of Bishop farm)
    Spencer Weaver 1796
    Abel Caulkins Jr.
    Geo.Calkins 1850

Gorden Pierce 1850 Moved from Whalen hill from place purchased from Butterfield in1802. He was a hatter by trade.

    DeLazon Pierce
    John C. Mott
    Otis D. Mott
    John A. Mott
    Robert O. Mott
    John A. Mott
    Jensen
    John and Carol Niedzialkowski

Old Fry homestead of 1788

Fry place West of Mott on Piermott Lane

Rhodes Fry, 1793, his son Ambrose Fry became a noted historian of his time. Delivered Fourth of July speeches in the town on two occasions fifty years apart and a writer of historical importance in the Freemans Journal

    Orlo Burch Sr. 1868
    L.M. Steere 1903
    Amos Barton
    Otis D. Mott
    William Kenny

Nicholas Steere home now owned by T. Polulech

Fields homestead built 1802 to replace earlier log cabin

Nicholas Steere 1794 remained in family until purchase.

Cook homestead now owned by John Briggs

Cook homestead (Cook Summit)

Built in 1805 to replace the log cabin built there in 1794. It was owned for many years by Mordington Cook. For many years it wore a coat of red paint until purchased by Paul Jones. For a while the builder ran it as a tavern and ran a distillery; purchasing corn, rye and other grain from local farmers. Now owned by John Briggs.

FIELDS HOMESTEAD

William and Nathan Field came in 1788 and built a log cabin. Enroute here they contracted smallpox and received medical aid in Cherry Valley.

The third year, having sufficiently cleared the land from trees, after 13 days trek in ox-cart they settled with their family in a new wilderness home.

The property was divided with Nathan north of the road and William on the south where he built this house in 1805. On this property is the oldest cemetery in our area. Besides several of the Field family) the remains of a revolutionary Col. Henry Wheeler rest here.

By: John Mott

Holden Inn—Trials and Results

Holden Inn, Maples Road near Junction with Chase Road, Town of Hartwick. In 1794 Stephen Holden arrived in the town of Hartwick with only $120. Within ten years he had cleared a large piece of land and built the well-known tavern. The first recorded town meeting in the township was held there in 1802. Travelers going westward through the county regularly stopped here. The Holden Inn had a plan and details characteristic of the first large frame dwellings with a massive central chimney.

From the hill over looking Holden Inn, a landmark of the community, can be seen the Hinman Hollow road as it winds to the SouthWest through the valley in the general direction of Milford. Beyond can be seen the Catskill Mountain range.

To the North East in the spring and late fall when the leaves are off the trees, one can catch a brief glimpse of Otsego Lake in the distance surrounded by woods. One can't help but wonder if Stephen Holden visualized all this when he started the clearing of the land, and the building of Holden Inn so many years ago.

Mr. Alfred T. Brown and his first wife, the former Lilith Record, were running a business in the State of Pennsylvania when they heard that Holden Inn was being put up for sale.

Mrs. Lilith Brown had been born and raised in the Hartwick locality. Thus having some knowledge of the place, encouraged Mr. Brown to come and look at it with hopes of purchasing it.

Mr. Brown well recalls the first time he came to look at Holden Inn. Being the spring of the year it was a rainy, nasty day, and the old narrow dirt road had become a bed of mud. Mr. Brown said he managed to reach Holden Inn, getting stuck only once, which must have been some sort of a miracle.

Having been unoccupied during the settling of the estate, the buildings had depreciated considerably, and the land had grown up to weeds and brush.

Many people looking at the old weather beaten house, with many of its windowpanes removed, the clapboards falling off, and sagging doors might have hesitated to look any further.

However, the Brown's were young people, and so ventured on into the house. Apparently, the outside had been good in comparison to the inside. They found a leaking roof had caused most of the plaster to crumble, wall paper hung in strips, where it wasn't entirely gone, and the old fireplaces had been boarded up and painted or papered over.

After looking the situation over they could see many possibilities in the place and proceeded to buy it. They moved in on the 25th day of May in 1931 and began the task of making the old inn livable once again. As they repaired, and restored much of its originality, Holden Inn's history continued to unfold.

The Brown's spent the next several years improving, and repairing the buildings, along with clearing the land, building fences, and trying to recondition it for general farming.

In 1938 Mr. Brown employed Walter, better known as Wattie, Renwick to work on the farm for him. Mr. Renwick continued to work for Mr. Brown for the next twenty-three years, until his death in May of 1961.

Mr. Renwick being a direct descendent of the Holden's through marriage was able to furnish Mr. Brown with much of its later history.

Other descendants finding out about the restoration of the old Inn became interested. They came to visit it, and continued to keep in touch with Lilith Brown down through the years.

In 1952 the Town of Hartwick had its Sesquicentennial at which time Mrs. Brown wrote a letter of invitation to Jonathan Holden. On September 23rd, 1952 she received the following reply, and I quote: -

"Mrs. Lilith Brown
East Hill, Hartwick, NY

Dear Mrs. Brown;
    Yesterday, on my return from a week's pilgrimage to the Plantations of Providence & RI during which I made my first serious exploration in my 71 years of life, of Old Warwick & Warwick Neck I received your letter dated Sept. 16 which was my 71st. birthday.

    "Holdens of Hartwick" compiled by me, a copy of which was in Hartwick library states, pg. 211 "Stephen Holden"— was one of a company which migrated in 1794 from Warwick, RI to Hartwick, NY on sleighs, and built the house which still stands, "the first Hartwick town meeting was held there."

    Unless something prevents it will be a great pleasure for me to attend the 150-year aniv. I am presuming that your invitation includes all Stephen Holdens namesakes of the Hartwick pioneer and all Randal Holdens namesakes of his brother, of which there are many.

    I would be interested in knowing if

tourist rooms are likely to be available at Sliters Hotel at which in 1932 we held a large reunion of Holden clan or elsewhere in Hartwick, Mt. Vision or Cooperstown, & if there is a bus to Oneonta & Cooperstown in case I do not come by auto.

Thank you,
Jonathan Holden."

As Mr. Holden had stated, Mr. Stephen Holden migrated to Hartwick, New York from Warwick, RI in the winter of 1794. He was one of a company that pioneered this area, coming through the untamed country by sleigh. He proceeded to buy some hundred acres of land from William Cooper, the father of the well-known author, James Fenimore Cooper.

Stephen Holden cleared the land on the side hill, overlooking what is now Holden Inn, and built a log cabin, which would house his family for the next few years while Holden Inn was being built. An Inn which down through the next 167 years, at least, would withstand the ravages of time, and the elements.

From its beginning it was a place of some distinction, and here the first town meeting was held, and possibly other events of importance took place down through the years.

The cellar, hand dug, still has a dirt bottom, is some 40 feet long, 30 feet wide, and some eight feet deep. The cellar walls are laid up from fieldstones, as are most of the walls under the buildings. They were taken from the land as it was cleared, and were laid up by hand with out the use of mortar. In the center of the cellar, also laid up from the field stones, and no mortar, is the two walls, each some 12 feet long, and some four feet wide which forms the support, with the side of heavy beams, for the 12 foot square chimney which is located in the center of the

house, running from the first floor to the attic floor.

The chimney itself, and its flues were made from handmade bricks, which Mr. Brown understands were made in an old brick yard which was located on the property now owned by William Powers Sr., on the Hinman Hollow Road.

At one time, this chimney, with its many large flues extended through the roof a few feet. At that time the fireplaces, of which there are six, were used for cooking and heating the large house.

A large fireplace graces the large East room on the first floor used by the Brown's as a living room. The original kitchen, now used by the Brown's for a dining room still contains the huge fireplace, and its adjoining ovens, with its smooth slate stone hearth that testifies to its usefulness of another era.

Eventually the big central chimney was dismantled down to the attic floor, for reasons unknown and two separate chimneys were built, one on either side of the main house, and another was built in the summer kitchen. These later chimneys extended only from the attic floor through the roof for a few feet. Stoves were then used for heating and cooking, with stovepipes running from them into the chimneys, the stoves being located in most of the rooms on the first floor. Mr. Brown recalls that it took a considerable amount of wood to run these stoves. Wood being cut from off the land itself took a lot of hard work, but was the cheapest fuel available, and the most practical from a farmer's point of view.

This probably happened in the early 1900's when for a time it became a two family house with Wells Renwick living on the West side of Holden Inn, and his parents, the Walter Renwicks, Sr. living on the East side.

Until the time of its purchase by the Brown's in 1931, Holden Inn had always remained the property of the Holden's and their descendants.

After buying the Inn for the next few years the Brown's also used these same chimneys, then in the early 1940's they tore down the chimneys, put new roofing onto the house, built a new chimney on the East side of the house, extending from the cellar floor level, to above the roof, along the outside walls of the house. At this time centralized heat was also installed.

The original house contained five large rooms on the first floor, with the same number of rooms on the second floor and an attic the breadth, and length of the house. A summer kitchen joined onto the south side of the house, beyond what was then the milk room and rear stairs. Beyond the summer kitchen was a small woodshed, attached to the kitchen for the convenience of the person doing the cooking, it is assumed.

Another building joined the summer kitchen, and woodshed on the east side. This building, some 30 feet or more by 20 feet or more, was the carriage house.

There are two staircases leading to the upstairs. One it is fairly safe to assume was the servant's stairs in the earlier days, and the other led to the large front bedrooms. The rear stairs are narrow and closed in, while the stairs leading from the front entry are, I believe, of Cherry wood and open. They run along the north side of the center chimney to the second floor, but the stair well extends to the attic floor, giving the hall a spacious look, as well as a complete view of the north sidewall of this huge chimney.

It is interesting to note that when the Brown's bought Holden Inn and started to repair it they were surprised to find all six fireplaces, that had been boarded up, were intact except for the mantle and framing around the one in the large west bedroom. This one had been removed. What became of it or why it was done still remains a mystery. The Brown's replaced it.

The original supporting beams under the first floor, and throughout the house are from hand-hewn trees taken as the land was cleared, as well as the boards in the plank walls. This is still the original wood. The original kitchen has the old, wide pine boards on its four walls, and surrounding the fireplace. Some of the cupboards and old doors are this same kind of wood, as are the floors.

The rooms have changed little in the Inn down through the years. The two large rooms facing the road on the first floor have doors on each end of the entrance hall, leading into them. They in turn have doors leading to the other parts of the house. For many years, I'm told our present kitchen was the milk room, where the milk pails, butter bowls, and. other utensils were kept. Mrs. Brown liked its size, and location where she could see the cows, and yard, while she cooked, so it became the kitchen, while the original kitchen made a very practical dining room.

The Renwicks, onto a new hand laid stone wall nearer to the barn, moved the carriage house that had been attached to the rear of the Inn around the year 1904. It was then used for a wagon house and horse barn. The space beneath was used for many years as a place to house hogs, while the upstairs was used for storage space and extra hay for the horses.

At about the same time the Renwicks moved the carriage house, they also raised the cow barn, which until this time had rested on the dirt floor. They set it upon a hand laid stone wall on the North side, and gave it some pole supports on the South side. In about 1953 Mr. Brown took out the pole support, and laid up a wall using mortar and cinder blocks. At the time the Renwicks raised the barn, they also extended it for some 36 feet.

For a short time after buying the Inn, the Brown's did use the summer kitchen. Then they converted it into a garage to house their car, and used the old woodshed for a storage place, around 1950.

The heavy snows in 1970 were too much for

both the garage roof, and the horse barn roof, both collapsing in a few minutes of one another. In 1970 another roof was put onto the house garage.

The Brown's found when they moved into Holden Inn that the hand dug surface well near the rear door was full to over flowing during the winter, and early spring. With the arrival of the summer months it dried up. Then it became necessary to carry water from a spring located down the Maples Road some quarter of a mile, on what is now called the Wishing Well Preserve.

In the early 1940's the Brown's had a deep well dug that would take care of their water needs for years to come.

At the same time the wiring of the house for electricity was started. It is possible that putting electricity into Holden Inn was one of the most difficult operations ever performed in this locality, in connection with electricity.

The Brown's were to discover before the operation was completed and the electric installed that not one contractor but three would be involved. Each would go as far as he could. Then another would take over where the previous one had left off.

It was a tedious, time consuming operation that took most of one spring to complete. What should normally have taken a few days ran into weeks.

Clapboards had to be removed in many places; channels had to be chiseled into the solid plank walls. In some places it was necessary to run cables beneath the floors, with many of the cables running through the center chimney. The Brown's were ready to celebrate the day the electric was finally installed completely, and turned on.

With the water being put in, and the electric; this seemed to be a good time to install a bathroom. A small unused bedroom on the West Side of the house was converted into the bathroom.

Lilith Brown died quite unexpectedly in October of 1961, but she had lived to see most of her dreams concerning the house become a reality.

Except for a few minor changes in the past ten years the house remains the same. A new rear entrance replaces the old one, while a new picture window has replaced the original window that was in the room now used as a kitchen when the Brown's bought it. Somehow the thoughts of parting with it was too much. So it was installed into the old original kitchen, which up until then had been a rather drab, dark room, having but one small corner window.

As I finish this account of Holden Inn and the years the Browns have occupied it. I'd like to think this was the way Lilith Brown would have wanted it told.

As Told to Hazel E. Brown by Alfred T. Brown May 3, 1971

Note: The Holden Inn burned down in October 1986 and a truly historic site was lost to the township forever.

THE FREEMAN'S JOURNAL/WEDNESDAY, Oct. 8, 1986—9

Congregational (Presbyterian) Church

The Congregational Church of Hartwick was located on the corner of West Main Street and Weeks Road. It was organized May 30, 1800 by the Reverend Jedidiah Bushnell, a missionary from Connecticut. There were sixty-eight constituent members. In the course of its brief history the church took in over three hundred and fifty members.

Originally the church was connected with the Union Association, which was later dissolved. In August 1822 it united with the Otsego Presbytery. It was incorporated as the Union Society of Hartwick as both Congregationalists and Presbyterians were in its original membership.

The church building was erected in 1810 at a cost of $250 and was 40 by 48 feet.

Henry Clarke Wright describes his memories of going to Sabbath services at this church in his autobiography *Human Life*. "Going to meeting on Sunday was as much a part of my father's life as his daily bread. It was in his view a duty from which none was absolved. The meeting to which he belonged was four miles from his house; and, rain or shine, summer or winter, hot or cold, he usually went to meeting and took some of his family with him. The great wagon, or sleigh, was taken out; the horses were harnessed to it, and brought round to the door, and there my father and mother and as many children as could be packed in, were loaded into the wagon and driven to meeting. Even the dogs and horses seemed to know when the family was going to meeting. Those who could not get into the wagon walked. The road to meeting ran through a valley beside the Otego Creek; a delightful ride. The meetinghouse was small and dingy; large enough, however, for all who came. It was usually called 'the house of God.' I never could tell why it should be called 'God's house,' while others were not. I used to ask myself if God did not dwell in my father's house as well as in the meetinghouse. My father owned a pew in front of the high pulpit, in which he and the older children used to sit; and the younger ones were sent up to the gallery to sit where and how they pleased; my father not thinking that, if any of his children needed his care, the younger ones did. But we were taught the mysteries of sitting still in the meetinghouse as well as in the schoolhouse. There we sat and heard the singing, the praying, the preaching and the benediction as silently, worshipfully and wakefully as we could; though many a sound nap did the parents and children take in that old meeting house in hot weather and many a time did they shiver and shake and look blue in winter for there was no stove nor fire and the thermometer was sometimes down to zero and the people must have extraordinary zeal to keep comfortable sitting still in meeting in such atmosphere. Soon as the minister had said his last Amen, the children in the gallery rushed for the door glad to be relieved from the confinement. We entered the wagon, drove home, put up the horses and then sat still in the house till sundown.

Rove, a great black dog of my father's used to perform his part of the Sunday service on this wise: In going to meeting he went before and cleared the road of hens, geese, pigs and cattle. While the family was at their worship in the meetinghouse, he would lie in the carriage to watch it; broiling under the summer sun or shivering beneath the cold blasts of winter. Then, as we started for home, he would usually leap into someone's wood yard and seize a stick of wood or a stake or rail from some fence and march before the horses carrying his burden in his mouth till he reached home. Rove was a wayward, reckless dog and many a dog, goose, pig, cow or woodpile had cause to remember him. But he regularly went to meeting."

The Congregational Church dissolved about 1852. Lumber from the old church building was used in the construction of a school building and a home, which have since occupied the site.

Pastors of the church were:

Whiting Griswold
    Sept. 26, 1806 – 1811
Henry Chapman
    Nov. 18, 1811–Died Aug. 30, 1823
John H. Prentice
    Dec. 30, 1824 – Dec. 25, 1829
Benjamin Gilbert Riley
    Feb. 25, 1840-1844
Mr. Spencer
    1844 – 1848
Chauncy Lee supply minister.

Deacons were:

David Willard	1800 – 1818
Daniel Potter	1802 – 1828
Jonathon Seymour	1812 – 1820
Sylvanus West	1812 – 1837
Jacob Bliss	1817 – 1826
Daniel Beebe	1826 –
Prentiss Brown	1837 –
Rufus C. Swift	1837 –

A membership list was recorded by Roger Butterfield from the church manual last known to be in the possession of Mrs. Lucy Adams Morse. That manual has since been lost.

Members listed: David Willard, Martha Willard, Benjamin Skiff, Elizabeth Skiff, Adah Skiff, Stephen Skiff, Daniel Potter, Molly Potter, Elijah Mason, Jonathan Seymour, Samuel Seymour, Abigail Seymour, Susannah Seymour, Nabby Mason, Hannah Willard, Benjamin Fuller, Christina Fuller, Josiah Brigham, Samuel Bates, Deborah Bates, James Gray, Isreal Dwight, Robert Dewey, Abigail Dewey, Lodowick Hotchkiss, Heman Comstock.

Luther Comstock (ex.), Salmon Comstock (ex.), Hannah Comstock, Abigail Comstock, Amasa Mudge (ex.), Sabra Mudge, Peter Goodsell, John Dunbar, Stephen Cook, Mary Cook, Jacob Bliss, Charles Bliss, Polly Bliss, Abigail Bliss, Jacob Harrison, Abigail Comstock, 2nd, David Morris, Spencer Weaver, Daniel Jewett, Rebecca Jewett, Stephen Maples, Isaac Babbit, Prudence Babbit, Levi Beebe, Lucinda Beebe, Seth Wright, Sarah Sherlock, Naomi Potter, Judith Craft, Hannah Bradley, Elizabeth Goodsell, Mary Foster, Betsey Griswold, Diantha Alworth, Sarah Peters, Ginne Bunn (ex.). All of the preceding joined in 1800.

In 1808 were added Isaac Pierce, Erastus Rowley, John Seymour, Patty Brigham, Clarissa Harrison, Martha Potter, Achsah Griswold, Abagail Seymour, Prince West, Ezekiel West, Hannah West, Lydia West, William Dillingham, Hannah Dillingham, Polly Dillingham, Anna Rowley, William Kelly, Delight Kelley, Syvanus West, Philo West, Weltha West, Jerusha West, Shubeal Button, Rebecca Dunbar, Elizabeth Mills, Ruth Seymour, Sarah Kerr, Marilla Wright,

Savina Ward, Sarah Butterfield, Daniel Beebe, John Williams, Sarah Williams, Peletiak Mills, Stephen Skiff Jr., Susannah Ward, and Abigail Alger.

In 1809 Nathaniel Thayer, Nancy Thayer, Hannah Pray, Anna Chase, Nathan Chapman, Susannah Chapman, Ruth Rawden; in 1816 James Chase, Susan Wilcox, Eunice Maples, Polly Root, Sylvia Edson, Oriel Wilcox, John Raynor, Josiah Maples, Lucius Thayer, George Seymour, Nicholas Sherman, Nancy Seymour, Mehitabel Seymour, Elizur Fairman, Calvin Babbitt, Oren Bliss, Aaron R. Bliss, Martha Bliss, Nathan Wentworth, Lindley Sprague, Donatus Babbitt.

Also Dana Allen, Sarah Wright, Asenath Casewell, Abigail E. Beebe, Matilda Alworth, Polly Alworth, Anna Runyon, Sarah Stimpson, Mary Sherman, Lydia Chapman, Betsey Brown, Nancy Lewis, Sophia Benjamin, Anna West, Sarah West, Susan Bates, Alice Allen, Sarah Chase, Polly Butterfield, Hannah Mix, Simeon Benjamin and Mary Benjamin, John Dunbar Jr., Lucy Dunbar, Rufus Hawkins, Catherine Beebe, Philena Foster, Sarah Foster, Ann Mix, William A. Thayer, Enoch Congar, Esther Congar, Lewis Beebe, Guy Davies, Simon Stimpson, Sarah Tracy, Laura West, Content West, Martha Barney, Anna Tracy and Jerusha Wilkins.

In 1817 Polly Weaver, Martha Botchford, Eunice Caulkins, Emma Darrow, Lucy Darrow, Caleb Thayer, Almira Thayer, Charles Bates, Charity Bates, Peter Wilcox, Anna Bliss, Elizabeth Reynolds, Joseph Camp, Sybel Allen, Delia Danielson, Newell F. Higgins, Daniel I. Cook, Amy West, Abigail Chase, Sarah Tyler, Sarah Crafts, Griffen Crafts, Elias Higgins, Daniel G. Sherman and John North.

In 1818 Asanath Weston, Talmon Hubbell, Augustus J. Wells, Henry C. Wright, Zeruia West, Cinda Hubbell, Josiah Elmore; in 1819 Mary Cheadle, Asanath Cheadle, Laura Cheadle, Hannah Day, Mary Crosby, Simeon Dillingham and John Dillingham.

Those who joined in 1820 were Philip Wells, Sally Wells, Delana Dillingham, Rebecca Butterfield, Betsy Tyler, Electa M. Babbitt, Mary Fox, Barnes Cooley, Lathrop Benjamin, Russell Benjamin, Silas Wood, Marcus S. Millard, Prince West Jr., William C. Bently, William West, John Crosby 2nd (ex.), William Alworth, Jacob Dunbar, Charles Bliss Jr., Jonathan Fisk, George Darby, (ex.), Chester Tyler, Elisha D. Sill, Titus Stebbins, Mary Benjamin, Ruth Tracy, Polly Smith, Fedelia Benjamin, Mary Potter, Mary Wilcox, Lura West, Sally Camp, Abigail Morse, Palmyra Peters, Rebecca Dunbar, Diantha Dunbar, Clarissa Dunbar (ex.), Almira Dunbar, Nabby Bliss, Camilla Bliss, Betsey Foster, Miriam Wright, Abel Caulkins, Hiram West, Sally Button, and Amasa Peters.

In 1821 Robert Camp (ex.), Mary Camp; in 1822 Amanda Potter, Theophilus Whaley (ex.), Elizabeth Winne, Eleanor Bliss, Marilda Sill, Martha Babbitt, Fannie Reynolds, Caroline Peters, Amos Barrows, Jerusha Barrows, Nathaniel Pierce, Lovisa Benjamin, Eliza B. Prentice; in 1825 Nancy Luce, Clarissa Sweeting, Maria Pulver, Eve S. Phillips, Cornelia E. Kittle.

In 1826 Delia Ann Grover; in 1827 Mercy Seymour, Martha Cook, Eunice Church; In 1828 Oramel A. Alger, Sophronia P. West; in 1829 Marcia Rose Chapman.

Joining in 1830 were Guy J. Chapman, Lavinia Chapman, Delia Chapman, Susan Chapman, John P. Thorpe, George Brownell, Dolly Peters, Sylvanus Willard, David Willard, Anah Louisa Peters, Sally C. Grover, William B. Douglass, Sylvester Merrill, Polly West, Sally McCane, Hannah Hubbell, Margaret Bradley, Bela Benjamin, Charles S. Benjamin, Mary Caulkins, Lucy Beebe, Eleanor F. Beebe, Caroline Abel, Nathaniel H. West, Asahel Benjamin, Lyman Dunbar, James M. Peak, Nancy M.

Fisher, Frederick A. Lee, Russell Caulkins, Horatio Bradley, Anna Smith, Hannah Smith, Sarah Williams, Jerusha West, Martha Willard, Louisa West, Lucy Sitser, Rhoda Farnum, Eleanor Hopkins, Julia Baker, Dama Harrison, Jas. Benjamin, Diantha Benjamin, Marilla Williams, Abiathar Gardner, Theodore Chapman.

In 1831 Hiram Harrison, Thomas A. Bacon, Chester Whitford, Sarah Gardner, Fanny Bliss, Hiram West, Lodema West, Chauncey Caulkins, Mary Ann Beaver, Lavinia Root, Miranda Bliss, Olive Bacon.

In 1832 Noah Farnum, Samuel Harrison, Dwight Harrison, Abigail Harrison, Amanda Burlingham, Mariette Tracy, Charlotte Tracy, Betsey Tracy, David R. Beach, Minerva Beach.

In 1833 Jesse Maynard, Sally Maynard, Silas Maynard, Elizabeth Maynard, Emarancy Maynard, Prentiss Brown, Weltha Brown, Grace Wells, John Irons, Maria Harrison, Aner D. Swift; in 1836 Rebecca Chase, Allen Bowen, Charles W. Dillingham, John Phillips, Chauncey L. Beebe, Anna Alworth, Phila Bowen, Susan

Beebe, Sally Farnum, Maria Farnum, Almira Benjamin.

In 1837 Celestia B. Peak, Celina Swift, Mary Rose, Abigail Ann Smith, Rufus S. Peters, Huldah S. Peters, Emily A. Culver; in 1838 Polly M. Chase, Rebecca H. Lee; in 1839 Huldah Chase; in 1840 Anna F. Riley, Samuel Story, Anne Jacobs, Nabby Patterson; in 1841 Clovis Steere, Mary Steere, Mariette Beebee, and George W. Potter.

A news report in the Hartwick column of a local newspaper in 1942 states "Mrs. James Goodenough, we hear, has moved with her daughter, Mrs. Samuel D. White, who occupies the Welcome Richards house. This house was built on the site of the old Presbyterian meeting house which, nearly fifty years ago, was used for a select school building and most of the lumber used in the present structure was taken from the old church which was purchased by the late Mr. Richards. II

Compiled by A. Harrison

House on corner of Weeks Road and County Route 11 containing materials from Presbyterian Church.

First Baptist Church

First Baptist Chirch—1995

On May 20, 1795, a scattering of Baptists of this region held a conference at the school house near Mr. William Baker's on the Otego Creek until August 19, 1795, whereby a council composed of delegates from Franklin, First Burlington, and Springfield churches were constituted a church. This meeting was held at the home of Ambrose Josters in the Town of Otego. Elder James Bacon was chosen as Moderator; Asard Whipple was chosen to be Clerk. Brother John Bostwick was chosen as Standing Moderator, and for the time being was put on probation for the work of the gospel ministry. The first communion was held on the first Sabbath in September, 1795. The church met the first Saturday of each month to prepare for the ordinance of the Lord's Supper and renew the covenant. Brother Bostwick and Brother Whipple were sent to Springfield as messengers from the church carrying a letter from the church signed by the clerk in the name of the church, The Baptist Church of Christ in the Town and County of Otsego.

During the May 20, 1795 meeting, the moderator proceeded to state concisely the object and business of the meeting, which was to seek for Christian union and fellowship in the order of the Gospel. The following items were voted upon and approved:

1. We will have no written form of articles at present but only a written covenant, and we will take the Bible as our only rule of faith and practice.
2. If any one should come forward and join himself to this Body, while lying under the imputation of moral scandal which is unknown to the brethren and sisters, (that one) shall be considered as an offender and subject to discipline.
3. Each brother and sister who have been members of other churches heretofore shall obtain as soon as may be, a letter of recommendation and dismission from their respective churches in order to complete fellowship.
4. We believe man is wholly depraved by his fall into sin and that his justification before God is wholly by Jesus Christ—and
5. All the outward means of grace without the Holy Spirit's agency and operation are not sufficient to change the heart of man from sin to

holiness, and that the Holy Spirit's operation and influence on the mind applying divine truth to the heart and conscience, is the only efficient cause of regeneration and sanctification.

6. No good work can be done by the unregenerate that is both morally and spiritually, both materially and formally good before God.

7. Every good work that is done in faith and from a principal of love and benevolence, we believe shall be faithfully and honorably rewarded in the Judgement Day.

THE CHURCH COVENANT

We do now as in the presence of the great eternal omniscient God, who knows the secrets of all hearts, and in the presence of angels and men, acknowledge ourselves to be under the most solemn covenant with the Lord, to be for Him and no other, and we do now renew our covenant with Him, and we do also by the assistance of Divine grace, unitedly give up ourselves to God with all that we have to be disposed of to His honor and glory and to one another in covenant, promising by the help of the grace of God to act toward one another as brethren in Christ, watching over each other in the love of God, guarding and watching against jesting, fightings and foolish talking, which is not convenient, and everything that does not become the followers of the Holy Lamb of God, and to seek the 'good of each other and of the church universal for the glory of God, and to hold communion together in the worship of God and in the ordinances and discipline of this church of God, according to Christ's visible kingdom, so far as the providence of God admits of the same, and submitting ourselves to the discipline of this church, taking the Scriptures which is the Word of God as our only rule of faith and practice according as we should be guided by the grace and Spirit of God.

The meeting was adjourned until the fourth Wednesday in June (June 24, 1795) next to be held at Mr. James Gray's barn beginning at ten o'clock in the forenoon, The following business was transacted: it was affirmed that the first day of the week was the Christian Sabbath: and the brother should not go to law with brother; letters were read of several brethren and sisters from their respective churches, all of which were accepted, who formed themselves into a Body and proceeded to receive a revelation of Christian experience from such as had not obtained letters.

On July 31, 1795, a meeting was held at the Schoolhouse, Otego, and a sermon delivered by Elder Bacon from I John 1:2.

There were twelve charter members; members joined by bringing a letter into the congregation requesting to be put into its watch and care; dismissals read the same. It is noted that some came from as far away as Rhode Island. Baptisms were performed after a brother or sister gave a revelation of their Christian experience. Members were dismissed for any misconduct, such as slander and intoxication. All the meetings up to 1804 were held in homes and schools.

The first building was erected in 1804 and stood on the same site as the present building. This church had box pews and a deep gallery on three sides. The land was donated by Comfort Cook and subscribers donated cash, grain, etc. for the purpose of building this meeting house. Elder John Bostwick, a veteran of the Revolutionary War, was the first pastor. He remained pastor until 1834 adding nearly 400 names to the church record. He moved his family to Pike, Wyoming County where he died in 1845. In the original building was a 1,000 pound bell which was rung at sunrise, noon, and night for the convenience of the people who lived within hearing distance. It was tolled for all funerals. This bell was cracked in ringing out the joy of the community when President Lincoln issued the Emancipation Proclamation. In 1864, a new bell was purchased at a cost of $300; Marcus Wells carved an inscription to be cast into the bell. This bell was later traded for the current bell.

Church and Parsonage—1935

The present house of worship was built in 1854 at a cost of $2,200.00 and had bench pews. The baptistery was installed with a pump in 1896. The beautiful stained glass windows were given in memory of former faithful members.

Stained Glass Window

The large front window was given in memory of Marcus Wells (born October 20, 1815 - died July 17, 1895) composer of the hymn "Holy Spirit, Faithful Guide," written in 1858. Mr. Wells was choir leader for many years. The first carpet was laid in 1894 at a cost of $84.

The 100th Anniversary was observed in 1895.

The first parsonage stands behind the church of today

The present parsonage was built in 1900. The dining room and educational room of the church was built in 1915-1916, funds and labor being contributed by the men and the Women's Society of the church.

In 1914, the church was incorporated as the First Baptist Church of Hartwick. The church was renovated and a new carpet laid in 1926 at a cost of $2,000.00. A memorial organ was purchased and dedicated in 1957 and is currently used. Funds were contributed by members and friends in memory of loved ones during the pastorate of the late Rev. Walter Miller. New carpet was installed in 1973 after the sanctuary was painted. The pews were also refinished at the same time. The stained glass windows were cleaned and repaired in 1961 and again in 1983 when many were releaded. In 1988, the church purchased a van to be used for picking up anyone who needed a ride to Sunday School and church. It was a big addition to the youth work, transporting youth to camp at Word of Life in Schroon Lake, NY. The 1st through 6th grade children are Word of Life Olympians. The Teens have a separate club. In present years the youth have attended summer camp at Camp Bayouca (Baptist Youth camp) at Marathon, NY. In recent years, the church has been made handicap accessible by the addition of a wheelchair ramp into the fellowship hall. Other renovations include replacing the roof on the fellowship hall.

FURTHER POINTS OF INTEREST

- In 1888 Pastor J. D. Roberts; salary was $500.00 per year.
- In January 1889 a week of prayer was observed with great attendance.
- On December 29, 1895, a revival meeting was held which lasted three weeks. The church was having great financial trial as was the whole country.
- From May 25, 1895 to May 16, 1896, 47 were baptized. The 23 years preceding, 57 total were baptized.
- 1896 - The church had 114 members.
- August 26, 1899, a building committee for the parsonage was appointed. Sept. 1900, it was authorize by trustees to borrow money to finish parsonage, paint church, and repair shed When completed, the cost was $1,250.00.
- In 1903, Memorial windows were placed in the church at a cost of $350.00. A furnace was installed at total cost of $80.00, a tin ceiling (current ceiling) was installed at cost of $80.00. Other repairs totaled $1,127.26.
- 1905, the church purchased a cabinet organ at a cost of $65.00.
- 1906, the barn on the parsonage lot was built. (current garage)

Taken from: First Baptist Church Hartwick NY 200th Anniversary 1795-1995 brochure

Reverend Booth and family in one of Hartwicks first automobiles Pastor of Hartwick Baptist Church 1905-1909

Virginia Scott, Betty Tedecco

Left side: Martha Clarvoe, Suzanne and Carolyn Clarvoe, Carol Niedzialkowski, Caitlin Niedzialkowski
Right side: Paul Clarvoe, Russell Clarvoe, John Niedzialkowski with son, Jay, Barry Grey

Grant Ward, Janice Gage, Ina Phillips

Rev. Hiram H. Fisher

Elder Hiram H. Fisher, famous artist, historian and pastor, was born in South New Berlin, NY, Feb. 22, 1826; converted at the age of eight, joined the church at age fourteen, and began his ministry at the age of twenty-nine years. His pastorate in Hartwick's First Baptist Church began in 1862 and terminated in 1870, but he resided in Hartwick many years.

During the eight years he was Hartwick's pastor many persons were taken into the Church. He officiated at the funeral of James Forbes in 1912 and at the marriage of Mr. and Mrs. Forbes forty-nine years previous. When Hartwick Church observed its centennial in 1895, Elder Fisher wrote a splendid history of the Church.

Elder Fisher was endowed with great talent as an artist. One day Miss Jane C. Jones loaned him her "Christain Herald" on which was a picture, "Jesus Blessing Little Children." She was a great reader of Christian literature and called his attention to the beautiful painting of the cover.

Thus he was inspired to paint his large masterpiece which hangs on the front wall of our Church today. When the task was completed, the magazine cover was returned to the owner and it remained folded among her scrap books and papers until, many years later, after her death, her things were auctioned and scattered. Mr. Fisher sold many of his paintings in New York City. He gave painting lessons in his home studio on West Main Street. He became pastor of Hartwick Baptist Church on April 1, 1862 with a salary of three hundred dollars and a donation. This pastorate lasted until 1870. During these eight years about sixty adults were added to the Church, he married sixty-one couples and officiated at sixty funerals. He moved back to Hartwick after an absence of twelve years and acted as supply pastor of the Church and did much church and Sunday school work.

His wife was Polly Dye whom he married in 1848. They had five children, two of whom survived him; Sidney Fisher of Ithaca and Mrs. Jennie Murdock of Hartwick.

Elder Fisher died October 13, 1914, after fifty years of faithful service to Baptist Churches in New Berlin, Burlington Flats, Chaseville, Schenevus, Burlington Green, Otego and Hartwick. Funeral services were conducted at Hartwick Baptist Church with Rev. John Courtright officiating and interment was in Hartwick Cemetery.

A beautiful memorial window pays silent tribute to the memory of this famous artist, historian and pastor who so wonderfully served Hartwick Baptist Church a century ago.

By: Nellie Balcom

Christian Hill Church

Christian Hill Church—Dedicated in September 1843. The first church building was built of stone in 1830, nearly across the road from this picture.

The First Christian Church in Hartwick Township was organized January 8, 1814 and was called "The Christian Church of Otsego and Hartwick." Later it was referred to as the "North Church" and also "The Christian Hill Church" as the area became known as Christian Hill. This church was one of the first Christian churches in New York State: New Baltimore, Green County having organized in 1812 and Charleston, Montgomery County in 1813 (History and advocacy of the Christian Church by J. R. Freese, MD).[1,2]

Jonathan Newman was the elder. Mr. Newman had been a Methodist preacher on the Otsego Circuit as early as 1790 and as late as 1797 (Hurd's "History of Otsego County"). These circuits covered up to 400 miles with preaching in each place once in four weeks. With a little imagination it is easy to see Elder Newman dismounting his horse and knocking at a settler's door to inquire if he could hold a meeting there. Whether the organization of the church was an outgrowth of earlier meetings here may never be known. A few years earlier Elder Newman had left the Methodist Church and lived a few miles below Hartwick. He was ordained to the Christian ministry March 9, 1814 at the Christian Church Otsego and Hartwick. Later he returned to the

Methodist Church.

The church met at members' homes or in the schoolhouse. The first mention of meeting at the Meetinghouse was in the June 5, 1822 minutes- according to an item in the newspaper "Watchtower," January 26, 1824. The Christian Meeting House and adjoining schoolhouse were destroyed by fire.

The church disciplined its members for everything from bad language and intoxication to family disputes. They followed the Bible instruction to judge their own and trials were held. Often members were excommunicated (suspended). If they repented they were reinstated.

There were two women from the Christian Hill church who were referred to as "female laborers." One was Sally Hedges who had been a long time [3] member of the Methodist church. She was married when she began to feel the call to preach but was denied the opportunity and dismissed. Sally Hedges then joined The Christian Church. The other was Ann Rexford who was three years old when her father bought a farm in the area in 1803. In 1816 Ann and her brother Leonard joined the church. Leonard began to preach in two years, soon followed by Ann. She often-shared preaching engagements in Central New York with Sally Hedges. By the time Ann was twenty she was preaching full-time, visiting many villages in New York[4] State. In 1824 she was in New York City for services. Later she married and left preaching. She remained a dedicated Christian until her death in 1891. These women had a full time mission – a hard life for anyone- especially with poor roads and many hardships. It was a time when few women were in public life. They did much to spread the "Christian Connection."

Gradually the membership dwindled and in 1905 the church was reported "extinct" by New York State Eastern Christian Conference. Some had joined the churches in Hartwick and others followed—and so ended The Christian Hill Church.

by F.H.

[1]Pg. 123—A History and Advocacy of the Christian Church by J.R. Freese, MD. published Philadelphia, Christian Book Concern

[2]Pg. 201—A History and Advocacy of the Christian Church by J.R. Freese, MD. published Philadelphia, Christian Book Concern

[3]Pg. 152—Memoir of Mrs. Abigail Roberts by Philetus Roberts Published at the office of the Christian Messinger & Christian Palladion by Moses Cummings 1850

[4]Pg. 47—Memoir of Mrs. Abigail Roberts by Philetus Roberts Published at the office of the Christian Messinger & Christian Palladion by Moses Cummings 1850

Sign erected at site of original Christian Hill Church, by the Historical Society, 1978.

Christian Church of Hartwick Village

The village Christian Church was organized February 1, 1853. According to the last entry in the New Lisbon (Lena) Christian Church Clerk's record, its members met with other interested persons in the old Baptist Meeting House to form a new church.

The Lena Church entry follows:

The Christian Church organized July 22, 1842 in Lewisboro having become somewhat scattered, feeble and discouraged came to the conclusion that it would be for the good of the cause to unite our strength with those in Hartwick Village who wished to organize a church on Gospel principles. Accordingly those in good standing took seats and was acknowledged in a church in that place with the determination to follow the Lord through evil as well as good report. — Church Clerk's book

The Lena Christian Church was first organized in New Lisbon Aug 30, 1819 (H S Bradley, The Christian Church – 1903)

Elder Samuel Haywood and Stephen Hitchcock were instrumental in organizing the Hartwick Christian Church. Elder Samuel Haywood was the first pastor. There were 48 charter members. The church building was raised July 5, 1853, under the supervision of Brazilla Thompson, at a cost of about $2200. The dedication service was held November 24, 1853.[1]

Reverend Gerald Holmes in *Were Called Christians First* has a more complete history of the church and its activities up to 1978.

In 1978 the church celebrated its 125th anniversary. Those taking part were Reverend Holmes and former pastors Reverend Roland Updyke, Reverend George Kyrk, and Reverend Lloyd Cobb. Reverend Larry Dean, who grew up in Hartwick, had part in the services. It was held October 14th and 15th with a concert Sunday afternoon. About 80 guests enjoyed the fellowship and dinner Sunday noon.

On August 5th, 1978 a service was held on Christian Hill. The last "Grove Service" had been held in 1942. Pastors of South Valley and Otego took part. Descendants of members of the Christian Church of Hartwick and Otsego were recognized. A short history of the Christian Hill Church was read. This service reminded everyone of the men and women who had served the Lord in this local church and community.

In September Reverend Holmes resigned. An Open House for Reverend and Mrs. Holmes was held at the Community Center. Reverend

Holmes had been active in many community organizations such as the Historical Society and the SOS Committee (a group who tried to save the Hartwick Grade Center from being absorbed by the Cooperstown Central School District). On October 1st Reverend Holmes, wife Margaret and Children, Scott, Beth and Lori left for his new pastorate at the Ogdenburg Church of Christ in Pennsylvania. [2]

In December 1979 Reverend and Mrs. George Storey and five children came to pastor the Church. Tragedy struck the family and the town March 19th, 1980 when Sarah Storey, aged 10 and her friend John Bodin, aged 12 were hit by a car and killed while crossing the street with other children. The two families were an inspiration to the town. Though his pastorate was short, (December 1979-August 1981) Reverend Storey was a consistent witness to the community. He also worked at the Meadows where he faithfully helped all. [3]

In 1980 the church was insulated at a cost of $1625. A Mother and Daughter Banquet was held with music from Practical Training School.

There were few dry eyes when Reverend Storey preached his last sermon here. The Storeys (George, June, Daniel, Jonathan, Mary Ellen, and Chip) went to Buffalo, Missouri, to continue in the ministry.

Don Phillie was ordained into the Christian Ministry April 10th, 1981. The examining council represented churches from the Tioga River Christian Conference. Reverend George Kyrk brought the ordination address. Reverend Don Phillie served as Assistant Chaplain at the Meadows for thirteen years and for the past eleven years has been Resident Chaplain, the position he held through 1996. [4]

Reverend Phillie was Interim Pastor from August 1981 till January 10th, 1982.

After having numerous candidates, it was voted to call Laverne Saxer to fill the pulpit.

Mr. and Mrs. Saxer and three young boys came from Sugar Run, Pennsylvania. On April 21st, 1983 an ordination council was held. He was examined at his home church, the Moxie Christian Church and ordained at the Evergreen Christian Church.

During the 1980's protective plastic was put over the outside of the stained glass windows and repairs done on them at a cost of $3954. An important occasion was a Bible Conference with Reverend Floyd Barukman. The parsonage was painted and the side porch repaired. The church dining room was also painted. A daughter was added to the Saxer family in 1983 and one in 1984. In 1988 the Semi-Annual Tioga River Christian Conference was held in Hartwick.

Churches are not exempt from problems. In 1987 the church needed painting and after numerous estimates, it was decided to put vinyl siding on instead. A contact for $8900 plus $800 for the roof was signed and work began. After advances were paid ($3067 and $800) the man stopped working. After numerous visits to the Better Business Bureau, the Consumers' Affairs Office and finally a lawyer, there was nothing to be done. There were too many judgments against the contracter so the roof was repaired in 1991 and Jack Croft was hired and finished the siding.

Through trials the church was drawn closer and much was accomplished for the Lord in the 90s.

Reverend Russell Killman held meetings in October 1990. He was a wonderful musician and evangelist from the "Heaven and Home Radio Hour" originating in California.

The parsonage was rewired in 1992 for $3200 plus $60 for the inspection. The church trim and roof were painted.

Special movies and videos have been shown at Sunday evening services and Youth Group Meetings.

Two members of the congregation, Tom and

Julie Dawes published a very interesting and informative monthly Christian newspaper called "The Christian News." Ten dollars a month was given to help this ministry along with collections and private donations. Also a concert by Tom Dawes and Poncho Washburn of Otego was held to help with this expense.

November 3-7, 1993 we had revival meetings with Tal McNutt, a forceful speaker with thought provoking messages.

1994 was a busy year with a new furnace installed in the parsonage *($2065)*, a new furnace in the church ($3266). Many minor repairs were done and the parsonage was painted *($2500)*.

Columbus Day 1994 the Tioga River Christian Conference again held their Semi Annual

here. It was a blessing to all. Everyone brought a bag lunch so all could attend all the sessions. The church served dinner at night.

In 1995 a cassette recorder and microphone was purchased so shut-ins, etc. can hear the messages.

1996 saw the old garage at the parsonage torn down and a new one erected.

In March 1997 it was voted to withdraw from the Tioga River Christian Conference. We continue to support the missionaries-now directly to the Mission Boards.

Fall 1998 found Steve Killmeirer putting a scaffold on the steeple. High winds and other circumstances prevented further work. In the summer of 1999, the steeple was resided and a

Work on Steeple

new weather vane was put up.

Kaps Krew rewired the church and put new lights along the sides of the sanctuary. Pastor Saxer, with the help of some of the men, installed a new ceiling in the dining room. Dennis Baker built a new bulletin board for the back of the church for Missionary displays.

In seven months the church lost four members, Emily Potter, Robin Wilsey, John F. Folds, and Carl Baker, and in 2000 our oldest member Minnie Mead, 94, went to be with the Lord.

Vacation Bible School was held with Lindy Drake as our guest missionary. It was a profitable time.

Christmas service's included a Singsperation with Otego and South Valley Christian Churches, and impressive Christmas Eve service and an excellent Christmas program. We concluded 1999 with a New Year's Eve Candlelight service. We welcomed the 2000th year of the Lord with prayer and the young people ringing the church bells.

In 2000 a new roof was put on the church and new tiles in the entry. In May Reverend Saxer, our Pastor of eighteen years, was diagnosed with Prostate Cancer and was operated on and received radiation. During this time we had a substitute pastor only two or three Sundays. Due to snow our New Year's Eve service was canceled, with the beginning of 2001 we are praising the Lord for answered prayers.

The Christian Church has always been interested in missions and supported them through the Conference Mission Boards. It wasn't until 1960 when we joined the Tioga River Christian Conference and became acquainted with some missionaries as a church that we started helping individuals.

Ten dollars a month was sent to Mr. and Mrs. Cloyse Drake (Village Missions) and Mr. and Mrs. Norman Fleet (New Tribes Missions in the Philippine Islands). During following years we took on Miss Louise Byron (India), Bryan and Shirley Burtch (Peru and Colombia... now at the Wycliffe Office in Dallas, Texas), Aubrey and Elsie Rogers (Missionaries to the Jews in Florida), Elwin and Arleah Fitch (with Spanish speaking people in Tucson, Arizona), Mr. and Mrs. Duane Hennings (Philippines), and Don and Jean Bodin (Venezuela). Other missionaries we have supported by special collections and prayer are: Lal and Lefa Din (Pakistan), Willis and Becky Ott (Bolivia, now in Kenya), Edmund and Grace Fabian (Papua New Guinea), Tim and Lorraine VanDyke (Colombia), Henry and Meiko Lake (Japan), and Lindsay and Carol Drake (Columbia). In 1994 we pledged ten dollars per month to Tim and Ginny Good (Poland), Amy and Jonathan Fabian (Papua New Guinea-second generation missionaries), Stanley Burtch (Peru), and Andrew Ott (Bolivia).

Since 1960 Cloyse Drake's church has become self sufficient, Fleets came off the mission field, as did the Jennings. Miss Byron retired but we continue to support her work in India. Lefa and Lal Din have both gone to be with the Lord. Their nephew reports annually on the state of the school in Pakistan. Our missionaries have become good friends and fellow workers for the Lord.

1993 was a sad year. A translator helper murdered Edmund Fabian. His wife continued his work and went back (1996) for another term and is still at work in 2000.

Tim VanDyke while serving as a house parent at the boarding school for missionary children in Columbia along with his fellow worker Steve Welch was taken hostage by guerrillas and months later was killed. All three men left a lasting testimony both here and on the field.

Vacation Bible School has been held almost every year since its start in 1930. For many years it was a combined VBS with all three Hartwick churches supplying teachers and meeting places.

Recently we have held our own at night because more teachers are working during the day. All children are always welcome. It had been a profitable ministry with children coming to know the Lord.

Over the years the church has been active in community affairs. The Boy Scouts, Girl Scouts, and Tiger Cubs have met at the church. While Shelter for Youth (SAY) was in operation the church supported it with a collection every second Sunday. Head Start met weekly here at one time and the Christmas gifts have been purchased for Head Start families for several years. WIC (Women, Infants, and Children) met at the church until more space became necessary and they moved to the Community Center.

The Christian Church of Hartwick has held morning and evening services and prayer meetings almost every week. May it continue to do so until the Lord comes.

By: F.H.

1. H.S. Bradley Paper " The Christian Church" Feb. 1,1903
2. H.S. Bradley Paper " The Christian Church" Sept. 19, 1917
3. Freeman's Journal March 20,1980
4. Freeman's Journal April 29,1981
Hartwick Christian Church Clerk's book

Ministry & Delegates at the Centennial Session of the New York Eastern Christian Conference, Held at Hartwick, N.Y. June 5-9, 1918.

Christmas Program 1984—Front row: Mellissa Woodbeck, Wendy Baker, Sarah Saxer, Jane Tedesco, Aaron Saxer, Brad Kelsey, Irene Matteson; middle: Billy Wood, Joshua Saxer, Lisa Woodbeck, Sally Tedesco in front of Lisa, ?; back: Pastor Saxer, Patrick Baker, Vernon Wood, Cathy Balcom, Crystal Wood, Laura Woodbeck, Robin Wood, a cousin of Wood's, Marie Saxer, baby Rebeka Saxer

Awana Group—Front row: Debbie Harper, Linda Ainslie, Terry Clark, Sandy Matteson, Marion Collar, Nancy Roberts; back row: ?, Valeria Campbell, obscured, Claudia Roberts, Linda Spickerman, Carol Goble

Hartwick Sesquicentennial, 1952—l to r: Evelyn Mott, Carol Mott, Ella Mae Harrington, Elizabeth Harrington, Ella Currey, Ella Bush, Agatha Harrington, Myrtle & Charles Spaffords

L to R: Julie Folk, Rebecca Walrath, Sarah Saxer, Megan Walrath, Rebeka Saxer, Nathan Saxer

2001 Picnic at Dennis & Judy Baker's

Bowe Hill Camp Meetings

From about 1805 to 1847, the camp meetings on the western slope of Bowe Hill, just below the summit and but a short walk from Arnold's lake, drew annually to its pleasant groves large numbers of people.

In the earlier history of these great religious gatherings the participants used cloth tents as a protection from the elements. Later on these coverings were succeeded more or less by cheap, temporary wooden structures. A most essential feature of the Bowe Hill camping grounds was a fine spring of water much utilized at the time for cooking and washing purposes. This was located near the southerly margin of the camp or what is the northerly border of the present (1847) grove where the latter day meetings were held; the older woods having disappeared long ago. It was a charming spot for these assemblages, the view from the summit of the hill being particularly grand and inspiring. The meetings were participated in by people drawn from several counties and were usually of about one week's duration. About 1822 Lorenzo Dow addressed a multitude there numbering, it is said, 10,000 people.

Ezra Stevens, a Milford boy, attended a camp meeting in 1824, a Reverend Mr. Gile being one of the leading exhorters upon that occasion. Bowe Hill was then often called Rye Hill owing to the great quantities of that cereal grain raised on its slopes, the product largely going to the numerous distilleries of Hartwick and vicinity townships.

The last camp meeting on Bowe Hill, according to E. K. Mosher, an old Laurens and Oneonta resident, was held in 1847.

The old schoolhouse on Bowe Hill was utilized by local Methodists for regular Sunday meetings. It is said the early Methodist Church Societies of Mt. Vision, Hartwick and Milford were all off shoots of the Bowe Hill School Organization.

It appears that among others drawn to this common center of public interest was one C—, a Hartwick tavern keeper; not so much through moving concern for his soul's ultimate welfare nor by a desire to hear the voice of the magnetic Lorenzo, as by the purely mercenary motive of deriving pecuniary profit from the congregated people irrespective of any and all rules of common propriety. In pursuance of his plan he had set a bar on the outskirts of the camp, installed himself behind the same with a barrel of whiskey and was soon doing a thriving business.

In the course of time and having made his appearance upon the preacher's platform, Mr. Dow's attention was finally drawn to the rival attraction presented by the obnoxious whiskey vendor and, annoyed by its proximity in such a place became more and more incensed as the busy publican continued his trade with every indication of callous indifference, if he perceived it at all, to the growing indignation of the evangelist. A little later the famous preacher took the floor and proceeded to address the assembled multitude; but before touching upon the subject of their soul's salvation took occasion to speak of his extended experience as a traveler. More especially of the usual opportunities that had befallen him for a close study of human nature in all of its manifold phases and which he felt he had not left unimproved. He stated that the audience before him unquestionably represented many types of character, a situation not remarkable in so large an assemblage. Yet, at the same time, in reviewing his experiences from the standpoint of twenty-five years observation, in many states and climes and after contact with people of all kinds, colors and conditions, the present occasion had revealed, even to him, an exhibition of innate depravity which was so unique in its way and fortunately one rarely seen. Then quickly turning on his heel and facing squarely in the other direction, Dow pointed his finger at the regenerate party and, in a loud voice and vividly denunciatory manner, exclaimed "For never in all my experience with the vilest and most degraded of human beings – search the ragtag and bobtail of creation as you will – never, I repeat, never have I before seen anything as low and despicable as the devil's two-legged dog standing over there!" But, alas for human frailty, it must be recorded as an illustration of the instability of the average man, that C—'s public exposure to such scathing blast, the cash receipts in silver and copper coin finally taken home by the local innkeeper more than filled a half bushel measure.

———

Compiled by Gladys Harrison from the Huntington Papers

Hartwick United Methodist Church

UNITED METHODIST CHURCH OF HARTWICK

Methodists were here in Hartwick more than 200 years ago! The settlers gathered in neighbor's cabins to listen and pray with Methodist Circuit Riders, who walked or rode horses along the trails of early Otsego County. Men such as Philip Wagner, Jonathan Newman, or Ebenezer White would stop at each cabin, visit with them, pray and preach; share a meal, and travel on. Their circuits would take weeks to travel—in all kinds of weather. (The grave of Ebenezer White is in the South Hartwick Cemetery) Some of these early services were held in the stone schoolhouse on South Street in the village.

The trustees signed the deed for the land on which the Methodist Church was built in 1839. The deed was recorded on March 11, 1840. We assume that the church building was erected at that time because during the winter of 1843, G. W. Andrews taught a select school in the basement of The Hartwick Methodist Church. He became the first pastor of our church. From then until now, the church has enjoyed the leadership of 56 pastors: a true blessing!

During the early days, many people were converted to Christian beliefs through participation in outdoor Methodist Camp Meetings. Families would drive horse and wagon from miles around to these daylong meetings. Families and neighbors brought meals for the day as well as their bibles. Bowe's Hill, The Pines, and George Teal's farm were some of the places for Camp Meetings. Many of Methodist's enthusiastic evangelists were speakers for the day.

In the 1855 census, when Reverend Joseph Shauk or Reverend W. Southworth were pastors, the church was in the Oneida Conference. The total value of the land and building was $1800.

It had 300 seats with an average attendance of 150. The pastor's yearly salary was $200 plus the use of the real estate (this implies there was a parsonage).

Even in the early years of our church, there were many changes and repairs made to the church building. In 1866 the church was temporarily closed for major repairs at the cost of $3400. A committee headed by George Robinson and Charles Russell resolved "that there be a belfry built suitable for a bell." A month later in 1867, the church was reopened with Reverend Bixby preaching.

In January 1879 a news item in the *Hartwick Recorder:*
"The friends of the M.E. Church are making preparations to repair their house the coming spring; a new and beautiful spire is contemplated."

In 1889, *The Otsego Farmer* item read:
"The friends of the Hartwick Methodist Church are making preparations for hanging a new 800 lb. bell in their church tower, with which they intend to call the people to a festival in the church yard on the evening of July 4."

In 1902, with Pastor Adelbert Finch, the building was repaired, and changed. The front stairs were moved, a gallery enlarged, stoves were put in basement, and the memorial windows were installed.

In 1924, the trustees contracted with Edwin Wood of Toddsville to remove the church steeple and roof over the base. He was paid $150.

Through the following years, repairs were made, new pews purchased, rugs and flooring were replaced—to keep a building safe and comfortable for its members and friends. Today, we are still working to keep our building comfortable, safe and attractive. Lately we have installed a chair lift, rebuilt the kitchen, installed new equipment and carpets, stair rails, fans, and restroom units. We are enthusiastic about improving our church home.

Our Sunday school has been active most of the time since 1864. That year we joined The Otsego County Sunday School Organization. We have a record book that shows our early Sunday School to be large and active. There have been many picnics, programs, concerts, and weekly classes for Christian instruction. One social event enjoyed by the Sunday school and the church was in 1877 a New Year's Tree.

An item from the *Hartwick Reporter* in 1877:
"The M. E. Church of this place gave their Sunday school the benefit of a New Year's Tree in their chapel January 2. The Programme was made up of vocal and instrumental music, and the distribution of presents, which were suspended from the branches of the trees, as there were two, one on each side of the altar, with their tops united together, thereby forming an arch, which, when decorated with the many toys and other more valuable presents, presented a fine appearance."

In later years, although smaller in number, the Sunday school has continued to be an important part of our church. They take part in the morning service, host coffee hours, help with suppers, and participate in all church events. They are receiving instruction from Mrs. Carol Ellis and Mrs. Colleen Webb.

Over the years, there have been many evangelistic activities in our church. In 1875, Pastor Shelland brought a "Praying Band." This group of 4 men from New York City led a series of prayer meetings open to all churches for 2 weeks. After they left, the 3 ministers continued with the Sunday Evening Services. Many came to believe. Later on, Pastor Gibby was one of the ministers holding services at the Laurens CCC

Camp with about 150 present on Thursday nights. Pastor W. Lyons in the 1940's began the idea of "The Lord's Acre." This was an acre of land donated by a church member (Stuart Ainslie was one) on which volunteers planted potatoes, cared for them, sold the crop, and used the money for the church's work for the Lord.

The women of our church, from the Ladies Aid Society in 1898 to the Women's Society of Christian Service in 1940, to the United Methodist Women at the present time have supported missions and helped their home church in its work. We have shared good food and fellowship with our church and with Hartwick.

With the guidance of Pastors: Reverend Nancy Adams, Reverend Isaac Mawokomatanda, and our present Pastor, Reverend Roger Yoder, we are becoming a closer, more active church family. We are also a member of the Northern United Methodist Parish. The Lenten services held in the churches of this Parish are well attended and truly inspirational. Some of the exciting events of our church were initiated by members such as the puppet Ministry, "God's Kids" by Janet McGrath's youth group. Because of a mutually supportive relationship between our church and its Pastors, we are able to grow in God's work in Hartwick and our parent church.

By: Eva Chamberlin

Bible School ca. 1930's

Hyde Park Churches

Hyde Park Methodist

Between the late 1800's and 1900's Hyde Park had a Methodist Church. It was located on the right side of State Route 28 going toward Oneonta. It was in the Hartwick charge. Pastors serving in Hartwick also served in Hyde Park. The Church was especially active between 1912–1930's. It closed in 1939.

Mr. Charles Campbell bought the church and was required to take the steeple off so it would not be used as a church. He ran a second hand store, antique shop, and even an auction room there. Later Mr. Colburn bought it and since 1994 Mr. Mark Anderson has rented it and operated the "Lonesome Whistle Toy Train Shop" there.

Faith Baptist Church

Now in 2001, Hyde Park has the Faith Baptist Church located on the opposite side of State Route 28. It was organized in 1981 by Reverend Arthur Kitchen with services held in the Cooperstown Milk Plant. This proved to be unsatisfactory so the church moved their services into the Pastor's home. They arranged two rooms so they could seat 50 people.

At this time they opened the Faith Christian Academy for grades 1 – 4. This also was held in the Kitchen's home with Mrs. Kitchen, teacher and Sheryl Baker assisting. This school was conducted for 3 years.

Because this church did not meet legal requirements and they also needed more space, the house was torn down about 1985.

A foundation for a new church was laid in 2 days. Then people came from a Southern Baptist Church in Georgia to help build the church on the plot where the house had stood.

They worked for two weeks.

A double wide was purchased for the Pastor's home.

Since Reverend Kitchen, the ministers have been: Pastor James Huffman, Interim Pastor George Bradford, and presently, Michael Gleason.

The church has evangelist services, special speakers, an active youth group, a younger youth group, the 'Captain's Club,' and weekly Sunday services.

Faith Baptist is an active church!

By: F.H.

Information is from the following sources:
Hyde Park Methodist information:
Methodist file in Hartwick Historical Collection
Mrs. A. Heller
Mr. R. Kelly
Mr. Robert Bailey
Faith Baptist Church information:
Pastor Gleason
Mrs. Alma Baker
Heidi and Mike Andela

F: R. Saxer, J. Field, Mrs. Glission, Preacher B. Glission, P. Glission, M. Andela
B: J. Carkees, S. Saxer, H. Andela, T. McFarland

Teen Leaders Mike & Heidi Andela

Ashley

Jessi, Rebekah, Sarah, Sarena

Jessi, Marissa, Julie, Casey

Heidi, Mrs. Glission

Evangelical Lutheran Church
Hartwick Seminary, New York

Lutheran Church

The Evangelical Lutheran Church of Hartwick Seminary is an active faith community of believers continuing the tradition that began when a group of their predecessors established the congregation on August 10, 1839. Forty members had extended a call to the Reverend J. D. Lawyer earlier that year on May 1, 1839. This action was taken to provide a distinct worship space, presumably to accommodate a greater number of people, separate from the chapel in the previously established Hartwick Seminary.

The Seminary was the first Lutheran Theological Seminary established in the United States as a legacy of John Christopher Hartwick. John Christopher Hartwick was born in Molschleben, in the Duchy of Saxe-Gotha, Germany on January 6, 1714. He was educated at the University of Halle and ordained a Lutheran Minister by the Reverend Doctor

Phillip D. Krauter in Holy Trinity Church in London on November 10, 1745. Within a year he arrived in what were then the "Colonies" and took on pastoral duties for congregations already established in Rhinebeck, Germantown (formerly East Camp), Livingston (formerly Tar Bush), and Wurtemburg (formerly Staatsburg). By 1758 he had left the Hudson Valley region. During this short time, as a newcomer to the New World, he had become acquainted with Native Americans in the region and notably some Mohawk Chiefs who appreciated his "restless nature and love of the wilderness." He initially purchased a large tract of land near Canajoharie in 1750 from a Mohawk named Sachem Hendrick. He had failed to apply for a required government license for the land acquisition and the sale was declared invalid.

Four years later, in 1754, Reverend Hartwick successfully purchased a comparably large tract of land comprised of 36 square miles that parallels what became and is now the Town of Hartwick, in the geographic center of Otsego County. In 1761 King George lll of England issued letters of patent to Hartwick and ten other individuals, seven of whom had already turned their shares over to Hartwick, making him the proprietor of eight-elevenths of the entire patent. He is credited with having been the first to refer to Otsego Lake by a name now familiar to us. Upon reaching the summit of a hill overlooking the lake, with two Native American guides, he saw the setting sun brilliantly reflected in the lake and was heard to say, "Das ist das Glimmerglass," giving name to the region later to become famous as the scene of James Fenimore Cooper novels.

About ten years before the American Revolution, Hartwick, believing that his property extended to the edge of Otsego Lake, commenced to clear some land on the present site of Cooperstown. Discovering his mistake, he abandoned the project. Nonetheless, Hartwick became the first "white" man to attempt a settlement of the lower shore of Otsego Lake, predating Judge Cooper by twenty years.

Despite his land holdings and love of the area he held pastorates from 1761 to 1783 for churches from Waldeboro, Maine to Woodstock, Virginia but stayed in one place no longer than six months. On July 17, 1796, he was journeying back to his beloved "Glimmerglass" when he died from an attack of asthma at the Clermont-on-Hudson home of Robert R. Livingston.

During his ministry, this highly educated and much traveled man won many friends in the new American colonies and the new nation. Among those friends numbered such dignitaries as Thomas, Sixth Earl of Fairfax, Virginia; the Honorable Frederick A. Muhlenberg, First Speaker of the House of Representatives; his father, Henry M. Muhlenberg, "Father of the Lutheran Church in America;" Jeremiah Van Rensselaer, Third Lieutenant Governor of New York; and Chancellor Robert R. Livingston, negotiator of the Louisiana Purchase and financial backer of Robert Fulton's steamboat, the "Clermont."

Hartwick's will was destined to preserve his name in the annals of the Lutheran religious denominations in America and in higher education. His eccentricity nearly defeated his in-

tent, for in it he left the major portion of his estate "To Thee Jesus Christ, Son of God & Man." This stipulation presented legalistic problems for his executors for years. The will provided for the establishment of a theological and missionary institute as well as directing that the remaining land of his patent be called "New Jerusalem." The original holding of 36 square miles had been so dissipated by lease and sale that his executors decided to devote the remaining resources of the estate to the creation of the school.

So thus, on Friday, September 15, 1797 the executors, the Reverend John C. Kunze, Frederick Augustus Muhlenberg and Jeremiah Van Rensselaer, met at the Albany Coffee House in New York City and founded Hartwick Seminary on that date. It was the first Lutheran Theological Seminary on the American Continents. The Seminary commenced operations in New York City five days later on September 20, 1797 with the Reverend Kunze as Literary Director and Professor of Theology. The executors also appointed the Rev. John Frederick Ernst "to preach for the inhabitants (of the Hartwick patent) and assist in the education of their youth" which he did from 1797 to 1802, settling in Cooperstown in 1799. An elementary school was established in Cooperstown in 1799 and an academy or preparatory school was established in Albany in 1801. Rev. Ernst endeavored to ascertain if there was land in the Hartwick patent suitable for a seminary. His efforts to form a Lutheran Church failed. From 1802 to 1815 it has been noted that preaching in the Hartwick area was largely neglected.

In 1812 it was decided that the far-flung educational operations should be consolidated on a site in the Hartwick patent, four miles southwest of Cooperstown. A two-story brick building containing eight classrooms with a kitchen and dining facilities in the basement was erected and completed and officially opened on December 5, 1815 (exactly 186 years ago today as of this writing on 12/5/2001!). The building was topped with a cupola containing the school bell, which is now installed and operating in the tower of the Yager Library-Museum building on the Hartwick College campus in Oneonta. The Reverend Doctor Ernst L. Hazelius was the first faculty member of the newly established Seminary and remained there until 1830 when the Rev. Prof. George B. Miller was elected as his successor. Rev. Miller led the Seminary starting in 1830 and continued until 1839.

In 1823 the Seminary Board met and it was suggested that there be "the building of a Chapel and took action to help the Lutheran residents of the community with funds to erect such a place of worship." Following the establishment of the congregation and the calling of the Reverend Doctor J. D. Lawyer in 1839, the church was erected the following year, in 1840, at a cost of $1,800. The grandfather of Faith Buechner, the second oldest member of our congregation (as of this writing in December of 2001) donated $12 for some of the lumber. A shed was erected on the north side of the Church to protect the horses and carriages during the worship services. The original contract for the construction of the Church was set at $1,400 and that amount was raised by subscription to discharge the debt. Later the cost was found to be $1,800 so a $400 mortgage was secured. When the mortgage note became due there were no funds to satisfy the demand and the Church was locked, It was only after "considerable trouble and contention" that it was again opened for worship. In order to liquidate the debt a "sinking fund society" was organized and it not only raised the money necessary to satisfy the debt but also contributed to the other expenses of the Church. The Sinking Fund Society later became the

Missionary Society and contributed to the department of Christian Benevolence until the death of one Lottie Miller.

The Church was intended to serve the students and faculty of the Seminary and the residents of the surrounding community. However, in 1840 the Rev. Dr. W. D. Stroble became the Principal of the Seminary and he preached to the students while Pastor Lawyer preached in the Church and there was "rival" preaching." Pastor Lawyer served the new Church until 1843. After Pastor Lawyer left there was no regular pastor for five years. In 1849 Pastor George Miller was invited back to preach in the Church and did so until 1870 when he was succeeded by Rev. William Schell who in turn was succeeded by Rev. Timothy Titus, who was both Pastor and Principal of the Seminary. Rev. Titus was in ill health. The Rev. James Pitcher did the preaching until 1873. Rev. Lawyer was the only minister of the Church during these years that was not a professor at the Seminary.

On February 8,1887 a sum of $500 was subscribed towards the total of $1,000 needed to renovate the Church.

On November 11, 1887 memorial windows from the manufacturer Mr. H. Stellwagon of Philadelphia, Pennsylvania arrived. The Church was raised 18 inches, the old gallery was re-

Memorial Windows

moved, a new entry was built in the front and an alcove was built in the rear. The Church sanctuary is now 34 feet by 48 feet and is furnished with 44 pews. Mr. H.R. Bowdish of Cooperstown was in charge of the carpentry work, Mr. John H. Weeks was in charge of the masonry work; Mr. J.E. Smith of Milford did the furnace and tin work and Mr. Charles H. Whitbeck oversaw the painting. The decorations were furnished by Messers Bullock and Becker of Albany. The seats, pulpit and altar furniture came from the Globe Furniture Company of Michigan and were made from black walnut. The pews were of oak and the interior of the church is of cherry wood. The remodeled Church was dedicated at an eleven o'clock service on the morning of December 22, 1887. On June 15, 1888 "commodious" sheds were erected for horses and carriages. Although the estimated cost for the remodeling of the Church was $1,000, the final cost was in excess of $2,000.

In the early 1900's, the Church was again rebuilt to "conform to Lutheran architecture." The pulpit and altar hangings were a gift from Dr. and Mrs. J.L. Kistler, as a memorial to their son, Ralph.

Pipe Organ

In 1921 the pipe organ was installed at a cost of $1,200 coming from the Moeller Organ Company. On November 3, 1956 the Hayes Room (beneath the Sanctuary) was dedicated as a memorial to the Reverend Doctor Harry Hayes. In October of 1977 a restoration of the stained glass windows was commenced at a cost in excess of $7,000. On June 24, 1979, the Reverend Doctor Edward Kirsten Perry, Bishop of the Upper New York Synod of the Lutheran Church in America, rededicated the windows at the eleven A.M. worship service. In September of 1980 the organ was extensively rebuilt at a cost of $2,000. In 1984 the single toilet "unisex" bathroom was replaced by separate rooms for the ladies and men with a combined total of three toilets! The furnace was replaced in 1999 with a smaller and more efficient unit and the kitchen was partially remodeled in 2000.

The Church became part of a three church parish formed by a covenant agreement in 1953 and pastoral services were shared with St. Matthew's Lutheran Church in Laurens and St. John's Lutheran Church in West Burlington. In 1985 this union ended and a very brief call was extended to the Reverend Maurice Gold, who elected to move out of the area. In 1986 Evangelical shared in a joint pastoral call, to the Reverend Arthur Henne, with Atonement Lutheran Church in Oneonta. This union dissolved in 1991 when Pastor Henne elected to serve only the congregation in Oneonta. A call was then extended to the Reverend Lynn Ash in collaboration with a former partner congregation, St. Matthew's in Laurens, in 1991. This union dissolved in 1995 when Pastor Ash decided to serve only St. Matthew's in Laurens. From the time of Pastor Ash's departure until the Reverend Paul R. Messner accepted a call in 1997 the church was served on an interim basis by the Reverend Richard Niebanck, recently retired from the pulpit of Immanuel Lutheran Church in Delhi (Delaware County). Pastor Messner is the Dean of the Foothills

Conference of the Upstate New York Synod of the Evangelical Lutheran Church in America. Pastor Messner continues to serve a merged parish in northern Schoharie County comprised of Zion Lutheran Church in Seward and St. John's Lutheran Church in Sharon in addition to serving the congregation in Hartwick Seminary.

The chronology of ministers who have served Evangelical Lutheran Church since its founding is:

Rev. John Fredrick Ernst	1797 - 1802
Rev. E.L. Hazelius, D.D.	1815 - 1830
Rev. Prof. George B. Miller	1830 - 1839
Rev. J.D. Lawyer, D.D.	1839 - 1843
Rev. Prof. George B. Miller	1844 - 1851
Rev. Prof. Levi Steinberg	1851 - 1864
Rev. Prof. George B. Miller	1864 - 1869
Rev. William Schell	1870 - 1871
Rev. Timothy Titus	1871
Rev. James Pitcher	1871 - 1873
Rev. Peter Bergstresser	1875 - 1876
????	1876 - 1880
Faculty of the Seminary	1880 - 1881
Rev. Alfred Hiller, D.D.	1881 - 1920
Rev. J.L. Kistler	1882 - 1893
(every 3rd Sunday)	
Rev. Archibald Dietz, D.D.	1920 - 1924
Rev. Frank Wolford	Local Pastors
Rev. John G. Traver	substitute
Rev. Charles Meyers	1924 - 1925
Rev. Bruce Charney	1925 - ?
Rev. Harry D. Hayes, D.D.	1934 - 1947
Rev. Paul M. Orso, Ph.D.	1947 - 1952
Rev. Charles Pope	1953 - 1955
Rev. William Rittberger	1955 - 1960
Rev. Theodore Warren	1960 - 1962
Rev. Louis F. Wagschal	1962 - 1967
Rev. William Wittcopp	1967 - 1968
Rev. S. Kenneth Arnsten	1969
Rev. Myron Jawenacke	1969
Rev. Robert Heffner	
Rev. Robert Maier	1970 - 1972
Rev. Robert E. Mansbach, D.D.	1972 - 1985
Rev. Maurice Gold	1985
Rev. Arthur Henne	1986 - 1991
Rev. Lynn Ash	1991 - 1995
Rev. Richard Niebanck	1996
Rev. Paul R. Messner	1997 - 2002

The Women of the Evangelical Lutheran Church in America (WELCA) has been a continuously operating organization within the Congregation since its inception in 1885 as the Women's Missionary Society. It faithfully undertakes several projects every year, recently including school kits and sewing kits for needy schools. Every Christmas, for a number of years, the WELCA has coordinated the collection of Christmas gift packages from the members of the congregation for the children of Migrant Workers in the program at the Bugbee School of SUNY at Oneonta.

Christmas gift packages from the members of the congregation for the children of Migrant Workers

The oldest member of the congregation is Amanda Bottke, who was born on January 29, 1907 in Germany and is 94. She recently moved into Woodside Hall in Cooperstown.

Amanda Bottke

The second oldest member of the congregation at the age of 93 is Faith Buechner, a native of Hartwick born on March 19,1908.

Faith Buechner

Faith moved from her home on State Route 28 into the Meadows a couple of years ago. Faith enjoys the distinction of being one of the last graduates of the Hartwick Seminary, in the patent, and one of the first graduates of Hartwick College when it was newly established in Oneonta. Her graduation from the Seminary was as a High School student, it being a parochial school, and from the college with her Bachelor's degree.

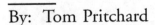

By: Tom Pritchard

Dr. Alfred Hiller, Pastor 1881 - 1920

Sources:

1. Hurd's History of Otsego County, pages 162 & 163
2. An Historical Record of the Evangelical Lutheran Church of Hartwick Seminary, NY from 1796 to 1989, Robert Geberth and Faith Buechner
3. Newspaper articles from the Climate Control Room of the Kinney Memorial Library in Hartwick, New York
4. "Hartwick College Pauses To Look Back At The Beginning", author unknown, The Daily Star, May 5, 1972, page 6 on the event of the College/Seminary's 175th Anniversary.
5. WELCA information from Betty Miller, Dorothy LaGasse, Esther Hughes, Ida Orlando, and Ginny Jaekes.

Standing l-r: Marjorie Nasholds, Elizabeth Miller, Patricia
Geberth, ?
Sitting l-r: Faith Buechner, Janet Kaiser, Lee Zoeller

Cliff Brunner in foreground

Lisa Hendricks, Katie Lane, Pastor, Paul Messner, Walter Clare, Dale Griffen, Palmer Clare, Tom Pritchard

The Manuscript Found

In 1820 in the house of John Davison, (later Jerome Clark's attic) lay an old trunk containing the hand-written script of a romance entitled *The Manuscript Found* by the Reverend Solomon Spaulding. This work was written in 1812, in Conneaut, Ashtabula County, Ohio, where the exploration of earth mounds containing skeletons and other relics fired Spaulding's imagination and suggested the idea for his story.

It was written in biblical style and for the purpose of intrigue was presented as a translation from hieroglyphics writing. The writing was found on metal plates taken from a mound, to which the author had purposely been guided by a vision. The story went on to relate the history of the settling of America by the last tribes of Israel.

Spaulding frequently read the manuscript to circles of admiring friends in Conneaut, Ohio. Later the script was taken to Pittsburgh and left with a printer named Patterson in the hope of having it published. The manuscript was finally rejected. Spaulding died in 1816 and in 1820, his widow married John Davison of Hartwick. She brought the trunk containing her first husband's manuscript with her to her new home with Davison.

In 1823 Joseph Smith announced that he had been directed in a vision, to a hill near Palmyra, NY where he discovered some gold plates curiously inscribed and containing a new revelation. This supposed revelation he published in 1830 as the "Book of Mormon."

Mormonism flourished and moved westward. In the course of time, a Mormon meeting was held in Conneaut, Ohio and out of curiosity was largely attended by the townspeople. Some readings were given from the book of Mormon. Some of the similarities between Joseph Smith's book and "The Manuscript Found" which Solomon Spaulding had read aloud to friends in the same town many years before were noted. They recognized the same peculiar names, unheard of elsewhere, such as Mormon, Maroni, Lamenite, and Nephi.

It was learned that Smith had closely followed Spaulding's story. To Spaulding's work he added only his own grandiose tenet about marriage and invented the theory of the great spectacles by means of which he professed to have deciphered the mysterious characters.

Spaulding's friends raised questions, which have never been cleared up, and were at last forgotten.

It was pointed out the Sydney Rigdon, who figured as a preacher and as an advisor of Smith among the first of the "Latter Day Saints," happened to have been an employee in Patterson's printing office when Spaulding's manuscript was there awaiting approval or rejection. But the matter was never brought to a definite issue, and nothing more came of it except a rather curious episode. Mrs. Davison moved from Hartwick in 1828, leaving a trunk in charge of Jerome Clark. In 1834 a man named Hurlburt found

Mrs. Davison and said that he had been sent by a committee to get "The Manuscript Found" written by Solomon Spaulding, so as to compare it with the Mormon Bible. He presented a letter from her brother, William H. Sabine, of Onondaga Valley, upon whose farm Joseph Smith had been an employee, requesting her to lend the manuscript to Hurlburt, in order "to uproot the Mormon fraud." Hurlburt insinuated that he himself had been a convert to Mormonism, but had given it up, and wished to expose its wickedness. On Hurlburt's repeated promise to return the work, Mrs. Davison gave him a note addressed to Jerome Clark of Hartwick, requesting him to open the old trunk and deliver the manuscript. This was done. Hurlburt got the manuscript, and not only did he never return it, but he never replied to any of the many letters requesting its return. The Spaulding manuscript has utterly disappeared.

By: Birdsall, Ralph
   The Story of Cooperstown 1917

Common Schools

As soon as the early settlers had their log cabins built, they thought about an education for their children.

Amasa Peters who settled in Hartwick in 1796 soon saw the necessity of a school. He gave land and built a school on West Main Street, just a short distance from where the Methodist Church now stands.[1]

The following must have been an incentive for two early schools: from "The Hartwick Suquicentennial Edition of the Otego Valley News," Oct. 10, 1952:

"There is no more typical early American institution than the one room schools. Letters, diaries, and other history contributions are filled with references to them.—There is a most interesting variation, which must find a place in our record.

Acting under the provision of Hartwick's will for the support of education the executors provided funds for teachers salaries in two common schools in the Patent, one each in the eastern and western parts. These schools were certainly open from 1799 until 1801 with young men from the resident families as teachers and the estate paying them upon certification from the local Trustees."

The Sundry Otsego County statistics from 1810 lists seven schools in the Town of Hartwick. Some of these may have been held in homes. In just four years the number had doubled, as in 1814, there were 14 schoolhouses in the township. We can assume some of these may have been log schools, since as late as 1855, there were still 313 log schoolhouses in New York State. According to "School House John's Otsego": Fields school #4 had a log cabin in 1802 and Pleasant Valley #14 had one in 1802; Chase #7, first meeting was held in 1813 and Potter school #5 records tell of a meeting held in the school house in 1814.

From the Watch Tower, (Cherry Valley Paper), Jan. 26, 1824: "Fire! on Wed. night last, the Christian Meeting House and the School House, adjoining, in the town of Hartwick (Christian Hill near Hartwick Village,) were consumed by fire. The fire originated in the Meeting House, and is supposed to have been 'set by design.'"

The "Watch Tower" supplied another bit of information of our early schools, Oct. 13, 1828, "The trustees of the common schools for the town of Hartwick are hereby notified that Saturday, the first day of November, next, is selected for the meeting of inspectors of the Common Schools of said town. It is hoped that the trustees of the Common Schools of each district will have their selection of a teacher, previous to that time.

Richard Fry
R.T. Comstock, Inspectors
Common Schools, Oct. 13, 1828"

It would seem in 2002, November would be too late to choose a teacher, but these schools had only 3 or 4 months of school, usually Nov.

1st to Mar. 1st. Men were usually the teachers. Then there was a summer term and "women generally taught then as the men and boys were busy in the fields as farmers took every available hand, children included.

A teacher qualified in all respects was hard to find. Clergymen were often the teachers. Some of the early farmer-teachers had learned to read and write back in New England. Some housewives and mothers had had the privilege to attend school and could read and write and do simple math. [2]

There were large families- therefore large schools. Often thirty or more children of all ages, crammed into our small district schoolhouses with one teacher! Often the oldest boys and girls attending school were older and bigger than the teacher. (In 1848- Whitehouse District #3 reported children 5-16 numbered 51, the number attending school was 48) To teach under these conditions would require strict discipline, much patience, good organization, and more hours than there is in a school day. It's amazing that our ancestors learned to read and write!

Laura Ingalsbe, a senior, in 1918, in the *Official Catalogue of the Hartwick Union School*: Vivid tales of the rigid rules of the old fashioned school masters are best told by our older citizens, who sat around the old box stove, and the Master's desk upon wooden benches of the most uncomfortable kind. The encircling benches nearest the wall were occupied by the older and most mischievous scholars who were always watching a chance to entertain the others when the masters head was turned. Those happy days were not without many a swing of the master's rod, but the old stone schoolhouse (stood on South Street where the one built in 1878 was, where the gazebo is now) and its associations that grew up around it can never be forgotten. Many a hard lesson was reluctantly recited near the brink of the red-hot box stove.

The next row of simple hard seats just in front of the older students were reluctantly occupied by the smaller students, who were forced to become the amusement of the tricky youths at their back. The younger ones sat nearer the master's chair. You must not forget the old bench where recitations were heard by the whimsy old master, whose long ruler played to get the most fearful study and work from the school."

As late as 1860, all that was required to become a teacher, was passing 8th grade and taking a test to qualify to teach. In the early 1900's, a graduate of High School could receive a certificate to teach if they could pass a test. Agatha Telfer Harrington graduated from Hartwick Union School in 1907 and immediately went to teach in Paines Hallow, driving herself there. Later she took courses at the Oneonta Normal and Training School and later at Oneonta State. [3]

Another example of a student going directly into teaching is told in an article in the Oneonta Star, Aug. 17, 1950:

"Elmer C. Talbot attended Hartwick School and later received his teaching Certificate from the same school. He taught six years and then farmed for twenty. After this he entered the feed business with the Burch Brothers, but sold his share after nine years.

He went into semi-retirement in 1917 when he took over the clerkship of the Hartwick Board of Education and became a regular member of the Board. He quit these two positions in 1924 to take over the duties of the school janitor.

Again, in 1932, he gave up the janitorship to again become clerk and a member of the Board.-- Now he is considering full retirement." And so will end 38 years of association with the Hartwick school system. Mrs. Martha Hollister Kinney was a clerk later.

A few of the many graduates of Hartwick Union High School and other local people who received more training were:

Lizzie Fields Marlette
attended Schuyler Teachers training class
Those who attended Richfield Springs Teachers Training School were:
Elenor Bradley Jones
Irene Jenks Brown
(Her father took her and she boarded there)
Cora Jenks Bowmaker
The following attended Morris Teacher's Training school:
Laura Tilly Bowmaker Mack and her brother Fred Tilly drove a horse each day to school.
Josephine Balcom Spafford
Cora Potter attended Starkey Seminary and Oneonta Normal and Training class
The following attended The Oneonta Normal and Training Class:
George Fuller
Myrtle Harrington
Florence Potter Groff graduated in 1896
Sidney Potter
Pearl Weeks
Nellie Weeks Balcom

It is interesting that in 1834, the State set aside $55,000.00 for starting Libraries in each district school in the State and each school was given $20.00 for this purpose. [5]

Potter School, District #5, immediately appointed a committee to go to Phinney's in Cooperstown to choose their books!

Field School #7 did even better — "Trustees to expend this and obtain additional subscriptions."

There was one district that voted that the books bought for the library were unsuitable and the committee was to return them, and another, appropriated the library money to the teacher's salary.

The Librarians were elected at the annual meetings so the district voters were in charge of the library in the schoolroom. Most of the school records state that the teacher became librarian in 1902.

It is surprising when you find districts outside of Hartwick paying money to Hartwick School.

In 1826 Hartwick #5 money received listed: Hartwick-$6.38, New Lisbon- $1.12 and Burlington - $1.26 – Total $8.76 (paid Lydia Wells, teacher; usually public money paid the teacher.) Potter District #5 had children from Burlington as the town line is just up the hill from the school and so district #5 was much closer than their Burlington school and the same was true of a New Lisbon family. When children attended from other towns, money was paid. This was true until the closing of the school. This was probably true in other districts.

The annual school meeting was held in the fall in the early days, three trustees were elected, later just one. Also elected were a clerk and collector and before 1902, a librarian. The trustees had the responsibility of hiring the teacher and seeing that repairs were made, supplier obtained, the school cleaned etc.

In 1867, #13 purchased a water pail and dipper. (Every one used the same dipper.)

Sometimes a voter would wish to be elected trustee as they had a relative or friend who wanted to teach in that district. In this case if there was another man with the same desire, sparks would fly! Usually by the end of the meeting all was calm. If a grudge remained, sometimes the teacher hired would have a much more difficult time teaching.

In District #3, Whitehouse, they "thought best for the trustee not to hire own daughter." (1903)

Wood was always needed to heat these schools. Sometimes one person would furnish all the wood and get paid for it. Other times those having children attending school did. One district required one third of a cord for each child to be brought when it was their turn. It was decided each year how it would be supplied. One year one district required beech, birch, or hard maple. They also wanted the wood cut in 17-inch length, the next year 20 and then 18. After that the length wasn't mentioned.

People often walked to "School Meetings" with their lanterns as the meetings were held after chores were done (at least in the Potter School). Then the lanterns were used for lighting. Children attended (if the mothers came) as this was before baby-sitters. Of course, until the 1930's the women couldn't vote. That was the first a woman voter was mentioned in the minutes.

In 1844 the Potter School, District #5 had moved their school from the bend in the road above the Potter farm to the corner almost directly across from it's former location. It is likely that this was nearer the center of the population. The district used ox teams and the carpenter was Barzilla Thompson. The school was situated on a small lot and in 1866 it needed more moving!

Dec. 21, 1866, "A special meeting was called to consider building a schoolhouse instead of a 'nuisance house.' It was voted that we move the building to make room enough to work behind it, and that two gallons of whiskey, be bought and paid for by the district to be used when moving said schoolhouse."

1877— The school had an 'end of the school year' picnic.—"July 8, 1877, Picnic held at the Balsom swamp, situated 2 ½ miles north east of Hartwick village. It was a union picnic with Buffalo School, Patent in Burlington, and Potter school. Whitehouse didn't show." [6]

A new school in Hartwick village was certainly needed (District 14). "Our district school is larger than common - 50-60 students. Lively work for teacher J. H. Jenks. For shame to the village that they have not a graded school!" [7]

The village needed a new school - but we find from a clipping in an old scrapbook, that a series of meetings were held before the village district could agree to build a new schoolhouse. "One party wants a house of sufficient capacity to seat about 75-80 in each department, primary higher English, while others want something smaller; not a few of the latter class are men of means but without children to educate hence the smaller house. On the other hand, a large number have children but unfortunately are without great means. We hope the backbiting and abusive insinuations will cease and they will build a house." [8]

This became a reality in 1878. "Work has commenced on the ground of our new schoolhouse. A portion of the building materials has arrived-Masons are at work on the foundation. Mr. A. Burch of this village is doing the work."

"Mr. G. W. Hall of Morris, who built the schoolhouse in this village, has just removed his tools and workmen, to a job in Burlington." [9]

1878, "Our new school house is ready for the winter school. It is a fine looking structure, lacking in only one particular, as public building - no appropriation was voted for a dome or tower." [10]

Hartwick Union School

District #17, on the west side (David Butler's home now) united with #4 after the new school was built.

A few early teachers in the Primary Department: Mrs. Gilbert Joslyn, Miss Lane, Mrs. McDonald, Miss A. B. Carpenter, Miss Clara Nearing, Miss Louise Bennett, Miss Martha Fields, M. Louise Potts.

Some early principals in the higher department: Mr. Wilbur (1878), Principal A. W. Ward, Mr. Cook, Professor E. W. Dow, Professor E. E. Beals and Mrs. Beals, Frank Burnell, Professors England, Pratt Babbit, Louisa Bean and Professor Studley. I found no information on the difference of professors and principals. [13]

The new school was often referred to as the Hartwick Union School although it wasn't until 1897 that the district voted to become a Union School. They also voted to raise $1300 to improve their school at this time. According to an article in the "Thermometer," 1918-1919, an addition had been added by 1918.

With the improved school, the school provided even more opportunities for the community to observe the student's progress; "A. D. Ward, principal of our Union School will close the winter term with a literary entertainment."

1883 -Mrs. McDonald, teacher in the primary department held a very interesting exercise last Friday PM consisting of singing, speeches, etc. The pupils, under her instruction, did credit to themselves and to their teacher." [11]

Even though the school had improved and increased the subjects taught - they could not give regents.

Circa 1885: Principal Prof. Dowd, Lelah Hopkins Bishop, Flora Jenks Davidson, Emma Phillips Cook, Nathan Brownell, Fred Hollister, Fred Field, Elmer Talbot, Fred Murdock, George McAngus, Nellie Barney, Lucy Wilson, Maggie Bowdish Wellman, Irene Bowdish Taylor, Lucy Seeley, Arthur Balwin, George Norton, Grace Green, Marcia Pratt, ???? Pratt, ????Hollister, Myrtle Arnold, M. Burlingham Barney, Charles Pratt, Myron Wescott

1897 – "Several students of our school are attending regent examinations at Cooperstown this week. Among them, Leon Porter, Glen Jackson, Edith Davidson and Fannie Harrington." [12] I remember my mother Susie Potter, always pointing to the house outside of Cooperstown and saying "I stayed there when I took my regents."

This problem was solved in 1898:

From the "Circular & Course of Study of the Hartwick Union School & Academy - Hartwick, New York 1899-1900."

"Hartwick Union School and Academy was established in March, 1898, through the efforts of the board of education & the citizens of the district on March 22,1898, the Academic department was chartered by the University of The State of New York as a Junior Academic School so securing the benefits of the regent system of supervision and participation of the apportionment of money by the University. They planned to introduce Latin and Algebra in the grammar grades."

The academics were improving but the school needed replacing. There was opposition just as there had been in 1878.

1915 – "The annual school meeting was held Tuesday evening at the school house. It was probably more largely attended than any previous meeting. The recent project of a new building having divided the district into two fractions, each side having a ticket in the field for the election of five trustees. Mr. Hintermister was made Chairman - after reports and other business - the following trustees were elected; A.M. Burch, Robert W. Gardner, George A. Fuller, Frank Berry and John T. Curry." [8]

1915 "Special School meeting at the school house. Three propositions were voted on; - The erection of a new school building, to cost $20,000 - large attendance. When the count was made, it stood 117 for and 153 against." [8]

As in 1878, it was finally voted to build a school on land bought from E. O. Rogers, at the end of Mill Street, the school was finished in 1920-1921.

In the last year school was held in the South Street School. Henry Murdock told in an interview in 1994 about this incident:

"A little boy had just started school a short time ago. He wanted to go to the toilet. The teacher let him go (of course it was an out side privy). He came back crying, "I can't find it." She said, "You've been there before." Then to another boy, "Billy, you go with him and show him where it is." Billy came back laughing. "Did you find it?" the teacher asked. "Yes, he put his

pants on backwards!" Billy answered.

Now in 1925 Hartwick had a school with more classrooms and even a playground. It was an exciting time for old and new students. One ninth grader climbed up the side of the school, just because it was a challenge.

Hartwick High School

"Our elementary department now consists of four rooms, two grades each.
1. Grade 1 and 2, 40 pupils, Mrs. Carr
2. Grade 3 and 4, 25 pupils, Miss Rowe
3. Grade 5 and 6, 25 pupils, Miss Jenks
4. Grade 7 and 8, 32 pupils, Mrs. Bowmaker
The Hartwick School system is well lighted, equipped, and supplied with competent instructors. For information write, or preferably call, on R. B. Alexander, Principal, South Street."

About 1930 - Districts #1, 3, 5, 6, and 10 of Hartwick and Otesgo's #'s 5, 13, and 17 were represented at a school fair. These were held several years during the depression. Races, broad jumps, and other contests were held on the H. H. S. grounds back of the school. Exhibits were shown in the E. M. B. A. Hall (now the Community hall). These exhibits were especially good. 1st prize was given to Mrs. Wo1oben's school, Otsego #17. Hartwick #5 and Otsego #5 tied for second place, schools of Mrs. Laura Bowmaker and Mrs. Hazel Fish. District #6 with Mrs. Moscrip, teacher, third.

4H exhibits were under the direction of Mr. Bray and Mrs. Teeter. [13]

There were also musical entertainments: Hartwick Reporter, Nov. 26, 1941:

"The annual Operetta by the grades of Hartwick High School will be presented at the Community Hall at 3:15 PM Friday Nov. 28. This year the operetta is based on Mark Twain's well-known story, "Tom Sawyer." Come and see Neilon Ainslie star as Tom Sawyer, Bertrand Roberts as that barefoot boy, Huckleberry Finn, and all the other characters dear to the readers of Mark Twain."

Soon we were in World War II. Many young men were enlisting and with them the principal Johnny Weinhauer. The student body also contributed to the effort of winning the war. [17]

In 1942, when the nation was putting its all into the war effort, the citizens of Hartwick were doing the same. Rationing of gasoline, meat, sugar, and butter was mandatory, and blackouts went into effect, and one needed to have a good reason to drive an automobile on the road. Everywhere there were drives for scrap metal and old tires. H. L. Harrington was chairman of the Hartwick Township Salvage Committee. [15]

A contest was announced for New York State schools to see how much scrap metal a student body could gather per person of their high school population. The contest to run for two weeks from Oct. 16 to Oct. 30, 1942. Townsfolk and farmers cooperated in spotting the scrap so that it could be collected by students. Will Gardner, Highway Supt., located 2 old metal culverts that could be dug out.

Stanley Hall, Agriculture Teacher, was in charge of collections, and Marion De Angelo, Soc. Studies Teacher, was chairman of the School Salvage Committee.

Students who were active included Dean and Douglas Wayman, Neilon Ainslie, Marvin King, Ralph Leach, Melvin and Ivan Risley, Charles Kenney, and Irving and Norman Jensen.

The winning schools were to send a student to attend the christening of a Liberty ship at Portland, Maine.

By bringing in 45 tons of scrap metal or more than a ton a person Hartwick High Schools 38 students placed second in the statewide contest. The winning school was Lake Placid Central School at Speculator. Pupils in 221 schools throughout the state collected 23,688,074 lbs. of scrap.

Hartwick student, Charles Kenney, gave the most time to the collection effort, but as an 8th grader was not eligible to attend the launching. Norman Jensen, a freshman was chosen.

A general town celebration was held at the school, and the Hartwick Township Salvage Committee took up a collection to defray the expenses for the party.

Someone penned a rallying song to the tune of "It's a Long Way to Tipparary" that went "It's a long way to Portland Shipyard, it's a long way to go" the rest of our words are lost to time, but we were pretty proud.

On Sunday, Jan. 17th, 1943 Norman accompanied by chaperone Marion DeAngelo, attended the christening of Liberty Ship "Lou Gehrig" by Christine Gehrig, Lou Gehrigs mother.

Among the notable people attending were NYS Governor, Thomas E. Dewey, Dr. George Stoddard, State Comm. of Education, and several Yankee baseball players, and sportswriters. The students from the three winning schools were presented to Governor Dewey.

Mrs. Gehrig presented to each of the three boys a volume of Lou Gehrig's biography signed by Lou Gehrig.

Expenses of the boys and their chaperones were paid by the American Industries Salvage Committee.

Hartwick High School, with the churches, was the center of the village. There was an active PTA with meetings and programs for all. Prize speaking was a tradition carried on from the days of the South Street School. In 1933 George Taylor, not only won first prize in Hartwick but also won first in the area at Otego. If that was not enough Thelma Smith won first in the girls competition. [13]

One of the ways the Senior Class earned money each year was the presenting of a senior play.

From the Class History in the 1934 "Hartwickian" we find the principle exciting & enthralling event of the year was the presentation of our play "And Mary Did." We all worried Mary wouldn't but she did and our budget was successfully balanced. The members of the class of 34 were Elizabeth Aplin, Oral Brown, George Dickinson, Charlotte MacDonald, Lee MacDonald, Irwin Matteson, Elsie Robinson, Margaret Schneider, Thelma Smith, and Virginia Turner.

In 1947, the senior play was entitled "Happy Days," and was presented in the Hartwick Community Hall. Members of the cast were: Victor Caskey, Selma Gage, Carol Hadley, Betty Grigsby, Robert Caskey, Beverly Fuller, William Hurtubise, Beatrice Gill, Donald Gas.

Production Staff:

Business manager	James Herron
Make Up	Mrs. Agatha Harrington
Properties	Carol Hadley & Beatrice Gill
Stage Manager	Fred Baker
Advertising	Beverly Fuller, Mary Jones
Tickets	Victor Caskey, Dorthy Marr, Lois Roberts
Prompter	Mary Jones [16]

Hartwick had 'assembly' programs where most of the grades and High School took part. September 22, 1946, "The 150th Anniversary of the adoption of the Constitution was celebrated with a very impressive assembly at Hartwick High. The program was opened with a selection from the school orchestra, directed by Mrs. Mulderig, playing "Young America." A portion of the 119th Psalm was read by Larry Russell, followed by the Lord's prayer. Salute to the flag - followed by the "Star Spangled Banner." James Svolos, principal explained the purpose of the program. The minuet was given by Donald Brown, Louise Bunn, Patsy Raimo, Esther Schidzick, Charles Smith, and Billy Bresee. Joe Truax, eighth grade read "The Making of the Constitution."

Charles Hadley, Ann Patterson, Francis McGrath, and Ruth Wirth sang "Constitution Day." Dorthy Vanburen recited "The Preamble of the Constitution," 5th & 6th grade sang "Washington," a selection from Washington's farewell Address, read by Melvin Risley, senior. "Hail Columbia" was sung by the 7th & 8th grade.

A quiz was presented on the "Constitution," Charles Kenny acted as Quiz Master, while the board of experts were Victor Caskey, Selma Gage, Beatrice Gill. The orchestra concluded the program with "National Spirit." The program was under the direction of Mrs. Agatha Harrington and Mrs. Madaline Eckstein, faculty members."[13]

Sports were also important. 1925 found the High School basketball team made up of Hayes, Fish, Gregory, Potter, Mills, Bunn and Porter. Several of these continued playing through the 1930's as a town team. [16]

The High School team in 1935-1936 was Gordon Matteson, Carey Wilson, Swen Peterson, Joe Fields, Stanley Frankewich, Fred Robinson, Durward Babcock, Stanley Chamberlin, Bernard Gillette, and Morris Frankewich. [17]

In the early days the basketball games were played upstairs in the Otego Valley Hotel (P.O.). At that time the building that later was moved back of the hotel was attached to the hotel and it was upstairs that basketball games, dances, etc. were held. When the E. M. B. A. Hall became available that was used.

1953 was a red-letter year for Hartwick High! In the March 6, 1953 "Sunday Press" published in Binghamton, they had a full page about Fran

(Bugs) Schweitzer and the Hartwick High sports. "The Hartwick School in this Otsego crossroads, contain 26 boys & no gym. Of the eligible males 23 play varsity or J.V. basketball in the low white wooden hall next to the feed mill. All 23 scored at least one field goal this season. The 23rd one scored was Chuck Smith, who in the final game, the 18th of the season,—dunked 3 while the crowd went crazy."

We learn that Hartwick had an unusual varsity team in 1953. Fran Schweitzer had arrived in Hartwick in 7th grade from Rahway, NJ, Fred Striesse originally was from Huntington L.I., Frank McGrath, North Bergen, NJ, Chuck Hadley, Patterson, NJ, Ray Polulech, East Springfield. The only hometown boys were Lee Beach and John Tubbs

Coach Dalrymple remembered back in 1948 when the gym (Community Hall) had been gutted by fire. That year they practiced in the snow but never gave up. They played their 'home' games on their opponent's courts. Not surprising they lost their first 16 games and then won two straight. The Hall was repaired and the next year was in use. During the time in 1948, that the boys were playing on a rival schools court:

Hartwick High School Huskies—1st row L-R: (Ballboys) Jim McGrath and Herb Schweitzer; 2nd row: Willie Grosslinger, John Tubbs, Fran Schweitzer, Fred Streisse, Ray Polulech; 3rd row: Frank McGrath, Lee Beach, Chuck Rollins, Bev Stevens, Chuck Hadley, and Coach Bill Dalrymple

some nights the principal and the coach had to pay the officials, but that wasn't the way when they played at home, (when they could play in the gym). There were seats along side of the court. They were always full. You had to keep your feet under the seats or some one would be tripped! The stage area would be packed. In 1953, at one game, $113.50 was taken in and the charge was 50¢ for adults and 25¢ for children. Hartwick loved basketball.

Baseball was also played. It was first played in town in 1878 and the team called themselves "Red Stockings." With a history of baseball in town, it's no wonder it was an important sport in the High School. The following played baseball in 1932:

High School		Grades
E. Tabor	catcher	C. Cook
M. Frankewich	pitcher	G. Mathewson
S. Chamberlin	pitcher	S. Frankewich
C. Wilson	1st base	R. Conklin
M. Frankewich	2nd base	G. Mathewson
S. Chamberlin	2nd base	S. Frankewich
S. Peterson	3rd base	A. Schneider
H. Bush	short stop	D. Babcock
H. Clark	right field	H. Irons
M. Hanson	left field	B. Gillette
J. Fields	center field	H. Fear

1944		1945
Frankewich	pitcher	Donald Hughes
Morehouse	catcher	Donald Morehouse
Kenny	1st base	Norman Jensen
Ainslie	short stop	Robert Telfer
Pizer	2nd base	Donald Jones
Carey	3rd base-	Henry Thering
Telfer	2nd base	Melrose Carey
Abbutullo	field position	Neilon Ainslie
Jones	field position	Ivan Risley
M. Risley	field position	
Ivan Risley	field position	

From the 1932 "Hartwickian":

"Our First Annual Athletic Banquet was held on May 6. There were fifty-nine present. Miss S. L. Johnson acted as toast Mistress. The music was furnished by Virginia and Genevieve Melius, which was very nice. Songs were sung and we also had cheers led by our famous cheerleader, Morris Frankewich. Other speakers of the evening were Stanley Chamberlin, Sophie Mele and Rev. Graig. The last of all was Donald E. Wilkes, who presented the Letters to the players of the basketball teams. We hope to have another next year." The Sports editor was Corabelle Bishop. The members of the boys' teams have already been listed.

The girl's team was made up of: Sophie Mele, captain, Helen Ainslie, Elizabeth Aplin, Orral Brown, Helen Dickinson, Deliah Jones, Elsie Robinson, and Margaret Schneider.

"The Oneonta Daily Star" summarized the sports activities in the 50's.

"Oneonta Daily Star" Spring 1957: "Era comes to an end" by Mead Parce:

Last Monday, a young Hartwick school pitcher tossed his high, hard one past enough batters to chalk up a 'no hitter' to win a league champership for his team. Herb Schweitzer, the hurler, who has been one of Hartwick High's stars in football, basketball and baseball this school year. In fact, the name of Schweitzer, has been somewhat a tradition at Hartwick High. Before Herb it was Fran Schweitzer who gained statewide fame as an athlete."

But as of June, there won't be any more Hartwick High School athletics.

The reason next year the High School students of this town will be taken to Cooperstown as part of a consolidation plan.

One of the reasons for the interest in the school's record in Tri-Valley and sectional athletics is that since 1946 Hartwick High's teams in three major sports have managed to earn 12 championships.

Baseball has been the Number one sport in Hartwick since the team has won the championship every year since 1952.

Schweitzer's no hitter capped the season this year and gave them their six straight title.

Six man football, a wide-open game featuring South Western grid style, has been a sport players and fans found to their liking.

In 1952, 53, & 55, Hartwick captured the Tri-Valley title on the basis of an 18 game winning streak. Two of those years, the team was unbeaten and untied.

Basketball, third sport played - produced a championship in 1951, 52, 53 and 55.

Championships started back in the days of Bill Dalrymple and continued through Eldaige St. Peters and D. Ron Schaertl, present coach.

Herb Schweitzer's no hitter, which ended the era was probably the most fitting "bowout," a school could have.

Since 1946, three other hurlers entered Hartwick's Hall of Fame with no hitter games. They are Neil Ainslie, Fran Schweitzer and Ray Polulech.

1952 Undefeated Hartwick High School Football Team—First row, seated, L-R: Lee Beach, Mike Gregory, Fran Schweitzer, Ray Polulech, Frank McGrath, and Chuck Hadley; 2nd row: John Polutech, Bill Bresee, John Henningson, Earl Roberts, Jim Hurtubise, Rich Mistretta, and Coach Bill Dalrymple; 3rd row: Herb Schweitzer—manager, Dick Conklin, Jim Campbell, and Jim McGrath—manager

However no story about Hartwick High is complete without Jim Hamilton, a sports fan, who can name off the heroes and all records, with the quickness of an IBM machine. That's why he has been Hartwick's "number one fan!"

So the winning era of the Hartwick High School ended as the high school students went to Cooperstown Central in 1957.

The last graduates of H.H.S. were: Robert Briscoe, Kenneth Bunn, Patricia Folts, Darlene Gill, Amelia Marion Lyon, James McGrath, Janet Mistretta, John Mott, Roy Nersesian, Barbara Norman, Helen Elizabeth Patterson, Herbert Schweitzer & Charles Wart.

At this time, Hartwick High had football, baseball, Junior and varsity basketball, girls basketball, and cheerleaders. Besides sports they had an active Student Council, a band, chorus, The Oracle Staff who put out a monthly paper -as well as the yearbook, prize speaking and of

The Last Graduates of Hartwick High School

course, the Senior play.

The last high school teachers were: Mr. Dennin, Miss Belding, Mrs. Derr, Mrs. Yule, Miss Telfer, Mr. Schaerth, Mr. Mascimbeni, Mr. Wassell, Mrs. McCarthy, and Mr. Bullock.

The grade school teachers were: Mrs. Laura T. B. Mack, Mrs. Delia Koletnik, Mrs. Betty Tedesco, Mrs. Susie Bunn, Mrs. Agatha Harrington, Mrs. Alger, Mrs. Phyllis Jamieson and Mrs. Bernice Patterson. [18]

Some of the principals were: Mr. Alexander, Mr. Herbert Fister, Mr. John Weinhauer, Mr. Newman Johnson, Mr. Jim Svolos, Mr. Charles Bowler, Mr. Peters, and Mr. Frank Slater. [19]

Twenty years earlier the high school teachers were: Mr. Herbert Slater, Mrs. Ruth Fister, Miss Sally Johnson, Mr. Henry Lottridge, Miss Eleanor Forrestel, Mr. Ashley Strong and the grade teachers were: Miss Linda Snyder, Mrs. Jessie Harrington, Ms. Grace Barnard and Mrs. Cora Bowmaker. [20]

Even though the town was sad at losing their high school, they were grateful that future Hartwick school age students would he able to have a larger choice of courses and, therefore, a better education.

It was a shock when the next year the 7th & 8th grades were taken to C.C.S. The last graduation exercise for the eighth grade was held in the school auditorium (gym) June 18, 1958:

"Music for the Processional and Recessional was played by W. J. Weaver on piano; instrumental selections were by a clarinet sixtette including Linda Grigsby, Barbara Lee, Marilyn Marlette, Carol Mott, Shirley Powers, and Elizabeth Potter.

The address of Welcome was given by Alice Smith; the farewell by Sharon Matteson. Other speakers gave a history of the districts in the Hartwick area, all of which are now closed. Class roll included: Mary Brown, Patricia Campbell, Carolyn Edwards, Phillip Lindroth, Douglas

Last Eighth Grade Class

Matteson, Sharon Matteson, Carol Mott, Robert Murdock, Mary Ellen Norman, Elizabeth Potter, Lawrence Rood, Ruth Rood, Alice Smith and Oakley Whitbeck.

Presentation of awards and diplomas by Robert Duke. The ceremony closed with the Eighth grade singing their original song "Farewell Hartwick School." Ushers were Shirley Powers and Bonnie Folts. A gift was presented to Miss Mary Telfer by the class."[21]

The next year the 7th grade joined the high school students going to Cooperstown.

Some concerned citizens, perhaps, had foreseen that Hartwick was going to be pressured, later on, to join a larger district.

From a clipping in the "Otego Valley News" (Jan. 1940): "Members of the Citizen Committee appointed to further the organization of a Central School in Hartwick and District Superintendent, Mrs. Naomi Bilderbeck were in Albany Jan. 15 filing briefs and petitions with Assemblyman Rapp, chairman of the Joint Legislature Committee on the Education System and Dr. E. R. Van Kleck, Assistant Commissioner of Education. The committee was assured that further consideration and study would be made by both departments."

This seems to have been a 'dead end' but it does show that Hartwick cared about their schools and their future, even back in the 1940's. There were interesting programs and much support for the Hartwick Grade Center.

Every Christmas there was a program put on at the community Hall with Mr. Millen in charge. The Hall was always packed for this entertainment.

Many students remember the gathering of the students in the hall and on the stairs, singing Christmas songs!

During this time the Grade Center had a day reminiscent of the Field Days held earlier, when all the grades played games together and were treated to watermelon by their teachers. [22]

1976 clipping "Grade Center Holds Concert." Hartwick—"On June 14, friends and relatives of the students of the Hartwick Grade Center were treated to concert celebrating Flag Day and America's 200th birthday. The gym decorated with flags depicting the first flag made in 1777 right up to the one we use today.

Mr. Millen, music director did a great job teaching the children songs representing different areas of history throughout our 200 years."

Some of the teachers at the Grade Center were: Laura Mack, Susie Bunn, Betty Tedesco, Kathi Chase, Sharon Matteson, Cora Alger, Mary Telfer, Delia Koletnik, Reggie Palmer, Agatha Telfer Harrington, Patti Banks and George Bouboulis.

Mrs. Bernice Patterson and Mr. David Thorn served as principals.

The last custodians were David Hollister, Ralph Matteson and Ed Utter.

Cafeteria managers, who followed Mrs. Mele were (Mom) Millie Schweitzer and Frances Wayman who served up delicious food with love for all. [23]

Rumors abounded early in 1977 that Cooperstown was going to close the Hartwick Grade Center. A group, "Save Our School" (S. O. S.) was formed and they investigated the possibility of a change in the school districts lines as one way of assuring that the Grade Center would not close. Mrs. Richard Conklin and the rest of the S. O. S. Committee were invited to address the Laurens School board on this issue. Nothing came from this attempt.

Cooperstown School Board had an open meeting, discussing a recent cost study done by the school administrators which showed that the school district could save $107,000 per year by the closing of the Hartwick Grade Center. So it was decided!

"Now it is a fight" the spokesman for the Save Our School Committee, Orrin Higgins said. "We still have an opportunity to give our community its school. [24]

The committee had already got petitions signed, organized marches and had put up posters in all the busy parts of the hamlet. The S. O. S. didn't give up. It was a losing battle and that fall all of our children were bused to C. C. S.

In the early days there were no buses, every one walked, or perhaps rode a horse if there was shelter nearby. In the late 20's or early 30's, one family of children drove a horse from a home in Burlington to Hartwick, put it in a church shed while at school. Some stayed in town with a friend and went home weekends. [23 & 16]

Then came the school bus. First they were horsedrawn. In 1921 District #5 voted to send the children to Hartwick instead of hiring a teacher (the following year they hired a teacher) Ralph Potter contracted to do this. He had to build that bus from specifications. It was a box-like structure on bobsleds for winter and put on wheels for the fall and spring.

Dorthy Manley Weeks wrote about "How the Outlying Kids Got to School" in the "Hartwick Conduit," Jan. 1, 1995 published by Mahlon Clark and describes the bus that took her to school, "I lived 2 ½ miles from school and we had snow and winters similar to the one last winter, only we didn't have snow plows. When I was seven years old, I can remember the truant officer coming and telling my parents we should be in school.

We had no way to get to school. We weren't allowed to walk to school because we would have been buried in the snow or frozen to death in the subzero weather.

I remember my father telling the Officer to take me to school and when school was out, to bring me home. Well, as you know, that didn't worry my father and Shirley Wright (Leonard Wright's father) called Albany and drove out in an old Model "T" Ford and they talked the Board of Education into paying someone to pick up the children and take them to school (H. H. S.).

John Bush ran a farm so he made a small bob sled and covered it with a roof, put seats on both sides of the sled. He carried his can of milk to the creamery and the kids to school. In summer he came with a covered wagon

The snow used to be so deep by Willam Kimmey's farm, he had to go thru the meadow. Sometimes we tipped over and away went the milk! Regardless of the hardships it was all worthwhile. I'm sure we learned more than they do today, and best of all, we developed life long friendships that still endure."

Other districts also had people bringing children to school. Ernestine Tabor Monroe (she lived up by Ferd Thering) remembers Fred Cook taking the children from one district to the Hartwick School. At night they would ride home on the trolley, getting off at Stop # 47. Also the Field District rode the trolley to Hartwick.

District schools had been consolidated with Hartwick # 4, Maples and Field as early as 1915. There were many early "buses."

Mrs. Thelma Phillips in 1940-41 contracted to take the High School students from District # 5 in Hartwick, (at this time she bought a four door Chevrolet for $900). She carried Edwina Manley, Deforest Whitney, Donald and Stanley Phillips. [25]

Another bus driver (this one of the regular yellow Hartwick High Schools) was Harry Perry. He had a garage in the old South Street School house after Clarks Garage moved in after the closing of the South Street School.

The older generation remembers what an exceptional climate for learning was created when home, school, and students were bound together in a secure, stable unit. Perhaps the teacher boarded in the homes of students but she or he was always accessible to the community and students whom she taught. The working conditions were not what they are today but teachers were respected. [26] That respect has to be State Mandated is a sad commentary on our modern

schools, but we are fortunate to have a good Central School in Cooperstown.

Today we have buses taking our Hartwick children to C. C. S. yet the fond memories of our "old" schools remain.

Bibliography:
1. Hartwick Reporter Oct. 6, 1915 "Hartwick Early Settlers"
2. Butterfield Papers
3. Diana Harrington Marlette
4. Families Obituaries
5. S. S. Randall   "History of Education- Common Schools"
6. ClippingOld Potter Scrapbook Pg. 1
7. ClippingOld Potter Scrapbook Pg. 5
8. Clipping Elisabeth L. Curry Scrapbook (owned by Linda Foody
9. ClippingOld Potter Scrapbook Pg.2
10. ClippingOld Potter Scrapbook Pg.3B
11. ClippingOld Potter Scrapbook Pg. 39
12. Clipping Old Potter Scrapbook Pg. 57
13. School publication
14. Hartwick Reporter

By: Frederica Hornbeck

15. Oneonta Star "Program of Christening of New York State Liberty Ship - written by Nadine Phillips
16. Play Program
17. Picture in Historical display in Library
18. Year Book 1937
19. Mrs. Marion Green
20. Year Book 1957
21. Eighth Grade Graduation Program1958 (Carol Goodrich)
22. Mrs. J. Palmer
23. Mrs. Wayman
24. Information from clipping
25. Stanley Phillips
26. Peggy MacGregor

The District School Information was taken from Clerks books, Hilda Augur's notes, and "Schoolhouse John's Otsego."

On left, Hartwick High School, 1936; Row 1: Stanley Fish, Bernard Guilette, Stanley Petewick; Row 2: Joseph Field, Robert Taylor; Row 3: Gordon Mathewson, Dorothy Manley Weeks, Clara Bishop, Ellen Pederson, Nelson Steere; Row 4: Madeline Smith, Rubie Sergent Conklin, Willard Griffin.

Hartwick High School, 9/24/24

Schoolhouse John

Ten years ago John Hall wanted another hobby. Stamp and coin collecting, hunting, fishing, making maple syrup, and nearly 20 years of baseball umpiring were not enough. His wife suggested he already had too many hobbies. John felt he simply needed to specialize in something. Then he came across a photograph of a one-room schoolhouse and has been researching them ever since. "I used to attend one. My interest was immediately sparked," explained Hall, who since has aptly earned the title 'Schoolhouse' John. "The one-room schools were by no means perfect, yet they did offer appealing qualities that can't be found in our modern-day system. Take Charlie, for instance." Hall said. "Charlie is in fifth grade and good in all subjects except math. Well, the teacher passes him because Charlie can still hear fifth grade math while in the sixth grade." Since John acquired that first photograph in 1978, he has collected more than 240 others and determined that 333 one-room school houses once served Otsego County residents. He explains that these single schools are as American as anything. Most children in Europe during the 19th century were apprenticed to trades. Education was reserved for either the rich or gifted. By contrast the school system developed here was very unique. John said. Public education in the New World was introduced in 1642, 12 years after the settlement of Boston. The General Court of Massachusetts ordered that selectmen in every town should have the power to take account of all parents and masters as to their children's education and employment. The selectmen's responsibilities were to see that all children learn to read, were taught to understand the principles of religion, and the capital laws of the country, and finally, to make sure the children were put to some useful work. Nothing was said, however about school. New Amsterdam (New York City) has claimed to have had a public school in 1633, although in a very limited sense. The school was for children of the Dutch Reformed Church and no others. Records show that 14 years later citizens were complaining that no schoolhouse had yet been built. In Otsego County the first schoolhouse was built about 1793 in Cooperstown. Under a plan devised for New York State in 1812 by Jedidiah Peck, schools then began being built two miles apart. Even then, if a child lived more than a mile from school, transportation was supposed to be provided. Peck has been called "The Father of the Common School System." Interestingly enough, Cooperstown founder Judge William Cooper, author James Fenimore Cooper's father, mistakenly caused the arrest and jailing of Peck.

"Another advantage of smaller schools was that the teachers had the aid of the older students to help instruct the younger." John said.

"Because the weekly teaching schedule was divided among each grade, much of the time spent in class was devoted to individual study when your particular grade was not being taught. School was in session through late spring, summer, and autumn. There was no running water in the classes, of course, and through the summer there was a continuous flow of children traveling across the pasture schoolyard for a dipper of cool water from the stream." John continued that in many schools, scripture time came at 4:00 PM. One publication written of old schools makes light of this event, quoting that short verses were liked by the children: "John, your verse," says the teacher. Up pops the boy like a jack-in-the-box, snaps out "Jesus wept," and with a grin drops into his seat. "Pray without ceasing," replied the teacher, searching the Bible to ensure the quote was direct. "Rejoice evermore," chorused the children. Since the schools were so close, graduation cards often read with many last names alike.

Mischievousness arose among these lifelong comrades. "I remember smoke flowing out from every opening in the school except the chimney on one occasion," John snickered. "That's because someone had climbed up on the roof and placed a rock on the chimney outlet."

Early schools were supported partly by subscriptions of the well to do, partly by the rental of lands set aside for this purpose, partly by tuition fees, and partly by taxes. School taxation in Massachusetts became mandatory in 1827. One of New York State's first direct involvement with the education process ordered all schools to group large windows together to provide ample light for studying.

The number of one-room schools in Otsego County increased to their peak about 1875, and then other systems began to emerge. Con-solidation, introduced with an analogy to farming that said we need to fertilize education, began absorbing one-room school districts into one complex. The Hartwick Union School building was an example of consolidation. Seven or eight districts were combined and many children rode to class by train. Hall explained that consolidation was needed to get more educated teachers to more students. More efficient centralization followed shortly after, becoming mandatory in 1938. Nebraska is the only state that has still not centralized. In some counties their children still attend one-room schools.

But the one roomers were built with whatever material was available," John said. "Some were built with cobblestone, field stones, or brick. However, the majority were built of wood. They all had attached woodshed and an outside toilet."

Some of the old buildings have become town halls, fire houses, homes, garages, machine shops, and camps. Many are disintegrating or are completely destroyed. There are some which have been moved. The Thomas Filer stone schoolhouse built in 1820 was completely dismantled, moved, and reassembled in 1944 at the Farmer's Museum in Cooperstown. The dunce cap and blackboard were not replaced in the school, however, because these items were not commonly used until after the civil war.

"You sometimes hit a dead end when searching." said Schoolhouse John. "One building I know of was moved completely to Syracuse. Lord only knows where it is.

Many school districts were named after the prominent family of the area: the Bowers at Bowerstown for instance. One story tells that the Lena schoolhouse in the town of New Lisbon was named after the first name of a former postmistress who operated the Lena post office. Line schools were those built on the border of two townships. Often there would be 40 students taught by one teacher, Hall explained. And often problems were caused because a woman teacher might be only 17 years old and some of her male students would be older. It could be especially unruly at times in these instances and others, when absenteeism could not be controlled. Excuses were not needed by students until 1890. Pay for teachers was always meager. The scale in Westford in 1930 was $10 per month.

Schoolhouse John Hall has filled more than 30 photograph albums with post cards and snap shots of Otsego County schools. He hopes to acquire a photograph of every one, but is sure that this may be impossible. In New Lisbon, for example, he has pictures of 15 of the 16 schools that existed in that district. The one that remains is the Newtown school, which burned to the ground in 1842 and was never rebuilt. In his suspendered trousers and checked flannel shirt Hall grins amicably and says, "That s just me - School House John. You get richer doing what you don't like to do in this world. I'll never be rich."

Most people feel richer just knowing Schoolhouse John. In 1997, the Hartwick Historical Society had a compilation of John's pictures and information on Otsego County schools printed under the title *School House John's Otsego*. John proudly autographed books at a special book signing held at the Kinney Memorial Library and Hartwick Historical Center.

An interview with "Schoolhouse John Hall" by K. O. Wilson

John Hall

Select Schools

There were several Select Schools held in Hartwick. It would appear that these were formed to either give the students more instruction in the primary grades or to prepare the older ones for higher learning. Big families were the rule so overcrowding of the public schools and teachers without training may have contributed to the growth of these schools. They were supported by tuition paid by each student.

In the Butterfield papers we read: "Samuel Morse and wife, recently married, moved into their log cabin on the Hartwick Patent (Christian Hill) in 1793 where Mrs. Morris soon afterwards, opened a private school." This was one of the first, if not the first select school in what was later the town of Hartwick.

The next private school I found was:
May 22 1815   TO THE PUBLIC
"The subscribers respectfully inform the public that they have procured the large white building adjoining the meeting house on Otego Creek, in Hartwick village, in which they design to open a school for young Gentlemen and Ladies. A good Preceptor will be procured to teach Reading, Writing, English, Grammar, Arithmetic, Geography, Latin and Greek, and any other branch of science taught in a private school. They will admit youth from 10 to 25 years of age or older if requested.

Good boarding for any number of scholars at a reduced price.

Terms of tuition
From three to five Dollars
The school will commence on the first Monday in July next.
Levi Beebe
Wm. A Boyd
Daniel Beebe
Sylvanus West
Rev. Henry Chapman, agent"[1]

A clipping in the Aug. 28,1817 Oneonta Herald tells that this school was still open in 1817.

"The young Gentlemen and Ladies Academy will commence Wed. Sept. 10 under the tuition and care of Levi Collins, Clergyman, and late Preceptor of the Academy at Monson (Mass.). All the various branches of Classic and Polite Literature will he taught, due care paid to the morals and manners of the students. Tuition from 3 to 4 dollars per quarter. Good boarding on the most reasonable terms in the bound of the village. It is expected there will be a female preceptoress in needlework and painting as soon as necessary.

Henry Chapman, agent   Aug. 12 1817"

This school was conducted on the second floor of the Thomas Pierce Tavern directly across from the Congregational Church (Presbyterian). This is the school Henry C. Wright attended and it had 40 students the first year. How long the school existed wasn't found but that corner was long known as the "Academy Lot."[2]

The next school I found was opened by E.J. Andrews in the basement of the Methodist Church and in late 1840's Elder Pattengill's school was there and was still there in 1851. [3]

In 1844 after the annual school District # 3, meeting's minutes, we read

"An unincorporated private school has an average attendance of 25, Public school has 58." (Was overcrowding the reason for the private school?)

Oscar Proctor was the Master of the school in the Methodist basement in 1852. [5]

The Presbyterian Church, formerly the Congregational, disbanded at this time and it was fitted for school use. Mr. Proctor moved there in 1853.

A letter of Mrs. Mary Shaul describes Hartwick in 1860— It tells of a select school kept by Henry J. Kellog. This school was in the Presbyterian Church. [6]

In an undated clipping calling attention to the advertisement of the 'Hartwick Hill Select School'

"The eighth term of this school is now in session. The Advantages here offered are sufficient inducement for public patronage. The services of Miss Lucina Barney in the musical Department are secured, positively, for the fall and winter term.

Good board can be obtained during the school week, Five days $1 or rooms furnished for those wishing to board themselves.

Prices per term as usual

Primary	$3.50
Higher English	$4.00
Latin	$5.00
Instrumental Music	$5.00

No extras or incidental expense in this school. A practical male teacher is employed in the primary Department. Pupils received at any time.

H.J. Kellogg, Principal" [7]

Following clippings were found:

Oct. 1870 "A Select School opened in West Hartwick, taught by Hattie Stevens." [8]

1877 "Prof. Thorp opens the second term of his Select School Jan. 2nd. He seems to be giving general satisfaction, which in this community, at least shows he is a workman."

"Prof. Thorp has organized a debating school for the benefit of his pupils."

In 1878, [9] we find two Select Schools in Hartwick.

1878 "The Select School of O.H. Babbitt closed last Friday night."

"Lynn H. Baily, Obituary

Son of Martha & Henry Baily-of 13 summers-The Select School of which Lynn was a member, together with their teacher O.H.Babbitt headed the procession as it slowly wended its way to the cemetery."

1878 "The last term of our Select School opened Monday after a weeks vacation. Mr. Rappleye has shown himself to be a workmen in this department being not only a first class teacher but a young man of Christian integrity who is not ashamed to work for the cause of Christ." [11]

We know this school existed the same time as the public school.

The following was in the same column of the paper:

"Our District school is larger than common"

Freeman's Journal   Nov. 16, 1871

"On Friday evening November 10th in the Baptist Church in Hartwick, occurred a Select School Exhibition under the management of Prof. E. Fayette Smith, a graduate of the class of '71 of Madison University. Though the weather was favorable, the church was filled with anxious listeners.

A school performance of this kind was a rare thing for the people of Hartwick, although the town has seen more years then many of the largest western cities. Hartwick is older than Chicago, Cincinnati, or Columbus – but not so growing or full of enterprise.

The exercises were opened with prayer by G. J. Travis, after which followed singing, recitations, declamations, and dialogues by the lads and young misses of this promising school. Of course there were defects in some cases, but they were comparatively few, on the whole the scholars gave great pleasure to parents and friends, and all interested in the institution, and this closed one of the most interesting exhibitions that we have attended in a long time. The controlling master mind of all was the teacher who has the power of imparting to his pupils, his own enthusiasm and right consentions and moulding minds which otherwise would have been latent."

The last item I found on Select Schools was in 1880:

"Miss. Mary Johnson has opened a Select School for juveniles in this village." [12]

There may have been many more but these are what I found. By this time the public schools had better trained teachers, buildings and all were receiving a better education.

Those that went on to college from the Select Schools were;

John J. Crafts, Union Stephens, Holden Yale, H.C. Wright.

The Select Schools had served their purpose!

By: F.H.

Bibliography

1. clipping in school folder in Hartwick Historical Museum
2. Butterfield Papers
3. Butterfield Papers
4. Butterfield Papers
5. Butterfield Papers
6. Weeks, Pearl "History of Hartwick"
7. Old Potter scrap book
8. Oneonta Herald, (Barb Potter clipping)
9. Old Potter scrapbook   pg.3,17
10. Old Potter scrapbook   pg.4,5
11. Old Potter scrapbook   pg.5
12. Old Potter scrapbook   pg.19

Brookwood School in Toddsville

The Brookwood School

The Brookwood School promotes a love of learning in a community that em braces intellectual curiosity, enthusiasm, and trust. We recognize individual learning styles and foster each child's self-esteem. The Brookwood School uses hands-on activities, experimental learning, and the region's many cultural resources in its endeavor to develop the full potential of each child.

The Brookwood School was formally chartered as a nonprofit independent day school in 1996, but the roots of the school date back to 1982 when the Christian Hill Montessori School for Preschoolers was founded. In 1995, founder Ann Weinke announced her retirement and a group of committed parents came together as a Board of Trustees to ensure the perpetuation of this fine program and to guide the expansion of the school.

The school now enrolls students from Pre K (3 & 4 yr. olds) through sixth grade. The youngest grades begin with Montessori-based, hands-on, interactive learning activities.

These educational threads continue through the upper grades. In small, informal classes, creative dialogue and independent study are emphasized. The curriculum is theme-based and interdisciplinary.

Brookwood is located in the village of Toddsville, approximately three miles from Cooperstown on Route 59. The school is situ- ated on five acres bordered by Oaks Creek. This country setting provides a suitable "lab" for science, wildlife study, and gardening. Year-round outdoor activities include sledding during winter months and soccer, softball, and other sports in spring and fall.

We are a small rural school with students who come from over fifteen communities, including Cooperstown, Cherry Valley, Cobleskill, Edmeston, Franklin, Milford, Oneonta, and Schenevus. At present there are 96 students attending Brookwood.

The parent body at the school is active and involved, making contributions on every level, from offering their talents and services in the classroom, fundraising, and student recruitment. Our families seek a school environment, in which their children are nurtured, where creativity is encouraged and where parent suggestions are valued.

_The three and four year old and kindergarten classes are based on the Montessori Method of education. The curriculum is designed to provide instruction and participation in specialized areas, helping children to develop fine and gross motor skills, aesthetic appreciation, and intellectual ability. Art and music further enrich the learning experience. Classes are child centered; the teacher is the guide and observer overseeing the child's exploration of the world, children learn in a pleasant and stimulating environment with carefully designed age-appropriate materials.

The classrooms are divided into five main activity areas. In practical life, which includes life skill exercises and creative arts projects, students develop organizational skills and become familiar with cognitive order, care of self, and their environment. In the sensorial area students learn to order, classify and describe sensorial impressions. The math activities use manipulatives, so that students may internalize the concepts of numbers, symbols, sequence and operations. The tactile math activities make it easier to memorize pertinent facts. In language arts students engage in many stimulating activities. Using manipulatives students learn to link sound and letter to better express themselves. Children also practice grammar in the context of oral and written expression. Additionally, we read children's literature and perform creative dramatics. In all activities, we encourage self-expression. Finally, children learn about the natural world in Environmental Studies, which combines the study of science and geography. We teach an awareness of global geography and of the many cultures of our world.

The 1 and 2 class has its roots in the Montessori tradition. Children learn in a natural, integrated and imaginative way. We seek to engage each child's interests and talents, in order to develop self-discipline, intellectual curiosity. Teachers are sensitive to each child and work to make each one feel secure and confident. The children have a wide variety of activities to choose from, and these activities are carefully designed to challenge and interest the child. We value each student's abilities and strengths. The program is designed to build on these strengths and to encourage the children to reach new levels.

We utilize manipulatives in every area of education, particularly in reading and mathematics. The incorporation of all senses enables the child to fully internalize what they are learning. We also use the "Explode the Code" series of books for language arts instruction. These books supplement the children's reading instruction. Science and geography are other areas of study on which we focus. The class learns about several continents in depth; they study the people, topography, language, food, history and much more. Science includes experimentation with physical properties, a study of the human body and a unit on dinosaurs, among many others.

The curriculum for grades 3, 4, 5, and 6 reinforces acquired skills while adding a new level of academic challenge. We encourage our students to question and investigate more fully the various subject areas as they take on more demanding projects and learn to apply organization, analysis and study skills. Language arts concentrates on reading, writing and mechanics. The curriculum is rich in children's literature and students acquire an appreciation of reading through exposure to many literary forms. Students learn to observe the rules of proper spelling and grammar as they write and express their thoughts. Our primary math text is "Building Mathematical Thinking," which adheres to the standards of the NCTM (National Council of Teachers of Mathematics). We also use a variety of supplementary materials to allow children to encounter and practice basic skills, problem solving, word problems, and thinking skills.

Manipulatives are often used to help students understand abstract concepts. Social studies are inter-disciplinary and thematic in approach. We take advantage of regional resources to help cultivate a sense of local and global community. Among the skills and concepts covered in the Social Studies curriculum are Mythology, Local History, Communities of Long Ago, Maps and Globes, Governments and Patriotism, The United States, and Geography. A variety of texts, literature, poetry, artwork, and documentaries serve to enhance the Social Studies program.

The goal of our Science curriculum is to create a sense of wonder about the sciences and the natural world. Our approach is theme-based and interdisciplinary, incorporating hands-on and multisensory activities. We use both the indoor and outdoor "laboratories," students learn the steps of scientific inquiry, sensory development, methods of experimentation, data recording, and proper use of science equipment. We cover a number of topics including Nutrition, Astronomy, Weather, Conservation, Physical Science, and Geology.

Computers are in use in all the classrooms from 3 yrs. through 6th grade. In the younger grades children become familiar with the computer through simple math and language activities. The older students can use computers for all of their subject areas, including research and documentation. The internet is available in the 3rd/4th, and 5th/6th grade classrooms, as well as in several central locations for the lower grades. We find this to be a valuable tool for research and communication.

At Brookwood, we recognize the visual arts and music as vital elements in developing the whole person. Children are powerfully affected by storytelling, music, dance, and the visual arts. These disciplines provide unique learning opportunities. In the visual arts a variety of materials and media are introduced at the earliest ages. For 3 year olds through K the emphasis is on creative self-expression and development of basic skills. Projects introduce the children to various media such as paint, collage, clay, and textiles. We also teach age-appropriate drawing. For all grade levels the goal is to develop the skills and understanding necessary for creating original work in order to communicate important ideas and feelings. The higher grades are introduced to art appreciation, history, and an expanded art vocabulary. As much as possible, art projects are integrated with curriculum themes and utilize the rich cultural institutions in the area. Themes such as local architecture, bookmaking, calligraphy, origami, and artwork from other cultures are part of the curriculum.

The music program for the younger children is full of movement and imagination. We encourage the children to develop keen listening and concentration skills, as well as physical coordination and self control. For the higher elementary grades the music curriculum integrates with academic themes where possible and students are exposed to the many diverse musical styles in an effort to encourage them to appreciate and participate in their own creative way. Students learn basic rhythm concepts styles through body movements, hand clapping, listening to different rhythms and playing instruments. The students in 3/4 & 5/6 receive both vocal and instrumental lessons twice a week. There is an ongoing presentation of music from different cultures, including folk songs and their origins, highlighting music history.

French is taught to all of our students two times a week by a certified teacher whose enthusiasm for the language is contagious.

Physical exercise is recognized as an important part of the school day, not only to maintain fitness but also to help students find a healthy outlet for their energy through physical activity. In addition to regular exercise the students receive at daily outdoor recess, the Clark Sports Center in Cooperstown is the site for weekly gym classes for grades K through 6. Three and four year olds end most of their school mornings on the playground, satisfying their love of movement and informal playtime with their classmates. For the elementary classes, during the formal gym period, students engage in exercises and activities, which develop co-ordination and team building skills while demonstrating good sportsmanship.

The goal of the Afterschool Program is to provide an interesting, relaxed afternoon with many choices of activities. Teachers use and model negotiation and conflict resolution techniques to help children to get along with one another. Each week we offer planned art activities around such themes as the seasons, the human body, shapes and colors, and dinosaurs. These projects encourage freedom and creativity and the development of small motor coordination skills. Every effort is made to provide and to introduce a broad variety of appealing books which are read at circle times or by students independently. There are games and outdoor playground time. Children enjoy wonderful opportunities to build friendships, talk, play games, dress up, and play.

Regular calendar events include Harvest Fest, the end of the year play and Grandparent's Day. We also have monthly all school lunch gatherings as well as weekly all school sessions for music and sharing.

Brookwood has a faculty consisting of 20 talented and dedicated individuals. Our teachers average 10 years of teaching experience. Teaching at Brookwood demands an appreciation of the intricacies of learning, the reality of multiple learning styles, a love of young people, and an ability to make use of the "extended campus." In addition, the school embraces the notion that teachers should be offered the freedom to teach and continue their own learning process.

Beginning with the kindergarten classes, the faculty makesuse of the remarkable physical and cultural resources in the area as part of "extended learning." We draw upon such institutions as the New York State Historical Association, TheFarmers' Museum, the Biological Field Station, The Clark Sports Center, the Cooperstown Library and the Discovery Center at SUNY-Oneonta to enrich our theme-based studies. In addition, Lake Otsego, the woodlands, the marsh ecosystem, and Oaks Creek provide valuable resources which help cultivate an appreciation of nature, a sense of stewardship for the environment and responsibility to the community at large.

In classroom discussions and through modeling by the faculty, students are encouraged to accept responsibility for their actions, respect each other's personal beliefs and values, and respect the dignity of each and every individual. When necessary teachers apply creative problem solving and conflict resolution to help students take greater personal responsibility and become better able to communicate their thoughts and feelings.

Students are expected to respect others and their property at all times. Students who steal or deface the property of others, or who intimidate or violate the rights of others, are put on notice. Subsequent offenses can result in disciplinary action, up to and including expulsion.

Brookwood follows a similar schedule to area public schools.

ARC Otsego Hartwick Treatment Center

On October 18, 1978 the Daily Star reported a meeting was held with the Hartwick Business Association and Matthew Goukas. Mr. Goukas is the executive director of the ARC. The plan was to set up a satellite station in the hamlet. A motion was approved with only one dissenting vote, from a member who felt more information was necessary. Mr. Goukas informed what the ARC has planned for the vacant Peter Pumpkin store. He also introduced Joseph Judd who is employed by the ARC and will be the project director of the Hartwick workshop.

The ARC feels that Hartwick is centrally located within Otsego County. As their clients are bussed to and from the facility, it is felt that the shortest time spent in traveling will afford the clients more time for their activities.

The Hartwick workshop would serve about 60 adults, ranging in age from 19 to 65 years of age, who have learning disabilities, physical handicaps, or are mentally retarded. "The goal of this program is to assist the client in preparing for and maintaining a personally self-satisfying lifestyle, and employment either in a sheltered setting or in a regular job in the community.

The ARC representative stated they had 90 percent of their funding and hoped to be in operation by mid-November. They are hoping to purchase the building.

ARC Facility in Hartwick

On October 1, 1979 the ARC held an open house. People who have an interest in the Association's work were invited to attend during the afternoon session when the clients were at their activities or during the evening hours.

Touring the center, one was impressed by the interest of the staff in their work, their enthusiasm and their knowledge of their subject.

The clients who are in the program come from Otsego County towns including Edmeston, New Berlin, Burlington, Burlington Flats, and Garrattsville. All are bussed to the site Monday through Friday for an activity day from 9 AM to 3:30 PM.

The center program aims to help with speech and language, community awareness, arts and crafts, an exercise program, simple music and dancing, kitchen awareness, recreation, self awareness, self expression and good grooming.

As the many years have passed the ARC has stayed around. The hours are Monday through

Friday from 9 AM to 2:45 PM. The program is structured into 4 core areas with 14 to 15 people to a core. Each core room is staffed with an instructor and 2 habilitation aides. The people who attend the program reside at Pathfinder Village, at Family Care Homes administered by the Otsego Regional Center, or with their own families.

HYDE PARK DAY HABILITATION

Hyde Park Day Habilitation is a program of The ARC Otsego. This is the third of three community-based day programs. It is located at 4861 State Highway 28 Suite 3, Cooperstown, New York 13326. With the onset of the Community Based Waiver Program set forth by the State of New York in 1995, the ARC Otsego developed a certified program to serve approximately 17 individuals with developmental disabilities not to exceed 15 people on any given day. The program runs 8:30 am until 2:30 PM daily.

The program opened on March 31, 1999 with a total of six staff. Cindy Carr, Site Coor-

The second annual Hartwick ARC Supergames opened with a flag ceremoney and music by the Morris Central School Band. In the background are members of the South Kortright Boys School Drum Corps.

dinator, oversees the program. Habilitation Assistants include Brenda Madison, Cathy Belrose, Christopher Dutcher, and Susan Flight. The Individual Program Coordinator is Heidi Slentz. Since the beginning of the

Linda Weidner, a member of the Cooperstown Central School Athletic Association, helps a client of the Hartwick Center maneuver through tires during the ARC Supergames. Miss Weidner was one of ten volunteers from the Cooperstown school who spent the day helping the clients participate in the games.

program only two staff have resigned and new people were hired.

The focus of the program is to provide individuals with a program that promotes individualism, inclusion, independence, and productivity. Activities include volunteering in the community, shopping excursions, touring local events and museums, coffee and current events, baking, group relaxation techniques, sign language skills, etc. The focus of the program is to have each individual achieve his or her own desired dreams.

By: Barbara Potter

Material from:
The ARC Otsego
The Oneonta Star
Heidi Slentz

Farming

Settlers with oxen and cart and their few possessions followed a rough path through the forest from the Mohawk River guided by the trail blazed through Cherry Valley by the Winsors and Field brothers who had arrived a month earlier. The Fields were delayed for some weeks in the pest house to be nursed with small-pox. The patent of Hartwick was valleys and hills of unbroken forest for miles. Mrs. Rhodes Fry, barefoot with babe in arms across streams and swamp, had been several weeks on the trail from New England beside her husband and cart. When they reached their destination a short way west of Fields darkness had fallen on a cabin still without a door.

A mile west was a neighbor they were yet to meet. James Butterfield survived the Cherry Valley Massacre and torture by Indians to be turned over to British at Fort Niagara. Following hostilities he settled on several acres of land on the northwest part of Hartwick land by Otego Creek. He built the inn painted white in 1792. It was said to be the first white house west of Albany. This for some time was temporary residence for new settlers.

Men came into the forest on foot a year or more before the move with axe and provisions for camping. Brush was cut and many trees felled in windrows to dry for burning the following year. Neighbors some times helped. Gathering charred remains of trunks for the second burning was a dirty disagreeable job. Ashes were care-fully gathered, leached and boiled into pot-ash. Ashes and these black bricks could be sold to the asheries of Samuel Waley (below Weeks farm) or to Joseph Holden at Sodom Point (South Hartwick). These were heated in the furnaces to high temperature to remove impurities to form Pearl Ash. Six hundred bushel of ash would make a ton of pearl ash worth as much as three hundred dollars in Montreal. The product was used in fertilizer, soap, bleach manufacture, and baking powder. There was demand in Europe for its chemical use until potash mines developed in Germany. This and maple sugar were about the only source of cash.

An alternative to burning was the girtling of trees that were left to die. These blazing torches were a familiar scene in the new land. A difficulty was the decayed parts falling on the crop beneath.

Every family had a patch of flax for the fiber woven into linen. Burned over soil was free of weeds. In division of labor children with their small feet could weed between plants.

Indian corn, beans, gourds, pumpkin, squash and grain were usual crops of the pioneer. Plots were shaded and wheat was affected with smut and rust. Rye remained the flour in addition to corn meal for the mainstay against hunger until the white flour of wheat became available from the Erie Canal.

Early mills were at such distance that it was too time consuming to leave, so most grinding had to be done with the home mortar and pestle. Harvesting was first done by sickle but a scythe with fingers to gather the stalk came into use. The cradle came into universal use. A good man followed by a man to tie bundles could reap four acres in a day.

Early threshing was done by animals treading on stalks placed on the floor. More common during our period were men handling flails. They beat out grain from the plant heads on the threshing floor. When the Badger endless belt was manufactured in Fly Creek, they were put to use to power a mechanical thresher.

Threshing by Horsepower 1898-1900 on Farm of George Chapman, Wileytown now Hartwick Road. From Back: unknown, unknown, Howard Chapman, Alvin Chapman, Arthur Eldred, Duane Eldred, Alvin Irons, George Chapman

Individuals owning a thresher followed a route among neighbors job by job. This was hard, dirty work requiring several men, so neighbors followed the route from farm to farm until all was finished. The host farmer always fed the work crew when they came to his place so this became a big chore for women of the house. When bad weather hit the season was extended by weeks. Lucky was the man who got his threshed first; but someone had to be last. With such an arrangement many bundles were stacked or stored in the barn until their turn would come. With dust and mold, wild-flax, paintbrush and thistles, air space behind

the machine was dark with all forms of these materials. This was a much-dreaded place to be, and some refused the spot while working for some one else. Owners of the machines charged by the bushel of grain coming from the chute.

Many farmers grew buckwheat as a cash crop. The grain will grow on the poorest of soil, requiring a short growing season. If seeded as late as July 1, a harvest can usually be made before frost. The stalks are tender to low temperatures. Because of the short season requirement, buckwheat could be substituted for failure of corn, oats or wheat. It was an uncertain crop and about the most yield that could be expected was around twenty bushels per acre. If extreme drought occurred at bloom there would much blasting and a lowered yield. The fragrant blooms were the source of strongly flavored dark honey. Buckwheat flour from mills in Hartwick and Mt. Vision were sold to local stores for griddlecakes.

Mudge Saw and Gristmill (later owned by Ainslie) was along Otego Creek in Peth (Hartwick). It was across from Williams foundry on the west and north of cheese-box factory by the bridge. A dyke of water for the mill fed from a dam above the North Street Bridge.

After flailing, grain was tossed into the air with a winnowing basket to clear away chaff and dirt. More cleaning was done by pouring from bucket to bucket in a breeze. A new patented fanning mill made cleaning much easier.

Settlers came with extra special skills to provide income besides farming. Seth Wright built the first barn below the village in 1792. Nathan Davidson purchased 200 acres along Susquehanna on the east side of the patent. Many preferred the high ground because of more ease in clearing and less danger of Ague (fever). Elms along the valley were cleared with difficulty by Davidson in exchange for his skill as a blacksmith. One year he made a thousand pounds of maple sugar from trees in front of the house. Settlers without benefit of modern spiles and buckets gouged channels about the trunk and guided the flowing sap into hollowed out log troughs. Slashing today may kill a tree; for them a weed to eradicate.

"Poverty was the greatest discouragement of the people. I erected a storehouse, during the winter filled it with large quantities of grain purchased in distant places. I procured credit for a large quantity of sugar kettles, which we conveyed as best we could, sometimes by partial roads on sleighs and sometimes on ice. By this means I established potash works among the settlers and made them debtors for their bread and laboring utensils. I also gave credit for their maple-sugar and potash, at a price that would bear transportation, and the first year after adoption of this plan, I collected in one mass forty-three hogsheads of sugar and three hundred barrels of potash, worth nine thousand dollars. This kept the people together and at home so the country soon assumed a new face" (Cooper).

In our new freedom following the War of Independence, men of the new Republic became obsessed with a plan to supply the world with sugar derived from the maple tree. In 1791, Gerritt Boon, a sugar refiner, purchased 265 acres near the present Cady farm as an extensive experiment in production of maple sugar. With the purchase of Louisiana, land became available for production of cane sugar. The idea of mass production of maple sugar declined.

On the cleared living site, cabins and sheds were of logs flattened on two sides and notched together at corners. With logs felled & ready a "bee" of neighbors had the dwelling assembled in forty-eight hours.

Early structures were covered with bark or shakes. As more frame buildings appeared, some men turned to making a few bunches of shingles for income. Window glass was a luxury in early homes. The panes were small and contained ripples. Oiled papers were used to some extent, or windows consisted of simple openings in the wall. Tallow candles or whale-oil lamps were used, but these were scarce until later. Great fireplaces supplied heat for cooking but couldn't keep the place warm in severe weather. Cooking utensils had long legs to support them over the coals. Pots were hung from cranes above the fire. After they became more established, large built-in ovens were used for baking.

In 1823, tin ovens began to replace brick ovens. Temperature of the tin oven was determined by distance from the fire.

Tea and coffee were hard to get. Substitutes were made of various roots and bark.

Flint and steel from the family musket was the main method of starting flame, or coals were brought several miles from home of a neighbor.

Albany was the chief market for goods and livestock and as the settlement grew so did hauling of products to and from the city. For several years roads and trails were without improvements and cattle and turkeys were driven to market on foot. Soon drovers worked at the occupation. People traveled by foot and on horses as they became more available and women became expert horsemen.

Grain was a bulky product to market in the beginning. Many distilleries sprang up to produce a more marketable product. There were

Seth Wright Barn, 1st in South Hartwick, 1790

seven stills within three-quarters of a mile in town before mills and churches were erected. By 1820, Hartwick had more distilleries than any other town in the county.

The "english" barn of New England and Britain became common in Hartwick.

This has a drive-in on one side perpendicular to the roof and roof line. The earliest had cattle on one side with a scaffold mow above. Above the drive-in is a storage scaffold for grain. A

Sheri Irving Barn, Christian Hill

mow area was the other side of the drive.

Sheds had shelter for sheep and oxen. Pigs had a separate house or were allowed to run at large. Horses were uncommon at the time or were of light draft.

By 1830, as more buildings were framed a boss carpenter would determine the type of building framing members.

Detail of Framing: Note the Complex Joinery

Timber length logs were often hewed on the spot. Braces, girts and outside sheathing were cut on the up and down saw powered by water. They were slow, cutting only on the down-stroke. This left a cross kurf across the board. This and hew

marks on timbers are marks of the age. A thousand feet of lumber in a day (if water held out) was a good day's work. These are some times called "up today, down tomorrow." A study of these old structures reveals ingenious varying joinery of family carpenters.

Once the parts were assembled and a trial of joint assembly completed, invitations were sent around for neighbors on the appointed day to raise the assembled frame under directions of the master carpenter. With this raising, the barn went up from foundation to finished rafter within a few hours. After the building was up and the last peg driven all took off and swung their hats and gave a cheer. Often there was hard drinking and many went away drunk.

Raising the Frame by a "BEE" of Neighbors was a Social Occasion

Breeds as we know them had not been developed for a special purpose. They were more hardy to survive the browse for survival on the frontier. Sheep were small and would produce three pounds of wool. Old breeds are preserved in some areas by a breed survival trust. The red Devon from that area of England was favored as oxen for their agility and hardiness. Some Merino sheep noted for fine wool were imported from Spain in the 1820's. The Ainslie, Potter, Loughs brought the Cheviot from Scotland to Scotch Hill, north of Hartwick at a time of improvement. They formed The Cheviot Sheep

Society of America. A few years back John Curry of White House had the "GOLDEN FLOCK" of America. For more than fifty years his entries were exhibited at the New State Fair in Syracuse.

By 1840 Hartwick had more sheep than any other town. Some farmers received as much as two thousand dollars for wool. The census in 1835 showed 215,149 sheep.

Sheep were washed and sheared, and wool picked by the family by hand in the evening. The fleece was greased and broke in soap and water, carded in rolls by hand and spun. All cloth in the home was made by hand and every home had a great wheel, flax wheel and loom. As families became established, young spin girls were employed as an extra part of the home. A woman could spin forty to sixty knots of yarn from dawn to dusk. Mills for carding and fulling soon replaced some of the work of the home.

In 1806 a mill opened in Toddsville by Todd and Steere, one of eight operating in Otsego County. A new mill opened at Hope Factory (Index) and Clintonville. Each employed several hundred people. Cotton bales were hauled from river ports at Catskill to factories by wagon and the completed product shipped in the same manner.

Early cotton factories did no weaving. Union Factory in Toddsville sent all its yarn into the country to be woven on private family looms. Yarn was carried out into the country and brought back by spinsters on horseback, bound on behind them. A woolen mill was operated by Rockwell in Sodom Point (South Hartwick) near the Lippitt Sawmill. In 1835, Toddsville produced 540,000 yards, Crockets factory in South Hartwick 260,000 yards and Hope Factory 500,000 yards of cloth.

Hartwick in 1835: 2 grist mills, 12 sawmills, 1 oil mill, 3 fulling mills, 2 cotton mills, 1 iron works, 1 distillery, 2 asheries, 3 tanneries, 2 card-ing mills, 1 triphammer, 15 school districts, 1 church, 4 stores, 35 dwellings.

Tow cloth could be made from coarse fibers in the hetchel for toweling and bedding. Flax is less adapted to machine processing than other fibers and with the coming of cotton mills in early 1800 weaving linen was disappearing. Processing of flaxseed into linseed oil became an important by product of the plant. The resulting linseed meal is an excellent feed along with grain for livestock.

Rufus Peters established an oil mill along Otego Creek across from Murdock farm in 1813. In 1840 few buildings received paint in town and people in Laurens would say "Live in Peth and starve to death" Homes commenced to be painted yellow.

Jonathan Newman, soldier of the Revolution came to Springfield and taught there. He was one of two circuit riders appointed to the Otsego circuit. This was a four hundred-mile long trip extending from Fort Plain down the Susquehanna. The round was made in a month with service for each class in a community once in two weeks. He was on this route and another until 1799.

Newman negotiated with J. C. Hartwick to come to the patent. In 1792 he leased to Jonathan and his brother Ezekial each a farm on the confluence of Oaks Creek and the Susquehanna. Hartwick was not clear on boundaries and found the site had a prior claim. He leased the Newmans 100 acres each in lot 14, a short mile south of Hartwick village and extending a mile from Otego Creek. (David Ward farm and house on corner of Stewart Eldred road). Here Jonathan lived until his death in 1828. He is buried in the old Hartwick cemetery. On his headstone is carved "12 years as itinerant and 17 as local preacher in Methodist Episcopal Church." The inscription does

Harrington's Tin Shop

not explain 12 years service in Christian Hill Church.

In 1810 Lyman Harrington had a tin shop located where the fire house stands that controlled seven wagons that traveled regularly into several adjoining states as well as his own. Progressive tinners would use this means to dispose of their wares. Formerly the peddlers cart was almost exclusively tin-ware. Soon they began to carry pins, needles, scissors, combs, buttons, small hardware and most any item that would yield a return. They would barter for any item that would sell. Linen rags were sold to the paper mill in Toddsville.

During the early years our farmers raised an acre of early flint type state corn (Indian corn) for meal and for fattening animals to butcher. In an area less susceptible to late and early frosts the well-harrowed ground was marked with team for planting. Marks were three feet apart across the field and then marked at a right angle in the other direction so hills on each corner of the square could receive a cultivator in each direction. A mixture of hen manure and phosphate and four kernels were dropped in each hill. If our young hands were too small we were given a large iron spoon for the task. Several cultivations and hoeing were necessary. When kernels commenced to harden after frost, stalks were cut with a sickle and tied into shocks to stand. Sometimes in the fall ploughed shocks were shifted to the side. When fall work slacked off, bunches of stalks were drawn to the upper barn floor for husking. When larger fields were planted neighbors were invited to a "husking."

Those who found a red ear could kiss the girl of choice. A few choice ears with straight rows extending well to the end were braided together and hung on the rafters for seed. Cows were fed corn meal to fatten them for slaughter. Hogs for butchering received corn with whey from the cheese factory.

Hops, the chief flavor ingredient of beer and ale, were introduced as a crop around 1820. The crop had a spectacular growth and by 1830 two-thirds of production was within a few miles radius of Cooperstown. Practically everyone went into the business and New York State grew more hops than any other region of the world until 1910. This was one of the most fascinating and speculative crops in this country. Fortunes were made and lost in a matter of a year or two and the social pattern of some communities were changed. James Clark at "Hop City" south of Cooperstown was the largest producer. Farms about Hartwick had a few acres that were harvested with help of neighbors. It was a time when a young man could earn a little spending money. It was the one cash crop for Gorden Pierce to finally pay off the mortgage.

Early settlers kept a family cow for milk, butter, and cheese. Their shingles, butter, tow-cloth, flaxseed and the like were exchanged for goods, since cash was a scarce commodity. Mills issued script that could be redeemed at the company store for goods. The gristmill kept some grain in exchange for service just as the tanner kept part of the leather from his processing.

From this leather the boot maker traveled the "whipping the cat." There was one size for each group of people with no left or rights. A fit was established by weather and wear.

In 1830 some residents (such as the Schneider

farm) had special buildings for cheese and butter. In a few years this progressed to creameries and cheese factories like one in Hartwick village, Raney factory above town and White House. They were run as cooperative neighborhood enterprises until the rail line made possible new markets for raw milk around 1900. Forty-quart cans of milk were picked up from platforms and delivered to International Milk Company in Cooperstown. This plant later sold to Nestles Food Company and later Dairymen's League.

Milk, like other food prices, is dependent on supply and demand, Demand remains more stable than supply, so with a good price the market becomes flooded and price return drops. Costs remain high so farmers are caught in the squeeze. During these times, some milk was returned without cause with much aggravation to shippers. In 1919 farmers organized the first great milk strike. For a short time milk was processed at home. With no settlement in sight milk was contracted with a creamery at Phoenix. Producers alternated with teams to make deliveries. Receipts to the creamery were not satisfactory so the old cheese factory at White House returned to use. We delivered in large shipping cans and picked up some of the whey byproduct to be fed out at home. Cheeses were stored on racks in a room above the processing until a buyer was contacted. The strike lasted for months and farmers narrowly survived the action. A cooperative that formed was always reluctant to resort to another strike.

Contracts were signed to form Dairymen's League Cooperative with a guarantee to accept all milk delivered. A small deduction per hundred was assessed from the check to capitalize the venture.

At the end of each year, part of the Certificate of Indebtedness was paid off at six- percent in-

terest. In addition to purchase of the plant in Cooperstown other plants were purchased to process milk not used in fluid form. During flush production, manufactured milk yielded lower return and we received a blend price. Strikes yield short-term benefits. The solution seems to be a quota system based on demand such as Canadian farmers adopted.

Cans of evening milk had to be cooled to at least fifty degrees to be accepted. Ours was cooled part of the year by cans of milk set in a trough with cold spring water flowing through. During hot months of summer, ice from the storage needed to be added to the tank. Every one had ice storage of some sort to preserve ice with

Hiding in the Leaves, Nelson Mclean, John A. Mott, Howard Toombs

insulation of sawdust between cakes. Ice was cut from near bodies of water in mid-February when it had gained in thickness. Will Weeks sold cut cakes from his pond near Otego creek. Several hundred cakes were stored to carry through the summer.

Times on the farm have changed from the time you could send any man into a field for work. New machines are more valuable than the old farm. A friend in town spoke of the time when he and other men went to the field with Grandfather Mott at sun-up with dew on the grass to scythe mow until mid-day. The man's worth was determined by his ability to lead or follow the pack. Dried stems were hand raked and bunched to pitch on the wagon rack. The most skilled hand was given the job to load with responsibility to keep all in place on steep side-hill. He did the pitch-off into a mow, since he knew how the load was built. Early barn plates were low for the pitch-in.

Dump Rake used to gather the hay into bunches.

After the system of hay track at the peak was installed larger barns and bay space was added.

We had a horse mower and dump-rake like our neighbor Bert Bristol. Mother and I and my sister rode miles on that rake making windrows to be bunched and pitched on. We were frugal for the harvest and re-raked many scatterings. We were the first at White House area to have a hay loader that had revolving slats to raise a windrow on the rear of the wagon. My job was to drive the team for the process. I had difficulty slowing the tough-bitted mules so not to bury the man loading.

In the barn a special harpoon hayfork was inserted into the load for conveying into the mow with a series of rope and pulleys. The fork load was pulled by horse team to a rail

car at the peak above the wagon and slid along above the mow. This when tripped

This later day threshing crew used steam power instead of horsepower.

fell below and was distributed and tramped. This was a tiring job pulling the tangle apart, especially as we neared the roof in hot July weather. Sweat ran in streams and we consumed gallons of ice-tea. Horse team driven by mother and the younger family drew up hay. There was work for all. When mows were filled often outside stacks were made.

Machines for threshing came early to our valley and neighbors went from farm to farm to help each other. Grain contained dust and shucks that were cleaned out by tossing into the air in a cross draft of the open doors; and further cleaned by slow pouring from

Grigsby combining on Mott farm.

bucket to bucket in strong wind. Soon the hand cranked fanning mill shortened the cleaning. During a much later time Mr. Grigsby of South Hartwick did the job for me with his field combine on a field of oats.

Our settlers were quite self-sufficient in providing food and shelter. Barns and outbuildings were simple for immediate needs. As several mills were built along streams and people became employed a market evolved for expanded barn and crops. With improved transportation creameries and cheese factories were built; and with the coming of rail lines we had a city market. Plants developed to handle the forty-quart cans of milk for down-city use. Dairy farming has become big business with hundreds of milk

Jerry Woods freestall barn.

animals and their replacements; large acreage of corn and other roughage.

Jerry Wood in South Hartwick is an example in contrast with the first barn in town by Seth Wright in 1792 and the freestall barn where each cow can find her stall in loose housing.

At milking time they go to the new parlor in the old barn to be grain fed and milked sixteen head at a time. Many cows can be milked in an hour this way in contrast to the old way of sitting under an animal for a long time.

Calves grow up in sanitary individual huts and older heifers have their own housing.

Calf huts

Large tankers make direct pick-up from the storage for transit to points of market.

By: John Mott

Information for this article has come from:

Jared Van Wagner "Age of Homespun"
Huntington Papers
Cooper Accounts
Roy Butterfield
Barns of New England by John A. Mott
Research of Darwin Kelsey – Old Sturbridge Village
Feeds and Feeding by Merric Olt
John A. Mott
"King Hop" by John A. Mott

The tractor in the foreground was symbolic of changing time in farming as it begin replacing our team Kit and Topsy on the hay wagon as horse power in the new age. My father provided a trial in plowing the field between two makes of tractors: a kid gloved smooth talking salesman for McCormick Deering and a field representative of John Deere for William Ainslie. The results were not even a close decision.

The new tractor Model D could be started by opening pet-cocks on each cylinder that were primed with gasoline, the gas line turned on and the engine cranked by a turn of the fly wheel. As the machine caught and started to pop with the characteristic of that make, the cocks closed. When the engine was warm the fuel line was switched to the kerosene tank. Use of this cheaper fuel was an important advantage of economy. With 27 HP on the belt and 15 HP for draft, we had more than sufficient power. On the up-grade pull the spade lugs on the wheels would spin us down before rubber tires came into common use, so we could find more use in our operations.

Hartwick Dairy Industry

The business of making butter and cheese was very important to Hartwick's early farmers. As most of the farms were small the local cheese factory or creamery gave the farmers a way to make a living with their excess milk.

In 1894 H. S. Bradley reported to the Otsego Co. Farmers and Dairy Association that: "The town of Hartwick has put on the market from their factories over 515,946 lbs. of butter and cheese. Also add to this a large number of farmers who do not go to the cheese and butter factories, but manufacture their own goods to supply special customers of their own, to say nothing of the large quantities shipped by patrons prior and subsequent to the factory season."

He further reported, "A local cheese-box manufacturer has turned out nearly 30,000 boxes the past season."

Mr. Bradley added, "to reach the market all of Hartwick's freight has to be carted to Richfield Springs, Cooperstown, or Oneonta. Had we the advantage of a through line of railroad our freight costs would be saved." This commentary was six years before the trolley line came through Hartwick.

A Hartwick news item in Feb. 1878 gave the following accounts. "P. Postel, of this village is doing quite an extensive business in the butter trade. Most of the shipments are made to Savannah, Ga."

Jan. 27, 1879 - P. Postel has shipped from this village to Savannah, Ga. this past season about 70,000 lbs. of butter for which he has paid the farmer cash at the market price."

Feb. 26, 1879 – P. Postel who has for the past two years located in this village, and has bought most of the butter shipped from this place, has recently gone to his home in Savannah, Ga. We are sorry to have Mr. P. leave our community, as he was the medium through which many hundreds of dollars came to our businessmen.

The following also appeared in the newspaper. May 28, 1878 –"Randall Arnold is doing a staying business at the cheese factory, running as high as 5,500 pounds of milk daily. Morris Brothers of Oneonta have engaged the cheese for the season. Randall makes number one cheese."

June 18, 1878 – "Patronage at the cheese factory is still increasing. An extra vat and press have become necessary. About 6,300 pounds of milk received daily, turning out 14 cheeses of 50 pounds each. Cheese in this factory commands the highest in market."

This factory was located on the north side of Main Street in back of what is now the Hartwick Market.

In the late 1890's butter and cheese factories proliferated in New York State especially in the Central New York area. Factories were often located on cross roads to accommodate as many farmers as possible in that area.

Hartwick had four cheese factories operating

in 1899. A half-mile above the village on what is now Rte 205 was a cheese factory run by the Rainey family. The factory was a large red building on a knoll east of the road. The building contained rooms for making cheese, weighing platform, cheese storage rooms, as well as living accommodations for the cheese maker and family. Originally known as the Rainey Factory it later was called the Hartwick Creamery. About 1920, Carrie Rainey Sill sold the factory building and premises to Wm. Weeks, and the factory was abandoned.

About two miles further north of the village was the White House Cheese Factory. Located on the crossroads, across from the White House, the factory was operated by Delos Lamb. It was in service as late as 1921, and was the last cheese factory to operate in the Town of Hartwick.

Both the White House and the Rainey factories were torn down in 1931 when State Route 205 was built.

A man by the name of Major Root from Gilbertsville owned 10 cheese factories in Otsego County, 2 of these were located in the town of Hartwick. One was the Hinman Hollow Factory. This was on the crossroads of what is now Co. Rte. 45, and Sweet Hill and Stevens Road. Thomas Millard operated the factory for many years, and lived in the house across the road. The house still stands.

Another C. P. Root factory was the South Hartwick factory, and was located at the foot of Bunn Hill on Pleasant Valley side. This was operated by Jon Allen and was sometimes called the Allen Factory. In later years it was operated by Andrew Gregory.

White House Cheese Factory

Rob Stohler delivering milk to White House Cheese Factory

MONTHLY STATEMENT.

M *F. S. Fields*

IN ACCOUNT WITH

C. P. ROOT,

MANUFACTURER OF

BUTTER AND CHEESE

For the Month of Oct   1897
So Hartwick   FACTORY

Average test your Milk,	
Pounds Milk delivered by you during month	2976
Pounds Fat delivered by you during month	
Whole number pounds Milk this dividend,	
Whole number pounds Fat this dividend,	
Whole number pounds Cheese,	
Number pounds Milk to one pound Cheese,	
Number pounds Butter to one pound Fat,	
Whole number pounds Butter,	
Total Money Received for Cheese this dividend, $	
Total Money Received for Butter this dividend,	
Total Expenses (for manufacturing and furnishing this dividend,	
Total Money to be divided,	
Average ratio per 100 pounds Milk,	60
Net price per pound Fat,	
Dividend,	17.86
Extras, 2¾" chen 9	25
Check,	17.61

In the 1890's, Morell Smith recorded in his diaries that he drew loads of cheese from the South Hartwick Factory as often as weekly to Oneonta, to be shipped to Albany.

With the opening of the trolley line in 1901 local dairy products began to be shipped from the Hartwick depot.

In 1902, F. H. Mead, a butter buyer, placed an ad in the Hartwick Voice for 50 tubs of butter on Saturday of each week for shipment to New York and Albany. Dorr Gardner's store on Main Street to be the central depot for gathering the butter for shipment.

Another news item tells that Meads shipped 79 cases of eggs by the freight line, butter is in great demand, and Meads wants more producers.

It seems that the arrival of the trolley line spelled the decline of cheese factories. Farmers now had a way to get their milk products to a larger market faster. However farmers soon faced a new problem. The big milk dealers completely controlled the market and the price paid for milk. The farmers had no guarantee their milk would be accepted. Milk was returned on the slightest pretext. The milk companies had a monopoly, and the farmers were faced with an impossible situation.

The farmers banded together and formed the Dairymen's League. By forming the League the farmers began to have a little leverage in controlling the situation.

On Sept. 24, 1920 the Otsego Farmer featured this headline—"Milk War Close To Home." The farmers, once organized, fixed the price of milk. This action threatened the dealers' monopoly, and they refused to pay the League's price. Nestle's Food Co. of Cooperstown and Bordens announced that as of Oct.1, 1920 they did not care to buy milk.

This action on the milk dealers part caused the Dairymen's League to look into the farmers pooling their milk together. This was the first step they took in getting control of marketing their own product as a group and to build their own milk plants.

The Hartwick Dairymen's League Plant

About 1929 and 1930 the League built two milk plants in the area. The first was built in Mt. Vision followed by the one in Hartwick.

Although these buildings were often referred to as creameries, neither butter nor cheese was manufactured. Rather these were gathering places for fluid milk that was shipped to New York and New Jersey. Both milk plants were built on the trolley line for rapid transport of fluid milk to market, however this was not many years before the decline of the trolley, and milk was soon sent to the cities by tankers.

The Dairymen's League gave farmers more control of their product, but they lived in dread of the city milk inspectors, who had the capability of having them shut out of the milk plant for whatever problem they might find. The inspectors were extremely critical of the way farmers handled the milk, and of their sanitary and cooling practices.

Frank Stewart worked at the Hartwick plant for 8 years. He had previously worked at the Richfield Creamery. He became the Plant Manager in Hartwick; as such he was also the local inspector. The following is his description of the steps involved in readying the milk for shipment.

Chilling milk as it flows over tubes of brine

Checking milk as it arrived at plant

When the milk reached the plant, it was first checked for odors, even tasted if necessary. The temperature of the milk was also checked. It was then dumped into a big vat and weighed, then sampled for butterfat content. Then smears were taken for bacteria, which was the result of poor cooling. Once a month milk was tested for sediment. A sample was obtained by a long pump that reached to the bottom of the can.

The milk was then cooled immediately to about 38 degrees by being pumped through a big cooler. The cooler had tubes of brine that were near zero or a little above. The milk was run over these tubes, and quickly chilled. Care had to be taken not to freeze the milk. The chilled milk was pumped into milk tankers, and shipped to New York or New Jersey.

The cans were thoroughly washed with caustic soap, steamed and dried. Each farmers cans were numbered, and the clean cans were always returned to the same farmer. If a can of milk hadn't passed inspection it was tagged and returned.

Some farmers delivered their own milk to the plant, or they might contract with a hauler. In the 1930's Gilbert Marlette hauled milk from South Hartwick. Howard Marlette remembers his father had a 1929 Brockway truck for hauling, and later a 1931 Ford. For people who can't remember those days, farmers had a milk stand by the road, and would have their ten-gallon cans of milk on the stand ready for pickup according to the haulers schedule. Mr. Marlette had a double route, first picking up milk on Rte 205, delivering to the plant, dropping off the clean cans on his return trip, then picking up for the farmers on Co. Rte 11.

Frank Stewart said that later on South Hartwick farmers went more to Jersey cows in their dairies which gave their milk a high butterfat content. This rich milk was sent to the Mt. Vision plant and shipped out in 55-gallon cans that went to New Jersey for the cheese and butter market.

Milk Trucks Delivering Milk to Plant

A living could be made by being a milk hauler, and routes were sometimes bought and sold.

Mr. Stewart mentioned some of the routes, and the names of some of the haulers. Howard Harrington drew out of Blue-Jay Hollow and New Lisbon. Also Albert Carkees drew from that vicinity. Bill Skubitz did Rt. 205, and loads came out of Hinman Hollow and off Scotch Hill. A load came from Whigs Corners drawn by Claude Bliss. The Wart Brothers drew from Christian Hill, Frank said they were just kids at the time. Their father, Walter Wart, had the oldest League membership in Hartwick at that time.

Frank also said that the haulers were an accommodating group, and some almost daily picked up groceries, a bag of chicken feed, or mailed a letter for someone on their route.

During the 1930's, 40's and 50's the plant was a busy place. The clanking of cans being loaded and unloaded was a familiar sound.

Things began to change as farmers installed pipelines and bulk tanks, and more and more tankers went directly to the farms for pickup.

The need for the milk plant diminished, and the plant closed in 1962.

The Hartwick Town Board submitted a bid of $2500.00 for the Dairymens League building, and the bid was accepted. Thus the town acquired the property with it's excellent well.

The building stood idle until 1976, when Hartwick's Town Barn burned, at which time the building and property were pressed into service as a temporary Town Barn. It was used by the town until the new highway buildings were built in 1980.

The building became derelict and the Town Board began to talk of tearing it down. Hartwick Historical Society made an effort to acquire the building for storage, and to house large pieces the Society might acquire. The Society also felt the building had great possibilities as a place for some Community Activities, for example a Farmers Market.

Desiring to make certain that the well on the property, which is now an important part of the village water supply, be protected, the Town Board made the decision to not allow any use of the building. It is currently slated for demolition.

As for the dairy industry in the town of Hartwick, this is the sobering fact, at the close of the year of 2001 there are less than ten farmers actively operating dairy farms.

By: Nadine Phillips

Information gathered from the following sources:

Pioneer Industries-—Pearl Weeks
"Recollections) —John Mott
The Otsego Farmer
N.Y.S. Map of Butter & Cheese Factories
Morell Smith Diaries
The Hartwick Voice
Oneonta Herald & Democrat
Interview with Frank Stewart

Hartwick Hatchery

Winter view of the hen house which houses 2,200 hens. Feed room is located in the center with cellar under it for cooling and packing eggs.

Hartwick Hatchery, located on the north end of School Street, was organized in 1922 by a group of Hartwick business men with Stanley Backus as president and manager. The Board of Directors also included Wm. Stilwell, O. W. Murdock, Chas. Stanton, O. A. Smith, Jay Babcock, and Charles Koffman. The business showed a substantial profit the first year selling 50,000 Better Baby Chicks. In 1924 plans for expansion were under way with Charles Koffman as foreman. The purpose of the hatchery was to produce a high quality White Leghorn chick. The members soon realized the value of an extensive breeding program and organized The Hartwick Poultry Farm to supply the rapidly expanding hatchery with the finest quality

pedigreed breeding cockerels. The breeding program produced the first 300 egg hen in Otsego County.

Beginning in 1927, and every year thereafter, the most promising pullets were put in trapnest pens. The weight of these pullets and their eggs were checked for three consecutive days each month from December through August to determine which pullets qualified as breeders at the end of their laying year. All pullets selected for the breeding program had to lay at least 200 eggs during their trapnest year, and their eggs had to average 24 ounces per dozen. The progeny testing program was carried on under the supervision of the Department of Poultry Husbandry of Cornell University.

In Dec. 1928 it was reported in the Farm Bureau News that Hartwick Hatchery has a hen that layed 312 eggs in 365 days. This is quite a feat for a hen. Day in and day out, winter and summer, spring and fall she keeps at the job rolling up profits for her owner. In a year of 365 days she took only 53 days off, and ended the year weighing 4½ lbs., and was laying eggs averaging 26 oz. per dozen.

There is good money in raising hens, said Stanley Backus, Manager. "Hens should be properly housed and given plenty of sunlight and fresh air. Litter should be kept dry and clean, and last but not least, be regular as to the time the hens are fed. Do not disappoint them for they will show their resentment in the egg basket the next day."

John Mott recalls attending a talk given by Professor Rice from Cornell. Using one of the hatchery's White Leghorn hens, the professor was explaining how to select a good laying hen. To everyone's surprise including the professor's, the obliging hen laid an egg in his hand.

The Hartwick Hatchery produced thousands of high quality White Leghorn chicks for sale throughout the state.

For many years Lynn Mayne supervised the daily operation and operated the incubators. When the incubators were in use twenty-four hour monitoring was necessary.

Stanley Backus remained president from the time of the hatcheries organization in 1922 until it was sold in June 1956.

Mr. Backus also owned and operated Backus Hardware for 35 years, was actively involved in the planning of Hartwick High School in 1921, and the installation of the excellent playground equipment which was in use during the 1930's and 1940's. He also built a fine house on School Street that is now occupied by Eleanor Sorbera.

Basil Grigsby operated a chicken farm in South Hartwick in the 1930's. According to his daughter, Betty Lacey, he helped organize the Nearby Egg Cooperative. He further expanded his chicken business and opened a hatchery.

In 1947, Kendall and Howard Marlette, started a hatchery, that they operated for about five years. Competition in the business was so great the brothers decided to close their operation.

By: NBP

Information for this article found in:
"The Oneonta Star"
A brochure "Facts about White Leghorns"
"Farm Bureau News"
Hartwick Hatchery, Inc.

Sheep

The Cheviot Sheep

A paper read before the Farmers and Dairymen's Association at Hartwick by Miss Lillie D. Curry.

One of the attractions of the great sheep show at Chicago was the Cheviots, for none of the mutton breeds that have recently made their appearance upon our shores are challenging more respectful attention.

The Cheviot is unlike almost any other breed of sheep in appearance. The body is compact, of splendid mould, and is well covered with dense medium wool, the whitest that grows. The face and legs are free from wool and covered with stiff white hair. The ears are wide apart and are carried erect. The eyes are large and lively and give the Cheviots particularly pleasing countenance. They are very docile. The tips of the nose and hoofs are black. The fleece is of superior quality.

First Cheviot in USA

George Lough, Sr., a farmer and breeder of full blood Cheviot sheep in Hartwick, was born in Kelso Scotland, April 2, 1815. In 1842 he brought eight Cheviot sheep with him across the Atlantic, the first Cheviot sheep imported into the United States. At a later date he imported other sheep of the same breed. His sons and his neighbors have bred these sheep, and the raising of them has become an important industry in Otsego County.

A well-known breeder.

William Curry is a widely known sheep breeder, of Hartwick. The Cheviot sheep has always been a favorite and through his long continued study of that breed, he has been able to produce some admirable specimens. During the past 10 years he has exhibited his flocks at the large fairs, such as the New York State Fair, The New England Fair, and the Western Fair (New York), and has taken 5 gold medals and 132 cash prizes, amounting to more than $2,200. In addition, his exhibits have captured many prizes at various fairs. At the World's Fair he took 17 prizes which included Sweepstakes on Rams, Sweepstakes on Ewes, and Silver Cup for the best flock. His flock is now known as the "Gold Medal Flock."

Tidbits On sheep.

Imported Cheviots –

Thomas and William Ainslie of Hartwick received from Scotland Tuesday two fine Cheviot rams bred in the famed Hindhope Farm. They were sent by John Ainslie of Edinburgh who spent last summer in Hartwick.

Thomas Ainslie had shipped to him from the city of Glasgow, Scotland, a few weeks since a fine Cheviot sheep, for the purpose of raising the fine standard of sheep.

William A. Curry would get off the train in Syracuse (a track ran into the fairgrounds) with a pail of grain under his arm and say quietly, "dick, dick, dick" and the sheep would follow him through the crowd on the state fairgrounds.

William Curry at State Fair

The Cheviot Association was organized in Hartwick. William Ainslie (Stuart's father) was elected a director and was a director the rest of his life.

In 1898, Fair of the Otsego County Agricultural Society – For the Cheviot special flock prize there are four entries; Thomas N. Curry, William Curry and Son, George Lough, and Edward S. Clark.

September 28, 1893 – County Fair

Sheep – Merinos – Best Ram over two years old, R. W. Potter $3; second best, R. W. Potter $2; Best Ram under 2 years old, R. W. Potter $3; 2nd best $2. Best Ram Lamb, R. W. Potter, 2nd best, R. W. Potter, $1. Best Pen 3 Ewes over 2 years old, R. W. Potter $3; 2nd best, R. W. Potter $2. Best Pen 3 Ewes under 2 years old, R. W. Potter $3; 2nd best, R. W. Potter $2. Best Pen 3 Ewe Lambs, R. W. Potter $2.

The Merino sheep were another breed that was also popular to the area. This is an article written by R. W. Potter.

The Merinos have staying powers surpassed by none. They were in evidence before most of the mutton breeds were thought of. The meat is much like venison with but little of the sheepy taste. The quality is excelled by none. They look wrinkly, their dense, oily wool

is a better protection from storms, and they are longer lived. They are very peaceable and orderly.

Merino Sheep

There are still sheep and sheepmen in the area. But sheep today make up only a small part of the agricultural economy, a far cry from the days about the time of the Civil War when sheep raising was a potent force in the economy and mutton and wool provided a healthy chunk of income.

In those days, history records there were about as many people in Otsego County (53,000) as there are today.

But the sheep outnumbered folks better than four to one, there being between 200,000 and 250,000 sheep in the county.

By: Barb Potter

Bibliography:
NY Farmer – January 1894
Cheviot Journal – 1990
Biographical Review – 1893
The Daily Star
Potter Scrapbook
Otsego Farmer

Cheviot Sheep

Bunn Hill sheep trail – 1918 sheep going up hill towards field   *Ainslie's barn and sheep*

Curry with Champion aged Ewe

Merino Sheep

Rufus Potter

Grace Potter

Rufus Potter

Rufus Potter

STATEMENT

New York State Sheep Growers Cooperative Assn., Inc.

300 West Genesee St., Syracuse, N. Y.

Nº 943

IN ACCOUNT WITH   Date _July 19_ 192__

Name _Ralph Potter_   P.O. _Hartwick_   Co. _____

Consigned with _Otsego_   County Sheep Growers Assn.   State _N.Y._   R. D. No. _____

Date	ITEM	AMOUNT	GRADES	Correspond. Bradford Count grades	LBS.	PRICE	AMOUNT	REMARKS
			Fancy Delaine	70's & above	✓			
			Delaine	66's to 70's	✓			
			Fine Clothing		✓			
			½ Blood Combing	60's to 64's	✓			
11-27-22	Cash Advance C2291	90.00	½ " Clothing		12	40¢	4.85	
	Interest on Advance		⅜ " Combing	54's to 58's	52	46¢	24.39	
	Local Assembling Charges		⅜ " Clothing		9	38¢	3.44	
	Transportation to Warehouse	2.47	¼ " Combing	50's to 52's	221	42¢	93.88	
	Membership Fee	.50	¼ " Clothing		✓			
			Low & Common	36's to 46's	✓			
	Overhead Expense (Rent, Insurance,		Tags		✓			
	Labor, Freight, Discounts, Supplies, Etc.)	11.03	Rejections Burry, cots, seedy, Etc.		✓			
					294			
			TOTAL CREDITS				126.16	
	TOTAL CHARGES	106.00					106.00	Figured by
			Balance (Check No. 1770)				22.16	Checked by
			Dated 7/14/22					

JELLIFFE, WRIGHT & CO.

LIVE STOCK   Mr. E. O. Rogers,

Commission Salesmen   Hartwick N.Y.

MAIN OFFICE:

DATE REC'D Sept. 14, 1920   284 WASHINGTON STREET

NEW YORK Sept. 14, 1920

ESTABLISHED 1850

OUT TURN CAR NO. 18789   CATTLE   CALVES   SHEEP 69   HOGS

NO. HEAD	DESCRIPTION	WEIGHT	SOLD TO	PRICE			
11	Yearlings	880	Wilson	.10	88 00		
21	Sheep	1950	"	.07½	146 25		
37	Lambs	2280	"	.13¼	302 10	536 35	
		ADVANCES					
	CHARGES	FREIGHT		68 93			
		COMMISSION		10 35	79 28		
	CHECK ATTACHED HEREWITH				457 07		

DETACH CHECK BEFORE PRESENTING

Hops

At the time my grandparents grew up in "PETH"(the important center of town and Otsego County), families were self-sustaining through their livestock and crops. Animals and fowl were driven to market in Albany on little more than trails for roads. On rare occasion a trek was made there for trade. Bulky grain was too great effort to transport with slow moving oxen so many distilleries were set up. Even Town and churches organized. Whiskey was more easily conveyed. Cash was hard to come by so trade was by barter until a rail line was built much later up through Otego Valley to other sources. Until other sources became available, my grandfather's income for the year amounted to less than thirty dollars.

Hops, (Homulus Lupulas) became a speculative and sometimes most rewarding of cash crops. Fortunes were sometimes made or lost in a single season. Hops have some medicinal and other uses but the waxy yellow lupulin (contained in base of petal of the blossom) preserves malt of beer and ale. The bitter flavour of Lupulin imparts the taste of the product. Vassar added three or more pounds of hops per barrels. A brewery I visited in London adds only one-tenth pound at present just as flavor.

Hops require a fertile soil similar to corn; which made the climate and sandy loam soils of our county ideal. Waterville, Cooperstown and Cobleskill became centers of the world for hop production by 1910. Many insects and vermin affected production and demand and the resulting price. Good years stimulated production with ruinous profits.

Farmer John's HOP Raising

No, I haint got no hop yard now, I plowed it up last year. The lesson that I Learned in hops has cost me plenty dear.
I'd been a couple thousand dollars better off today if I had never seen a hop. I tell you it don't pay.

The first year that I raised my hops an got em picked an dried, I had about a couple tons and some pounds besides.
A dealer offered thirty cents; I wouldn't let em go;
I THOUGHT THEY'D GO UP HIGHER YET;
my neighbors told me so.
I kept my hops a year and sold for just five cents a Pound;
I thought I'd try another plan when next year came around; An so I sold for seven cents; but it was just my luck,
For hops went up to forty cents, an once more I was stuck.

I went so for several years. it seemed to be my fate,
To sell my crop of hops too soon or hold on too late.
I always took the lowest price instead of the highest one,
An tha 's about the way I found most all my neighbors done.

Sary'n I both worked ourselves to skin and bone;-
We tried to save, an so we done what work we could alone;
But spite all that we could do, we had to run in debt;
A mortgage fastened on our farm we hain't got rid of yet.
An I plowed the hop yard up and bought a lot of stock,
Young cattle, cows and hogs and sheep, a pooty good-sizes flock.
We saved a little money now; the mortgage's growing less.
An in a half dozen years we'll wipe it out I guess.

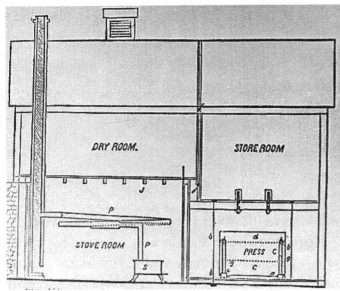

Hop House

Hop picking at Austin Moran's; Back: Peter Coon, Clarence Shaul, Howard Chapman, Peter Sternburg; Center: Carree Parr, Susie Shaul, unknown, unknown, unknown, Greeley Bishop, Bert Shaul; Front: Myrtle Scott, Mabel Drake, Lulu Bishop (Wells)

Yields of a ton or more in New York in the 1830's caused a shift to this area. New England, which had long enjoyed a monopoly on the product, could no longer compete.

For several years hops became the main cash crop in Hartwick and my great grandfather paid off our mortgage. Much labour is involved in setting and tending plants, providing and setting poles, stringing yards to support vines, and then in picking and processing for market. Lupulin in hops are volatile and requires a skilled person in the drying kiln. Neighbor John Parr did well because he knew when to sell. It took a couple of years for a yard to bear.

The only yard I knew at White House was that of Austin Moran in the early twenties. Area farms had a small acreage and neighbor helped neighbor at harvest and used everyone available. Sometimes friends and relatives came from a distance.

My mother came to her Uncle Willie Green's farm on Christian Hill where my father and she first met. I guess most had their own kiln but for some it was a joint venture, My father said; "This was the one time I could earn a little spending money." Women did most of the picking while men tended box and pulled poles.

Hoppickers at Lynn Greens

Box containers for picked hops were large, but some women with nimble fingers made a hard-earned wage. They wore wide brimmed hats for shade and long sleeves as protection from the rough vines and insects. Large supplies were baked ahead and extra housing arranged for the boarders. It became a sort of yearly social event during the few weeks of harvest. Our chief remembrances are of the dances and fun events. In general, farmers who continued in the business had fair returns.

Many claimed the demise of hops was due to the "Blue Mold", but this could he controlled. The 18th Amendment prohibited making and

Back Row: Lena Eldred Palmer (daughter of Delos Eldred), Clarence Shaul (son of Lenych Shaul), Ellen Sloan Beckley (daughter of Simon Sloan); 2nd Row: Mrs. Thomas Longton, Nellie Ainslie Reynolds (daughter of Rob Ainslie), Ella Doney Baker, Nellie Wart Bishop; Front Row: Pearl Eldred Coupe, Ethel Ainslie Sargent (daughter of Rob Ainslie), Lulu Bishop Wells, Austin Moran and dog Nero

sale of alcohol for a short time. Uncle Willie Green who continued until the 1920's said: "There just is not any money in it."

New plantings in Oregon and Washington on virgin soil produced double our yield and could be harvested the first season.

The opening of the rail line offered new markets in dairy and poultry with less intensity of labor.

By: John Mott

Kinne Hop Yard in Hartwick Seminary

HARTWICK VILLAGE

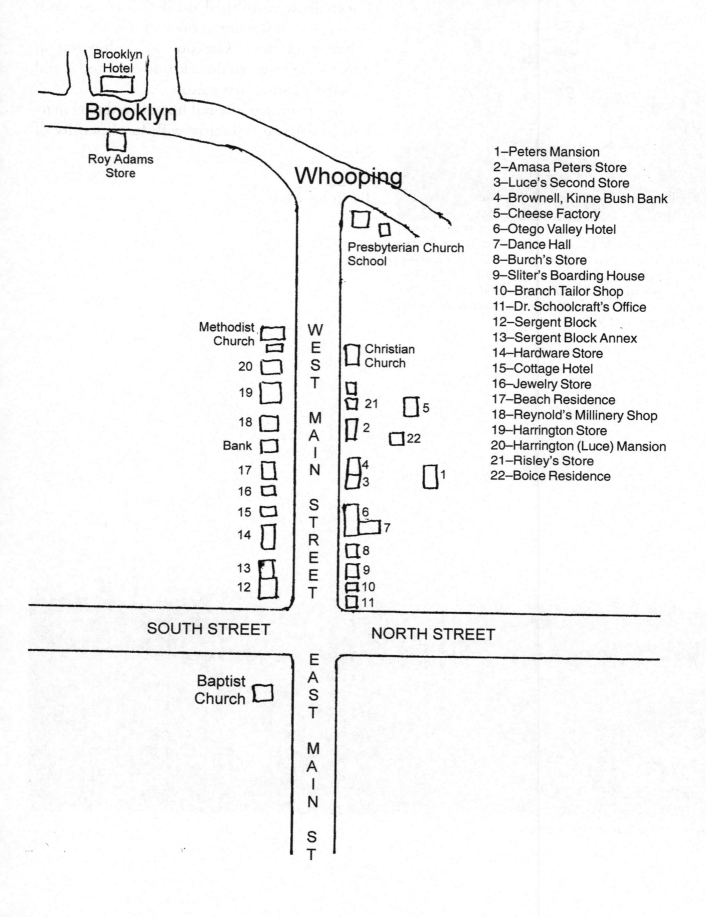

Brooklyn Hotel

Brooklyn

Roy Adams Store

Whooping

Presbyterian Church
School

Methodist Church

20

19

18

Bank

17

16

15

14

13

12

WEST MAIN STREET

Christian Church

21

2

4
3

6
7

8

9

10
11

5

22

1

SOUTH STREET

NORTH STREET

EAST MAIN ST

Baptist Church

1–Peters Mansion
2–Amasa Peters Store
3–Luce's Second Store
4–Brownell, Kinne Bush Bank
5–Cheese Factory
6–Otego Valley Hotel
7–Dance Hall
8–Burch's Store
9–Sliter's Boarding House
10–Branch Tailor Shop
11–Dr. Schoolcraft's Office
12–Sergent Block
13–Sergent Block Annex
14–Hardware Store
15–Cottage Hotel
16–Jewelry Store
17–Beach Residence
18–Reynold's Millinery Shop
19–Harrington Store
20–Harrington (Luce) Mansion
21–Risley's Store
22–Boice Residence

Notes on Village Commerce

Amasa Peters came to this area from Connecticut. In 1809 he obtained a permanent lease on a parcel of property on what today would be the north side of Main Street. Amasa set about farming the land and while plowing discovered large veins of a gray claylike substance. He further noticed that his plow blade became brightly polished as it passed through the clay. Amasa began to mine and sell the clay as Peters Polish. Whether Amasa was well to do or not when he came to Hartwick, he certainly had a head for business and was soon a wealthy man for this time and place. A large house constructed on the Peters property was known as Peters mansion. It was an imposing place and when first built was set in a grove of trees and had a wide lawn that ran all the

Amasa Peters' Mansion

way to Main Street.

It had an iron fence and wide iron gates extending along the street. A wide carriage drive led to "The Grove", a picnic area used by the community, located in back of the mansion along the Otego Creek. The architecture of the Peters mansion, the Luce mansion and a house located at the foot of West Hill, south of the Brooklyn House, now gone, were built to the same blueprint and by the same builder. The roof of the Luce Mansion was later raised and a third story added and a porch enclosed, giving it a totally different character.

Unfortunately over time businesses have been built between the Peters Mansion and the street, shutting this former showplace from view of the passerby. Amasa started the trend when he built a building and opened a store south and west of his house on Main Street, just east of the Hartwick Market. This was many years later to become the Commercial Hotel.

Amasa died in 1821. His son, Rufus, though still under age, was soon in charge of the business. In 1825 Rufus had two teams hauling produce in winter to New Haven, Connecticut, thus turning a profit on local farm surplus taken in trade. The teams returned with oysters, clams and other seafood. (This explains how the little hamlet of Hartwick so often put on huge oyster suppers at various lodges and churches.)

Rufus was a good business man with a finger in diverse Hartwick enterprises but he died at the age of 38. Rufus was well liked and it has been told that his funeral was so large that people were still in the church when the funeral procession reached the cemetery one mile away.

The next year the Peters property came into the hands of Rufus' sister, Eliza, and her husband, Torry Luce. Luce was a successful store keeper in Gilbertsville. He took over the operation of the Peters store and operated it in the same location for fifteen years. Torry and Eliza lived in the Peters mansion and raised five children: Rufus, Caroline, Cynthia, Dolphus and J. Henry. In 1853, Torry acquired the block next to the Otego Valley Hotel. This parcel already had a well established store that had been operated by George and Jarvis Caulkins and later by James Newton, Jr. Torry opened his store in this location. At this time he was known as the wealthiest man in the village.

In 1855 he turned the store and the business over to his sons, Dolphus and Rufus and in 1867 sold the building to Dolphus. Dolphus died in 1876. Rufus continued to operate the store for two years then he bought out the large Harrington store on the south side of Main Street. This part of the Luce story will be explained in the history of the Harrington block.

Now to go back to the store west of the Otego Valley Hotel formerly operated by the Luces. After Rufus moved his old store continued under different management. Henry Robinson was to operate this store for many years as well as being postmaster. Dr. McClellan bought the building in 1895 from Henry Robinson's widow. Over the years it saw use as an annex to the hotel, was a bakery and in the 1930's was operated as a Victory chain store by Webb Chamberlain, followed later by Leslie Leach. The building has since been torn down and the area is now a part of a parking lot.

The building next door that was to the left as you faced it from the street also housed many businesses. The date it was built or by whom is uncertain. Rob Brownell's name appears on an early map. The Kinne Bush bank opened in this location. When the bank vacated the building, Ben and Blaine Talbot opened their dental offices there. In the 1930's The Tipple family opened the Blue Bird Tea Room, a nice gathering place for after-schoolers as well as a social spot for locals. Later the Hamilton family first opened their print shop there. Soon after, the building became a two family rental property and later was torn down.

Building west of Otego Valley Hotel that was later operated as a Victory chain store.

Now we go back to the Peters Mansion. This fine looking building passed out of the hands of the Peters-Luce family. Orrin Fitch acquired the land when he bought the store in the 1850's. In the 1870's Randall Arnold owned the mansion and property and built a cheese factory to the west of the mansion in back of the present Hartwick Market.

The thriving cheese factory called in a steady stream of farm wagons loaded with milk and contributed to a business boom along Main Street.

Arnold later rebuilt the cheese factory to the north of his property near the Grove. After Randall Arnold a man named Wing acquired the property, followed by a series of owners and renters. Some kept the place up and others didn't care. Buildings along Main Street mostly shielded it from view. In the 1950's Fred and Louella Earl acquired it and started restoration. Today it is owned by the Schilling family, has a new roof, new paint and (from a certain angle) can be seen from the street.

The large building long known as the Otego Valley Hotel in the center of Hartwick has had a long and varied history. At an early time, date unknown, Walter Kerr had a tavern on this site.

View of North Side of Main Street

Sometimes it is hard to determine the exact date of the building of early structures. The Otego Valley Hotel is one of these. Pearl Weeks in her "History of Hartwick" states the hotel was built in 1805. 'The Special Oneonta Leader', December 14, 1901, states "The Otego Valley Hotel was built about 75 years ago by Andrew Elbridge." This would make it built about 1826. Either way we can conclude it was built at an early date.

Research reveals the following owners. Peter Olendorf in 1833, Elisha Wentworth in 1841, Sidney Ballard, Russell Andrews, Waterman Eldred 1851 to 1865, R. B. Brownell, Haskel Harrington with E. Norton in 1886. He held it until his death in 1923. Later his widow sold it to L. A. Scram in 1929. It was sold again to Charles Gaywitz in 1933, then to Lester Dawley who sold it the same day to Rensselar Stevens. Andrew Kerzinski and family were in the hotel after Stevens. Monroe Burch bought the hotel at a foreclosure sale in 1938.

The operation of the hotel was usually carried on by the owners. Waterman Eldred, Rob Brownell, Harrington and Norton, Pratt and again Brownell. Brownell was the exception as he had a long succession of leases and managers during his second ownership — Bard 1887, H. Wood 1892, Olson ??, P. Irish 1893, George Freelan 1898 - 1900, R.L. Holbrook 1901, H. Wade 1902, Howard Bedford 1908, Eli Kimball 1910, Samuel Vunck 1911 - 1912, Eli Kimball again 1913, Elmer Miller. Later a Samuel Justice and a Mrs. Burns acted as managers as was disclosed in the following news clipping "Fire was discovered creeping through the roof of the Otego Valley Hotel but it was put out by the prompt arrival of the firemen. The hotel is under the management of Samuel Justice and Mrs. Burns."

Over the years the hotel has gone under the names of various owners and managers - names such as Harrington and Norton, Kimball's Hall, Vunck Hall, etc. Mr. Bard was the first to call it Otego Valley Hotel. Even though there have been other names, The Otego Valley Hotel is the one that survived.

The back part of the hotel was moved to a lot to the rear. The time of the move is uncertain, possibly after Monroe Burch purchased it. The upper floor was used as a dance hall and was referred to as Burch's Hall in the late 1940's.

Before Hartwick High School consolidated with Cooperstown, it became necessary to place some classes in an outside location from the school building. For a time one of the lower grades classes was held in Burch's building. This continued until the Hartwick High School consolidated freeing up space for all the grades to meet in the Hartwick Grade Center.

The last owner of the back building was Jim Hurtibise. The building began collapsing. The hoops for a basketball court were still up, a forlorn reminder of past use. It slowly fell down in the 1990's and finally has been leveled and is being used as a parking lot.

The main part of the Otego Valley Hotel is standing firm in 2002. It is now owned by Chester Winslow. It houses the Hartwick Post Office as it has for over 50 years. Also a comparatively new business to Hartwick, the Otego Optical Company, operates there. There are apartments upstairs and hopefully the building has a long future in our village.

Across a narrow alley from the Otego Valley Hotel stands a building that has long been a store. In 1860 James T. Barney and Frederick

Orlo S. Burch, Orlo G. Burch, A. Monroe Burch in front of store.

Wilcox opened a general store. Theodore Norton was their efficient clerk and soon be-

came a partner. In 1874 Orlo S. Burch took over the store, followed by his son, A. Monroe Burch and later by his son, Orlo G. Burch. This historical gem of a building is still in the possession of family members.

To the right of Burch's store a building stood for many years. It is understood that Orlo S. Burch had his first store there. When Poplar Avenue opened shortly after 1900 to make street access to the trolley lines office building, this Main Street building was moved to the avenue (4th house on the left). In it's place the present building was built by Menzo Sliter who operated a meat market there for years. In 1919 it was advertised as Sliter's Hotel and in 1925 was known as Sliter's Boarding House. Mae Sliter was to run the boarding house well into the 1940's. Jack Briggs acted as an assistant manager. It was later owned by Roland Hurtibise and at the present time is home to the American Legion.

To the right of the Legion Hall is another very old building that has housed a lawyer's office and many businesses. In 1882 William H. Branch had his tailoring establishment here as well as serving as Town Supervisor. Later, in 1898, his son, H. O. Branch, continued the tailor shop as well as carrying a stock of cloth. Later the building housed the post office with Bert Branch as Post master. Also, at varying times it has housed the telephone office, a harness shop and a shoe repair shop. In the 1950's

Scott Hester built the low addition in front of the building to house his coffee shop and later his barber shop. At the present time it is adding to our Main Street as a charming little dwelling.

The corner lot that now serves as lawn and flower garden for the next door house on North Street, once had a building with a long history. It has served as a private dwelling. At one time Jane Jones ran a millinery shop there. Dr. George Schoolcraft had his office there for over forty years. After Dr. Schoolcraft passed away, Walter Block bought the house and tore it down.

Behind the boys standing on the Baptist Church lawn can be seen Dr. Schoolcraft's home and the Block home.

On the south side of Main Street there stands a large white building on the corner. It is uncertain when it was built as it doesn't appear on the village map of 1868. However a news item in the 'Oneonta Herald Democrat' of May, 1878 tells that "Leroy Sergent has put up a large two story addition on the west side of his store fronting on Main Street." The new addition soon filled with businesses. Cassius Maples opened his law offices upstairs. The two lower rooms were occupied by Loren Ingalsbe's shoe shop and Henry Harrison's jewelry store.

In 1879 Mr. Sergent's son, Elmer, kept his father's store in the corner building. Another news item of 1879 tells that "L. R. Sergent is in New York buying his winter stock of goods."

In 1889, Frank Bresee set up a store in the Sergent Block. His was a very ambitious project for such a small village but he conducted it with success. He was to start an even more ambitious project in 1899 with his highly successful Oneonta Department Store.

Dorr Gardner took over the operation of the Hartwick store for Mr. Bresee, first as clerk then as partner-manager. Gardner ran it from 1901 until 1914. Being an astute businessman he had a hand in several enterprises. He had a wagon operated by Emmett Bliss on the road. His corner store was the gathering place for butter and eggs from local farms. These were shipped by the new trolley line to reach the Albany market. Mr. Gardner also built the imposing gray stone house with the wrap around porch that stands on South Street.

For several years the corner building was Hartwick's Post Office. In addition to housing a store and post office the upstairs rooms were used for a variety of social gatherings. A men's group gathered for readings and debates and a drama club put on plays.

The new addition also was to see a variety of businesses as the years passed. During Dorr Gardner's time there was a livery stable in the rear. Years later, in the 1930's Claude Tilley ran a feed store in the back part. Other businesses fronted on Main Street. At various times a series of barber shops occupied this section. Among the barbers were George Bresee, Bill Bryant, Millard "Barb" Clark and Albert Edgett. In the upstairs of the addition a variety of lodges and fraternal orders met - the Eastern Star, the Macabees, etc. In the 1920's the silent movies were very popular entertainment. These were accompanied by suitable music hammered out on a piano by local musicians. Among the names of the pianists recalled are Claudine Edgett and Grace Bryant Beach.

In the early forties the company that pulled

View of south side of Main Street businesses

up the steel rails of the trolley line had their temporary headquarters there. In the late forties the building was used as an auction room.

Chester Winslow bought the corner building and it was home to his law office for many years. It is still owned by a member of the Winslow family. The annex part of the building has been torn down and the space is now part of the ARC parking lot.

Where the ARC building stands a pair of buildings and many businesses once thrived. The first building housed a hardware store for many years. The first owner that we have knowledge of was Elisha Robinson. He sold his interest to George MacClellan Augur in 1889. Mr. Augur operated the store well into the 1900's. At one time Smith Chittenden, a gold smith, operated a jewelry store in the eastern part of the building, carrying a full line of clocks, watches, jewelry and stationery. Later an old post card shows that same shop to be a millinery store. It has long been told that the upstairs of this building was once the Baptist Church. In an article printed in the "Freeman's Journal," December 23, 1882, it states that this building once occupied the site of the present Baptist Church and was the pioneer church. In later years Stanley Backus had the hardware store and carried on the business until 1948.

Next door to the hardware stood a narrow building with a 24 foot frontage and 238 feet deep. We find it first mentioned in a deed from Augustus Gilbert to Peleg Gardner in 1893. In the deed it states that Gardner had been conducting a hotel there for some time. It appears to have had the name of the Cottage Hotel from the beginning.

An incomplete list of proprietors reads as follows: Virgil Holbrook, 1901, E. W. Marsh, 1902, Claude Dudley, 1908, Howard Bedford, 1909, William Wilson, 1910, and L. H. Brown, 1919.

The Cottage Hotel building was attached to the hardware store at the second floor and a narrow alley ran between the two. This gave access to the hotels' livery stable.

After its heyday as a hotel, an overall factory was opened on the second floor. This was about 1920. Thelma Tilley Phillips was sent for two weeks training and then worked as a floor lady for $18 a week. The factory had 30 machines and several local women worked there for $11 a week. The following are the names of a few of the workers: Ella Curry, Anna Eldred, Elizabeth Curry and Minnie Mead. Ford Risley, a teenager at the time, recalled working after school folding overalls and tying them into

Main Street, Winton store on right.

bundles at 10¢ a bundle.

Later the Thomas family operated a bakery on the premises with living quarters upstairs. Thomas' Bakery daily turned out a nice selection of baked goods. This author remembers half moon cookies, molasses cookies with a glazed top, breads, doughnuts, and much more. After the Thomases, Bill and Catherine Garvin took over the bakery and continued to turn out the same excellent baked goods.

In the 1950's Joseph Fields bought the whole building complex. He incorporated the buildings into a large store operating a hardware, a bottled gas business and a full line of groceries complete with meat counter. After operating the business a few years he sold to Carter Harrison, Sr. Harrison razed the whole complex and built a modern supermarket which included a liquor store and a laundromat. This business was operated by Carter Harrison, Jr. After a time the market was bought by a grocery chain and was known as "The Peter Pumpkin". The store soon closed permanently and the building is now the center for ARC clients.

The next building was a small two story affair that looked like a dwelling. It had a porch and stood close to the street.

A. Mr. Bottsford either had a home or business there. In the early 1900's Mr. and Mrs. Winton had a jewelry store. Later Mrs. Winton ran it alone and had a variety store and lunch room. Clara Bishop Scavo remembers that her sister, Cora, helped out after school. Later George Buzzie had restaurant there. James Byard, well known lawyer, bought the building, modernized the appearance and opened a law office. After Mr. Byard's untimely death the Hartwick Fire Department obtained the building. They opened the front and installed two large doors to allow entry of fire trucks and equipment. This building sufficed as the fire hall for a number of years until the new fire house was built. The old building was then torn down.

The next building, that is now an apartment house owned by Ray Polulech, was for many years owned by the Beach family. First by Bert Beach who operated a livery stable in the back of his premises; later by L. Dean Beach who operated a coal business in Cooperstown and was Town Supervisor and had his home there.

The house beyond the bank has been occupied by various families for many years. The 1868 map shows it to be the millinery shop of Laura and Rebecca Reynolds. Mr. and Mrs. William Varney are the present owners.

The block where the present fire house stands has a long and varied history. It was the site of one of Hartwick's oldest businesses. Lyman Harrington's tin and sheet metal business was housed there as early as the 1820's. Today when we have aluminum, stainless steel, ceramics etc. for a great variety of needs it is hard to imagine the importance of tinware to the early settlers. Lyman Harrington advertised for 6 to 8 peddlers to take his wares about the countryside to sell. The following is a list of wares that probably was Lyman's as it was found, handwritten, in the upstairs of his establishment many years ago. This list points out how important tinware was to early farms and townspeople alike.

10 Quart pans	Culinders
6 Quart pans	Flour scoops
44 Kettles	Spit boxes
12 large and small skimmers	
Pepperboxes	
48 Straight pails	Blow horns
12 Covered pails	Patty pans
6 Pint basins	Dust pans
Gallon coffee pots	Flat pans
1/2 Gallon coffee pots	
Small barrels	
Large tea pots	Milk dippers
Old maid tea pots	Flat staves
Quart and pint lamp fillers	
Tea steapers	
Candle molds	Cake cutters

The 1848 financial report of School District # 4 shows that a tin dipper was purchased of Harrington for 17¢. This school was "kept" in the ancient stone building on South Street. This helps to establish the date of Harrington's tin shop.

Lyman Harrington also built the beautiful house next door to his establishment. Lyman died in 1850 and Sheffield Harrington and Elisha Robinson converted the business into a general store when the metal craft business declined. Elisha Robinson gradually withdrew from participation to look after his hardware and foundry business. In 1865, Chester L. Harrington, Lyman's son, business man and adventurer, returned after fifteen years on the west coast where he had pursued mining and merchandising ventures. He moved into his father's mansion and entered the firm. In 1872 Rensselaer Dunbar was listed as a partner. C. L. Harrington was also to try his hand at making and selling several patent medicines.

In 1887 Rufus P. Luce, who had been operating the thriving Luce store across the street, bought the large Harrington business, store and mansion. Rufus moved his family into the mansion and operated the store until his death in 1902. Rufus' son, George T. Luce, ran the store until 1917 when he left the store to become Hartwick's post master. Torry B. sold the store to Lew Knochs in 1927 who operated it for three years before he passed away.

Don Perrine operated the grocery store through the 1930's. A very congenial man, he sold meat, fresh fruit and vegetables. He was the son-in-law of Earl DeMett who had operated meat markets in the village for years. Perrine closed the store about the time of World War II.

Sometime after the war, Mr. and Mrs. Emmett Hamilton moved across the street and opened their print shop in the upright part of the old building. Mrs. Hamilton worked with her husband and she was also a poet. She published some booklets under the name of Mary Morgan.

In the western end of the building Hartwick Free Library was located. Mrs. Hamilton acted as librarian and several members of Hartwick's influential citizens were on the board.

The property was acquired by the Hartwick Fire Department and the Harrington block was torn down to make way for the new fire house.

About the same time that Jim Byard opened his law office in town, he purchased the Luce Mansion. The Byards were in the process of refurbishing the place when Mr. Byard was fatally injured in a horrendous auto accident and Mrs. Byard was left handicapped. She continued to live there for a time with her daughter, Lulu, before moving to a smaller house on North Street. Today Barry and Kay Brick own the mansion, which has been beautifully restored.

Risley Store

We will now cross Main Street to bring us full circle. The building presently housing the Hartwick Market has a long history. The building originally stood on the south side of Main Street, the second place west of the Methodist Church. According to the town maps of 1850 and 1868, Matthew Halbert (or Hulbert) had a tin shop here. Later Harvey Porter used it for a furniture and undertaking business. Porter had the building moved to its present location in 1889. At the turn of the century Vernon C. Porter ran a hardware and had a line of furniture for sale. The building, then known as the Porter Block, had a large floor space and could provide for more than one enterprise at a time. It has accommodated barber shops, butcher shops, a meeting room for the Maccabees, and at one time provided a room for the fire company's hose cart.

Interior of Coolen and Ostrander Store

Earl DeMett had a barber shop there and likely a butcher shop too. Will Risley purchased the block from DeMett about 1915. Mr. Risley dealt in farm machinery and conducted a grocery store. He was to operate the grocery store for over 30 years. He was assisted through the years by his wife, Ethel, and his son, Ford. During World War II when Ford was in the service, Ford's wife, Anna, helped in the store. After the Risleys retired from operating the store, Peg Coolen and Charlotte Ostrander bought the business and ran the store for several years. After Coolen and Ostrander closed in the 1980's, the building stood idle for nearly ten years.

In 1996, Joel and Marilyn Habercorn reopened the store. They had put months of work into painting and refurbishing. At the writing of this article The Hartwick Market is the only business on Main Street that carries groceries. The Market also has a going business making subs, sandwiches and light meals.

We now return to our point of origin, the original Amasa Peters-Torry Luce store. After Torry moved his store down two doors Orrin Fitch continued at Torry's store. We don't know for how many years or who was to follow him. We know names associated with the building but that is about all. At some point in time the building ceased to be a store and began to be operated as a hotel. Bob Brownell, Steve Brown, Howard Bedford, Ellis Bard and others have all been associated with the building. It is believed Howard Bedford added a third floor about 1898. Soon after, in 1900, with the arrival of the trolley all hotels began to

Commercial Hotel

flourish. This building was known as the Commercial Hotel and was to operate under this name into the late 1920's. Leon Bard was the proprietor into the early thirties but it is uncertain when it ceased to be a hotel.

In the 1930's William Peterson opened a restaurant called "The Peth" and operated it for several years. In the early 1940's Bill Eggers took over the restaurant. Others to operate a restaurant were the Harris family, Bob Grant and Marshall Lisisky. Soon after, probably in the 1950's, the old building was torn down.

The dwelling that still stands in the former alley was once the home of Frank Boice who printed and published Hartwick's very own newspaper, "The Hartwick Reporter."

Interior, Roy and Lulu Adams Store on Brooklyn side around 1934

Some additional notes from John Mott on the Brooklyn side,

An early trail from Otsego Lake went over the hill to the west to Toddsville and Christian Hill to Butterfield's White House. The path continues south on the west side of the Otego Creek to the hamlet called "Peth", a center of importance in the town and county. The tale is that John Christopher Hartwick hoped this would become the county seat but Judge Cooper, anticipating the move, journeyed by fast horse to Albany to secure the location at Cooperstown.

"Whooping" Hill

A downgrade into town caused a team to go into Brooklyn just 'a-whoopin' and the location of entrance was known as "Whooping."

A school stood along Whooping adjacent to the Presbyterian Church on the corner with Main Street. Across to the south was a distillery that fed their mash to their cattle. Above was a school for fine ladies. Parm Williams operated a foundry along Otego Creek across from Mudge's saw mill and a cheese box factory was located at the creek crossing.

Roy Adams Store

A grocery and general store, commonly called Roy Adams Store was located in Brooklyn across from the hotel. Frederick E. Bissell bought the site in 1837 and probably built at that time. His sons, Edwin and Theron were long connected there. In 1882 E.J. Weeks and son were proprietors. A.H. Field owned it 1903. Later Roy Adams was there until his death in 1919, then his widow, Lulu Adams Morse, continued for many years. Subsequent owners include George and Grace Benjamin and Beulah Barrett. The final storekeepers were Harold and Sylvia Merrihew. The building stood empty for several years, was used for a short time as a Youth Center and later burned down.

By: NBP

Sources:
Maps 1858 and 1868
Oracle, v. 5
Dr. Butterfield
Kenneth Augur
Frederica Hornbeck
John Mott
Interview with Ford Risley
Pearl Weeks "History of Hartwick"

History of Hartwick National Bank

The Hartwick National Bank was the out growth of a private banking concern known as Kinne, Bush & Company, Bankers, which was organized on June 20, 1908, by the following: D. E. Siver, J. Warren Lamb, H. L. Brazee of the village of Cooperstown, NY, Lee Kinne of Hartwick Seminary, NY, Dwight Aplin of the Town of Hartwick, NY, and Robert M. Bush of Cooperstown, NY. Mr. Bush was at that time the Cashier of the Cooperstown National Bank and also a Director of that bank. D. E. Siver was Vice President and a Director of the Cooperstown National Bank; J. Warren Lamb and Lee Kinne were also Directors of that bank, and H. L. Brazee was a Director of the Second National Bank of Cooperstown, NY, and later became President of the Second National Bank. Dwight Aplin was a prominent farmer of the Town of Hartwick.

Kinne, Bush & Co., Bankers, was a project of Robert M. Bush, a man at that time about 60 years of age. He had been a practicing attorney in Spencer, Iowa, for many years before he entered the banking business. He was familiar with the promotion of small private banks of which there were many in the Western States at that time. Edward D. Lindsay, later Assistant Cashier of the National Commercial Bank & Trust Co. at Hartwick, was at that time Assistant Cashier of the Cooperstown National Bank, and Ora W. Murdock was a Teller at the Cooperstown National Bank. Both of these men assisted in the organization of Kinne, Bush & Co., Bankers. Mr. Lindsay placed the initial order for the stationary and supplies to use, and Mr. Murdock was appointed as assistant to Mr. Robert M. Bush, who had been appointed as manager. Mr. Murdock assumed full time employment at the opening of the bank in Hartwick, and Mr. Bush undertook to spend two afternoons a week at Hartwick and more time when needed. This arrangement continued until September 26, 1919, when Mr. Robert M. Bush retired from the co-partnership and the name was changed to Kinne, Burch & Co., Bankers. Mr. Orlo S. Burch entered the firm at this time. Orlo S. Burch was a merchant in Hartwick, the father of A. Monroe Burch, who later became President of Hartwick National Bank. The co-partnership of Kinne, Burch & Co., Bankers, continued until March 26, 1920, when the Comptroller of the Currency granted a Charter to the Hartwick National Bank.

The first President of the Hartwick National Bank was Orlo S. Burch, with Ora W. Murdock as Cashier and Byron L. Fuller as Teller. (It may be interesting to note that the President received no salary, and the salary of the Cashier was $2,200.00 per year, and that of the Teller was $1,000.00 per year.) Byron L. Fuller had entered the employ of the banking firm of Kinne, Burch & Co., Bankers, about three years before the organization of the Hartwick National Bank, and continued with the bank until his death on May 4, 1959, after the merger with National Commercial & Trust. He served successively as Teller, Assistant Cashier, Vice President, and President, and at the time of his death was serving as Chairman of the Advisory Board of the Hartwick Branch. The success of the Hartwick National Bank was due in a great measure to the ability and energy of the first Cashier, Ora W. Murdock, who planned and carried out its organization and served as Cashier and Director until his untimely death in April, 1925.

On April 28, 1925, Mr. Harry D. Bilderbeck was appointed Cashier and Byron L. Fuller, Assistant Cashier. Mr. Bilderbeck was at that time a Director of the Bank and Supervisor of the Town of Hartwick. Mr. Bilderbeck served as Cashier of the Bank for eighteen years, and resigned June 30, 1943; at which time Edward D. Lindsay was appointed Cashier and a Director of the Bank. Byron L. Fuller remained as Assistant Cashier. During Mr. Bilderbeck's incumbency as Cashier, Orlo S. Burch died, and Dr. George E. Schoolcraft was elected President, and served in that capacity from June 30, 1939, until his death February 27, 1944.

A. Monroe Burch was elected President to succeed Dr. Schoolcraft on March 7, 1944, and served as President until his death May 5, 1954, during which period the business of the bank showed a healthy increase. Mr. A. M. Burch was a man of great natural ability and sound judgment, and he enjoyed the respect and confidence of the people of Hartwick and surrounding territory.

No successor to A. Monroe Burch was elected until August 3, 1954, when Mr. Orlo G. Burch, the son of A. Monroe Burch, was elected President. He held the position until December 28, 1956, when he resigned. On January 8, 1957, Byron L. Fuller was elected President and served in that capacity until the merger in July 1958.

The charter members of the Board of Directors of the Hartwick National Bank were Dr. George E. Schoolcraft, Elmer L. Sergent, Chester R. Burch, Ora W. Murdock, Orlo S. Burch and Eber O. Rogers, all residents of Hartwick, NY. These men were leading citizens of Hartwick, and considered of good reputation and financially responsible. The Presidents of the bank served in an advisory capacity mostly, and, with the exception of Byron L. Fuller, were not engaged in the daily work of the bank.

Terms of the Presidents of the banks were as follows: Orlo S. Burch — March 26, 1920, to June 30, 1939; Dr. George E. Schoolcraft — June 30, 1939 to February 27, 1944 (at the time Dr. Schoolcraft became President, the Board of Directors consisted of A. Monroe Burch, H. D. Bilderbeck, John R. Parr, William H. Stilwell and George E. Schoolcraft); A. Monroe Burch — March 7, 1944 to May 5, 1954; Orlo S. Burch — August 3, 1954 to December 28, 1956; Byron L. Fuller — January 8, 1957 to July 11, 1958, the date of the merger with National Commercial Bank & Trust Co.

Edward D. Lindsay

Directors of the Hartwick National Bank at the date of the merger with National Commercial Bank & Trust were Byron L. Fuller, John K. Harrington, David L. Dorfler, Edward D. Lindsay and Chester J. Winslow, Jr. Mr. Winslow also served as Attorney of the bank. These men were continued as the Advisory Board of the Hartwick Branch, and Mr. Winslow continued as Attorney.

Kinne, Bush & Co., Bankers, of Hartwick, NY, opened in temporary quarters in a wooden building across the street from the present office of Hartwick Branch of Key Bank. The building now occupied by the bank was designed and constructed for the use of the private banking firm of Kinne, Bush & Co., Bankers.

After the private banking firm was succeeded by the Hartwick National Bank, an addition was built on the back of the building to house the bank vault and to provide a director's room. The ceiling of the banking room was lowered a few feet, as it was found to be hard to heat the building before this alteration was made. The bank building was designed by Linn Kinne, architect of Utica, NY.

At the time the bank opened as Kinne, Bush & Co., Bankers, there was a great deal more going on in Hartwick than at present. The trolley railroad company had its headquarters here, and the powerhouse, car barns and general offices were here. Many of the employees of the railroad lived in Hartwick, some of whom owned their homes and some lived in hotels and boarding houses. At one time there were four hotels in operation. The railroad had several different names during its existence, such as Oneonta, Cooperstown and Richfield Springs; Otsego and Herkimer, and finally the Southern New York. The railroad finally went the way of many others, and now is only a memory as far as Hartwick is concerned, although a number of residents are still receiving railroad pensions as a result of their former services.

In 1978 there were rumors the Hartwick Bank, a branch of the National Commercial Bank and Trust Company was closing. The Hartwick Business Association assisted by Don Webster, manager of the Hartwick Branch, the Hartwick bank directors and the town board worked hard to keeep it open. With the backing of Victor J. Riley, Jr., President and Executive Officer of the National Commercial Bank and Trust Compnay it was kept open!

"The Bank" was the title of the bank for only a few months before it became Key Bank, Hartwick Branch in 1980.

In 1995 the bank celebrated the 75th anniversary of the chartering of the Kinne, Burch and Co. Bankers and also the 15th year it had been a Key Bank.

Marie Saxer was bank manager and Carole Donahue, supervisor. Carole was the great grandaughter of one of the founders, O. S. Burch.

In 1997 Key Corp sold the smaller banks to Albank – a division of Charter One and in 1999 the bank became Charter One, which it is in 2002.

Freeman's Journal June 28,1979; Aug. 12, 1979; April 16, 1995

_____

By: Marie Saxer

Hartwick Supervisor Carol Donahue, left, and bank manager Marie Saxer cut the cake at the 75th anniversary of Hartwick National Bank and the 15th Anniversary of the Key Bank branch at the bank.

Business section, Main Street

The Trolley

SOUTHERN NEW YORK RAILWAY

READ DOWN SOUTHBOUND TRAINS—Utica to Oneonta TIMETABLE EFFECTIVE APRIL 26, 1925. NORTHBOUND—Oneonta to Utica READ UP

20	16-18	14	54-56	12	10-12	6-8	52	2	STATIONS	Miles	5-7	55-57	9-11	13	113	115	15	17-19	21
Sun. Only See Note	Dly	Dly	Sun. Only	Sun. Only	Dly Ex. Sun.	Dly (*)	Sun. Only	Dly Ex. Sun.			Dly Ex. Sun.	Sun. Only	Dly	Dly	Dly	Dly	Dly	Dly (*)	Sun. Only
PM	PM	PM	PM	PM	AM	AM	AM	AM	Via N. Y. State Rys.		AM	PM	PM	PM	PM	PM	PM	PM	AM
7.00	7.00	2.30	12.30		9.30	7.00			Leave UTICA Arrive		10.30	1.00	3.30				8.00	10.00	
7.51	7.51	3.21	1.21		10.21	7.51			Ar. MOHAWK Lv.		9.39	12.09	2.39				7.09	9.14	
8.27	8.27	3.25	1.19		10.27	7.59			Lv. HERKIMER Ar.		9.48	12.16	2.45				6.58	8.43	
8.37	8.37	3.33	1.25		10.37	8.09			Lv. MOHAWK Ar.	0.00	9.38	12.06	2.38				6.52	8.33	
8.55	8.55	3.50	1.42		10.56	8.25			McCREDY'S	5.83	9.25	11.53	2.26				6.38	8.19	
9.01	9.01	3.56	1.48		11.02	8.31			HENDERSON	7.72	9.19	11.47	2.20				6.32	8.13	
9.06	9.06	4.01	1.53		11.08	8.36			JORDANVILLE	10.10	9.14	11.42	2.15				6.27	8.08	
9.20	9.20	4.17	2.10		11.24	8.50			RICHFIELD SPRINGS	15.35	8.59	11.27	2.00				6.12	7.54	
9.27	9.27	4.25	2.18		11.30	8.58			LAKE HOUSE	16.72	8.51	11.19	1.51				6.04	7.46	
9.29	9.29	4.27	2.21		11.33	9.00			CANADARAGO PARK	17.78	8.48	11.16	1.48				6.01	7.43	
9.37	9.37	4.35	2.29		11.41	9.08			SCHUYLER LAKE	21.25	8.39	11.08	1.40				5.53	7.35	
9.48	9.48	4.46	2.40		11.51	9.16			OAKSVILLE	25.09	8.29	10.58	1.30				5.42	7.25	
9.51	9.51	4.49	2.43		11.54	9.19			FLY CREEK	26.89	8.26	10.55	1.27				5.39	7.22	
9.57	9.57	4.55	2.48		11.59	9.24			TODDSVILLE	29.39	8.22	10.50	1.22				5.34	7.17	
10.02	10.02	5.00	2.53		12.04	9.29			Arrive INDEX Leave	30.94	8.17	10.45	1.17		4.28	5.05	5.29	7.12	
10.28	10.28	5.03	3.25		12.36	9.58			Leave INDEX Arrive		7.51	10.18	12.46				6.41		
10.13	10.13	5.15	3.07		12.17	9.41			Arrive COOPERSTOWN Leave	34.02	8.04	10.31	1.02				5.16	6.58	
10.15	10.15	4.47	3.11		12.21	9.44			Leave COOPERSTOWN Arrive		8.02	10.29	12.58		4.39	5.15		6.53	
10.45	10.43	5.20	3.40	12.55	12.55	10.15	8.00	5.55	HARTWICK	36.89	7.36	9.58	12.29	3.24	4.11		6.26		12.40
10.54		5.29		1.03	1.03	10.23	8.08	6.04	SOUTH HARTWICK	40.15	7.26	9.46	12.16	3.16			6.16		12.31
11.00		5.35		1.09	1.09	10.28	8.13	6.09	MT. VISION	42.83	7.21	9.41	12.11	3.11			6.11		12.25
11.14		5.46		1.20	1.20	10.40	8.24	6.21	LAURENS	47.01	7.07	9.27	11.56	2.57			5.57		12.11
11.26		5.59		1.31	1.31	10.54	8.35	6.35	WEST ONEONTA	51.28	6.55	9.15	11.44	2.45			5.45		12.00
11.30		6.04		1.36	1.36	11.00	8.40	6.40	JUNCTION	52.91	6.50	9.10	11.40	2.40			5.40		11.55
11.40		6.14		1.45	1.45	11.10	8.50	6.50	Arrive ONEONTA Leave	54.91	6.40	9.00	11.30	2.30			5.30		11.45
PM	PM	PM	PM	PM	PM	AM	AM	AM			AM	AM	AM	PM	PM	PM	PM	PM	PM

(*) Trains 6-8 and 17-19 do not carry baggage Mondays to Saturday inclusive, account of Railway Postoffice. Note: On Decoration Day, Independence Day and Labor Day, Train 20 will be run on Sunday schedule. **NOT RESPONSIBLE**—This Company is not responsible for errors in timetables, inconvenience or damage resulting from delayed trains, or failure to make connections. Schedule shown is subject to change without notice.
A. J. STRATTON, General Manager, Oneonta, N. Y.   E. D. CONKLIN, General Freight & Passenger Agent, Oneonta, N. Y.

An important part of Hartwick's history was the trolley line that ran through the town in the early 1900's. The trolley line that was to become so important to the town and village lasted less than fifty years, but it played a great part in the rise and fall of the economic growth of the area.

The story of the trolley line really began 18 miles to the south in the 1880's on the streets of Oneonta. Before the advent of the automobile, Oneonta had a horse drawn trolley line operat-

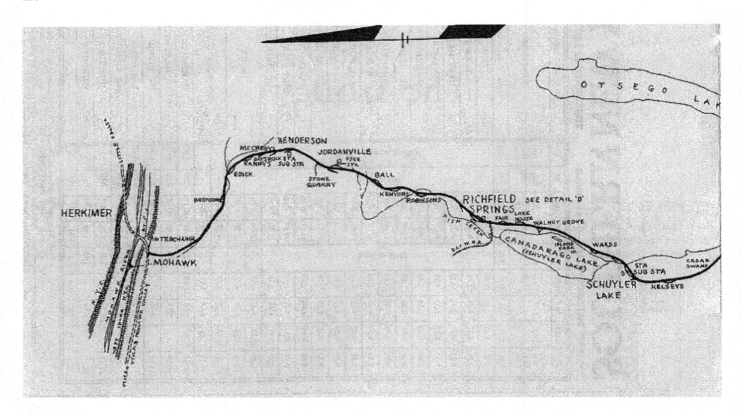

ing on the city streets. This line was known as the Oneonta Street Railway. In the early 1890's plans were formulated to turn the route into an electric railway. This line was to be The Oneonta and Otego Valley or O&OV. Its powerhouse was constructed on Market Street in Oneonta.

Hartwick anxious to have the trolley come up the Otego Valley formed a citizens committeee that was active in promoting the undertaking financially and otherwise. They worked at securing the rights of way, to be without cost to the expanding line. The new line grew by leaps and bounds, and in no time was extended to West Oneonta, and started pushing north to Laurens. As the line advanced rapidly many laborers were needed to man the picks and shovels for

Work Gang

Work Gang at Hope Factory

the back breaking work of construction. The common laborers were predominately Italian immigrants and were desperately in need of work.

The fast paced construction moved north and reached Laurens by July of 1901, and this part of the line was immediately put into use. A huge celebration was held and enjoyed by locals and laborers alike.

The fast pace continued and the line pushed through Hartwick in the summer of 1901, and then on to Cook's Summit, through Chase to

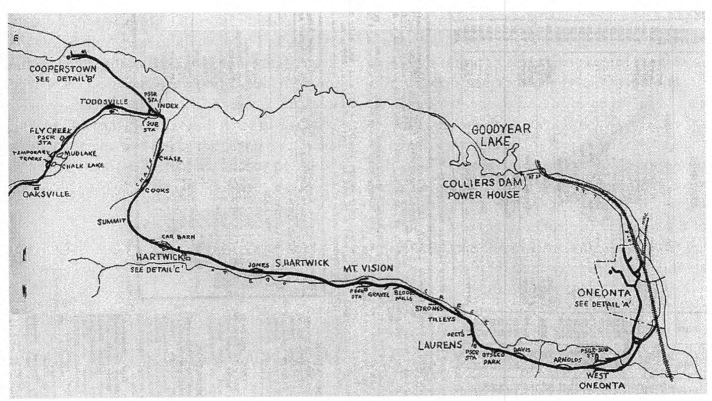

Index. A spur line reached Cooperstown late in the summer of 1901. The trolley line was now to be known as the Oneonta, Cooperstown & Richfield Springs Railway.

Powerhouse

As the line grew it wrought many changes in the tiny village of Hartwick. The Brooklyn side of town had been considered the business section, but with the arrival of the trolley line, the focus of the village shifted to the east side of town.

W. J. Hotaling began constructing stations along the trolley route. He built Hartwick's wooden depot building, and was later to supervise the building of the powerhouse and the car barns. As Hartwick was about midway of the line, it was to become home to the offices (Tamany Hall), house and repair the rolling stock (car barns), and provide electric power (powerhouse).

The construction of the trolley line was financed by capitalists and financiers from New York City. They were represented by Henry T. Jennings, a very able man who took many steps to facilitate the construction. He did an impressive job of coordinating the finances and the work force, but there were many occasions when the line faced bankruptcy.

Jennings proved apt at solving problems and

emergencies, but as the laborers building the line had little if any representation, they were the first to suffer. On more than one occasion there was not enough money to pay the construction workers. As the line pushed north the workers lived in tents and shanties along the route. One of their shantytowns was located below where the powerhouse was to be constructed. There also were boarding houses in Laurens and near Hope Factory in Index. A news item of the time tells of the arrival of the trolley at Hope with 62 Italian workers aboard. An army of picks and shovels and a gang boss awaited their arrival.

In 1903 a large group of unpaid workers attempted to halt the passage of a trolley car south of Hartwick blocking the tracks on either end. A confrontation between sheriff, deputies, company men and laborers took place, a riot ensued in which clubs, stones and firearms were used. Men on both sides received wounds, and one laborer was fatally wounded. Several of the workers, Rosario Lava, Ramonte Lofardo, Giovanno Remsivic, Romento Aldelfe, Centro Lavengo, and others were all arrested for inciting a riot, and taken before the Justice of the Peace and remanded to the custody of the Sheriff of Otsego County. The case was to go before the Grand Jury, but in September 28, 1903 it was decided that no crime had been committed and they were discharged. The treatment of these laborers was not one of the proudest moments in the trolley lines history. The dispute was settled and the laborers were paid, but the situation was to be repeated.

The first power house was of wooden construction. According to recollections of Henry Murdock, the timbers were sawed at a mill located on Wells Avenue, now known as School Street. The mill operated by Howard Murdock and Russ Bresee stood on the site now occupied by the present school building. The trees for the powerhouse timbers were cut locally. A dam was built, flooded and frozen to transport the trees to the mill. The powerhouse was built below the village. The builders walked to the site from the Brooklyn side of town, and crossed the Otego Creek on a wire walkway. The wooden powerhouse was of short duration and burned in 1904. The second powerhouse was constructed of brick and lasted as long as the trolley line.

Powerhouse

The line reached Mohawk in 1904. The company was in financial difficulties, and went into receivership. A new company was formed and the line became the Oneonta and Mohawk Valley or O & M V.

In the meantime Hartwick village was seeing a business boom. Trolley line personnel found the village centrally located, and there was a great demand for housing and lodging. On the west side of Otego Creek located at the foot of West Hill and the Gulf road stood the Brooklyn House. A three-story affair it housed a barbershop, rooms for lodging and a ballroom on the third floor. A very busy hotel in it's heyday.

Three more hotels and a boarding house were operating on Main Street in the center of town. On the north side of Main Street was the Commercial Hotel, which stood to the right of what is now the Hartwick Market. The large pillared building that now house the U.S. Post Office was the Otego Valley Hotel. Beyond that in the American Legion building was the Sliter Boarding House. Across the street where the ARC building now stands was the Cottage Hotel. From 1910 to 1920, Main Street, Hartwick from the Brooklyn House to the trolley depot was flourishing and probably at its peak.

Some excerpts from a letter written by Walter Andrus describes a bit about the village at this time.

"I can still remember the thrill I got when my mother would take me to Cooperstown or Oneonta on the trolley. Then about 1911 I got to spending my time around the Hartwick Station, my Dad being Agent. I picked up enough work so that 1912 I was on the payroll. As I was a minor my Dad had to sign my bond with a bonding company so I could handle money. I worked between school hours.

Later I was named, Assistant Agent, going to school with permission to leave during the day to carry the mail at certain hours. Daily with the exception of Sunday I made five round trips a day between the station and the post office, and my salary was three dollars a week. Later I was made Agent at $9.23 a week plus commission on express charges. I graduated in 1915 and worked as Agent with an assistant until I quit in 1917."

Station

The trolley made several stops in the town as well as the depot in the village. If there were passengers or mail the trolley would stop at South Hartwick, Jones Crossing, Fields Crossing, Cooks Summit, Chase, and Index. There were

Hartwick Station and Dispatchers Office

post offices at South Hartwick, Chase and Index each with their own postmarks.

At the South Hartwick stop there was a tiny station building, and the mailbag would be thrown off or the trolley would slow so a mailbag could be thrown on.

These stops also enabled students of the outlying district schools to catch the trolley to travel to Hartwick or Cooperstown to attend High School.

The trolley kept to a rigid schedule, and its dedicated employees averted many a calamity. Ice and snow storms, cows on the track, downed power poles were all taken in stride, but the unexpected could cause a tragic accident, and this happened more than once.

One such unexpected tragedy happened in South Hartwick in March of 1925. The trolley track approaching the South Hartwick station from the south was on a sharp curve, so the motorman's view rounding the curve was obstructed. About the time the trolley was expected, Mrs. Kent Myers, whose job it was to carry the mailbag from the post office to the trolley station, was waiting for the trolley to arrive.

As she looked south to watch for the train she saw her seventeen-year-old son Charles checking his trap line. As she watched she saw her son, who was prone to epileptic seizures, fall between the rails. As she ran frantically toward him, The trolley came around the curve striking the boy killing him instantly. The trolley traveled over fifty feet before it could be brought to a halt. The heartsick parents attached no blame to Motorman Elmer Genter and Conductor Howard Hyde, the crew of the trolley.

The trolley had a sad history of other accidents all along the line, from Oneonta to Mohawk, but along with tragedy the trolley brought excitement and opportunity. For a short run, fare could be as little as 5¢ or a trip to Oneonta 25¢.

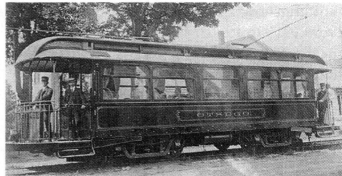

The palace car Otsego was finished in African figured mahogany and had a toilet, ice box and bar on board.

Excursion Car

Excursion trains ran south to Otsego Park, which was an amusement park below Laurens,

Otsego Park

built by the railroad, or north to Canadarago Park on the lake which was a very popular spot in the 1920's and 1930's.

For 15¢ extra fare one might ride in the Parlor Car which was elegantly furnished, and had an observation platform with a highly polished brass

Parlor Car

rail. Many dignitaries rode in the Parlor Car and it was also used for conveying wealthy families to their summer homes.

By 1907, due to more and more demands for electricity the PowerHouse at Hartwick couldn't keep up. More electricity was needed so a hydroelectric dam was constructed fifteen miles away on the Susquehanna River. Portions of the towns of Portlandville and Milford Center con-

Colliersville Dam

taining over 600 hundred acres were to be flooded, and a dam built to fill the need. Construction started in 1907 and continued through the winter months. Workers earned $3.30 a day. A power line was built to carry 13,200-volt currant to the trolley line.

Car Barn

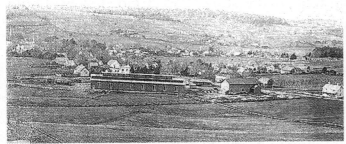
Car Barn

In 1910 the car barns in Oneonta burned, and five cars lost. The car barns in Hartwick now housed the entire rolling stock.

Offices of the Otsego & Herkimer Railroad, Hartwick, NY

The offices and general warehouse for the railroad line were located by the tracks on land pres-

ently occupied by Phillips Lumber Co. The offices were transferred to Cooperstown in 1912. Land next to the station was donated by the line, and the former office building known as Tamany Hall was also donated, and was to be moved to this new location. The relocated building was to be the clubhouse for the Employees Mutual Benefit Association, and is still known today as the EMBA Hall. The moving of this structure was a major feat, and required many teams of horses, many men, and a great deal of planning. It was watched with great interest by many people. The hall's auditorium measured 40 by 90 feet, and had a wide stage that was used for plays, lyceum courses, vaudeville acts, etc. The hall still serves the community today for a variety of purposes.

In 1918 the line requested the Public Service Commission to change its name to the Southern New York Power & Railway Company. Until it's demise the line continued to be known as the Southern New York.

For over 25 years the electric line meant just about everything to Hartwick's economy. Four or five daily mails went out in both directions. There was fast and frequent express service. Heavy freight could be handled economically.

In 1917 no less than 45 persons were employed in various capacities by the company, and had residences in the village, most with families.

The employees of the line kept the trolley to a close schedule, but there were occasional mishaps or acts of nature that raised havoc with the schedule.

In February of 1920 a blizzard brought the trolley to a stand still. According to the Hartwick Reporter not a car was moving on the main line of the Southern New York. The company manned the snow plows trying to break through the mountainous snow drifts piled high by strong winds. No mail reached Hartwick from Saturday night until about Tuesday noon. Monday night the line was open between Hartwick and

1920 Blizzard

Richfield Springs only. Snow plows were working all night long in an effort to break through to Herkimer and Oneonta. The tieup of this road has never been so complete, and it is taxing the ability of the company to relieve the situation. In central and northern New York scores of trains have been stalled more than 24 hours in snow drifts.

The safety of the trolley, its passengers and freight lay not only with the crew, but in the dispatchers office located in Hartwick. The line was a single track all the way, and the dispatchers were kept busy. While the law allowed an eight-hour workday, the company permitted the dispatchers to work no more than six hours.

The trolley crew itself, while relying on the dispatcher's office, could also tell by the dimming of lights if another trolley was approaching.

Hartwick could tell if a trolley was laboring up Chase Gorge as it would cause lights to dim in the village. Village residents were used to power surges.

Minnie Mead told of her rescue by the trolley's crew in the 1920's. She worked in Cooperstown and drove back and forth to Hartwick. On one occasion as she left work there was a snowstorm, and though it was snowing heavily, she felt she could make it home. As she drove, the traveling grew worse and there was no other traffic on the road. She slowly made her way up Index hill, through Bissell Hollow, and up Chase Gorge.

She got as far as the cape below where Fedinand Thering lives now, and her car could not make it through the drifting snow. Sitting in her stalled car, watching the snow steadily piling up, listening to the howling winds she weighed her chances of leaving her car, and making her way to the nearest farmhouse which would have been where Therings live. She decided to stay with her car, as she felt that either way she might freeze to death.

In the meantime the trolley was also making its way to Hartwick. Equipped with snowplows it was slowly making progress against the drifting snow. After making the grade up Chase Gorge, it was proceeding across the flatter area, where the track came quite near the highway at the cape. There the crew spotted Minnie's car buried in the snow, and decided they should check to see if someone was stranded. James Maxwell struggled through the snowdrifts to the stalled car. Once there he recognized the car, and seeing someone inside pulled the door open, and said "Is that you, Min?". Wonderful words to hear when you've reconciled yourself to possibly freezing to death. Her rescuer helped her across the field to the trolley. Inside was a hot fire in the firebox where she was able to get warmed through, and thanks to the trolley crew arrived safely in Hartwick.

There were other acts of courage and dedication of the men who worked on the line, men whose names were once well known from Oneonta to Mohawk. The names of these men are now but a distant memory in the minds of the very few old timers left.

From 1910 to 1920 Hartwick flourished and was reaching the peak of its boom years. The trolley remained vital to the area, even though the line itself was having financial problems. The advent of the automobile was draining away the line's lifeblood, and it was struggling to keep afloat. Then on March 27, 1925 the line suffered a devastating blow. Fire struck the car barns at Hartwick. The wood brick structure burned quickly, and could not be saved. Eight cars were

Car Barns

lost in the fire, and much of the passenger service was curtailed.

The loss of the building, and rolling stock was estimated at $200,000.00. The remaining equipment was transferred to the PowerHouse where it was to stand outside exposed to the elements. Plans for a new car barn never came to fruition, and the line, little by little, curtailed its services. More improved roads were being built, and trucks and automobiles were usurping trolley revenues. In 1928 the line carried 61,403 passengers, and by 1931 it carried only 14,118. Passenger service was discontinued in 1933. More and more mail was being transported by truck, and the mail contract was lost.

By the 1930's the crews of laborers who built the line were long gone. The motormen and conductors had found other jobs. The need for the dispatchers, switchmen, and wiregangs no longer existed.

Through the 1930's the trolley operated as a freight line. It carried feed and coal north, and crushed stone south from Jordanville. Ironically the crushed stone was used to build the highways that were strangling the line's existence.

The trolley's trips north grew fewer and fewer.

Trips fell from once a day to twice a week. One lone man now kept watch of the tracks for signs of trouble. Baggio Cardone, probably one of the original Italian laborers, now a lone figure operating a push car, patrolled the tracks checking the ties and rails, keeping the route safe for the occasional trolley.

The Associated Gas & Electric sold the line in August 1939 to the H.E. Salzberg Corp. of New York City.

The last shipment of coal was delivered to the Beach Coal Company in Cooperstown on September 16, 1940. In late 1940 a request for abandonment of 44.1 miles of track was granted leaving 1.5 miles of track between Oneonta and West Oneonta still doing business with five employees.

Once abandoned the line fast became derelict. In 1941 when the nation was at war there was a cry for scrap metal. Children were let out of school for scrap metal drives. Fields and woods were searched for old metal. Farmers parted with old machinery, housewives gave cherished aluminum pots and pans, and the rusting tracks of the Southern New York were being pulled up.

Copper and steel needed for the defense effort were reclaimed from the lines right-of-way. About 75 tons of annealed copper was salvaged from the wires. The Horton Construction Co. from Taunton, Ma. ripped up steel rails. Acetylene torches were used to cut the rails apart. A caterpillar tractor nosed down the roadbed ripping the rails loose from the ties. Workman with pinch bars and sledges removed spikes. This was followed by a bulldozer gouging out the old ties so trucks could drive in and load the rails and scrap iron. A crew of a dozen men cleaned up about two miles of track a day.

Approximately 4,000 tons of number one steel was reclaimed. Some of the track was to be relaid elsewhere. The remainder was to be melted down for building locomotives, battleships, tanks or cannon.

When the trolley line had first been proposed in the 1890's the towns along the route secured the rights-of-way free of charge to the builders. In the 1940's the rights-of-way reverted to the original farms or plots of land.

The Powerhouse continued to stand for a few years, but eventually was torn down. The 185-foot tall smokestack continued to stand. The rugged built foundation walls were four foot thick. On May 16,1953 people gathered on Route 205, and watched as Ben Wells and Carl Eggleston of Morris set off the dynamite charge that caused the smokestack to crumble and drop. The bricks were reused in a building on Chestnut Street in Oneonta. Hartwick Rod and Gun Club owns land where the PowerHouse stood, and their clubhouse stands by the old PowerHouse Pond.

On October 21, 1954 the remaining 1½ mile remnant of the Southern New York received another terrible blow. The railroad's 50-ton diesel engine pulling an empty freight car from West Oneonta collided with a 12-ton cement mixer truck in Oneonta's West End. The truck passing in front of the slow moving train got by safely except for the last foot, which glanced off the train causing the truck to overturn on a passenger car waiting at the crossing.

All five employees were on board the train. Four men were inside the train, with James Maxwell, conductor- flagman standing on the front

of the diesel engine. He was fatally injured in the accident. Affectionately known as Jimmy Maxwell, he was a long time resident of Hartwick, a former town of Hartwick Supervisor, and had been conductor for the trolley line for 43 years.

The line continued to operate with five employees, providing, as needed, service to only a half dozen customers.

On Dec. 5 1969 a petition to abandon the final mileage left of the line was filed by the owners H.E. Salzburg & Co. There was vigorous protest against ending service, therefore the Public Service Commission opposed the closing. However the Dept. of Transportation advised that an expressway was soon to sever the line in the West End anyway.

Soon after the Southern New York had an offer of $10,000.00 for the line, trackage, business and equipment.

In 1973, the West Oneonta Depot, the last parcel, was sold to Joseph Capra by the Queens Railroad Company and is now the offices of Capra Business Consultants.

By: Nadine Phillips

Bibliography

In Old Oneonta—Ed Moore—Vol. 2 & 3
The Leatherstocking Route—David F. Nestle
The Oneonta Daily Star
The Otsego Farmer
The Freeman's Journal
The Hartwick Reporter
Transportation—Dr. Butterfield
Recollections of——Minnie Mead, Henry Murdock
Letter written by Walter Andrus (Loaned by Dave Petri)
Justice Criminal Docket

Polish Beds

There are at least three and possibly more stories recorded about the discovery of the wonderful polishing qualities of the blue clay found to exist under the earth along South Street.

One story involves a Mrs. Alsworth who ran a boarding house near a brickyard some distance south of the village. She noticed some of the bluish substance on the floor of her kitchen on a rainy day when the men had returned for a noon meal. Stooping to remove it, she observed its peculiar composition and rubbing some of it across the blade of a knife, revealed its power to polish.

Another story concerns Rufus Sargent who in 1840 was having a cellar dug for a home on the east side of South Street. The workers noticed their picks and shovels were becoming very well polished. They experimented and found the blue gray clay they were digging through made a wonderful polish. The beds on the east side of the street never proved to be profitable.

A third story about the discovery of polish in Hartwick is that Rufus Peters brought home a sample of the odd clay he found while plowing. Mrs. Peters determined it made excellent silver polish and it was marketed in small packages as "Peter's Polish". Later Mr. Peters sold it by the barrel to silverware manufacturers where it was used in the final buffing process.

Manley Bresee is also given credit for selling the polish in 3 oz. Packets for 25¢ to farmers wives on his peddler's route.

Sheffield Harrington began digging polish on the west side of South Street where larger deposits were found. He was the first person to ship barrels of polish to manufacturers of fine furniture and caskets in the New England States, especially Connecticut. Most houses on the west side of South Street have steep banks in their back yards, reminders of the blue grit that was removed.

The process of mining polish was exacting. A layer of covering gravel and dirt four to eight feet in depth had to be removed before the vein of polish was revealed. Great care had to be taken to keep dirt out of the clay itself and the men were required to wear clean clothes and covered boots when they worked in the pits. The clay was removed in large chunks and transferred to a drying shed. In earlier days, the polish was removed with picks and the pieces thrown to the workmen above. As the pits grew deeper it was necessary to suspend scaffolding and the chunks were thrown upward from one to another until the surface was reached. The horse and pulley later supplanted this labor-intensive method.

The pits had to be reopened each day as the clay and the surrounding gravel were extremely unstable and tended to cave in during the night. Eighteen hour workdays were common to take advantage of the open pits before they caved in on themselves, a continual hazard to the workers.

When dried, the clay could be pulverized into

a fine, flour-like powder. It was usually packed in barrels of 300 to 400 pounds capacity. Annual production ranged from 1200 to 2200 barrels.

The polish was mined and shipped for about one hundred years until the 1940s when cheaper polishes lessened the demand and profitable veins of the clay became harder to find.

———

By A. Harrison

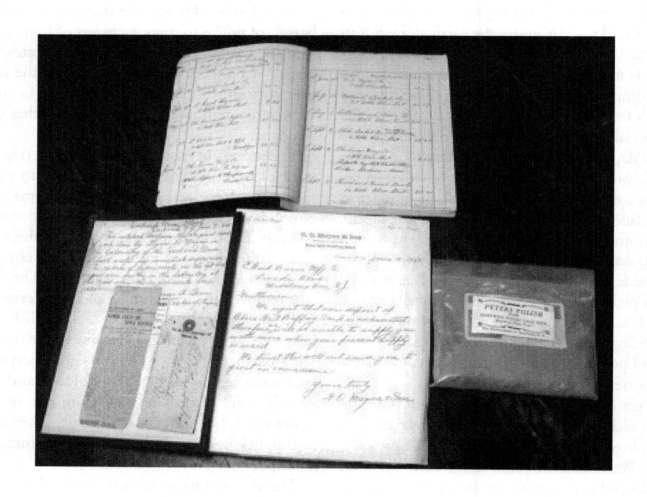

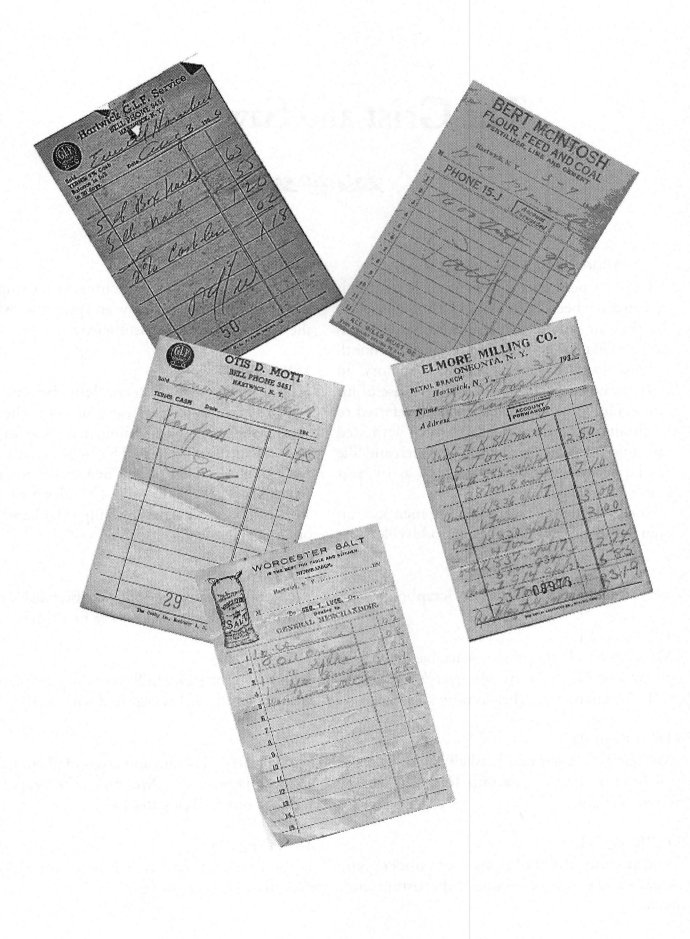

The Grist and Saw Mills

1806 – The Huntington Papers

The first permanent gristmill of Hartwick is said to have been built around 1806. Prior to this time an early settler named Richards was in the habit of taking a bushel of corn once a month to what was later known as "Hope Factory" in Index to be ground into flour for the use of his household. The Hartwick gristmill referred to was built not far from the date which witnessed the building of the Presbyterian Church and like the latter was presumably located at or near Hartwick Village.

The Chenango County History mentions an even earlier gristmill located in Toddsville.

Items From Old Potter Scrapbook

1878 -pg. 14

Mr. Cassius Maples of this place has rented his gristmill to Albert Avery. Mr. Avery's son Melvin will take charge of it this coming season.

1878 – pg. 91

Mr. Summer Alger and Haskell Harrington are proprietors of the gristmill formally run by Cassius Maples.

1878 -pg. 33

The gristmill at this place has been under going repairs and is now beginning to do custom work again.

1878 -pg. 19

Mr. Card and Alger contemplate putting in steam power to run their saw and grist mills when the supply of water is insufficient.

1880 -pg. 34

School Street sawmill items. John Bowdish of Milford is about to erect a steam mill in the village for the purpose of planing, matching, molding and slitting lumber. The building is to be put up at the head of the new street recently opened by E. W. Wells on the Maples premises. The foundation for the dwelling is laid and another is being laid.

1880 – pg. 7

The steam whistle of John W. Bowdish's new planing mill was blown for the first time.

1884 -pg. 40

John Bowdish's steam mill is running on full time with six hands and is crowded with orders.

1892

The Hartwick steam and saw and planing mill changes January 1st. Mr. Aplin the proprietor has sold out to Delos Robinson.

1894 – pg. 73

Delos Robinson has traded his steam mill for the Channing Naylor farm.

1892 –

Howard Murdock and Russ Bresee owned the sawmill on the lot on School Street where Peter Soberas house now stands. They sawed lumber and etc. using steam power.

The mill burned in 1904.

Howard Murdock and Russ Bresee Sawmill: Howard Murdock in white shirt and suspenders, Russ Bresee with vest and white shirt next to Howard. The rest are unidentified.

Grist and Sawmill built in 1802 by Samuel Mudge; the year the town of Hartwick was organized (March 3, 1802). This picture taken before 1880. Melvin Avery with hand on grain bag, Cassius Maples on steps with hat raised in hand, Thomas Jenks directly behind pile of bark, Milan Seely bareheaded with pole in hand, Reverend Fratenburg at right wearing derby, Summer Alger at extreme right. From 1862 to 1867 Lewis Beach and his brother George Beach ran the grist and sawmill. One of the old millstones in this mill (1942) was still there but had not been used for years. The mill got their power by digging a ditch ½ mile long and connecting with a dam in the Otego Creek located just up the stream from the North Street bridge on Route 205 at the edge of the village.

1898 – Hartwick business Folder (local history)

Delos Robinson recently opened for sale of all kinds of feed at the old Bissel stand westside.

1898 – Dec. 29 Otego Valley News

A.D. Beach in connection with his livery business keeps a line of feed at his barn on Main Street in the rear of L. J. Jackson's barbershop.

1903-pg. 116-Old Potter Scrapbook

Louis Lake has opened for business the gristmill and sawmill that has been closed for the past few months. He is prepared to do all kinds of grinding and sawing at the old stand.

1914 - Old Potter Scrapbook

Marked improvements made to Deacon Bissel's saw and gristmill since it has fallen into the hands of Mr. Lake. Includes engine, building and machinery.

1922 James Ainslie O. B. 1967

Louis Lake had gristmill near Otego creek (where Jim Millea built his house).

Jim Ainslie

Ainslie brothers bought the mill. They did grinding for farmers for awhile then did lumber business.

James Ainslie (Jim) was in business for 45 years.

Jim Ainslie's Mill

Phillips Sawmill

1932 – Sept. 8 Hartwick Reporter

Ainslie brothers will open our cider mill for business as of October 1st. Price per gallon for making cider 3 cents. We also begin to grind buckwheat for flour at that date.

1915-1917 Hartwick Reporter

The feed store managed by Burch brothers changed name to Burch Brothers and Talbot. This was later Harrisons feedstore by the railroad tracks.

Harrison Feedstore. Cool Storage in Rear

1925

Paul French had feed, coal, fertilizer and lime store. Paul was killed while hunting in the North Woods.

1922 – John Mott paper

G. L. F. formed.

Companies grinding and mixing rations were at liberty to substitute any product to the mixture that would provide a profit and there was no means to know what was included. A group of farmers here and at other locations met with H. E. Babcock under sponsor of Grange and Dairymen's Leagues to form a cooperative buying organization to insure quality and savings. This cooperative known as Grange League Federation (G. L. F.) was owned and operated by farmers through the local committee. All rations sold had contained a tag on the bag with guaranteed analysis of content.

Otis D. and Mrs. Harriet Mott

Old RR Dispatcher Office and Freight Station purchased by Otis Mott for G.L.F. Feedstore

In the beginning Otis D. Mott acting as agent buyer sold feed direct off the freight car with shipments arriving on the siding just south of the rail depot. Here farmers who were notified of the arrival loaded the feed into their vehicles.

For a short time Mr. Mott relinquished handling to Mr. French of the existing feed store. Sales did not continue to benefit the new Co-op so Mr. Mott resumed handling of the product. For a number of years this arrangement continued until the old trolley stock room was obtained for storage so that sales became more regular to customers. After the demise of the rail line the depot was purchased for business.

G. L. F. expanded into other products and these were trucked in from Albany and some freight cars on siding in Oneonta. As an operating farm Co-op dividends from sales were paid to farmers who were issued stock.

G. L. F. combined with Eastern States Farm Co-op to form Agway. With the passing of Mrs. Mott, Otis decided to sell the business to W. J. Weaver and the business continued under Agway management for several years. During that time the competing feed dealer was bought out.

The feed grinding and mixing store started by Burch went through several owners; McIntosh, Roberts, Harrison. Carlton Roberts was last acting manager for Harrison.

Ralph Bush grinding grain for Agway

1949

Webb Weaver came as agent buyer for G. L. F. and bought the store from Otis Mott at that time. The store was once Hartwick's trolley depot. Later Agway bought Harrison feed store August 7. The town office building now is built there on the site.

1976 or 1979

Agway closed June 30, 1978 in Hartwick. Store manager was Jeffery Haas of Norwich. He succeeded Kendall Marlette. Kendall was transferred to Milford Agway store. Kendall was last working in Cooperstown.

December 1980 The Daily Star

Anthony Schlieser bought the Agway store from Webb Weaver. Schlieser converted part into a self-service Laundromat. The remaining 9,000-sq. ft. houses the new Feedbag feed store.

1988

Orrin Higgins now owns the building and the Grain and Tool Shed is managed by Roger Wright and sells Blue Seal feed and etc. The only feed store in town year 2001.

———

By: Eva Murdock

Maple Industry

The making of maple syrup was a basic industry for early settlers. Large stands of maple trees in the area provided the pioneers with wood for fuel, lumber for shelter and in the spring of each year sap for making maple syrup and sugar.

From Beardsley in "Growing Up In Cooper Country" the proliferation of maple trees led the pioneers to the practice of tapping the trees in the early spring, then felling the trees, and burning off the land to make a cleared area in the wilderness.

In pioneer days a sugar camp would be set up in a grove of maple trees and occupied during the sap season. Early methods of making maple syrup was a far cry from the sophisticated systems of today but the process of boring a hole in the tree and placing a sap spile is still pretty basic. Today maple producers have pipelines and huge holding tanks, where the early settlers attached homemade wooden buckets to catch the sap. When large amounts of trees were tapped and the sap running, a person could be very busy gathering. Also boiling the sap near where it was gathered was most practical, so the camp was active both day and night during the season. Depending on the trees and their location de-

termines the sweetness of the sap, but it takes about 32 to 40 gallons of sap to make a gallon of syrup. Large caldrons of sap were kept boiling over a roaring fire. Eventually it was discovered that large flat pans made boiling more efficient to reduce the sap down to syrup. Remains of old sap arches can still be found in some woods today. The settlers relied entirely on maple sugar and honey, and many never in their lives tasted the cane sugar we have today.

Most every farm had a sugar bush, but there were some farms with bushes that were outstanding producers. Hartwick had what was considered to be the best sugar bush in Otsego County. It was on the Abe Marsh farm north of Hartwick, on the farm currently owned by Tom Weeks. The first evaporator used in Otsego County was on the Marsh farm, and people came from afar to see it.

Though making sugar was an exhausting and sticky business, as soon as spring was in the air, most farm families eagerly looked forward to sugaring time. Donald Eldred remembers that his grandmother boiled sap on the pinnacle on their farm. That must have been a sight to see, not only for the one boiling sap on the pinnacle, but for the people in the valley below.

Susie Phillips told the following story of old fashioned syrup making. After days of tapping, and gathering, and boiling, her family was nearing the end of maple season and had a large flat pan of syrup ready to be purified and canned. The boiling had been done in the yard, and as it was late in the evening, it was decided to pull the pan from the fire, cover it, and finish the final steps the following day. Boards were used to cover the pan, and all went to bed. In the morning the family was up early, but the family goose was up earlier. It had gotten on the boards, and been tipped into the pan of syrup. The goose was so weighted by the sticky syrup it couldn't move. The syrup was ruined, and the hated goose was exiled to the chicken yard. So ended days of hard work.

Another sad occurrence that sometimes befell maple syrup production was fire. Occasionally a person overseeing the boiling process would be overcome by exhaustion and would fall asleep while boiling and the pan or evaporator would burn up, sometimes the building also.

In present day Hartwick there are very few sugar bushes left, and the process is much changed. Today pipelines carry the sap to holding tanks, and from there it is trucked to a sugarhouse for boiling in a large stainless steel evaporator that is computer operated. The final steps are monitored closely to produce the best quality syrup possible.

Bruce Phillips is presently Hartwick's only maple producer.

By: Nadine Phillips

Dismal Inn Sugar, Hartwick. In five short years, Bruce Phillips built his operation into an efficient sugarhouse, running over a thousand taps.

Dismal Inn Sugar, Hartwick

*Methodist Church
Lord's Acre sugar house*

Meat Markets and Delivery Routes

The face of Hartwick's Main Street changes from decade to decade, even year to year, businesses come and go. Hartwick village is checkered with ghosts of former businesses. At one time almost any item one needed could be bought locally. Today, when we cannot even purchase produce or fresh meat in the village, it is hard to believe that a hundred years ago many local businesses were competing for the housewife's grocery dollar.

A news item of 1907 tells "Hartwick has 3 meat markets, either of which is selling 3 times as much as 25 years ago. Dorr Gardner, Sliters and DeMetts are having a hustling trade. (Earl DeMetts market was in the small storage building by Thamer Harpers house.)

Another news item "E. 0. Rogers and John Bingham have started a meat market on the west side and make regular daily trips canvassing the village. Meat eaters ought to be able to get all they desire with three meat markets in town."

Also in 1910 this item appeared; "Clayton Babbits implements have arrived and his meat market in the basement of Marvins harness shop is now opened." The harness shop was on the north side of Main Street where a parking lot is located at the present time.

From a taped interview with Ford Risley: his father, Will Risley, built a home on South Street and ran a meat market in a little shop in front of his house. In 1915 he opened W.E. Risleys General Store on Main Street and sold groceries and fresh meat for more than 30 years.

Jim Telfer started Telfers Meat Market sometime in the 1920's, in the cellar of the Telfer home on South Street.

Telfers raised their own meat for the market. Beef, pork, veal, lamb and poultry were raised on the farm. There was a smokehouse for curing bacon, dried beef and ham. Telfers had an outstanding recipe for sausage.

Two large rooms were built in the basement for the market. One room was the cooler where the meat was hung, and it had a compartment from floor to ceiling that was packed daily with ice. As the ice melted the water drained outside to a dry well. The ice supply was cut during the winter from the Powerhouse Pond.

For years Andy Telfer was the butcher and meat

Earl Demett – 1913

Meat Delivery

Elevating Ice in Telfers Icehouse

cutter. He presided over the meat block, and would cut your order while you waited. Later years Bill Carvin took over this work.

Telfers had a delivery truck on the road. Bert Shaul made deliveries, and took meat orders, which he would fill the next trip through. The delivery route closed in 1935.

After Jim Telfer died in 1938, his daughter Mary Telfer took over the meat market and dairy operation with the help of Bill Carvin. Joe Lynch was another employee at Telfers doing much of the dairy work. Donald Phillips and other local fellows worked for Mary Telfer, Lynn Persons remembered as a young teenager washing bottles for spending money. Betty Lamphere, who taught high school science, helped during the summer. Miss Lamphere tells that they did a big broiler business, processing 20 or 30 a week. Summers were busy, as haying and growing and harvesting other crops were very important to the businesses.

Just before World War II, Telfers stopped butchering, and closed the meat market.

Mary continued the milk delivery business, and for years delivered milk door to door in the village.

When the meat market was still in operation customers would generally place a meat order when Mary delivered their milk. Mae Sliter, who ran Sliters Boarding House, was a regular customer. One day her meat order was "I want only five pork chops this week instead of six, as last week Dr. Schoolcraft put the extra chop in his pocket."

Miss Lamphere explained how the dairy operation was run during the World War II years. After the milking, the cans of milk were im-

mersed in ice water in a large vat in the milk house. The milk bottles were washed and rinsed, and Mary had a bottling apparatus that would fill 12 bottles at a time. There was a capper to seal the bottles. The Telfer dairy was certified, and all state health rules were followed. When state health rules required pasteurization Mary changed much of the operation. She no longer did the bottling, but getting up at 4 A.M. took the chilled cans of milk to the Oneonta dairy for pasteurization. Then returning to Hartwick did the route as usual.

Many of Mary's customers would leave instructions of where or how they wanted their milk delivered. Several would ask her to put their milk in their icebox if they were going away. Mary got a chuckle over the following incident. A certain Hartwick lady left her a note saying that she would be out of town for three days. She did not want to leave her milk tickets on the porch as someone might steal them. "Mary please leave the milk inside, and get the tickets off the table, as I have left the house unlocked."

Eventually Mary sold the milk business, and took up a teaching career, as a Science and Agriculture teacher for Hartwick High School.

In a long gone building located where the REA presently has a parking lot Art Allen opened a meat market and luncheonette in the early 1930's. Backed by well-to-do businessman E. 0. Rogers, the market was called Maplehurst, and served lunches as well as selling meats. Mr. Rogers was involved in many local business ventures, and built a fine home now occupied by the REA. Across the road were many barns and out buildings, all painted cream color and trimmed with white. All the level farmland now owned by Kallans was part of the farm, and it was indeed a showplace when you drove into the village. Mr. Rogers passed away in the late 1930's, and the farm was broken up and sold, and Maplehurst Meat Market was closed.

About 1945 Scott Hester bought the Rogers tenant house along with the Maplehurst building. Hartwick had just come through the deprivations of World War 2, and many items that hadn't been available for years, were again coming on the market.

Kallan barns before the fire.

For a brief time Scott Hester did a landslide business selling fresh bananas to the village residents from the old Maplehurst building.

100 firemen battle flames that destroy Hartwick barns

Sometime in the 1960's the Rogers tenant house and Maplehurst were torn down. The big farm had several owners until acquired by the Kallan Bros. who raised crops and used the barn for storage until it burned in 1969.

Delivery to Icehouse

Another familiar face around town in the 30's was Stanley "Puff" Brown who ran a delivery route. A genial person, he sold cold meats, and a good selection of fresh fruits and vegetables. Later, his wife Enna was the friendly Grand Union lady, selling Grand Union products door to door.

Ice Harvest – Filling Icehouse

Before modern refrigeration, the dairy industry, the meat industry, village folk and farmers all depended on ice for cooling.

Ice cakes on Double Bob Sled

Many people had icehouses that they filled in winter with blocks of ice cut locally. The ice was packed in clean sawdust for insulation, and would keep well into the summertime.

Frederica Hornbeck remembers her father filling their icehouse with ice cut from a small pond on their farm on Scotch Hill. Neighbors worked together cutting the ice into blocks by hand with an ice saw.

A 1913 news item from Elizabeth Curry's

scrapbook states "A. D. Beach, E.O. Rogers, and M. D. Sliter have had forces of men very busy these past few days putting ice in for the coming seasons. —Good thickness and usual quality."

Another news item of Feb. 1923- "Ice harvest nearly over and fine quality gathered."

Mrs. Orville Main who lived on South Street wrote in her diary Jan.22, 1936-"Ice house nearly full. Jim Ainslie drew 180 cakes of ice, 2¢ a cake for drawing."

Jan. 29, 1936 – "Drew 2 loads of sawdust and finished covering ice."

Stuart Ainslie said that as long as the Powerhouse was in operation hot water was discharged into the pond and it never froze over. After the powerhouse closed the pond became a major source of ice for Hartwick village.

Clifford Stohler had a buzz saw on runners to cut ice. Ice sold from 3¢ to 5¢ a cake at the pond.

Henry Murdock remembers drawing ice with a Model A Ford truck. He said it was not a money-making business.

When cutting ice on a large scale an ice plow was used. David Petrie explains "There were a couple kinds of ice plows. One kind just cut ice, the other type cut a row, and at the same time scored the ice for the next row. This made uniform blocks. The ice saw didn't always cut all the way through, and the ice had to be broken apart with an ice spud. An ice spud could have one, two or three prongs. The floating ice was dragged from the water with long ice tongs. Austin Thompson had a homemade ice saw and rigged an elevator ramp for loading, and cut ice as a business.

Before electric refrigerators and freezers, the housewife kept food cool in an icebox. Not the efficient machines we are used to, the standard for chilled foods was far different than today.

In the late 1930's and early 40's Whites from West Oneonta had an ice delivery route. They came through Hartwick twice a week. If you wanted ice you put a card in the window. The deliveryman brought a cake of ice (I think about 25 or 35 pounds, and costing 35¢. He would carry it with ice tongs, and deposit it in the top of the icebox. As the ice melted the water ran down a drainpipe to a catch pan in the bottom. The catch pan was forever overflowing and had to be mopped up.

These were the good old days!

Nadine Phillips

Milliners

The milliner was a craft person during the late 1800's and early 1900's. Their styles and skills in making women's hats had a competitive market. One such store was located in the end of the Augur Hardware and later I remember one located on Main Street.

The milliner on North Street was Mrs. L. P. Shaul. She had formerly had a shop in the red house that was the second house from the library. Later the Shauls moved to the brick house, which is now in the Farmer's Museum, where Mr. Shaul sold pianos and Mrs. Shaul conducted her Millinery Shop.[1]

Earlier milliners were Laura and Rebekah Reynolds. Their home and millinery shop was in the Wolben house (now Varney's). [2] Rebekah was mentioned in a letter about Hartwick in the 1860's from Mrs. Mary E. Shaul. [3]

Another milliner was Jane Jones. She owned the property on the corner of the south side of Main Street but soon purchased the house on the opposite side of the street known as Dr. Schoolcraft's. This building has now been torn down. [4] In Jane Jones' obituary we find she was a milliner in Hartwick for 30 years.[5] She advertised in the "Hartwick Visitor" on May 13, 1902. Behind Ford Risley's store (now the Hartwick Market) was Mr. H. G. Miller's blacksmith shop and Mrs. Miller's Millinery. In 1895, Mrs. H. G. and F. Miller invited the local ladies to come and view "these latest Fancies in Fashion. Direct from New York."

Clipping June 19, 1899 – " Mrs. Flora Garlock has finished her work at the Millinery store of Mrs. Sabra Miller and has returned to Welcome."

Mr. and Mrs. Miller moved to Cooperstown about 1903 and Mrs. Miller continued her milliner work. [6]

Mrs. Aval Pratt, formally Inez A. Kinney conducted her own shop. In 1915 she advertised in the "Hartwick Reporter."

Bertha Aplin was a milliner before marrying Wm. Ainslie.

One of these frilly creations a century ago sold for as much as three dollars and a woman would turn out two or three a day.

It was a stiff price for the times. Although making the hat itself took only an hour or two, there was a lot of time spent in the selection of materials. The customer would come in and look at the box of feathers and choose the fabric and style that would look best.

Feathers were a prominent part of headwear and it was said by some men "A bonnet was an excuse for a feather." A woman put great store in the appearance the right hat would give for the season.

By: John Mott and Frederica Hornbeck

Bibliography:
1. Elenor Jones memories
2. 1868 Atlas of Otsego County
3. Pearl Weeks "History of Hartwick"
4. 1868 Atlas of Otsego County
5. Nadine Phillips blue scrapbook
6. Nellie Balcom's scrapbook (Barb Potter)

Fig. 1-A Shirred Brim frames The Face Attractively

Fig. 2-A Chic Effect In White Velveteen

Fig. 3 - Black on White Makes A Striking Combination

Blacksmiths

No artisan was more needed in developing a frontier community than a blacksmith. His role in working iron and steel was much wider in earlier than in later times. He was called upon to make hinges, latches, bolts, axes, hoes, "iron" wagons and sleds and other related tasks, in addition to the shoeing of oxen and horses, the setting of wagon tires and all the repair jobs our older generation have witnessed. There was work for many of his kind; many were available and their shops stood, not only in every village and hamlet, but often solitary on country roads.

Nathan Davidson was located in Hartwick about 1780. He came from Massachusetts. He came down the lake from Springfield on Otsego Lake, late in the spring, ice covered with water, which rendered the journey, to one unaccustomed to the lakes, not at all pleasing. As he approached the shore, and at last found himself safely on terra firma, casting a backward glance, he exclaimed, "You'll never catch me on that ice again." He was a blacksmith by trade, and during the Revolution assisted the colonial cause by shoeing the horses of the soldiery, making swords, etc. He was a useful man in the new settlement, working at his trade for the pioneers, who in turn assisted in clearing his land. He is thought to be the first such workman in the town.

Samuel Bissell located in 1791 a short way out of Hartwick Village (Bissell Hollow), he settled just west of the Chase burying ground, the road then came out at the Oliver Weeks place. His father built the Curtis Chase place. It was built for a hotel, Sarah Bissell Carr was one of his daughters. In 1801 he moved his home to Chase Creek with his shop right across the stream from the "Chase" school house. His descendants followed the trade there certainly for more than seventy years. Asahel Armstrong, from Bennington, Vt., was not far east of Bissell in 1791 on the road up the west side of Oaks Creek near Toddsville. Elihu Wentworth, who had come to a nearby farm with his father as a boy of twelve about 1794, and also from Bennington, learned this trade and followed it all his life in this town and elsewhere. William Eddy had a shop in 1803 not far west of Toddsville. Elihu's son, David Wentworth, had the same calling, and for a long time his shop was on the Milford road directly south of Arnolds Lake. Joseph B. Luther, a blacksmith, was twenty-one when he arrived here from Swansea, Mass. in 1814, so he doubtless had already acquired the trade. His family soon acquired a considerable property here, and it is not known that Joseph ever did any local blacksmithing. He knew how!!

A prominent pioneer was Deacon Ziba Newland, who came from Norton, Massachusetts and settled in what is now South Hartwick, in about the year 1792, then 24 years old. Deacon Newland was a nail-maker by trade, and soon after locating set up a shop and forge, which business he followed in connection with farming. He married Lucy Henry, and had a family of nine children. A grandson Henry Newland, resides in Otego Village.

David Kendall was a Hartwick Village blacksmith as early as 1813. He accumulated considerable real estate, and was an esteemed citizen, a commissioner of deeds, an executor for several estates, a clerk and chorister at the Baptist Church for thirty years. His stone shop stood in 1827 on the Main Street of Hartwick a little way from the Grist Mill. John Webster is mentioned as having preceded him. There were too many in this craft to enumerate all, so only a few comments will be accorded this topic. In 1872 there were eleven blacksmith shops in the town, five in the village, two at the Seminary, and one each at South Hartwick, Toddsville, Chase and Clintonville. Robert W. Gardner was a village blacksmith from 1868 until 1922, a period of over half a century.

Adelbert D. Petrie, son of Davis and Maria (Van Slyke) Petrie, was born in Hartwick Seminary, Sept. 5, 1849. His home had been in that vicinity all his life. He was a blacksmith by trade

Albert A. Avery

and operated a shop at Hyde Park for many years.

Albert A. Avery was a long time Hartwick blacksmith. He built in 1856 the house on East Main Street owned by Mrs. Grace Auger, now owned by the late Swen Peterson.

James H. Barney was located on North Street (St. Hwy. 205). His shop was on the lot next to Frederica Hornbecks house, in about 1868. Also R. A.

Sherman had a blacksmith shop on the west side near Bissells.

G.B. Ashcraft of Oneonta has purchased the dwelling and blacksmith shop on the old furnace site, west side of Otego Creek. (Across from Jack Burch's house.)

Blacksmiths
1872-1873
Gazeteer and Business Directory
Of Otsego County

James D. Sherman	Hartwick
Dewit Prece	Hartwick
Edwin Pickens	Hartwick
Robert Gardner	Hartwick
Robert Schermerhorn	Toddsville
Asa Pride	South Hartwick
A. D. Petrie	Hyde Park
Mercer, Son and Co.	Hartwick Seminary
Horace J. Beckley	Hartwick Seminary

Shop of Edwin Pickens on Brooklyn side

Albert Avery	Hartwick Seminary
Orlando B. Ashcroft	Hartwick Seminary

H. G. Miller & Son
Blacksmithing & Carriage Making
   -Repairing & Horseshoeing & Specialty
   -Hartwick, NY July 2, 1892
   -Received 75¢ for Shoeing

Henry G. Miller for many years a blacksmith

of Hartwick, who for 2 years or more has made his home at Cooperstown, where his wife has been engaged at millinery work. He died of paralysis in 1906.

On Monday noon 1913, William Jones brought his team to John Horan's blacksmith shop.

In South Hartwick 1914, Asa Pride suffered a stroke while shoeing a horse of A. Munson.

In a clipping on July 21, 1915 – The partnership heretofore existing between Ralph Bouton and Charles Bingham has been dissolved, Mr. Bouton continuing the blacksmithing shop in the rear of

Robert Gardner in his shop behind Methodist Church

Robert Gardner

the Commercial Hotel, and Mr. Bingham moving to the shop on the corner over in Brooklyn.

Robert W. Gardner was born on the Ainslie farm north of Hartwick, the son of the George and Eleanor (Weeks) Gardner. His occupation was that of a blacksmith and he occupied a shop in one location for 54 years, closing it about four years ago due to ill health (1919).

Horace C. Tabor was born in 1883 in the Town of Middlefield, son of Simon and Lucinda (Taber) Tabor. He resided in the Town of Hartwick for 38 years as a blacksmith. He died from a heart ailment, and his funeral was held at Patterson Funeral Home.

We still have a lot of horses within our town and in outlying towns. There is a call to have the shoeing of these horses and in our town of Hartwick we have Dan Conklin, who has a traveling shop on his truck. He even has a forge to do hot shoeing. So we still have our Blacksmith (Farrier).

By: Barb Potter

Bibloiography:

Hartwick Seminary – Otsego Business Directory
Gazeteer & Business Directory of Otsego County
Hartwick History
Hurd's History of Otsego County NY
Potters Scrapbook
Kenneth Augur Manuscripts

J. SIMMONS,

THE WEST SIDE.

Horseshoeing

AND

General Repair Shop.

HARNESS !

Nothing looks better than a fine
new Harness when out driving.

TO LOOK THAT WAY WHY NOT
COME AND LOOK AT MY
. . ASSORTMENT . .

PARR'S HARNESS EMPORIUM,
NORTH ST.,   HARTWICK, N. Y.

CLEANING UP TIME

is here and you will
need Harness Oils and
Dressings, Horse Clip-
pers and extra parts.
I have them in stock.
Will grind your clip-
per knives while you
wait.

I can repair your
Harness so that it will
do another season's
work—maybe longer
if you will bring it to

W. I. GARDNER
COOPERSTOWN. N. Y.

BLACKSMITHING
and
REPAIRING

THE MILLER SHOP
New Shoes, 35 cents and up. Cold set
60 cents per horse. Recalking 80 cents.

ALL WORK SATISFACTORILY DONE

Lyman Snyder

Aug 7
1917

H. G. MILLER & SON

BLACKSMITHING & CARRIAGE MAKING.

REPAIRING & HORSE-SHOEING A SPECIALTY.

Hartwick, N. Y., July 2 1892

Received Seventy five
cents for shoing
H. G. Miller

Leather Workers

Like all early settlements, Hartwick had both cobblers and harness makers. John Mott in his "Recollections and Stories about Hartwick" writes; "The early men of crafts traveled from cabin to cabin 'Whipping the cat', staying with the family until the work was completed. He worked from a "last" according to the size of the people's feet. There was no left or right as we have now. The boot had to be fitted to the foot according to the wear and weather. By 1837 shoemakers tended to establish permanent quarters."

Pearl Weeks in "Pioneer Industry" and "The History of Hartwick" tell of John Irons, early shoemaker (before 1813), The Fox Harness Shop, (early 1800's), Lyman Brooks (1823), and Deacon Cones, shoemaker. (1823).

The Odd Fellows (I.O.O.F.) required men, requesting to join the order, to give their age and occupation as well as answer questions. The first one in their record book was: 1848 Hawkins Smith, age38-Harness maker. In a letter from Mrs. Vivian Brandel, Michigan to Town Historian, Anita Harrison we learn that Smith Hawkins, born in 1809 in Hartwick married Lucy Gardner. He went to Michigan about 1865 when about age 56 or 57. He was on the Board of this newly settled area and was the first elected supervisor. He named the new Township Hartwick, after his birthplace. Mrs. Brandel wrote that she had learned that Smith Hawkins had served as Town Clerk in Hartwick, NY from 1837 to 1842. In Hurd's "History of Otsego County, NY" Hawkin Smith is listed as Town Clerk 1837- 1842 in Hartwick. It would seem that the name had been inverted in one Hartwick or the other. The village of Hartwick in Michigan is gone now but it's interesting to know a harness maker remembered his birthplace and named the new town, "Hartwick."

Others who joined the I.O.O.F.
1845 Henry Arie, age 58, shoemaker
1852 Harvey Algers, age 26, shoemaker
1852 Jacob Luce, age 45, shoemaker
1854 Thomas Halstead, age 23, shoemaker
I found no information on these shoemakers.
Speres Ward & Robert Telfer ran a harness shop in the Bissell block (1860).[1]

In the 1868 atlas we find a Harness Shop on the west side of the village run by F.H. Bissell. Horace Jacobs, shoemaker was in District # 5.

The Otsego County Gazateer (1872—75) lists John L. Luce & Loren Ingalsbee as shoemakers. Our harness makers were Mason Arnold and Bissell & Sons. In 1882 we find Mr. Ingalsbee conducting a shoe shop in the corner block and Mr. Arnold had a harness shop in the Sergent Block. Later "Charles Holbrook opens a Harness shop in the room lately occupied by M.D. Arnold." [2]

The1892, Freeman's Journal printed Mr. Richard Russell's obituary, born 1882, he owned a shoe shop, first in Cooperstown and later in Hartwick.

Horses in Harness

A harness shop proprietor who followed lived on North Street, 5th house from the four corners on the left (Pat Ennis lives there in 2001) and had his shop there. His name was William C. Parr. Elenor Bradley Jones (1891—1985) remembered that Will Parr had scarlet fever when young and his legs never grew. He sat in a wheelchair and had very strong arms. Elenor told how he would pull himself up on the bench with his arms. He moved his shop to Main Street in 1894.[3] He also sold ice cream & confections at his shop.[4]

In the 1902 "Hartwick Visitor", Mr. Parr's advertisement reads:

"Parr's Harness Emporium
Nothing looks better than a fine new harness when out driving
TO LOOK THAT WAY, WHY NOT COME & LOOK AT MY ASSORTMENT."

With the coming of the automobiles (two ads in 1915 "Hartwick Reporter"), in Parr's ad in 1915 you can see how the harness shop adjusted to the change, A big advertisement for Milwalker Mowers & New York Champion rakes is noted. Later in 1917, Parr added bicycles and motorcycles. So we see the change from horses to motorized vehicles.

"The Oneonta Leader" published Aug. 15, 1901 at Oneonta, NY tells us of another Harness Shop. "The Horsemen of Hartwick and Farmers throughout that section, find that their wants in the line of all kinds of horse equipment, can be supplied at E.S. MARVIN'S. He is the leading Harness Shop of the Otego Valley and he is enjoying a well-deserved prosperity. Besides a fine line of harness blankets, robes whips etc. he deals in wagons of various makes. Mr. Marvin is sole maker of the famous <u>David Russell Scotch Collar</u>. Mr. Russell, a native of Scotland, made these collars for years in Hartwick and at his death Mr. Marvin secured the pattern and the right to make the collars. Nothing like the Russell Scotch Collars are made anywhere in the county. Mr. Marvin hoped by the means of the trolley, to extend the sale of these very desirable articles of horse equipment."

Now that the local stores were carrying more shoes, we find shoe repair shops taking the place of cobblers. In 1915, "Mr. Barney Petri of Mohawk will open a shoe repair shop in the Theron Bissell house. He has a large patronage from the railroad employees—".[5]

In the 1922 Daily Star Directory, E.W. Mack, North Street, Hartwick, is among the Harness makers.

The last harness and shoe repair proprietor was Mr. Thomas Sweet. He was a Lutheran Missionary in Canada. When the Mission closed, Mr. & Mrs. Sweet came to Hartwick and bought a farm in Hinman Hollow. He started his first Harness Shop upstairs over the Post Office, when it was on the corner of Main & South Street (Later Chester Winslow's office). Mr. Sweet advertised in the Hartwick Reporter. Some of the years he advertised were 1917, 1919,34, 38 & 41. Around 1920 Mr. Sweet wrote his friend, Mr. P. Peterson in Canada, telling him there was plenty of work here. Mr. Peterson came down by himself and partitioned off living quarters upstairs by Mr. Sweet's shop. Later Mrs. Peterson & Swend came to join him after a trip to Denmark. Later they lived in the house that burned (Stevens lived there in the 50's), between the R.E.A. and Frances Weaver. From the shop over the Post Office the Harness Shop was moved to over the Victory Store (Chaperlins). After this it was moved to the small building by the Legion. It had been a lawyer's office & later the P.O.

In 1917 foot wear was added to the harness & shoe repair shop. After Mr. Peterson had been here awhile, Mr. & Mrs. Sweet moved to Mass., with Mr. Peterson taking over the shop. [6]

In the Mar.14, 1923 Hartwick Reporter the following appears:

"The Hartwick Harness Shop
Have in stock a general line of horse furnishing, goods at reasonable prices.
HAND MADE HARNESSES & TRACES MADE TO ORDER.
Harness & shoe repairing.
Agent for USL storage batteries.
P. Peterson"

In 1937 Mr. Thomas Sweet advertised "(Workshoes- Reduced)"

Men's work shoes were	$1.69	now $1.49
Men's work shoes	$2.29	$2.19
Men's 16 inch boots	$4.00	$3.85
Men's 15 inch hoots	$3.00	$2.79

I believe through all these years there were neighborhood men who repaired their own harnesses & others. Mr. Bill Powers told me Hinman Hollow was very fortunate. Mr. Frankewich repaired harnesses for his neighbors and did a professional job. It was very handy to have someone nearby who could repair things in a hurry and the farmers could get back to harvesting or whatever.

In the middle 30's, I remember Mr. Sweet coming out of his shop, and warning me, in a friendly manner, that I was ruining my feet, wearing sneakers all the time.

The 1941 ad for the Shoe & Harness shop emphasized the "Wear u Well" shoes and rubber foot wear and still advertising all kinds of repairs for shoes and harnesses.

I believe Mr. Sweet was still carrying on his business in 1948 when both Mr. & Mrs. Sweet were killed instantly when their Model T was involved in a 3 car crash near Laurens, NY [7]

That was the end of the Harness & Shoe Shops in Hartwick.

By: F. H.

Bibliography:
1.   Weeks, Pearl, "History of Hartwick" pg.75
2.   Old Potter Scrapbook pg.20
3.   Old Potter Scrapbook pg.73
4.   Old Potter Scrapbook pg.20
5.   Elizabeth Curry Scrapbook
6.   Swen Peterson
7.   Oneonta Star

Garages, Gas Stations and Farm Machinery

As Hartwick entered the mid 1920's the streets took on a different character. Automobiles were stirring up the dust. New businesses were born—garages were replacing livery stables, and gas pumps were replacing hitching posts.

Automobile Livery Service
DAY OR NIGHT
Reliable Cars and Drivers.   Reasonable Rates.
CLARK'S GARAGE,   HARTWICK, N. Y.

About this time Millard and Harold Clark opened a garage off South Street. This was located in back of the house, which 50 years later, was known as Dr. Steffi Bakers office.

Union School turned service station on South Street.

After the new school opened on Wells Avenue, the old school building on South Street stood idle. At some point the Clark brothers moved their garage to the old building. They installed gas pumps, built a grease pit, and serviced cars. They also sold Ford cars, and some people recollect that they sold Buicks too.

Eventually the Clarks opened a Ford Garage in Cooperstown, and Clifford Stohler ran the South Street garage.

During World War 2 when gas rationing was very strict, gas stations had little if any gas to sell, nor could they get oil products, tires, or parts. Bill Powers remembers that the South Street garage opened nights as a farm repair shop. Elmer Bloomer taught a welding class, and farmers attended to repair their irreplaceable farm machinery.

Sometime after the war, Harry Perry came to Hartwick, and operated the garage, and drove the school bus.

In 1958 and 1959, Leonard Wright ran a service station, and operated his John Deere business in the old South Street building while his father, Shirley Wright was erecting a new farm machinery building on North Street.

After Leonard moved to the new location, the old building again stood idle. The premises were owned by the Oneonta Fuel and Oil Co. Bill Powers remembers that Chester Winslow, acting as the Town's Attorney worked out the legal aspects of the situation, and the building and land was given to the Town with the proviso that it was never again to be used as a gas station. The old building was torn down and the Town built a small Park complete with a gazebo.

Getting back to the early 1930's, gas was selling for 25¢ a gallon, or 5 or more gallons for a $1.00. Gas stations were springing up all over town. On Main Street Risley's and Burch's stores had gas pumps out front, as did Backus Hardware and the GLF. Now not only are the gas pumps gone but so are the stores. As of this writing the Hartwick Market is the sole surviving store on Main Street.

Risley's Station with Gas Pumps

John Parr built a gas station on South Street where the Quick Way now stands. This station was to have many proprietors over the next 60 odd years.

John Parr in front of service station he built.

The following is an incomplete list of owners and operators.

1930's Tom Riley

1940's Chauncey Barton

According to Pam Persons her father Bill Dean purchased it from a Mr. Gould in 1949, and

added a lunchroom.

Service station with lunchroom added.

Rock and Ruby Conklin - operators

Stan and Audrey Phillips owned it in 1957

Fred and Luella Earle owned and operated it for 19 years

Doug Robertson bought it from John Karakaris and started operating the station as "Doug's Community Service in 1978. In 1979 he was served notice by the DOT that two brick posts with antique "Mobilgas" signs located at the entrance to the station were on the states right-of-way and would have to be moved. Doug's position on this was that the signs were of historical interest and served as a tourist attraction, and were important to his business.

One of the old signs in front of Doug's Community Service at Hartwick.

Hartwick Historical Society also took up the cause, and designated them as historical landmarks.

Doug tells that he took his case to Washington and with the help of Tony Casall and Don Mitchell and because he had been in the military he was allowed to keep the landmarks as long as he ran the station. He ran the business for about four years before selling it to Mid-

State Fuel.

The old station was torn down in the 1980's and the modern Quickway was built by Mirabito, and is presently the only gas station in Hartwick village.

Back again to the 1930's there was another little gas station built on the site presently occupied by Tedescos Meat Processing Plant. It was operated by Lawrence McLaine, and sold Blue Sunoco gas. The little building stood for many years and ended up as a dwelling and burned when Lavern DeForest lived there.

Lawrence McLaine pumping gas.

Further down Rte. 205 in the Pine Woods, Gilbert Bunn, built a gas station and restaurant in the 1930's. Gilbert's father, Clarence Bunn, ran the gas station for several years.

Bunn's Gas Station in the pine woods

The restaurant was of shorter duration, but continued to sell candy and soda pop, when they had picnics or ball games on the baseball

field up in back of the station. Later the station was purchased by Mr. and Mrs. Aluffo, and the station building is now the private home of Dave Sprague.

Still further down Rte 205, a unique small building still stands. Howard Marlette remembers that it was built as a gas station in the 1930's, but he does not remember who the builder was.

Back in South Hartwick, kitty corner from the cemetery, Herm Hughes, grandfather of Doris Powers, ran a garage in the 1930's. A natural born mechanic and tinkerer, he kept many an old fliver on the road.

For years Boggy Hoose had a gas station at the foot of Index hill. Bill Powers explained that Boggy had a unique setup at his station. His storage gas tank was across the highway and up the hill by the old trolley tracks. The gas would gravity flow from the tank down to his station. While other stations had to actually pump gas, Boggy merely had to put the hose into the auto, and gas would flow right into the tank.

Now to return to Hartwick village to the west side of town. In the late 20's The Brooklyn House was past its glory days. The following is a newspaper account written by Lula Morse.

"Whatever Became Of 'The Brooklyn House?'

Three and one half stories above ground and a half story below ground. A Hostelry that accommodated traveling salesmen and cared for their horses and trunks before we dreamed of the Southern NY Railroad.

Whatever became of the Brooklyn House

Some of the proprietors of the well-known hotel were Rufus Conklin, Mr. Eldred, Alta Irish, and George Freelan. Then came "No Liquor-License," and Clayton Elliot rented the place. After Prohibition, it was rented as a dwelling place until Mr. "Al" Bresee arrived.

"Al" was a resourceful man. He saw the possibility of a Gas Station. He took the best of the hand-hewn timbers and lumber of seven years seasoning, built the "Gas-station" afore mentioned.

All went well, until one day his son, "Mac," was servicing a car, the motor running. BANG!!! A spark lit the gas, the tank blew up—and with that the fire did it's worst.

Was "AL" licked? NO! He took the best of what was left of the standing Brooklyn House, and built again—the present station and residence of Mr. and Mrs. Paul Ferrara.

Ferrara's Gas and Service Station

And the station has done a flourishing business ever since."

Paul and Manolia Ferrera, very accommodating people, operated the gas station for many years. Paul was an avid baseball fan and played for the Hartwick Town Team.

In October 1955 to 1957 Leonard Wright leased and operated the station and sold John Deere machinery. As there was not enough room for the machinery Leonard moved the business to South Street.

In the meantime Paul Fererra returned to run the station for a brief time. Anita Harrison remembers that Ferreras were running the station when they moved to Hartwick in 1957.

Others who operated the station were Floyd and Geniveve Bresee, Joe Neil and the Seeheusen family.

Don Schweitzer bought the old station in 1980. It was in a rundown condition, and after extensive renovations the Schweitzers moved in 1983, and it is an attractive private home at the present time.

Through the years many other garages have been open for business in and around Hartwick village.

Ron Clegg had a garage on Main Street.

Ralph Weeks had a garage at Jones Crossing.

Walt Monroe operated a garage just off South Street from 1947 to 1969.

Red Lyons had his garage in Hinman Hollow from 1947 until 1977. Doris Beers remembers that Red taught a car maintenance class for women during World War 2.

Owen McManus had a garage on Christian Hill.

In the 70's Rod Wellman ran a garage on Gulf Road before opening "Hartwick Garage" on Piermott Lane in Jan. 1979. He continues to have a busy operation as well as servicing REA vehicles.

Wayne Bush started a welding shop in back of his residence on Main Street about 1980. His son, Junior Bush, joined Wayne in business, and Junior presently operates a welding shop on Scotch Hill.

Dietmar Jaeck has had a garage on Gulf Road since 1993. The business "Phoenix Restorations" specializes in European car repair and restoration.

Tim West opened "West Transportation" north of the village in April of 1997 and is presently doing an expanding business.

Another new garage is Greg Horths "Rte 205 Auto and Fleet" south of the village.

One of Hartwick's early manufacturers of farm machinery was Palmer Williams Iron Foundry. Williams made horsepowers, plows, cultivators, and threshing machines. The foundry was located in the village, on the west side of the Otego Creek, across the street from the Burch family home. This description of the foundry was found in Pearl Weeks "History of Hartwick."

"Casting day is usually Friday. The owner and his assistants, with uncovered arms and chests, catch the molten stream in huge iron dippers as it flows from the furnace, and transfer it to the molds, which are made in sand. All is noise, steam, and confusion. The constant puff, puff of the escape valve can be heard a quarter mile in all directions."

An 1878 news item tells, "P. O. Williams shipped a new threshing machine to Oswego, and has four more ready. They are fine looking machines and work as well as they look."

Another news item of August 1878 describes a near fatality at the foundry. "P. 0. Williams, prop. of the foundry, while running off a heat of castings last week, came near being burned to death.

He was carrying one end of a large shank ladle of molten iron, from which the new cannon for Mt. Vision was to be cast, when his foot caught an obstruction and threw him to the floor. Had it not been that his brother, an experienced foundryman, carrying the other end of the ladle, the result might have been of a very serious character. Mr. Williams escaped with one foot and one hand considerably burned.

Those who never witnessed an accident of this kind, where the boiling liquid is flying and popping in all directions, would be sufficiently amazed after one experience."

Monday July 8, 1878—news item
"A mowing machine trial came off in the meadows of the George Lough, Jr. farm. The following named machines were tested: Warrior, Kirby, Buckeye, and Champion. The latter after testing was found to be imperfect, hence failed to come up to recommend.

Another test was given the same day on a hill. This time P. S. Jenks, agent for Champion, put a perfect machine to the test in lodged grass, and as a result sold three machines on the spot. Also one of the Kirby and one of the Buckeye were sold as a result of both trials."

In the 1920's Hartwick was saying goodbye to the horse and buggy days. Up until then Hartwick's streets and businesses had been geared to the needs of horses and horse drawn conveyances. There were hitching posts, watering troughs, and the hotels all had livery stables. Every church in town had a church shed for sheltering horses during services.

Hartwick's first dealership for John Deere was started by Will Ainslie in 1927. According to Stuart Ainslie the first John Deere tractor sold in Otsego County was bought by Otis Mott from the new Ainslie dealership. For a few years Will Ainslie conducted the machinery business from the family farm on Scotch Hill. Stuart was ten years old at the time and he remembers growing up helping to service John Deere equipment. In 1932 the business was moved to the village to the little building next to Thamer Harpers house.

First John Deere tractor sold in Otsego County. Sold to Otis Mott

Stuart graduated high school in 1934, and worked mostly as service man, and his father was the salesman. They continued the business on the same location until Will Ainslies death in 1942. Stuart carried on the business until 1946 then went to full time farming, though he continued to service any tractors they had sold. Stuart is a loyal John Deere man at 86 and still owns a John Deere tractor.

In 1955 Leonard Wright became Hartwick's new John Deere dealer. In 1960 he opened a new facility on North Street, and operated his

Leonard Wright's John Deere Store on North Street

business there until 1980. Having completed 25 years as a John Deere dealer, he retired from the dealership, but continued to operate the facility as a repair shop and gas station for another five years, retiring permanently in 1985.

The premises were sold to the ARC about 1989.

McCORMICK-DEERING FARM MACHINES
F. S. FIELD
HARTWICK, N. Y.

FARM MACHINERY

Engines, Manure Spreaders, Separators, Plows and all kinds of Repairs for International Harvester Co.'s Machines.

F. S. FIELD
Hartwick, N. Y.

Another farm machinery dealer was Fred. S. Fields who sold McCormack Deering from his farm on East Hill in the 1930's. The farm is presently owned by John Thorn.

Also in the 1930's Stan Backus sold Massey-Harris farm machinery from his hardware store on Main Street.

By: N.B.P.

Funeral Homes

The present day funeral home is a far cry from the way funeral arrangements were handled a hundred years ago. After death, bodies were not sent to a mortuary, but rather the undertaker was summoned to a home, where he would conduct the funeral from the home or deceased's church.

A crepe was placed on the front door. A crepe was usually a spray of flowers and black cloth fashioned for the purpose. This would serve notice that a death had occurred, and prevented people from unknowingly intruding on the grief stricken within.

The body would be kept in the home for the viewing, and family and friends would keep vigil until the funeral.

As the undertaking profession was sporadic, it was usually necessary that a mortician pursue a second occupation to make a living.

In the Otsego County Directory of 1872 it is noted that Wm. C. Alger was an undertaker and clock repairer.

In an 1880's newspaper, H.S. Bradley, who was a local undertaker, advertised that he kept on hand Imitation Rosewood and Black Walnut Coffins. He also kept on hand Merino and

Muslin Shrouds.

Harvey Blackledge Parker was another local undertaker in the 1880's. He lived on Weeks Rd. in the house now occupied by Nancy Smalley. He was also a furniture dealer.

In the 1890's, Edgar Higbie advertised as a Funeral Director and Furnisher and Practical Embalmer. He was also a dealer in Fine Furniture. Selling Parlor and Chamber Suites. He also dealt in Road Wagons and Carriages.

Mr. Higbie's place of business was on West Main Street. William Stilwell opened the Stilwell Funeral Home in the same location in 1909. He was in business there for 32 years. He was an astute businessman who served on the board of directors of several Hartwick businesses, including the Hartwick National Bank and The Hartwick Hatchery.

Upon Mr. Stilwell's retirement in 1941, J. Donald Patterson bought the property and business. Mr. Patterson resided in Hartwick, and was owner and manager of Patterson Funeral Home for 43 years, retiring in 1982.

Patterson Funeral Home

Dependable 24 hour Service.

Patterson Funeral Home

Phone 3511   Hartwick, N. Y.

For a brief period after Mr. Patterson's retirement, Ingalls Connell & Dow operated the business before closing it permanently.

Another funeral home on Main Street was located where Bruce Clinton resides. This was the Maxwell Funeral Home, and was opened in 1932 by James Maxwell. Mr. Maxwell operated the funeral home until his untimely death in 1951.

Maxwell Funeral Home

J. A. MAXWELL

FUNERAL DIRECTOR

Ambulance Service

LADY ASSISTANT

Phone 3331

HARTWICK,   NEW YORK

A Masonic service was held for him in the funeral home. This was to be the last service held there as the funeral home closed with Mr. Maxwell's passing.

By: NBP

All information from the Oneonta Star and Hartwick Reporter

Printing and Publishing in the Township of Hartwick

From Pearl Weeks "Pioneer Industries," we read of an "Otsego County Gazetteer" newspaper c. 1870's which was edited and printed in the brick building by the stone house on the corner of North and East Main Street. A few years ago Corinne Pollock got the information from an old scrapbook, dated c. 1885 or 1890, loaned to her by Mrs. Florence Groff and Miss Lina Potter of North Main Street. No copies of the "Gazetteer" have been found yet.

Since paper is necessary for printing and supplies to make it important to this area, the following is submitted: Mostly from "Recollections of an Early Mill Town – Toddsville" compiled by Lawrence W. Gardner, 1974. In 1788 Samuel Tubbs purchased of Judge William Cooper c. 300 acres. He built a log cabin and gristmill on the Hartwick side of Oak Creek. Tubbs sold back to Richard (eldest son of William C.) Cooper. In 1796 Jehiel Todd purchased the south part of the Tubbs patent from R. Cooper with flow rights.

In Elihu Phinney's "Otsego Herald" of April 10, 1806, "A Papermill is being opened by Jehiel Todd on the Otsego side of Oaks Creek. Some town of Hartwick residents worked for the mill. Elisha Butts of Toddsville was a paper maker.

William W. Wilson of Toddsville was an agent for the mill. Many others indirectly helped keep the paper mill running. In 1831, Layman Harrington's Tin Shop advertised for 6 or 8 men to peddle tinware and goods. They took a lot of their pay in rags. 940,000 lbs. of rags were used annually. Also huge quantities of chloride of lime and 1000 cords of wood were used every year. In 1853 rags were worth 3 and 4 cents per pound. Paper was 9 cents per pound.

In 1805 H. & E. Phinney advertised in their Otsego Herald for sheepskins to bind books with. Hartwick had the sheep, and sheep and wool outranked dairying till 1826. In 1824 there were 5960 sheep in Hartwick. In 1810 H. & E. Phinney advertised for 1 to 2000 sheep hides, well tanned. An 1844 diary of a Post Rider delivering newspapers from Cooperstown, through Hartwick, S. Hartwick, to Morris, mentions Robinson's Tannery c. 1818.

Zera (Zira) Todd ran a store, book-binding and printing plant (with E. Phinney) in connection with the woolen mill in the house now known as the 'Old Dr. Almy House' across Oaks creek from the paper mill.

Besides Pearl Weeks and Roger Butterfield, Hartwick has had other writers and publishers. One of them was Henry Clarke Wright who, in 1849, wrote *"Human Life"* illustrated in My Individual Experience as A Child, A Youth, and A Man." He was born on August 29, 1797, in the town of Sharon, Litchfield, Connecticut. At 4 years of age he moved to the 'western country' which was Hartwick. He attended school from 5 to 12 years of age. In 1850 he was going to write another book titled *More as A Man.*

In 1858 Marcus M. Wells wrote the words for his famous hymn, "Holy Spirit, Faithful Guide." Then he sat down to his melodeon and composed the music. It was translated into 15 different languages.

Marcus Wells

Marcus Wells House

Miss Nelly Sergent, who graduated from Hartwick Union School in 1901, wrote a widely read book "The Younger Poets."

The Honorable Jedidah Peck wrote persuasive articles for free schools for "all the children of all the people." He is known as Founder of the Common Schools.

"The Life of Abraham Lincoln" (1866) and "Life of Benedict Arnold" (1879) were published by Isaac Newton Arnold. Isaac was born in Hartwick on November 30, 1815, the son of Dr. Arnold.

The Theological Society was established in Hartwick Seminary in 1822. A "Catalogue" of officers and students was edited and published in the Seminary and was printed in 1827 by J. H. Prentiss, printer of " The Cooperstown Federalist." The "Hartwick Seminary Monthly," four pages with a supplement, was published around the 15th of each month of the academic year at 25¢ per year. Volume 1. No.1, 1880. Willis S. Winman was editor and William E. Hull proprietor. This paper was printed from stencils made by Edison's Electric Pen and Duplicating Press. This method was used including the issue of July 1881, Vol. 2, No. 7. The next issue, October 1881, Vol. 2, No. 7, (note same as above) was doubled in size. As the students did not have the time to print it, it was let out to a letterpress printer. They had been printing about 250 copies and to pay the costs without raising the price, needed 200 more subscribers.

The Electric Pen Press was a means whereby an electrically controlled needle punched holes in a stencil, exactly copying the writing. Then one layed the stencil on the paper to be printed and with a brayer covered with felt and some ink, it was rolled over the stencil. It made a clear copy, slow but faster than writing each by hand. The stencils could be saved to reprint back copies.

"The Hartwick Visitor" started Thursday, May 1,1902 with Vol. 1, No. 1. It noted that it was "A pleasant May Day to start a Hartwick newspaper." Published and printed by C. S. Hitchcock for $1.00 a year. Also from the paper: "The Hartwick Visitor" makes its bow to the citizens of this and surrounding towns, as is usual on the occasion of a first appearance, and hopes to become better acquainted during the year to come. The proprietors have put in a Printing Plant which all may be proud of, as it will enable you to secure at home all that may be needed in the printing line, and give you a paper which we trust will find a welcome in every home.

Another useful item was the railroad timetables for the O. C. and R. S. R. R., the D. & H. to Cooperstown and C. V. R. R., and the Lackawanna R.R.

On Thursday, November 6, 1902, Vol. 1, No. 28, the name of "The Hartwick Visitor" changed to "The Hartwick Review and Visitor" with A. D. and C. S. Hitchcock editors and publishers.

"The Hartwick Reporter" started with Vol. 1, No. 1 on April 14, 1915, by A. D. & C. S. Hitchcock Printing Company

Old carrier's story of how the 'Freeman's Journal' reached us by special horseback rider.

"The fall of 1844, when the writer was 13 years old, witnessed one of the most exciting campaigns in history records. In that year Polk and Dallas, Clay and Frelinghwyn were the candidates respectively for president and vice-president. I was living then with my uncle, Jas. H. Kenyon, at Jacksonville (Mt. Vision) and he was the proprietor of a newspaper route running southwest from Cooperstown.

Each Saturday morning that fall I left home on horseback for Cooperstown, over Burk hill. Reaching the county seat about half-past ten o'clock, my first call would be at the Freeman's Journal office. Col. John H. Prentiss was the editor and proprietor, and from him I obtained from 175 to 200 copies of the Journal. From there I crossed the street and called on Andrew M. Barber and got 150 copies of the Otsego Republican. In the latter office the late L. P. Carpenter, then 16 years old, was serving a 5-year apprenticeship.

I would get away from Cooperstown about 1 o'clock PM with big saddlebags full of papers. My first stop was at Hope factory, where I left several copies. From there to Hartwick village, the houses were far apart and I made but few stops. I remember Elisha Fields and a few others. At Hartwick I recall Rufus Conklin, Dr. Head, Sheffield Harrington and Deacon Bissell and then on down to the Robinson tannery, where there were several copies taken. Then down to Linus Shepherds where I crossed the creek to a Mr. Brownell's and then came back and down to Thomas Wilcox's store at South Hartwick where I left a number of papers."

This was just the route for our area.

"A pleasant May day to start a newspaper," wrote the Editor of the Hartwick Visitor Vol. I No. I of his new business enterprise, begun in our town on May 1, 1902. The idea must have been catching because by the next week another paper called the Hartwick Review also begun publication. They began on the above optimistic note, and an editorial in the initial offering of the Visitor stated that, "Hartwick has arisen from its Rip Van Winkle sleep, rubbed its eyes, stifled its last yawn and is now wide-awake and wondering how it had been content to simply vegetate all the years gone by. Now it is taking a step forward and Hartwick is to have a newspaper, a real live paper that will endeavor to look out for the best interests of its patrons and be helpful in all things which will aid in the advancement of our village."

by: Homer Martin—Retired Printer at The Farmer's Museum

Information from:
Archives Hartwick College Library

Country Kitchen

The following article was published in the last edition of the "Freeman's Journal" (July 10, 1996). The news brought to light the closing of the Country Kitchen Restaurant not for a few days, but forever.

30 years celebrated by Country Kitchen

HARTWICK - On Monday, July 9, 1966, Richard and Corinne Pollak unloaded several bags of groceries and said a lot of prayers, as they opened their little business - The Country Kitchen Restaurant. With a young family of three to provide for, the Pollaks opened at 6:30 a.m. and worked until 9 p.m. seven days a week. It was a lot of work, but they enjoyed people, and soon the little kitchen caught on, serving all walks of life. A lot has happened since then. Memories of power outages, which lasted many hours, triggered terror, with freezers and refrigerators stocked with food.

Art Jamieson, then manager of the cooperative, would call in the wee hours to see if the Pollaks could fix up some sandwiches for the crew, which had worked feverishly to get the power back on. By candlelight, sandwiches were prepared. It was all quite an adventure in those early years. Back then, there were heavy snowfalls, and Richard Pollak would fire up his trusty John Deere AR by a flywheel, which took many turns before she kicked off. The plow was operated by a manual lift and drop system and took a lot of "ups and downs" to clear the parking lot, which became smaller and smaller with each snowfall.

The new underground cable for the New York Telephone Company was being laid then, and it took a lot to keep the men going. Much of the work was done in the cold of winter and some during deer season.

Then it was like working on the front lines. The kitchen worked on a voucher basis, which was sent in each month, and then the bills got paid. There was nowhere else then on Route 205 to eat or make a phone call, so both parties helped each other,

Corinne Pollak fought to get the first outdoor pay phone. It stood its ground until April 29 of this year. NYNEX servicemen dismantled it and in 25 minutes, the old glass enclosed booth was in the truck and headed down the road to be trashed. It apparently did not bring in enough money to help pay for the Bell-

Atlantic buyout by NYNEX. As an outdoor emergency phone, it had served the rural area well in its time, much like the Pollaks have done.

The Pollaks said, "It was amazing how many truck drivers just made it to the Country Kitchen when there was a problem."

Over the years, the Pollaks prepared and served good, wholesome food, with homemade breads, pies, and muffins. A hearty bowl of homemade soup or chili and homemade bread would stick to your ribs. As the years passed, eating habits changed; health and weight problems entered the picture.

Additions to the menu where made to suit those needs. Food not only tasted good, but it looked good and was served with a smile. Soon, the little kitchen was bursting at the seams. Some good fortune made it possible to add a beautiful, airy and bright dining room with an extended counter area for the folks who had to get in and out.

The Pollaks always encouraged people to enjoy, relax, and they did. They still see families who started coming in the 1960s. They have

seen the children grow, graduate high school and sometimes college. Some of them married and returned with their young families. In some cases, grandma and/or grandpa had passed away, but the routine of stopping at the Country Kitchen had not.

Comments such as "You don't remember me do you, Mrs. Pollak?" or "See you are still here" or "I used to stop here with my grandma and grandpa when I was little." What great memories for everyone.

Richard Pollak hadn't forgotten his time when he played Clarabell the Clown for Vita Smith of Howdy Doody Productions of 11 West 42nd St., New York City. He still joked around and now used the horn just to get one's attention when the words don't come out just right due to the loss of his voice. He was diagnosed with ALS, or Lou Gehrig's Disease, in March 1995. Can't keep a good man down.

Corinne Pollak is still writing for a number of publications. Her column, "What's Cookin' in Hartwick," ran for 13 years in the Pioneer and then the Freeman's Journal and was picked up by the GRIT out of Williamsport, PA. The newsy column was in each week for several years. She has contributed to a number of area publications such as The Daily Star, the Pennysaver, Mount Vision News, Banner, Christian News, and now the Voice of Stamford. She seeks out opportunities to put her thoughts on paper.

Health problems bothered both Richard and Corinne. In the early 1980s, Corinne's allergic reaction to smoke brought about New York's first non-smoking restaurant, for which the American Red Cross awarded the Pollaks with a commendation. Richard still survives numerous challenges. Just ask him.

Well, the years have been good to the Pollaks. Their family is all grown and they have even had a 9-year-old grandson who thinks his grandpa is a great guy. What will the future bring now for the Pollaks? They have gone from a seven-day week to a five-day week with occasional holidays off; from 15-hour days to seven-hour days. Most of the time, their days off are spent doing business anyway. In the last three years, they have gone from a two-week vacation to a month during January, which this year turned into four months. Upon arriving in Florida, Richard found his sister gravely ill. They stayed and did what they could, but liver cancer took her at age 59. Who knows what they will do this year?

The Country Kitchen reopened May 1 with an extended menu and shorter hours, for the Pollaks say they are semi-retired and are taking time to "stop and smell the roses.' Sundays and Mondays, they are closed, and that time is spent in many different ways. The last week of June, they entertained their grandson,

Kenny; or is it the other way around?

Hopefully, they will arrive on July 9, when they can say, "We made it and we thank you all for your support in the good times and the bad times."

Their favorite greeting remains, "God loves you, and so do we."

(Editor's note: The Country Kitchen closed unexpectedly Saturday, June 29 just nine days shy of their 50th anniversary.)

Richard Pollak, who fought ALS with all he had, could no longer work and decided to close the restaurant when his physical abilities gave out. His wife, Corinne, cared for him at the home in part of the same building as the restaurant. He lasted till 6:15 AM, Valentine's Day 1997, when his family were all present. Corinne never reopened the restaurant and still lives there.

Hands & Hearts United—
Laura's Restaurant is Built

The property was purchased from Gilbert and Marion Bunn on Route 205 just south of the village in April 1986. Willie Wust dug the foundation and brought in the fill. Loitsch Company of Otego poured the foundation. Thering Farm Supply of Route 23, Oneonta, was the building contractor. Friends, relatives and community members put hands and hearts together and had the building framed in by the end of a sunny Saturday in May. This was not the end, but the beginning of a very successful Hartwick business for the next 13 years.

Friends from near & far after a hearty breakfast - 1999

Laura's officially opened on June 12, 1986 and was open seven days a week serving breakfast and lunch and specials each Friday night. The kitchen, designed by Laura herself, featured lots of workroom but the best spot to be

was the baking area where she would prepare as many as 14 pies at a time for her Friday dinners. Unbeknownst to her, many a piece would be hidden by her helpers to enjoy at the end of her sold-out dinners.

Early mornings would find her turning on the coffee pots in the pre-dawn hours and popping her turnovers into the oven so she'd be ready for the first town road crew to arrive shortly thereafter. After a busy morning local business people, residents, tractor-trailer drivers, county crews and tourists would stop to enjoy a hearty lunch special or one of her huge hamburgers. Friday night specials often sold out. Laura may best be known for her generous portions and start-from-scratch preparations. Among favorites were chicken and biscuits, fresh pork, roast beef and leg of lamb, to name a few.

Due to health concerns involving heart surgery and diabetes, the restaurant was sold to its present owner, Richard Brooks, in September of 1999. Laura is still called upon by community organizations to assist in preparing for community functions. . . and to serve a few of her pies!

By: Laura Kane

Everett & Laura pounding nails

Who's the boss?

Her first buffet

All wrapped up

Building the cellar stairs

Grandchildren - Future Carpenters

Raymond Manley & Laura - checking on progress.

The sign goes up.

The Finished Product

Post Offices

The earliest Hartwick residents of 1786 had no post office nearer than Cherry Valley. An official government publication states that in 1790 there were but 75 such offices in the nation. New York City is listed as having the only one in this state but there are clear references to an Albany post office in 1784 and mail seems to have been coming to Cherry Valley the following year.

At any rate, under our present Federal constitution a Postmaster General was appointed in 1789 and the department well organized in 1794. In that year a post route was established running from Canajoharie through Cherry Valley to Cooperstown. Letters addressed, not only to Hartwick, but also to Morris, Unadilla, Harpersville, Oxford, Union and even Painted Post were soon being advertised as held there. Mail for such distant locations were carried by Post Riders and by chance travelers as a matter of accommodation, left at a tavern or store and so usually reached their proper destination. As settlement progressed additional mail lines were constantly laid out, providing new interactions and causing changes in lines. The government preferred stages for this purpose and these were always used between populous communities but to reach the smaller outlying districts post riders also held contracts for many years.

A Post Office was established in Cooperstown in 1794 and Hartwick settlers received their mail there. It has been thought for a long time that the first Post Office within the present town was opened at Hartwick Village at an early date but how early had not been established. For many years 1809 was thought to be the approximate date, because it was known that Levi Beebe, who with his son, Daniel, kept store in the west end and is known to have been Postmaster of Hartwick during the period of 1809-1819. Now new evidence shows an earlier date for a Post Office at Hartwick. In a letter dated Hartwick, July 9, 1806 to Daniel D. Caulkins, Amenia, Dutchess County, State of New York. To be left at Poughkeepsie Post Office.

"Dear Brother

I rec. your letter of the 30th of June and was glad to hear that you and the rest of my friends in Amenia are well, we enjoy the same blessing. I am neither mad, jealous, nor delirious at present, but have the same respect that I ever had for you and Anne which you never had any reason to think was not sincere unless it was in the deficiency in my letter to father. The reason that I was not more particular are in the first place, because I was in a hurry to get the letter to the Post Office, the mail going eastward the same day. I did not know that there was a Post Office at "Peth" til Abel came to my hut the same morning. I expected I must go to Cooperstown til Abel informed me of the above office and not knowing the hour I sat down and wrote what I did.

Dear brother, permit me to subscribe myself your sincere friend and affectionate brother.

Hezh Caulkin

We now know that Hartwick's Post Office was established on September 20, 1804 and Levi Beebe was Postmaster until December 25, 1821.

In 1809 the route was circuitous—Cooperstown, Hartwick, Milford, Otego (Laurens), Unadilla - once a week, south on Fridays and back on Saturdays. In 1825 it was long - 110 miles by stage once a week, Utica, Bridgewater, Plainfield, Exeter, Otsego (Cooperstown), Hartwick, Unadilla, ending at Oxford. By 1833 there was a change worth noting, Cooperstown, Hartwick, Mt. Vision, Laurens, Oneonta, 28 miles once a week, twice by 1837.

Around 1835 Hezekiah Watkins was carrying mail between Oneonta, Cooperstown, Laurens, and Hartwick, the service being exclusively performed by horseback and furnishing the only mail facilities for the time being.

An item of 1843 may indicate additional service. James H. Kenyon, Post Rider, carried mail from Cooperstown to Louisville via Hartwick, Jacksonville (Mt. Vision), Potter Schoolhouse (the one at Lena), Hard & Peck's Store (New Lisbon) and Noblesville. A postal Map shows offices in the town at Toddsville, Chase, Hartwick, and South Hartwick on the Cooperstown - Oneonta run. The fastest modes

Early horse drawn post delivery

of delivering mail were embraced and so as they became available the steam and electric roads secured the contracts.

Today the motorized Highway Post Office has taken over this function.

Free street deliveries from offices in the cities and the larger villages began in 1863 and in 1896 the government began to extend this accommodation to rural areas.

Rural Free Delivery Route # 1 was established from Hartwick Village in 1907 all on unimproved roads until 1921 about as much as could be covered daily by horsepower, about 25 miles long. Route # 2 followed in 1909. These were consolidated in 1938, giving a 48-mile course with 170 boxes. By that time a horse was a rarity on a highway and roads were indeed better.

Levi Beebe, having become interested in local cotton manufacturing, left the village store and post office to his son, Daniel, and removed to Hope Factory. There he was Post Master at Hopeville in 1822. This office was later located

Post Office	Established	Postmaster	Discontinued
Hartwick	1804	Levi Beebe	Maintained
Hartwick Seminary	1828	Clark Davison	1994
South Hartwick	1850	Chester W. Rockwell	1942
Toddsville	1850	Andrew H. Todd	1918
Chase	1890	Hosea Chase	1910
Hinman Hollow	1893	Duane Salisbury	1894

at Phoenix Mills and in 1902 the Index office was opened under Joseph L. Field.

In these days when postage costs are going up, one can take comfort in recalling what they were when Hartwick was new country. Rates then depended on the distance a letter was carried. The schedule in 1792 was:

Under 30 miles - .06
30 – 60 miles - .08
60 – 100 miles - .10
100 –150 miles - .12 ½
150 - 200 miles - .15
200 – 250 miles - .17
250 – 350 miles - .20
350 – 450 miles - .22
over 450 miles - .25

This was for a single sheet, folded and secured by sealing wax, no envelope, two sheets, double cost; a one-ounce letter, a four sheet charge. The postage was marked on the outside and was usually collected from the recipient. In later years rates were constantly lowered:

1845	– ½ ounce	.05	300 miles
1851	- ½ ounce	.03	3,000 miles
1883	- ½ ounce	.02	throughout U.S.
1885	- 1 ounce	.02	throughout U.S.
1944	- 1 ounce	.03	throughout U.S.
1958	- 1 ounce	.04	throughout U.S.
1963	- 1 ounce	.05	throughout U.S.

Adhesive stamps became available in 1847 and their use was made mandatory in 1856. Postal services have constantly increased. Postal money orders could first be bought in 1864, a postal savings plan was instituted in 1910, and the Parcel Post system began in 1913.

The following Post Offices have been in the Town of Hartwick: Chase, Hartwick, Hartwick Seminary, Hinman Hollow, Hopesville, Seymour, South Hartwick, and Toddsville. Only Hartwick remains to this day.

Chase was named for the Chase family. Comfort Chase settled in the area in 1800. Hosea Chase established the Post Office in the area known as Bissells Hollow, on 6 February 1890. The Post Office was discontinued on 31 January 1910. The patrons were served by the Cooperstown office after the closing. Hosea Chase was the only Postmaster.

Hinman Hollow was named for Joshua Hinman, an early settler, but the Post Office lasted only 3 months, from 16 November 1893 until 16 February 1894. Service was from the Milford Post Office after that time. Duane Salisbury was the Postmaster.

Another short-term Post Office was Hopeville, which started 1 January 1822 with Levi Beebe as Postmaster. It closed in February 1824.

Hartwick Seminary's Post Office was established on 6 March 1828. South Hartwick had a Post Office from 15 January 1850 until 31 December 1942. The Mount Vision Post Office now serves that area.

A Post Office was established at Toddsville on 23 September 1850. It was named for Jehiel Todd, one of the first settlers in what became Toddsville. He also built the first papermill in the area. The name changed to Seymour for a year, 7 January 1886 – 30 December 1886. Then was changed back to Toddsville. According to "Recollections of an Early Mill Town, Toddsville", "The late Samuel M. Shaw succeeded in having the name changed to "Seymour" in memory of the late Horatio Seymour, governor of New York. A petition was quickly drawn and the name speedily restored." This work also reports some of the locations of the Post Office. "In 1856 the Post Office was located in the store west of the 'oldest house in Toddsville' opposite the hotel. In 1868 it was located in the Stone Store opposite the Union Cotton Factory. In 1904 it was located in the same Stone Store. Later it was located in a house opposite the school. This house was one of two that burned in the 1940's." The Stone Store mentioned above is now in the Farmer's Museum in Cooperstown and has a Post Office section which shows what these early Post Offices were like. The Toddsville Post Office was discontinued on 30 April 1918 and the postal patrons are served by the Cooperstown Post Office.

Everett Pope was the first rural carrier, beginning November 16 1907. The route was basically the same, south to Jones Crossing, then north to Wileytown. Then into the town of Burlington and over the hill to Patent and back to Hartwick. He served 100 boxes over his 25-mile route. He started out with the mail loaded in a soapbox strapped onto a sulky drawn behind a horse named 'Bessie.' When the snows came he switched to a cutter. When conditions were bad he was forced to cut through hay lots and pastures to avoid 6-foot drifts. He went to Boston and purchased a 'Metz' auto 'knocked down' and in a crate complete with blueprints for assembly and driving instructions. He learned to drive it in his back yard. Hartwick was the first town in the area to have a motorized mail route. He was a carrier for 12 years then appointed Postmaster on February 18, 1924.

Seymour Robinson, rural carrier in the 1920's attempted to solve the problem of delivering the mail in winter to patrons on the back roads by buying a Model T Ford equipped with tracts. It was the snowmobile of the times. He had to drive mainly in low gear. The first day Mr. Robinson drove it he didn't get through his route until after five.

He only used it for about one winter. The car was wider than the sleigh tracks and proved impractical. Mr. Robinson went back to his horse and sleigh.

April 5, 1978 – Stuck in Mud

Hartwick: "Genevieve Bresee had a bout with the mud while on the mail last week and the mud won. Temporarily at least. Going up East Hill which is usually a dirt road, but has become chocolate pudding of late. The road gave way under her jeep and the front went down in and stayed there. Ginny did a bit of walking through the pudding to a phone and had a town truck come to haul her out. It was nip and tuck for a while but they freed the jeep and Ginny continued on her route – just a bit late!"

Waldo Potter receiving commission as Post Master

POSTMASTERS
HARTWICK POST OFFICE
OTSEGO COUNTY, NEW YORK

POSTMASTERS	TITLE	DATE APPOINTED
Levi Beebe	Postmaster	09/20/1804
Daniel Beebe	Postmaster	12/25/1821
Lyman Harrington	Postmaster	10/01/1829
Sheffield Harrington	Postmaster	02/17/1849
Thomas McIntosh, Jr.	Postmaster	06/16/1853
Dolphus S. Luce	Postmaster	11/27/1855
Frederick Wilcox	Postmaster	04/23/1861
Elisha Robinson	Postmaster	09/20/1871
Henry D. Robinson	Postmaster	04/07/1879
William H. Branch	Postmaster	08/25/1885
Hubert 0. Branch	Postmaster	06/25/1889
George McC. Augur	Postmaster	07/25/1893
Hubert 0. Branch	Postmaster	09/18/1897
George T. Luce	Postmaster	01/31/1917
Torry B. Luce	Acting Postmaster	05/06/1919
Torry B. Luce	Postmaster	02/14/1920
Everett W. Pope	Postmaster	02/18/1924
Dorr Gardner	Acting Postmaster	03/10/1936
Dorr Gardner	Postmaster	02/04/1937
John Richard Byard	Acting Postmaster	10/29/1940
Claude 0. Weidman	Acting Postmaster	04/07/1942
Claude 0. Weidman	Postmaster	06/12/1942
John A. Bush	Acting Postmaster	04/05/1944
John A. Bush	Postmaster	12/13/1944
Roscoe E. Conklin	Acting Postmaster	10/31/1958
R. Waldo Potter	Acting Postmaster	03/17/1961
R. Waldo Potter	Postmaster	09/04/1962
Thelma Bunn	Officer-In-Charge	09/13/1975
Frederick J. St. John	Postmaster	05/07/1977
Connie L. Tedesco	Postmaster	08/31/1985
Mary B. Powers	Officer-In-Charge	05/07/1991
Helen Olmstead	Officer-In-Charge	06/26/1991
Carol D. Brown	Postmaster	10/19/1991
Richard Martucci	Officer-In-Charge	10/13/1995
Chris Davis	Postmaster	02/17/1996
Ruthann Perrie	Officer-In-Charge	08/16/2001
Mary B. Powers	Postmaster	

HARTWICK SEMINARY POST OFFICE
OTSEGO COUNTY, NEW YORK

POSTMASTERS	TITLE	DATE APPOINTED
Clark Davison	Postmaster	03/06/1828
Ebenzer Chaffee	Postmaster	02/13/1844
William C. Davison	Postmaster	03/17/1854
Levi Steinberg	Postmaster	10/06/1856
Mrs. Ann E. Miller	Postmaster	12/13/1860
William C. Davison	Postmaster	03/01/1865
John L. Kistler	Postmaster	04/29/1904
John E. Luther	Postmaster	01/03/1912
Harold A. Ingoldsby	Acting Postmaster	09/02/1926
Harold A. Ingoldsby	Postmaster	01/28/1927
William D. Field	Acting Postmaster	10/04/1928
Mrs. Jessie B. Field	Postmaster	12/07/1928
Robert D. Field	Acting Postmaster	04/30/1946
Robert D. Field	Postmaster	04/15/1947
Mrs. Dorothy L. Field	Acting Postmaster	09/24/1954
Mrs. Dorothy L. Field	Postmaster	02/25/1955

Discontinued December 31, 1994, Mail to Cooperstown

TODDSVILLE POST OFFICE
OTSEGO COUNTY, NEW YORK

POSTMASTERS	TITLE	DATE APPOINTED
Andrew H. Todd	Postmaster	09/23/1850
Rufus Steere	Postmaster	06/26/1852
John T. Wilson	Postmaster	06/21/1853
Rufus Steere	Postmaster	04/24/1861
Sands Shumway	Postmaster	04/15/1869
Orlando Shute	Postmaster	01/29/1874
Welcome Murdock	Postmaster	11/17/1880
Lovina Potts	Postmaster	09/27/1881

Changed to SEYMOUR on January 7, 1886

Lovina Potts	Postmaster	01/07/1886
Granville J. Quackenbush	Postmaster	08/18/1886

Changed to TODDSVILLE on December 30, 1886

Granville J. Quackenbush	Postmaster	12/3 0/18 8 6
James H. Finch	Postmaster	09/22/1904
Burton H. Jackson	Postmaster	11/17/1909

Discontinued April 30, 1918; mail to Cooperstown

SOUTH HARTWICK POST OFFICE
OTSEGO COUNTY, NEW YORK

POSTMASTERS	TITLE	DATE APPOINTED
Chester W. Rockwell	Postmaster	01/15/1850
LeRoy R. Sergent	Postmaster	03/16/1854

Thomas Wilcox	Postmaster	04/18/1859
Henry C. Bunn	Postmaster	01/19/1870
Lacell L. Hubbard	Postmaster	04/10/1870
Putnam E. Van Buren	Postmaster	05/18/1874
Schuyler Osborn	Postmaster	01/21/1880
George W. Joslyn	Postmaster	07/12/1883
Arthur E. Manzer	Postmaster	10/31/1884
Frank H. Bresee	Postmaster	02/09/1886
William B. Card	Postmaster	12/06/1887
Harvey R. Holbrook	Postmaster	04/01/1890
Charles W. Tilyon	Postmaster	10/27/1915
John L. Adams	Postmaster	03/27/1917
William M. Carr	Postmaster	07/22/1918
Ada M. Carr	Acting Postmaster	02/17/1922
Ada M. Carr	Postmaster	02/28/1922
F. Belle Fitch	Acting Postmaster	12/29/1922
F. Belle Fitch	Postmaster	01/11/1923

    (Married, may 10, 1924, Name F. Belle Sherman)

Marian J. Matteson	Acting Postmaster	06/16/1939
Marian J. Matteson	Postmaster	07/01/1939

    (Married, Name Marian J. Bunn)

Post Office discontinued December 31, 1942

CHASE POST OFFICE
OTSEGO COUNTY, NEW YORK

POSTMASTERS	TITLE	DATE APPOINTED
Hosea Chase	Postmaster	02/06/1890

Discontinued January 31, 1910; to be supplied by rural delivery from Cooperstown

INDEX POST OFFICE
OTSEGO COUNTY, NEW YORK

POSTMASTERS	TITLE	DATE APPOINTED
Joseph L. Field	Postmaster	03/08/1902
Charles W. Stephenson	Postmaster	07/22/1903
Thomas Higgins	Postmaster	09/12/1905
Virginia L. Connor	Postmaster	12/14/1907

Discontinued October 30 1915: Mail to Cooperstown

———

By: Barb Potter

Information attained from:
Otsego County Postal History
    by Dorothy Scott Fielder
Potter Scrapbook
National Postal Archives – Washington DC

Rural Electrification

Otsego Electric office building

President Roosevelt himself was the catalyst which produced the Rural Electrification Appropriation Act of 1935, (a measure designed to relieve unemployment) including rural electrification as one of eight categories of projects eligible for funds. On May 11,1935, President Roosevelt signed *Executive Order No. 7037* to create the Rural Electrification Agency and appointed Morris L. Cooke as REA's first administer. REA's first loans were approved on July 22 of the same year and went to borrowers in Georgia, Indiana, and Tennessee.

On January 6, 1936, Senator George W. Norris of Nebraska and Representative Sam Rayburn of Texas introduced bills to continue REA for 10 years as an independent lending agency. And on May 20,1936, President Roosevelt signed the Rural Electrification Act of 1936 (the Norris-Rayburn bill). It was not until July of 1939 however, that REA was placed in the United States Department of Agriculture.

It took some time for the borrowers of REA funds to actually build the lines and energize them once the program was underway. REA assisted the new co-ops in a number of ways besides loaning money.

The REA staff found they needed more than loan specialists and engineers. The emergence of cooperatives as the dominant type of borrower shaped REA into something more than just a lending institution.

Most states had no legal precedent for electric cooperatives. Before 1935 only Iowa had a statutory provision for distribution of electric power by a nonprofit membership enterprise. State laws covering agriculture marketing cooperatives were not satisfactory for REA borrowers. One of the first chores for the new federal agency, therefore, was to hire attorneys to draft a "model" statute for states to adopt as a vehicle for rural electrification. REA lawyers also drafted model bylaws for adoption by the new cooperatives.

Engineers hired by REA discovered that the electric power technology had been developed for the cities. The construction and the individually engineered system design were too cumbersome, too slow and too costly for thinly populated rural areas. REA, in coordination with its borrowers and cooperative manufacturers and suppliers, had to develop entirely new designs, standards, materials and procedures for engineering and construction in rural areas.

REA staff accountants also had to improvise procedures that would link the special bookkeeping problems of non-profit membership organizations with the large scale lending operations of an agency using government funds and with the established accounting practices of the utility industry and regulatory bodies. REA devised for its borrowers a Uniform System of Accounts and a correspondence course to train rural electrification accountants.

Assistance in building the lines and supplying power was only part of the battle for rural electrification. REA also helped farmers and rural households learn how to use their new electric power by putting on a Demonstration Farm Equipment Tour during the years 1938 through 1942. A team of REA agricultural engineers and home economists went into 20 states with a tent that would seat 1,000 persons and with a large collection of electrical equipment and appliances transported in trucks and trailers. This traveling "electric circus" was for many the biggest show ever to come to town. Hundreds of thousands of rural people learned from the exhibits and demonstrations how to use the new "wire hand" (later NRECA'S Willie Wiredhand) for milking cows, cooking dinner, farrowing pigs, doing the family wash and ironing, pumping water and performing dozens of other farm and home chores.

As was the case with nearly every social and domestic program, the war years of 1942 through 1945 for the most part suspended the progress of the rural electric program. While there was a shortage of labor and materials, copper wires, etc. during the war years, the leaders of the rural electric cooperatives were not idle and on March 19, 1942 they founded the National Rural Electric Cooperative Association to help obtain materials.

Within four years following the close of the war, however, the number of rural electric systems in operation doubled, the number of consumers connected more than tripled, and the miles of Energized line grew more than fivefold.

The history of Otsego Electric Cooperative, Inc. is as rich and interesting as that of the REA program itself. Nine local rural residents and farmers had heard about the new federal program called the REA and learned that loans were being made that would permit construction of the distribution network.

The first meeting of the subscribers of The Otsego Electric Association, Inc. met at the Farm Bureau Office in Cooperstown on July 22, 1941. These incorporators were Marshall G. Shultis, David Brown, Winfred C. Arnold, John J. Ahern, Alfred Monson, Mary Kabosius, Fritz E. Stockigt, Glenn Mathewson and Marjorie L. Sprague and were all of the members of the Otsego Electric Association. These nine people were also the Directors of the Association. At this meeting bylaws were adopted which were taken from the model bylaws of REA.

On August 7, 1941 the directors met, again at the Farm Bureau Office. At the meeting the Secretary reported that there were 383 completed applications for membership on file and that the membership fee of $5.00 for each application had been turned over to the Treasurer. At the next meeting, held on August 18, 1941, the Board of Directors resolved to make application to REA for a loan for the purchase of materials to begin construction. At the September 4, 1941 meeting, less than one month after the first meeting of the Board, the Secretary reported that a total of 833 membership applications had been received. Mr. Shultis, who had been hired by his fellow Board members to be the Association's "Coordinator", reported on the progress of canvassing for memberships and right-of-way easements along the route of the proposed lines. (You can bet that the woman of the house was very involved in persuading the man of the house if he were at all hesitant about joining and paying the $5.00 membership fee!) Incidentally, Mr. Shultis soon resigned as a Director because, in the recently adopted bylaws, a director could not also be a paid agent of the corporation.

At its meeting on November 22, 1941, the Board authorized an application to REA for a loan in the amount of $432,000 to construct the electric transmission, distribution and service system. Also at that meeting, the Board appointed Frederick W. Loomis as legal counsel to the corporation. (Several years later, in 1962, Mr. Loomis became Otsego county and family courts judge and resigned as counsel to the cooperative. At that time Richard Johnson was appointed as counsel.)

The Otsego Electric Association, Inc. filed a petition with the New York Public Service Commission for authority to construct an electric plant in portions of Otsego, Herkimer, Madison and Chenango counties. At that time, six such associations had filed similar applications with the PSC. Those six were: The Oneida County Electric Association (which later became the Oneida Madison EC); The Genesee County Electric Association (which dissolved as a result of spite lines being built); The Chautauqua-Cattaraugus Electric Association (which subsequently merged with the Steuben EC); the Delaware County EC; the Steuben REC; and, of course, the Otsego EC.

On April 29, 1942, the Governor of New York State approved an act allowing these cooperatives, non-profit membership corporations to be organized as cooperatives under Chapter 566 of the laws of 1942. All of the

six associations petitioned to withdraw their pending petitions before the PSC, and this was granted. Under the New York REC Law, these cooperatives were exempted from the jurisdiction of the PSC. On May 11, 1942 the Board of Directors resolved that the corporation be converted into a cooperative, nonprofit, membership corporation pursuant to the Act. This was accomplished and a new set of bylaws was adopted.

At a meeting on August 4, 1942, the Board met to consider lease of office space in the village of Hartwick. This building was rented for the sum of $400 per year.

However, on August 11, 1942 a special meeting was held. At that meeting the Board was informed that the War Production Board had denied their petition for a priority rating on materials necessary to construct the electric lines. The Board then decided that any further effort to maintain or lease an office be discontinued until such time as further need for an office should arise.

In April of 1943, the Board met to consider re-applying to the War Production Board for materials and further to consider a "Food Production Survey" of the farms, which would be served by the lines they planned to build. As many of you know, most things were rationed at that time, due to the war effort. In September 1943, the War Production Board authorized the cooperative to purchase a typewriter if manufactured before 1915. The War Production Board, however, found it doubtful if one could be found in satisfactory condition and, therefore, advised that the cooperative rent a typewriter - but it had to have been manufactured before 1935 and must come from the local ration board.

As the year progressed, some materials became available for construction and the Edens-Marson Company of Indianapolis was hired to begin construction of the system. The first substation site was purchased in Oaksville from a Mr. Pushlar for the sum of $100.00. Mr. Harry Bilderbeck was hired as the right-of-way agent and later became the acting superintendent. Mr. John Kissel was employed as the first manager of the cooperative in December 1943. In January 1944 the Directors approved a contract with the New York State Electric and Gas Corporation for the purchase electric power and energy. June 24, 1944 was the date when the first substation and approximately 16 miles of line were energized. Members of the Co-op turned out in substantial numbers, in spite of lowering skies and intermittent

— BEFORE POWER WAS TURNED ON

— & AFTER!

drizzle for an all day celebration.

The Co-op's Board President, Dave Brown, threw the switch symbolizing the start of electric service. A shout of joy from the gathered crowd of members and their families and friends began a new era in the rural areas of Otsego County. That night, a dance was held in the hall over the Co-op's office. This event was filmed by cameramen from "The March of Time." It was the first REA financed line to be energized in the state. A copy of a news article about the event discusses the members and their new Co-op. "They're dairy farmers

mostly. On their rich meadow lands graze fine herds of Holsteins or Guernseys. Twenty-thirty-even fifty milk cows to the herd. Once they milked them by hand without too much difficulty. Families were large-labor was plentiful. But then their sons and hired men went off to war or else were drained into the smoking war industries that dot the Mohawk Valley. Then these farmers, their wives and their little ones tried to do the job alone. They milked long after dark settled down over their quiet hills. They pumped water and carried it to thirsty demanding cattle until the job became a torment. Now they will have electricity. Electricity to milk their cows and pump their water. Electricity to cool the milk and turn their grindstones and make one man's labor serve the work of two."

The reason that the War Production Board authorized the building of a total of 1,200 miles of line by the 5 co-ops in New York was... "to help the Empire State's farm families raise more dairy products and other food for the huge metropolitan markets of the eastern seaboard, and for our soldiers and allies abroad."

We found it interesting when our Field Representative - Buddy Bunt - met with Richfield Town Supervisor Jim Kurkowski regarding a service request in 1993. Mr. Kurkowski told Bud that during World War II he was in the Philippines and was watching a film called "The March of Time." As he watched it he suddenly realized that the band playing in the film was his high school band, and he recognized several people in the film. It was the film taken at the Oaksville substation when it was energized. In those early years, labor and equipment were difficult to obtain. Why, for a short time, members' services were connected even though no meters were available. Those members' bills were simply estimated until meters could be obtained.

By the way, the Oaksville substation was completely reconstructed in 1984 almost exactly 40 years after it was first energized.

Since those early years the cooperative has grown steadily. We now have a total of six substations and a seventh is scheduled for construction soon. The Co-op has approximately 680 miles of line. All of the Co-op's main lines are now three-phase lines. The Co-op now has nearly 3,700 member/customers and we employ a total of 20 employees. The Co-op serves rural areas of Otsego County and portions of Chenango, Madison, and Herkimer counties as well.

The Board of Directors, which is elected from the membership, by the membership, totals nine members. Mr. Winfred C. Arnold, one of the original incorporators, served on the board until his retirement in 1996. At that time, he was the only remaining charter member of the Co-op and had served on the board, in varying capacities, since that very first meeting held in 1941.

I started with the Co-op in 1974 as an apprentice lineman. I became a journeyman lineman and progressed into field engineering, purchasing and member relations. In the spring of 1986 the Board of Directors appointed me as the General Manager of the Co-op. The Board and the employees are all great people and are a genuine pleasure to work with. Each of us is committed to providing the best possible service to our members at the lowest possible cost, consistent with sound business practices.

CONCLUSION

Like our local rural electric cooperative, Otsego Electric, most rural electrification is the product of locally owned rural electric cooperatives that got their start by borrowing funds from REA to build lines and provide service on a non-profit basis. But even those rural areas which receive service from power companies owe a debt to REA, since much of that service was extended only after REA financed systems proved once and for all that the job could be done.

Today about 99 percent of the nation's rural areas have electric service. There are nearly 1,000 rural electric Co-ops serving over 12 million consumers - farms, residences, churches, commercial enterprises, etc. REA systems own fifty percent of the poles, wires, etc. in our country yet serve only ten percent of the population. The average Co-op serves only 6 customers per mile of line while investor owned utilities serve 32 customers per mile and municipal utilities serve over 40 per mile. Due to the nature of the areas we serve, cooperatives' costs are higher to supply electric service to our customers. In most states, the Co-ops' electric rates are higher than the investor-owned utilities due to these economies of scale. Here in New York, however, we receive "preference power" from the New York Power Authority which helps us to maintain rates that are considerably lower than the investor-owned utilities.

BY: Bill Powers

BIBLIOGRAPHY

Rural Electric SOURCEBOOK
1990 National Rural Electric Cooperative Association, Washington, DC
THE NEXT GREATEST THING 50 Years of Rural Electrification In America 1984 National Rural Electric Cooperative Association, Washington, DC
Otsego Electric Cooperative - Meeting Minutes

Other information derived from the personal observations and experiences of the writer.

Telephone

Trying to trace the telephone companies serving Hartwick around 1900 has been confusing.

First I found the following items:

"Another extension of the telephone line is under consideration, running from some point on the line to Snowdon Hill, then on to Burlington Green, assumes a favorite out look."[1]

1882 "Today the poles are being set for a telephone line between Oaksville, weather permitting, Cooperstown will be reached at an early date— giving us connection long desired by the Hartwick business men."[2]

1882 "Ellis Bard has charge of the telephone office in the Otego Valley Hotel."[3]

"H. S. Bradley has a telephone line in operation between his dwelling and the post office."[4]

None of these clippings tell us which company is doing the work.

We find that there were at least 5 different companies serving Hartwick between 1900 and the 40s. Sometimes two at the same time.

In an item Feb. 4, 1939, we read: "The first telephone company operating in Hartwick was organized by Dr. G. E. Schoolcraft, Monroe H. Fields, H. O. Branch and L. Sergeant. It's switchboard was in Mr. Branch's block on Main Street (I believe this was where the P.O. was and later Sweets Harness Shop). The first telephone operator was Mrs. Elmer Genter. The properties were soon taken over by the "Otsego Home Independent Telephone Company" of Cooperstown and operated by that company until sold to the Otsego and Delaware Company in 1911. Mrs. Harry Ingals succeeded Mrs. Genter as operator. In 1914, Mrs. Mary B. Pickens became agent and has continued to the present. In 1926 the center office was moved to its present location on Wells Avenue."[5]

Mrs. Beatrice Gill Griffith, granddaughter of Mrs. M. Pickens adds more:

"Mrs. Mary Bradley Pickens was an operator of the Otsego and Delaware Telephone Company. One of the places she operated from was the powerhouse, which was located down where the Rod and Gun club is now. Then they put her office up over the Post Office. (Later Sweets Shoe Shop). Then they sent her to Cooperstown but I don't know what part at Cooperstown. They moved her back to Hartwick and put the office in the Lina Potter house on Wells Ave. where it was when I was born and there until the office was closed.

It was very interesting work. The office was what would have been our living room. On the right hand side of the rooms was a wall that housed a large transformer that was all coils. Then there was the switchboard. This is where your calls come in. They were called 'plugs' and when you plugged in the switchboard a number would light up. They might want number 10. So then you would plug in number 10 and then my grandmother rang the number so they could talk. Then kind of kitty corner across the room was a large table that was to do business with the people. Then in the back corner to your left was a telephone booth where people could go in and talk privately and make their own cells.

Then there was the messenger work. Mary had to walk wherever the message was meant to go. The message could be about a death, wedding, new baby or someone just coming to visit. She walked sometimes up West Hill and East Hill or South Street. Sometimes she'd just get home and get another message to go back to the same area.

Myrtle Sarah Gill was Mary's daughter who helped Mary with the telephone switchboard. It was a very nice business, working with many people and made many friends. To grow up with a business like that was very interesting and made many nice memories.

The office was taken out in 1939. My grandmother felt bad and cried. Mrs. Grace Beach was an operator working with Mrs. Pickens when the office was in the old P.O. building. Minnie Mead was also an operator in the telephone office." [6]

New York Telephone Company had built the brick building between Irene Matteson's and the corner in 1939. At this time there were about 70 customers who now had dial service. The new exchange will handle local calls automatically. Long distance or other calls requiring the assistance of an operator will be taken care of by the Cooperstown telephone office. Mrs. Mary Pickens, agent for the Telephone Co. will receive a pension. [7]

Another company was the New Lisbon Farmer's Telephone Co. This company was formed by John D. Gregory. John D. Gregory, a teacher and blacksmith, formed the New Lisbon Farm Telephone exchange. Mr. Gregory lived at Welcome and one night a member of his family was sick and he had to drive to Garrettsville to get a doctor. On the way he

thought, "why not have a telephone system?" in 1902 he invited several neighbors together. They formed the New Lisbon Farm Telephone Company. Twelve subscribers made up the new firm and E. E. Steel served as the first president. The first line was strung in 1903 by John B. Gregory, lineman. Will Harrington became the first operator following his death, the Gregory's moved to Garrattsville. Mrs. Gregory assumed the duties of operator. The telephone was thought a necessity but the lines weren't very reliable. [8]

1913 "The New Lisbon Farm Telephone company is at work dividing the heavy loaded farmer lines. The new lines have been from Garrettsville and nearly every line is divided—leaving 10 or 15 people on a line: where previously the lines had as high as 35 subscribers. The Hartwick village line contains only business." [9]

Mr. Bill Powers took care of the Hinman Hollow New Lisbon Farm single wire line. He used a crank magnet to energize the ringing bell, 2 batteries in the phone to talk on. There was a line from Scott's farm on Arnold's Lake road over the hill to Fred Edgett (that was a private line). It had been up so long the wires had grown into the trees (rust acted as an insulator). All wires were on trees. Bill used an old radio earphone to see if the line was alive. Mr. Gregory said if Bill wanted a telephone, he would have to maintain the line. Every snowstorm or windstorm the line went down! Mr. Powers had to climb up the mountain, carrying heavy pliers and an adapter— squeezed together to fix the broken line. They gave him a whole box of adapters. There were 7 or 8 on a line (Bill's folks didn't have a phone but his mother could tune in her radio and she could listen to the phone. The New Lisbon line covered to the Milford feed store, Laurens, Morris, Mt. Vision and Hartwick. In some places the New Lisbon could hook into the Bell phone but you couldn't do that in Hartwick.

Mrs. Madge Hughes could call her sister in New Berlin for free, but her sister couldn't call her!

The New Lisbon Telephone connected farmers with their neighbors and doctors long before other phones were available to them. It was a very important part of the life of people living on the outskirts of Hartwick.

The old wooden wall phone had a handle you turned to ring. There was a certain ring for the operator and so many rings for each phone on the party line. You were allowed 5 minutes for each call as a subscriber. If you went over 5 minutes each additional minute cost 3¢. I believe the rent for the year was $12.

The office was later in the house next to the Presbyterian Church in the middle of Garrettsville. Some of the operators were Nell Reynolds, Lulu S. Stickles, and Mabel Chase. They were considered friends by the subscribers. [10]

When we first moved to Hartwick, we were visiting and the phone rang. It wasn't their ring but the daughter, a dignified, proper person, hurried to listen. My husband was shocked. He asked her why she did it and the reply was "it was a known fact, everybody did it." It was the truth but it did often work for good. If one neighbor was sick or injured, the word was spread and instantly food, or help to do the chores or whatever was needed was on the way,

In 1946 the New Lisbon Farm Telephone Company was sold to the New York Telephone Company for $5000 which included their entire equipment. It had done its work.

In a scrapbook we find the Bell came to Hartwick in 1913.

1913 "farewell party for Frances Main. Miss Frances Main has won many friends during her short residence here. She has occupied the position of night operator for the Bell Telephone Company."

From advertisements in the Hartwick Reporter we find that the Bell and the New Lisbon were both used by the Talbut Bros., dentist, Mr. Stillwell Funeral director in 1915. Some businesses only had one. Even in 1933 we find Ferrine's I.G.A. had both phones. So both were serving the village at the same time.

New York Telephone Company served Hartwick from 1939 till 1997 when it was sold to Bell Atlantic. In 2000 Bell Atlantic became Verizon.

By: F.H.

1. Old Potter Scrapbook pg. 8
2. Old Potter Scrapbook pg. 8
3. Pearl Weeks, History of Hartwick pg. 40
4. Old Potter Scrapbook pg. 35
5. Eva Murdock's Clipping
6. Beatrice Griffiths Own Words
7. Murdock Clipping
8. June 18, 1946 Oneonta Daily Star
9. Elizabeth Curry Scrapbook
10. Murl and Warren Gregory

Hartwick Town Insurance Company

Since 1886 the Town of Hartwick has been the home of one of the smallest Co-operative insurance companies in New York State. Hartwick Town Insurance was formed on April 10, 1886 with 37 members carrying a total amount of insurance of $73,100. Under the certificate of incorporation the reason the company was formed is "to insure dwelling houses and their contents, farm buildings and their contents and other buildings and property including stock, cattle, horses and sheep against loss or damage by fire and lightning." The original territorial limits of the company were established to be in the Town of Hartwick only. Insurance coverage at the company's formation ranged from $3500 to $300. Charles M. Augur of Hartwick Seminary was the first Secretary-Treasurer. The Directors of the company were Andrew N. Todd, Charles N. Chase, Chester B. Steere, Monroe H. Field, Oscar Bradley, Ezra Blanchard and Charles M. Augur.

When the company was formed insurance policies were issued for 1 year or 2 years or 3 years to stagger the dates the policies renewed. The policies however were renewed as they were issued until there was great confusion. One person might have 3 policies each with varying policy length. A big policyholders meeting was held in Hartwick where, to eliminate confusion, it was decided that all policies would be renewed for a 3-year period. The policyholders are the owners of the company. An annual meeting of the policyholders is still held once a year as was established in 1886. Directors are elected for a 3-year term from policyholders. The directors then elect a President and a Secretary-Treasurer for a 1-year term.

For many years policyholders were assessed an annual premium based on estimated expenses for the upcoming year. If a loss larger than the company had assessed for occurred, the directors then went to the bank and took out a loan to cover that loss. The policyholders would then be assessed for the amount of the loan. The company was not allowed to keep a surplus of money on hand. In later years the State changed its laws and the company began to accumulate premiums through annual assessments to cover future losses.

The usual losses that occurred in the early days of the company were lightning striking animals or buildings as well as chimney fires. Changes in the company's by-laws also reflect changes in the lifestyle of the policyholders. In 1912 a change was made stating that, "no person holding a policy shall use or allow anyone to use any steam engine within 50' of any property insured by the company and the smoke stacks of any such engines used shall be properly secured and nothing except soft coal used for fuel." Also, permission was given at the same meeting to use electricity, acetylene or gasoline for lighting purposes provided the Fire Underwriters Association has approved the wiring for electricity. In

1914 permission was given to store automobiles in buildings covered by the company but at a fee of $4 per year. All gasoline tanks however had to be 50" away from an insured building.

In 1965 a Charter change was approved expanding the territory eligible for coverage from the Town of Hartwick only to all of Otsego County. The company today still writes fire coverage with lightning, damage by aircraft or vehicles and (providing the premises are also insured under the same insurance policy), against theft of livestock from the insured's premise. New York State limits the amount of coverage that the company can write to 10% of its surplus. In 2000 the maximum amount of insurance coverage that could be written was $12,000 on any one building or group of buildings. Some of the policies can be covered for more than the stated maximum if the buildings are more than 60' apart. There were 70 policies in effect in 2000 with $698,845 of coverage. The operation of the company has changed little over the years. The company has an annual assessment that is due October 1st each year. Rates charged for the annual assessment have not changed in many years as the number of losses have been small. In 1998 William Powers retired as secretary-Treasurer after serving in that position since July 25,1957. He has maintained his position on the Board of Directors and has served as President since 1998. Mary Balcom was elected Secretary-Treasurer in 1998 succeeding Mr. Powers. Current members of the Board of Directors are Eileen Balcom, Chris Briggs, Donald Eldred, Donald Elliot, Fred D. Field, Ralph Goodrich, Kim Gruchacz, Orrin Higgins and Pat McBrearty.

By: Bill Powers and Mary Balcom—Information gathered from policies and past meeting notes

Fire Departments

How horrible it must have been in the early days when a fire broke out. Neighbors came with buckets. In settlements the bucket brigades at times were successful, at least saving the out buildings. Outside the village there were often only family to man the buckets. After the telephone came, neighbors could be summoned. They could save some of their possessions. How thankful we should be for our fire equipment and especially our trained volunteer firemen.

Even in 1940 things were much different than today. There was a house fire about two miles out of town. The roads were snowy. Half way up a steep hill the driveway was worse. The pumper couldn't get in. The men fastened ropes to the pumper and pulled it into the driveway. It was hard but the men succeeded. The house was lost but nearby buildings were saved!

There is mention of an early fire company on the west side. "The Neptune Hose Company kept its equipment in the shed behind the Brooklyn House."

In an 1898 clipping we learn that the Hartwick Hose Company will hold a field day with many sports and then later it was reported $78 was raised.

1899 – "The Hose Company had their first experience of wetting down their first blaze one day recently. The shingle roof of H. G. Miller's blacksmith shop caught fire from sparks but was quickly discovered and put distinguished."

In a later clipping we learn of an early Fire Chief Mr. Clark Beach. In 1896 Mr. Clark was the Fire Chief. His son Clifford made the sign (1940's) that hung outside of the firehouse when it was in the building that stood next to Dean Beach's (Polulech apartment house). It probably is the one hanging outside of the present firehouse.

The Fire Department moved into this building after rebuilding it in 1946.

Another place that housed the fire equipment was the former Dr. Baker's barn in the 1930's after Clark's garage had moved to the former school. A 1914 Pierce Arrow hand truck was purchased in 1920. The bell that was on it is used in 2002 to call meetings to order.

1934 seems to be the year our present volunteer fire company was organized. Fire department President Donald Chase at the dedication of our present firehouse July 4, 1969 reported eighteen men got together May 3, 1934 and decided to form a fire district. "Two people who were at that meeting are here today and active members. They are Orlo Burch and Floyd (Speedy) Mead" Chase stated.

In 1982 at the banquet honoring Wayne Griffith as 'Fire Man of the Year', Orlo Burch gave a history of the fire department reporting a group of firefighters organized in 1902 but until 1934 there was not a fire district.

1934 the treasury was empty but with a 10¢ fine for every absence from a meeting and with the help of a spaghetti supper (35¢ a plate) a fund was started. Their equipment was a second-hand pumper, a siren they bought for $19, and two pails!

Hartwick Fire Department has raised money toward their equipment from the first.

1934 Notice –

"Fires are Costly

Attention Citizens of Hartwick

Fireman's Ball EMBA Hall Oct. 12

This money is for new equipment.

A worthy cause—Say 'YES' when a fireman approaches you Sept. 19, 1934

This dance became an annual affair.

Card parties have also been an annual fundraiser for over 50 years.

On October 8, 1945 the town board voted to separate the Fire Company and the water works and have separate taxes assigned.

Later in December 1945 the first new pumper was purchased, a Seagrave for about $7,695 and a new siren.

The new fire truck had not arrived in December 1945 as firemen led by Fire Chief Carl Thomas responded to a fire at the foot of Hemlock Hill in New Lisbon. They didn't take their aged pumper as Mr. Thomas explained, "the Hartwick pumper built in 1918 is so worn it is not taken outside of the village." A milk truck owned by Albert Carkees loaded with cans of water joined a caravan of cars and a Harrison Feed Store pickup truck, all loaded with firemen and hand equipment. The house was fully involved when they reached it but firemen prevented the fire from spreading to the barn and henhouse.

In 1967 the volunteer firemen purchased the property on the south side of Main Street formerly the Perrine store and later occupied by Hamiltons. By the spring of 1968 the volunteers had the ground ready for the builders. Henry Murdock donated the gravel to fill in the cellar hole.

The whole community joined in fundraisers, $11,000 was raised and $13,000 was borrowed.

Firemen and the auxiliary held rummage sales, card parties, bake sales, three barn dances, two barbecues and two auctions.

The American Legion and Auxiliary held a smorgasbord and the Rebekah Lodge held a two-day rummage and bake sale. Much labor was donated. Carter Harrison Sr. of Arizona and Hartwick drew up the plans without charge.

"It is all volunteer labor that transformed this lot into this structure. We are fortunate because two of our volunteer firemen are professional builders." Thamer Harper, Fire Chief, explained in the September 23, 1968 issue of the Oneonta Star. These men were Clyde Tuller, carpenter, and James Millea, who is a mason. They worked long hours.

November 25, 1968, Oneonta Star states, "The Hartwick firemen have a new home," James Renwick, Jr., Town of Hartwick supervisor and a fireman said, "We knew the community would come through." "I would like to offer our sincere thanks to Hartwick Company No. 2 and the Garrattsville Fire departments, who came on Veteran's Day and helped us put the deck up," said Donald Chase, department president. Phillips Lumber Company was thanked for the use of equipment used in installing the heavy beams and the Town Highway Superintendent, Stanley Griffith, for his cooperation.

July 5, 1969 The big day arrived!

The new firehouse was dedicated. Congressman Samuel Stratton was the main speaker. He praised the Fire Department and the community for doing it themselves "without federal funding" "as we celebrate the nations independence we can see right here in the operation of the fire company – something of what it requires to have a free and independent country – hard work, not much pay, and plenty of risk."

Leonard Wright, Fire chief, also praised all and challenged the community to larger participation. He especially praised Charles Schroeder and the new emergency ambulance squad. A much deserved badge was presented to Mr. Wright by Allen Beach, Otsego County Coordinator, who acted as Master of ceremonies for the entire parade and dedication.

Daily Star – January 1969

"The Town of Hartwick sold the old fire house and lot to Carter Harrison, owner of the adjacent Hartwick Supermarket for $1,000. Proceeds from the sale will be turned over to the Fire Department's fund toward the cost of the newly completed firehouse. Thamar Harper tore down the building and rebuilt it across from the restaurant on 205." Irene Mozolewski reported more than 4000 came to see the new fire hall.

"Before the dedication in May the department had received the ambulance from New Berlin for $3,500. It was equipped with only a stretcher – but now is in compliance with New York State laws."

In addition to Captain Schroeder, other officers are Carl Schidzick, first Lieutenant, Anita Harrison, second Lieutenant, Kay Tarbox, secretary, and William Graham, treasurer.

Squad members are Minnie Schroder, Minnie Mead, Floyd Mead, Genevieve Bresee, Donald C. Phillips, Peter Sorbera, Joseph Gerecht, James Renwick, William Harrison, Robert Telfer, and Norma Telfer.

Hartwick in 1973 had a new president of the fire department. This time it was a woman, Mrs. Kay Tarbox. The first woman fire company president in our area.

This was the year the Otsego County Fireman's Convention was held here. They had the usual activities. Many visitors attended. Hartwick No. 1 with Jerry Tarbox, Fire Chief and Hartwick No.2 with Larry Lamb worked together with help from other companies. Hartwick No. 2

sponsored a chicken barbecue. The parade had more than 80 units!

Besides being president of the Volunteers, Kay Tarbox taught First Aid in Hartwick, Garrattsville, Cooperstown, and Springfield Center. She was awarded a Commendation Certificate from Cooperstown Emergency Squad; also two engraved silver trays, one in appreciation from the First Aid Training Squad County Fire Department and the other from a class she taught at Bassett Hospital.

At this time she received emergency calls at her home and could activate the siren from there also. Hartwick had two others, Fannie Irons and Minnie Mead, who could do the same. Since they were in the same neighborhood, a horn was installed outside so they could hear all calls. This system worked so well that it was still used in1976. One phone was in John Bush's, one in Leonard Wright's and one in Minnie Schroeders. At one time the switchboard for the emergency squad was in Gene Ward's home. Walkie-talkies were added in 1973. [19]

1976 was the year that Hartwick purchased a 1952 Ward LaFrance pumper with a 500-gallon booster tank. The truck, which has under 1500 miles, was purchased from Armonk, NY for $2895 and is now in service.

The Hartwick Department is also revising a 1946 Seagrave fire truck, which has served the town well for nearly three decades.

"The department in 1976 has six pieces of equipment: a 1969 Ford with a 1000 gallon booster tank, a 1200 gallon tank on an army truck, a panel truck used to transport equipment, the Seagrave pumper and the 1968 Cadillac Ambulance used by the twelve member emergency squad.

Officers are John Bush, Fire Chief, Ronald Clegg, first assistant, Ronald Kane, second assistant, and Robert Stickles, third assistant. Department officers are Orlo Burch, president,

Donald Phillips, Vice-president, Linda Walrath, secretary, and William Steer, treasurer. The company averages about 20 calls a year."

In 1976 there was a tornado. Live wires and trees blocked many roads. The firemen worked continuously removing fallen trees and guarding "live" wires. 8302 man-hours were put in by the Hartwick No. 1 firemen in 1976.

Also in 1976 at the parade in Cooperstown celebrating our County's 200th birthday, Hartwick won with the oldest fire engine, also most men in line within the county.

The Seagrave pumper (1945) has participated in parade after parade but in 1978 the Seagrave took part in a funeral!

Daily Star – January 20,1978
"Ralph Spicer, 79, the grand old man of the Hartwick Fire Department was paid tribute by his fellow townspeople.

After a service at Ingalls, Connell, and Dow Funeral Home (Patterson's) the casket was borne to the venerable 1946 white Seagrave pumper of which Mr. Spicer had been especially fond. With six firemen flanking the casket the truck was driven slowly up Main Street to the Hartwick fire hall draped for the occasion.

At the fire hall the procession was brought to a halt and the fire siren sounded in a last salute to Mr. Spicer, then the procession continued on to the cemetery.

Fire Chief, John Bush said, "Ralph loved that old truck."

Former Chief Tom McGrath added "there is a lot of sentiment connected among the townspeople to the old truck and those same people will deeply miss the kindly old gentleman."

Gib Bunn who was always at the wheel of the Seagrave when Spicer rode beside him said, "I don't think anyone knows when he joined. The old records were lost in a fire in the fire hall when it was on South Street." Mr. Spicer had no known survivors but he had the Fire Department.

While Edie Conway was captain of the Hartwick Emergency Squad in 1978 the Town of Hartwick purchased a 1975 Van Ambulance for $13,500 to replace the 1968 Cadillac. The van has 4000 miles on it. It is roomier than its counterpart and has a power inverter to 110 volts.

1980 saw the Hartwick Emergency Squad equipped with pagers. The Town purchased 11 pagers and the fire department 11 more to equip the entire ambulance crew and the fire officer. Mike Basile was Captain of the squad at this time and Ronald Clegg, Fire Chief.

Hartwick Emergency Squad held an open house Sunday for their brand new ambulance, which went into service in mid-November. (It had made over 35 runs already.) Squad members on hand to answer questions were Caren Kelsey, a past captain, Deborah Clegg, first Lieutenant, and Captain Mike Basile. The modular vehicle, which cost $48,000, and is expected to last at least ten years, is much larger than the old ambulance and easier to handle. They also thanked the community for its support."

Daily Star – May 29, 1996
In 1996 – Hartwick Fire Department No 1 bought and rebuilt a four by four 1986 pickup truck to use as a grass fire vehicle. The cost was $3,500 for the vehicle and the improvements.

Fire fighters who volunteered time on the truck project included John Bush, Ronald Clegg, Roger DeLong, Raymond Miller, Bruce Adams, Mark Hopkins, Reverend Laverne Saxer, Joshua Saxer, Ronald Monroe, Charles Monroe, Chico Sprague, Duane Hotaling, Wayne Griffith, Chris Reller, T. J. Wellman, Peter Chase, Rick Miller, and Richard Thompson.

In 1995 a new ambulance was purchased and is in use today. Also purchased recently was the Freightliner Rescue Vehicle.

In 2001 the new meeting and training room was dedicated to Dr. Steffi Baker, our Doctor and friend for many years, who bequested money to the fire department. The room is very attractive and comfortable and is being used by the community as well as the fire department.

In 2002 the fire department now have 8 junior firemen between the ages of 16 and 18. They are New York State trained as all the firemen are and also trained by the local department. They do all that regular firemen do except enter a burning building, drive the vehicles, and have a key to the firehouse. The junior firemen are active and the program very successful.

The fire department has sponsored many activities. Among these are: an annual banquet honoring the fireman who has put in the most hours, etc., a contest to choose a fire queen, open house in October with free blood pressure screening, an annual chicken and biscuit dinner in March, an annual C.P.R. training class. The fire department has sponsored the boy scouts for many years and holds an annual Halloween party.

Hartwick is very fortunate to have an active fire department with loyal, well trained volunteer firemen and a dedicated emergency squad. Over the years the auxilliary has put in many hours raising money and serving coffee and food to the men fighting the fires.

Equipment in service January 2002:
1995 Ambulance, 2000 Rescue truck, 1990 Ford pumper, 1995 International, 1968 Pumper, 1986 Ford 4 x 4 pickup for grass fires, and a 1946 Seagrave for parades.

The following list of past chiefs of Hartwick No 1 is from the plaque in the meeting room.

John Morehouse	1920-1932
Orlo Burch	1933-1939
Carl Thomas	1940-1945
Arnold Kolliker	1946-1949
Floyd "Speedy" Mead	1950-1957
Leonard Wright	1958-1960
Rod Wellman	1961-1963
Donald Phillips	1964-1966
Thamer Harper	1967-1968
Leonard Wright	1969-1972
Jerry Tarbox	1973-1974
Lyle Jones, Jr.	1974-1975
John W. Bush	1976-1978
Ron Clegg	1979-1981
John W. Bush	1982-1984
Wayne Griffith	1985-1986
Ron Kane	1987-1993

Parades

Caren Kelsey, Ron Clegg, Darlene Roe, Lynn Loomis

*Flag- Chuck Hascup, Chris Reller, Dan Shute, Dave Butler,
Ron Kane,chief, Cindy Thompson, Deb Clegg, Caren Kelsey*

*Glenn Morrison, Flag,?, Flag, Terry Bunn, ?, Ken Carson,Sr.,
Owen McManus, Bernie Zeh, ?*

Sesquicentennial Parade 1952

John W. Bush   1994-present

HARTWICK
FIRE DEPARTMENT COMPANY 2
OVER THE YEARS

As the story has been told by the old timers over time, on or about 1948-49 a few of the concerned citizens of the hamlets of Hyde Park and Hartwick Seminary started talking about fire protection in these areas, because of the distance of the Hartwick Fire Department.

Some of these gentlemen started attending meetings with the Town Board and meetings and drills of Hartwick Fire Department to get information and formal training.

This went on for approximately two years and the first recorded meeting of Hartwick Fire Department Company Number Two was held on June 20, 1950.

The 14 present were Kenneth Aney, Henry Aney, John Aney, Clark Miller, Kenneth Meade, Frank Cowels, Dick Ofield, Charles Bice, Porter Backus, Harry Ingalls, Charles Hadcock, Clifford LaGasse, Frank Collison, and Arthur Collier.

At this first meeting elections were held and the following where elected Frank Collison, Chief, Clark Miller, 1st Assistant Chief, and Arthur Colliers, Secretary-Treasurer. The minutes also reflected that a committee of 3 was elected to look at and investigate an alarm systems of sorts.

They continued to hold meetings in homes that had the newest invention called television. These meetings were held on Wednesday nights the same night the program Wagon Train would be on. At 8:00 PM the minutes would actually show they took a break and eats would be served, the show would be watched then at its end the

meeting would restart. Then they would adjourn and a friendly game of cards would begin.

Along this same time a building was acquired at the old site of Hartwick Lutheran Seminary. It was a small building used as a garage and meeting hall. A trailer loaded with hose, portable pump, nozzle, and simple fire fighting equipment was also kept here. This would be pulled by farmers with their tractors to the scene of the fire and hold it until Hartwick Company One could arrive and bring it under control. The members that were around at the time of the call would be summoned by the ringing of the Church Bell at the Lutheran Church and telephone calls.

The first motorized fire truck was a 1940 Plymouth pickup truck. It's color was green with red doors with department name on them.

This very small building was rebuilt and an extension was added for the extra length of the truck. During the summer months meetings would be held at the Fire Barn until darkness would fall.

Dinners were held and monies saved to buy a real fire truck and build a real Fire Hall. The truck was a 1954 Willys Jeep pickup that was real Fire Engine Red. This truck is still in service at this writing.

At the July 1957 meeting, land was staked out that had been donated by Floyd Kitts and the C. J Strong family to the Town of Hartwick to build a fire hall at its present location..

Hartwick Fire Department Company 2 became known County and State wide as Hartwick Seminary Fire Department due to the fact of it's beginning at the Seminary and is still known as that today.

The new Fire Hall was built in the summer of 1958 by the membership. The head carpenters and masons were "The Ryan Boys", Cliff, Francis Sr. and John along with Bob Bailey. Backhoe work done by Jackson Schultz, Sr. Slowly and surely it started to become the real thing.

In early fall 1960 there was a major fire in the area across the roadway where the Hartwick Commons stands. Known as the Snood House, said by older locals to be the oldest house in this area of the Town of Hartwick, burned to the ground. This really stimulated the men to get serious, rigid, formal training through Fire Chief Scanlon of Oneonta. A water truck was purchased from West Oneonta Fire Department, a 1948 International Tanker, retired fuel oil truck from Reinhardt Oil. This served the Company until 1965 when a new Ford F-600 chassis was purchased from Smith Ford of Cooperstown. The tank from the old tanker was placed on the new truck.

In 1969 a new custom tank was fabricated by Jack Myers of Morris, a welder and fabricator of fire exits.

In the spring of 1970 under the guidance of Supervisor, Jim Renwick and Hartwick 1st Asst. Chief Carl Schidzick, a surplus 1952 Ford Seagrave pumper was offered to Company 2. Within a short period of time and a little tender loving care this truck was ready to fight fires and how it did.

This may well be the real beginning of what Hartwick # 2 is today, a true Fire Company not just a second station. Hartwick Seminary became a mutual aid company to Hartwick, Cooperstown, Milford and all area Fire Departments.

In 1973 a small van was donated by W. L. Taylor Oil of Cooperstown to be used as an Emergency Rescue and Equipment unit. At this point members saw the need for First Aid training, the new horizon of Emergency Services.

In 1974 the Fire Company had outgrown its station and needed more space. Trucks and equipment were being housed in other areas of the community.

Plans were laid and land was purchased to build an addition at a total cost of $50,000.00 to the taxpayers.

The membership of this Company came together and did the interior work to save money.

The fall and winter of that year many hours of work were spent putting up ceiling, lights, and heat. The following year concrete was ordered, poured, and worked to it's smoothness.

In October, 2000, Hartwick No. 2 celebrated their 50th anniversary with an open house.

2002 officers are Donald Roseboom, chief, Larry Lamb, 1st assistant, Mike Basile, 2nd assistant, Peter Chase, 3rd assistant. They presently own a 1971 Mack pumper, a 1995 International tanker, a 1990 Chevrolet emergency van, and a 2000 Dodge Dakota 4 x 4 brush truck.

By: F. H.

Bibliography

Old Potter Scrapbook
Elizabeth Curry's Scrapbook
Henry Murdock
John Bush
Oneonta Star July 5, 1969
Freeman's Journal December 22, 1982
Oneonta Star July 5, 1968
Hartwick Reporter September 1934
Town Board Records
Susie Potter's Brown Scrapbook
Susie Potter's White Scrapbook
Oneonta Star September 23, 1968
Clipping, Henry Murdock
Oneonta Star May 5, 1969
Freeman's Journal August 7, 1973
Daily Star April 26, 1976
John Bush Scrapbook
Daily Star July 2, 1980
Freeman's Journal February 5, 1986
Cooperstown Crier March 23, 2000

Dedication of New Hartwick Fire House Ribbon Cutting
July 5, 1969 - Left to Right:

Front Row: C. Schidzik; D. Chase; D. Phillips; F Mead; L.
Deforest; C. Tuller; J. Tarbox
Second Row: L. Wright; M. Burch; D. burch; O. Burch; S.
Phillips; P. Sorbera; J. Millea
Back Row: W. Steers

LEFT TO RIGHT:
Otsego County Fire coordinator-Allen Beach; Hartwick Fire
Chief - Leonard Wright; Town Supervisor - James Renwick,
Jr.; Congressman - Sam Straton; Hartwick Fire Auxiliary -
Pres. Rose Tuller; Hartwick Fire - Pres. Donald Chase.

Hartwick Fire Chief Leonard C. Wright; First Assistant Carl Schidzick; and Town of Hartwick Supervisor James Renwick Jr., pause
to admire the intricate control panel on the new Town of Hartwick tanker-pumper. Purchase of the machine was made possible by a
$5,000 grant from the Clark Foundation and the balance of the $21,000 cost of the truck will be financed by the town.

Hartwick #2 Fire Department

1954 - Willy's Jeep

1954 - Willy's Jeep, Ford Econoline Emergency Van, Pumper E20, Tanker TA76

1970 - Earl Walrath, Sr.; Frank Miller, Sr.; John Lamb; John Miller; Larry Lamb

Hartwick #2 Fire Station before beginning construction of addition.

Hartwick #2 Fire Station after addition added in 1976

The Hartwick Waterworks Company

Hartwick, NY, Viewed from the East

Hartwick Water Works Company was founded in 1896. The purpose was to create a sustainable supply of water for businesses and to provide for improved fire protection. In addition, residential water service was also provided to village residents. Over several years the water lines were extended to eventually serve the entire village. The stockholders, officers and directors faced many challenges during the seventy years of operation such as low pressure, problems with water purity, a case of typhoid and water turbidity. The original sources included both Cooks Pond and the Willis Spring on East Hill.

As the town grew these sources could not pro-

Old Spring that Fed the Town Reservoir

vide a sanitary source and tended to go dry during the summer months and during periods of prolonged cold. In 1925 a dam was constructed on the land where the Hollister and Phillips farms were located on East Hill. The new reservoir was the main source of water for the village until the mid 1960's. In 1964 the Barney Gulf Resevoir went dry. With the help of the Hartwick Fire Department the Water Works was rescued. However, the events of the fall caused the Town Board to create a Water District and to acquire the water system.

Orlo G. Burch purchased all of the outstanding shares of stock of The Hartwick Water Works Company during the late 1960's and the corporation was dissolved in the early 1970's.

Officers at the time the Barney Gulf Dam was constructed were: Jacob N. Bush President; Orlo S. Burch Director and Vice President; A. Monroe Burch, Director and Superintendent; L. H. Bresee Director

By: Orlo C. Burch

Fire Department and Highway workers assisting in pulling the pipe from the old East Hill well after the pumping shaft broke in the fall of 1964.

The Stage

Stage routes were established along the well-populated Atlantic Coast even in colonial times. With settlements proceeding rapidly westward from Otsego Lake soon after 1790 similar services for mail, passengers, and small package freight became available.

Stage lines ran throughout this region and some continued until superseded by railroads and other modern forms of transportation.

Phinney's Almanac, published in Cooperstown, in its edition for 1803 describes a post route extending to Painted Post in Steuben County. Starting at Griffin's Tavern in Cooperstown the first stop was at "Ellsworth's" on the old Otego Road east of South Hartwick. It continued by Morris, Oxford, and Unadilla. This route soon shifted to pass through Hartwick Village, where a post office was established that year. John and Andrew Winton's line in 1820 was from Cooperstown through Hartwick and Laurens to Morris. Johnson and Wakefield succeeded as proprietors in 1825. The southern terminus became Oneonta as soon as 1835. Waterman Eldred was driving this route in 1860 and Frank D. Briggs daily in 1875. The trip was then accomplished each way in an exact five hours, leaving Cooperstown at 5 AM and Oneonta at 1 PM. This line ceased operations with the opening of the electric railway in 1901. Previously it had been owned and operated by Albert D. Beach for many years until he sold out.

New Berlin Pioneer June 11, 1859

Stages and Stage Routes
Z. E. Allen, Proprietor
Stages leave the Eagle Hotel, New Berlin daily and tri-weekly as follows:

For Utica	8 o'clock AM
Oneonta	4 o'clock PM
Norwich	4 o'clock PM
Cooperstown	8 o'clock PM
Sherburne	12 ½ o'clock PM

The Cooperstown stage leaves New Berlin only 3 times per week, viz; Tues., Thurs., and Sat: returning on Wed. – Fri. – and Mon. The other lines run daily.

Z. E. Allen
New Berlin, May 17, 1859

Taken from the Potter Scrapbook 1876-1900's
P 11 –1899 - Clesson M. Cook has taken the stage route from this place to Cooperstown to run till April 1st, 1899. Orson Fields, the proprietor, being unable to drive it during severe weather.

P 64- Virgil Hollbrook is again able to drive the Cooperstown stage after several weeks of severe illness.

P 79 -1890- Charles Sheldon of Oneonta has purchased an interest in the stage line from Oneonta to here and is now the general driver on this end of the line. He expects to move here the 1st of April.

P 99-1913- Hartwick - June 4th, Clarence Gardner, for many years a blacksmith of this village, has bought the Barton shop in Garrettsville and will soon move to that place. It is understood that he will run the stage route to Mt. Vision keeping Robert Miller in his employ.

Ella May Harrington's Scrapbook
(owned by Historical Society)

The stage plying between this place and Cooperstown failed to get through to the above named place last week Tuesday and was forced to return before getting two miles out of this village on account of the snow blockage. The roads were in bad condition yet over 300 hundred voters were at the polls in this district.

1892- Lester Davis has been driving the Hartwick to Cooperstown stage the past few days. Orson Fields is not yet well and Mr. Harris, the former driver, having commenced his work at Williams Cheese Factory.

898-Otis Holbrook of Otsdawa has been visiting a few days his son, Robert L., the proprietor of the Oneonta and Hartwick stage route.

Freight- R. H. Price of South Hartwick runs regularly 3 times per week with freight and express from here to Oneonta, which is a matter of quite an accommodation to our businessmen.

Joe Fields book- Hartwick Past- Stage stopped at Holden Inn.

Otego Valley Hotel Stage Stop

Hartwick History Notes – Transportation

Stage Co. – 1908
   Two stage lines: Cooperstown – Fort Plain
   C-town 6:30 AM – 12:30 PM
   Ft. Plain 9AM – 1 PM

C.V. to Richfield

Highways – 1798
   Great Western Turnpike
   Second Great Western – 1801

Robert Holbrook – One of the village's most highly respected and beloved citizens. Born in Otego, May 26, 1868, Mr. Holbrook was a son of Otis and Mary (Harris). He was married to Cora M. Allen of South Hartwick, Sept. 28, 1897, and then lived at Hartwick and for 4 years. He drove the stage from Hartwick to Oneonta. Later he was employed as motorman on the electric railway.

By: Barb Potter

Bibliography:
Hartwick Visitor
Old Potter Scrapbook
Ella May Harrington's Scrapbook
Hartwick History Notes
New Berlin Pioneer

Little Old Hartwick

In a little place called Hartwick, a town that's known so well.
That has three good churches, and four places they call hotels;
Is a little dinkie railroad, with its car shops and its barns,
That carries the farmers' produce, as they bring it off the farms.

There's a little Kill O'Watt factory, about a mile below the town,
That furnishes the power, for miles and miles around.
It keeps a gang of men that labor, night and day,
To make the towns along the line, look like the Great White Way.

It keeps the cars a-running, almost every day,
If we do not have a snowstorm, and cows keep out the way.
And if they drop a motor, or a car goes in the creek,
They put a brand new tie in, and it always does the trick.

For the man that does the head work, is a man that is well known.
And the boys on this ere pike, all call him Daddy Stone.
But he has to have a helper, each department has a head,
And the man, that is the super, to the boys is known as Fred.

Then we have our freights and tariffs, and other things going on,
So have a man from Richfield, and the boys, they call him John,
But Charlie tends the Kill O'Watt factory, as it grinds from hour to hour
For to run the New York Southern, we have to have the power.

And when we have a snowstorm, or the cars get acting mean,
We start right off for Hartwick, to see friend George Killeen;
So among all the fellows, you never hear a kick,
For the cars always get there, but it sometimes takes a week.

H. O. Hintermister
January, 1918

Town of Hartwick Highways

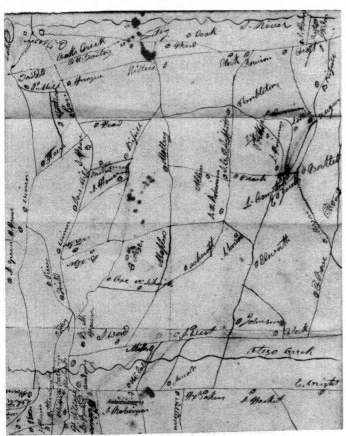

Original in the Department of Rare Books and Special Collections, University of Rochester Library. Not to be reproduced without permission. ca. 1815

In 1980 Hartwick's new town barn was built, followed by the new Town Hall in 1995. Hartwick citizens were pleased with the modern and spacious complex. Amazing changes have occurred in Hartwick, town and village, to bring the community to this point.

Lets examine the great changes brought about by time for the workers and travelers of our town's highways and byways over the past 150 years.

When the pioneers came they blazed trails through the wilderness. More people followed and the trails became the beaten track, and with time formed a network of roads which in some cases are the same country roads we follow today. Before the days of snowplows and sanders, of road graders and ten-ton trucks, how were our roads kept open?

According to research by Roy Butterfield, "the first real highway to traverse the town was doubtless the old Otego Road laid out in 1773 to supply, from Canajoharie, the settlement in the making in the vicinity of Laurens. It began north of Laurens, ran up the west side of Otego Creek, crossed the stream, on north to a point a mile south of South Hartwick, then northeast through the town over roads still mostly in use, reaching the River Road about a quarter a mile north of the Seminary and on to the foot of Otsego Lake. It was referred to in 1809 as "the great road from Otsego to Wattles Ferry," now known as Cooperstown and Unadilla. It is reported to have been in good repair in 1785.

The River Road (now Route 28) is said to have been in use before 1777. Certainly Clinton's foot soldiers went that way in 1779, camping over night at (Cully's) Milford Center, at the end of the first days march from the lake."

The above taken from "Transportation" by Dr. Butterfield.

Freeman's Journal – May 13, 1833
Notice to Bridge Builders
The undersigned, commissioners of the

towns of Hartwick and Otsego give notice, to the inhabitants of the above towns, to meet at the house of Hezekiah Lyon, in Hartwick, on the 23rd inst. At one o'clock pm for the purpose of contracting a Bridge across the Oaks Creek, near Hope factory.

Com'rs. Of Highways

| Jabez Chapman | James Johnson |
| H. Burlingham, Jr. | Comfort Chase |

As early as 1844 and before a system was in use to work the roads, the township was divided into 45 wards or districts, and had three Highway Commissioners. Each district was headed by an Overseer or Pathmaster of Highways, whose job it was to see to the maintenance of roads in his district. The overseer was provided with a list of names of men to provide the labor. All free males, 21 years of age or older, were obliged "to work on the roads" at least one day a year. Freeholders had to give additional days of service according to their assessed ratings. The number of days to be worked was conferred to each name on the list, and even widows were required to furnish ½ days work. Two thirds of the required work was to be done before July 1st, and the rest by Nov. 1st. Noxious weeds were to be cut down by July 1st, and again by Sept. 1st. Loose stones lying on the beaten track were to be removed at least once each month from April 1st to Dec. 1st. Bridges were also built or repaired as needed.

In 1853 the number of wards was expanded to 48, and by 1861 again expanded to make 50 wards. The number then stayed the same as long as the ward system was in use.

The Town of Hartwick Clerks Record details the progress of maintaining town roads over the past century and a half. The following are facts and incidents culled from these records.

The Overseer of Highways had many duties, and it would seem to be a thankless job. Over the years many men in each district held the job, some men held it repeatedly for years.

The Overseer had to keep an accurate list of who worked, and actual time worked. A fine was imposed on anyone failing to do his requirement, and it was the overseers' duty to determine and collect the fines.

Also commutations were granted, which was money paid rather than laboring on the roads. This was also to be accurately recorded, and the monies collected from commutations and fines was turned over to the Commissioner of Highways. Failure to carry out any of the above resulted in a penalty against the overseer of $5.00. This being a sizable sum in the mid 1800's.

In 1846 it was voted that the overseers furnish plank for bridges to the amount of $5.00 to be charged to the Commissioner of Highways, and the wards will put the plank on the bridges free of charge.

In the early days there was a road that ran across the Otego Creek less than a mile below the village. It connected what is now County Rte 45 and County Rte 14 (Hemlock Hill).

In 1857, Chauncey Gardner, who was liable to be assessed for labor petitioned to close the road as it had become old and useless, (if that road had been kept open it probably would have been well used today).

Again according to Roy Butterfield, what is now North Street in Hartwick village, did not exist until 1838. The problem was the swamp near the North Street Bridge, and the creek bed there is underlaid with Hartwick polish making an undesirable foundation for a bridge. Twelve freeholders certified in 1837 that a highway there was "necessary and proper" and the commissioners approved. An opposing group objected to the expense of construction and acquiring land. On appeal the road was ordered built. Until the bridge was built people coming into town from the north entered Hartwick by what is now the Weeks Road, and into the Brooklyn side of town.

Jan. 5, 1879–E. A. Wells has bought the Harvey Maples property, and we learn that a street is to be opened running north from Main Street. (This was to be Wells Ave. or School Street.)

In 1894 the highway in Ward 50 from Hartwick to Burlington Green was damaged, and there was not sufficient funds to repair. It was resolved that the Commissioner of Highways repair immediately according to law.

The following men furnished labor and materials.

Irving Petri—6 days sanding mason	$9.00
Wm. Dean—6 1/4 days mason work	15.62
Cyrus Wellman—Stone for wall	2.00
Mark Weeks—½ day mason work	1.37
A. Marsh—120 bushels sand	6.00
Chas. Huse—6 days mason work	15.00
———Bissell—Furnishing stone	18.00
Chas. Tanner—½ day mason work	1.37
M. Weeks—4½ days mason work	11.87
A. H Fried—Plank, stone, fill, & sand	30.89
S. H. Chapin—6 3/4 days mason work	16.87
John Smith—6 bushels cement	6.00
	$133.00

In 1893 Hartwick bought a "road machine," a grader drawn by two or three span of horses. This did better and faster work then men working with plows, harrows, hoes, and shovels.

About 1900 the district or ward plan of maintaining the roads was receiving more and more criticism. A petition was filed at the town clerk's office signed by some 40 leading tax payers asking the town board for a vote by ballot to change the system for working the highways from the labor system to the money system. At a special town meeting in 1902 the electors voted to tax themselves for this purpose. There were some dissenters, so in

1906 it was again voted on, and by a decisive vote road districts became obsolete.

A motion was made in 1902 that the Supervisor levy a tax on all taxable property of $780.02. Also a poll tax of $1.00 on each and every male inhabitant except which is exempt by law which such amount to be $464.00. Making a total of $1248.02 to be paid to the Commissioner of Highways to be used for working town roads.

In 1907 state aid for highways became available and Hartwick received $892.50 of such.

March 1907- A motion was made to buy 2 used road machines and one new machine. The used machines were $50.00 each and the new machine was $200.00.

Feb. 1908 - A resolution was passed that teams used on the road scraper shall weigh not less than 2200 lbs. per team and the price for work of each team and man shall be 55¢ per hour, and eight hours for all days worked. Also the price for teams and men with plows and drags shall be the same. Also two men to haul scraper at $1.75 each per day of 8 hours. Also day laborers 15¢ per hour.

May 13, 1908 - a special appropriation of $100.00 was granted for completion of east Main Street to the four corners. A newspaper item at the time suggests that a road sprinkler would be a great addition to our busy Main Street. The dust accumulates so fast and is so disagreeable.

The Waterwagon – June 1915   Main Street was ankle deep with dust that whirled behind each vehicle. Deep ruts froze during winter.

March 22, 1912 - Resolution adopted that compensation of Supt. of Highways shall be $3.00 per day for all highway works performed during his term of office by him with no further compensation for expenses.

About 1912 the first hard road in the Town of Hartwick was the River Road (Route 28).

1920 - Highway Supt. to purchase Tarvia from Barret Co., for finishing highway through Hartwick village from depot to bridge by Ainslie's mill. $1,650.00 or as much as necessary from general fund for the same.

June 13, 1921- The elements have destroyed many sluices and extraordinary highway repairs are necessary.

It was voted to purchase of E. H. Risley his gravel bank. The bank was on one acre of land east of Dean Macks. (This would be south of Old Hartwick Cemetery behind Dean Shepards house). The bank to be paid for at the rate of 20¢ per load until the amount of gravel equals the amount of purchase price $150.00. At that time Risley to give town a good and sufficient deed and easement of right of way to and from gravel bank. (Henry Murdock states that the bank turned out to be too stony to be usable.)

In 1921, macadam was extended to the western end of the village, and by the end of 1922 the hard road reached Jones Crossing. By the end of 1923, the road from Hartwick to South Hartwick was all macadam road.

Feb 9, 1924 - Motion carried that Highway Dept. buy a York Power and Stone Rake of York Machine Corp. for $1085.00. Also purchased a one ton Ford truck equipped with steel dump box and hard rubber tires on rear wheels

Feb. 9, 1924 - Town Highways Superintendents pay to be raised to $5.00 per day for labor.

Feb. 17,1928 - All the forces of equipment of town is required in the coming months in the construction of Hartwick Index Road.

Also the North Street Bridge in the village, and other bridges in the town are in greater need of repair than other years.

July 21, 1928 - Motion to buy a 75-horse power Linn Tractor to be delivered at once.

The Hartwick Index Rd. was in use as early as 1788. The original road followed a bit different path then the current road. It went past the Chase Cemetery and what was known as the Kinney farm coming out on the far end to again join the Hartwick Index road or what is now known as Co. Rte. 11.

The modernizing of this road was completed in 1928. Wm. Bryant, who was a workman on the project, told how crushed stone was obtained for the roadbed. As you leave Hartwick the steep bank on the right, looming almost straight up from the road, is largely composed of shale rock. The rocks were dynamited, and chutes were built to convey the pulverized stone down the steep incline to wagons waiting below.

The expense of improving this road was borne mainly by the County as part of the County Aid System of Highways. Also in cooperation with the Southern New York two railroad crossings were eliminated. Known as "Twin Crossings" it was a very dangerous section of road located between the home of Lynn and Pam Persons and the cape below the Ferdinand Thering farm. The trolley line crossed the highway twice within that short distance and these crossings were eliminated by laying out a new route.

In 1929 the Town Board decided that a building should be constructed to house town highway equipment. A storage building on the Gulf Road had been in use for some years, but was inadequate. A decision was made to buy a piece of land and, erect a building. Several building sites in and near the village were considered, and the final site was on Poplar

Bridges in the Town of Hartwick.

North Street Bridge

North Street Bridge

Stone Arch Bridge at Chase

West Main Street Bridge

Avenue on land owned by Hosea Jones. The requisites were for a plot 150' x 150', and price not to exceed $400.00.

Old Town Barn

Jesse Card, Highway Supt. was in charge of constructing a 36' by 40' building.

Poplar Ave. Aerial View

Poplar Avenue probably came into being, when the Trolley Office building was built about 1902. A news item in the 'Hartwick Voice' mentions the need of more housing and even suggests that Hartwick build an apartment building to house trolley line employees and their families. This idea never happened, but three new houses were built, and three houses were moved to the street. The first house on the right, owned by Ray Polulech, was built on the spot, as were the third and fifth. The second house was moved from Wells

Avenue. The fourth house originally stood where the American Legion Hall stands.

Third house from left site of present Legion Hall, moved to Poplar Ave.

House moved from Wells Ave. to Poplar Ave.

The last house on the street now houses the office of Phillips Lumber Company. This building was also moved there, and is said to be a composite of a couple of buildings, one section said to be part of an old fire station, or something of like style.

Phillips Lumber Company now occupies the site of the trolley office building. Giles and Robert Phillips started Phillips Lumber Co. in 1947. It is still a family owned business, and is presently operated by Bruce and Jim Phillips.

Nov. 1929 - Proposed to buy a snow plow and snow sled for the tractor. These accessories were purchased at a cost of $277.50.

April 4, 1930 - A petition signed by 112 people, 70 who were tax payers requesting a stop and go light on the four corners.

New State Road

June 1930 - A committee was appointed to purchase, install, and maintain a stop and go light.

Also the purchase of a Rome Grader with straight wheels and a Climax Grader for $1000.00 was authorized.

1931 - A contract was made with NYS Electric & Gas to furnish lights for Hartwick streets.

Nov. 1930 - A motion to discontinue paying for water troughs on Hartwick streets. (Autos were outnumbering horses.)

Dec. 1930 - The Town Barn was ready for wiring and lighting.

Also an agreement to keep street lamps lighted each and every night from ½ hour after sundown to ½ hour before sunrise.

May 1931- Construction began on the dirt road heading south from Hartwick village. The road that was to become State Rte. 205 was a narrow muddy dirt road. The Keller Corp. from Massachusetts did the work, and completed seven miles of new state road by November 1931.

Aug. 1932 - Gasoline pump and tank were installed at the new town barn for use of highway equipment only. Superintendent to be sole custodian.

Aug. 1932 - State Dept. of Public Works would not give authorization to operate a stop and go light at the four corners, but would permit a yellow blinker light.

Construction on Route 205 going north out of Hartwick village began in 1932 and was completed in 1933. The work was done by Rite Way Construction Co. of St. Johnsville, NY. Work on this portion of road proved to be difficult. The North Street Bridge was a challenge for the modern construction workers as it had been for the early road builders in the 1830's. The vein of Hartwick polish running along the creek in that area made building a firm foundation a problem. Again and again their work washed away, but the bridge and new state road were finally completed in December 1933.

Petition to remove yellow blinker light, and have the state install legal stop signs on each side of Route 205 at the four corners. The light was removed and stored in the town barn.

June 7, 1934 - Special meeting of Town Board called for purpose of discussing the possibility of purchasing a Linn Tractor and Snow plow, as old tractor has several parts either broken or badly worn, and therefore would cost a large sum of money for repairs. A resolution to purchase of Linn Corp. of Morris, NY one factory rebuilt Linn Tractor equipped with 75 H. P. Wankesha Engine, dump body and hoist, electric lights and starter, high speed reverse and pneumatic tires. Also Linn Frink Snowplow at a total price of $6275.00.

April 1937 the following item appeared in the 'Oneonta Star.' Work has started on the Hartwick-Milford county road, four miles of which will be built this year. The road will follow the route of the old dirt road, which joins route 205 south of the village.

When the new road replaces that built by the pioneers, several arched bridges, broken by heavy, modern traffic, and the remains of an old corduroy road, will disappear."

In the 1940's during the World War II years, no roads were improved or macadamized, and even repair work was kept to a minimum.

April 7, 1943 - The Town Board reported that there were insufficient funds for highway improvement. Repair only roads most in need of repair. This same entry was to appear again in the Board minutes for 1944-1945-1946.

Also very little in equipment purchases were noted. A Universal Tractor Shovel with ¾ yard dip and 75' of ½" cable was purchased in 1943.

In April 1944 the highway employees received the following rate of pay. Motor equipment operator, truck driver, and mechanic received 60¢ an hour, and a laborer 50¢ an hour.

Oct. 1955 - A newspaper article gave the following summary of Hartwick Town Highway Dept. The department takes care of 65 miles of dirt road, 35 to 40 miles of hard top, which includes plowing and sanding of county roads. During the summer the department built .9 miles of Erwin roadway on the Wiley Town Road, making a total of three miles finished in the last three years. The Erwin road is 16' wide with a 12" base and 5' shoulders. Many of Hartwick's dirt roads became improved roads with the Erwin Plan. Will Gardner was Hwy. Supt. in the 1950's and he said that the Greenough Rd. south from Toddsville, and portions of Scotch and Christian Hills were slated for improvement under the Erwin Plan. He also said they had completed repair work on two of the largest bridges in the town, both in Toddsville. The work on the Oaks Creek Bridge was shared with the Town of Otsego.

In the early 1960's the western end of Mott Road now Piermott Lane was reconstructed, Harold Beach was the Highway Superintendent at that time.

The section of road between St. Rte. 205 and the bridge on Mott Road had high banks

Harold Beach, road supervisor

that funneled deep snow in the roadway sometimes making it necessary for travelers of that route to take to the fields. John Mott donated a gravel bank to fill the roadbed bringing it up to level. At the same time the bridge was reinforced, and the creek bed straightened.

John Mott took a series of photographs of this project, and more of these interesting pictures can be seen in an album at Kinney Library.

June 1962 - Resolved to raise School Street with macadam topping and lay sluice way and piping to take off water in the spring of the year.

Nov. 1969 - The central New York area was hit by a heavy snowstorm that spread damage over a fifty-mile area. Communities were dark and silent as power lines were down. Area counties suffered from cold and lack of water.

Working On The Roads In The Town Of Hartwick

Henry Murdock and Harold Beach starting creek bed on Mott Rd.

Raking road surface

Linn tractor at snow time

Cutting a sharp corner on Mott Road

Henry Murdock grading culvert under supervision of road commissioner Beach and Stanley Griffith

Early road equipment

People dug themselves out, and nicely got back to normal when a second major storm hit in late December. Roads were closed and highway workers were again pushed to the max. In Hartwick townsmen were pressed into service to man equipment to open snow clogged roads. The Linn tractor was dispatched to the most troublesome areas. With Highway Supt. Stanley Griffith operating the Linn, and several other men with trucks and shovels, they were attempting to open the Mateunas Road on Christian Hill. Going up the hill from the corner of Bush and Petkewec Roads they were building ever-higher snow banks. The fumes from the tractor filled the cab and Stanley Griffith and high school student-football player Mike Phillips were overcome. They were taken to Bassett Hospital and admitted suffering from carbon monoxide poisoning. Beatrice Griffith recalled that her husband was in the hospital for three days, and released on New Years Day 1970. As his term of office was up he never returned to the job.

Soon after the storms of 1969, the Town Board received the following report by Acting Highway Supt. Floyd Bresee. "Three to four feet of snow fell just after Christmas causing considerable "tie-up" and hardship. Continual drifting and small amounts of additional snowfall added to the difficult process of opening the roads, plus breakdown of machinery. With no thaws, snow stayed until spring. Bresee gave an oral inventory of snow removal equipment owned by town, and present condition of same. The age of equipment ranges from 9 to 30 years, and is much in need of extensive repairs."

Feb. 23, 1970 - The Town Board voted to buy 1 rebuilt 1955 Oshkosh Snowplow Truck with power steering, dump body with heavy duty hoist, and 440 Frink plow and wing for $12,500.00. 1 used 1954 Chevrolet 4 wheel drive dump truck with snowplow for $4500.00.

Early Sunday morning on Nov. 14, 1976, The Hartwick Town Barn was destroyed by fire. The blaze, started by an overheated furnace, destroyed the barn, six of the ten vehicles in the town fleet, causing an estimated $135,000 in damages. Vehicles lost in the blaze were two four-wheel drive snowplows, three dump trucks with sanders, a bulldozer, plus hand tools parts and supplies.

The alarm was activated at 5:25 AM by Joe Fields whose propane gas business was located directly behind the town barn.

Highway Superintendent Thamer Harper and crew used trucks that were parked outside to tow other vehicles away from the flames.

The fire was fought by Fire Chief John Bush and the Hartwick crew of firemen, assisted by the Mount Vision Fire Dept., who brought a pumper and tanker. Hartwick Fire Co. No. 2 responded with thirteen men, a pumper, and a tanker. Laurens and Garrettsville were on standby. Due to the response of all these men and equipment, and due to the lack of a high wind the fire was contained to the town barn and equipment.

According to Supervisor Bill Powers, Hartwick faced the coming winter with one 4 wheel drive snowplow, a ten wheel dump truck, a front end loader, a backhoe, a grader and two small dump trucks. Almost immediately Hartwick's old creamery building was pressed into temporary service. As it turned out the temporary status was to continue for several years.

Plans for a new town barn began to be formulated. Land for a new building site was acquired from Agway. The newly acquired land had been the site of the carbarns of the long defunct Southern New York.

Two proposals for a new town barn and office were presented to the voters at an informational meeting in Sept. 1979. The

Hartwick Business Association stated that while not opposed to building a new structure, the Association was opposed to the cost figures offered by the town board for the construction costs. At the November election both propositions were soundly defeated.

In May 1980 the Town Board again met to consider costs and proposals. In a surprise move the board decided to enter into a contract with Ferdinand Thering of Mount Vision for the erection of two steel buildings at a total cost of $64,492.60. Dimensions of the buildings to be 40' by 112' and 40' by 96'. Construction work went rapidly.

New Town Barn

Completion of the new facility was signaled by a free barn dance held for the community on Oct. 11, 1980.

In the early 1990's the employees of the Highway Dept. were unionized.

New office building

A new Town Office Building was completed in May 1995. The masonry building has of-fices for the Town Supervisor, Town Clerk, Town Assessor, Planning Board and Town Justices as well as an arraignment room and a conference room. The $275,000.00 project was over five years in the making. "The wait was worth it" declared the then Town Supervisor, Carol Donahue.

An Open House was held at the new Town Hall on Saturday June 24, 1995.

In September 1997 the community was stunned when a freak accident took the life of 36 year old Randy Hopkins, when a tire on a front-end loader exploded. A husband and father of three children, he was struck in the chest by a blast of air, and died of massive internal bleeding.

Many men have been involved in keeping Hartwick roads open over the past century and a half. The men of the 1800's whose highway labor was assessed without compensation, and the Superintendents and their crews who have seen great improvement in roads, equipment and their maintenance. Highway workers are called upon to respond at any hour of day or night, depending on weather or the unexpected. The Highway Superintendent spends long hours watching the weather, determining when to call out the road crews.

At least two of Hartwick's Road Superintendents died while in office. Harold Beach in 1965, and Steve Raimo in 1987. Ed Rood, a highway employee for 13 years, filled in Steve's remaining term of office. Ed has since been returned to office by voters in several elections and has been endorsed by Democrats and Republicans for the election year of 2001.

By: Nadine Phillips

Bibliography:
The Freeman's Journal; The Daily Star; Transportation—By Roy Butterfield; Hartwick Town Clerks Records ; The Hartwick Reporter; History of Hartwick—By Pearl Weeks

Physicians, Dentists and Veterinarians

The practice of medicine is as old as mankind, primitive though it may have been. Sound medical practice is a constantly evolving thing. Two hundred years from now our modern medical miracles will probably be viewed as pioneer steps.

The following article tells a bit about the men who practiced medicine in this area since the early days of Hartwick.

When Otsego County was young few of its physicians attended medical school. Rather, unless they were European trained immigrants, most of our early doctors served an apprenticeship with a qualified practitioner, observing and assisting him, compounding his medicines, and reading in his library. At the successful end of such service he would receive a certificate of proficiency. From that point his ability largely depended on putting into practice what he had learned, and keeping abreast of medical advances through reading, attending lectures, and his own observations.

Dr. Nathaniel Gott was one of our earliest local physicians, coming to the area in 1792 and to Hartwick about 1797. He was to practice here for nearly 30 years. It is noted that his wife died in Hartwick in 1797.

Dr. Gott was descended from one of that Puritan band that landed at Salem in 1628. He was born in Wenham, Ma., served in his hometown militia, and responded to the Lexington call. He was an eccentric man, and wore the colonial costume of knee britches, three cornered hat, and buckled shoes to the end of his life.

Dr. Gott appeared to have had a classical education, was versed in Latin, and had had some medical preparation. He was skilled in preparing his own remedies, and was a Charter member of The Otsego County Medical Society. A learned man, his library was presented to the University of Michigan upon his death.

Hurd's History of Otsego County" lists the following physicians as members of the Otsego County Medical Society.

1806	Nathaniel Gott	Otsego
1818	Walter Almy	Hartwick(Toddsville)
1819	Paris Pray	Hartwick
1830	Welcome Pray	Hartwick
1831	F.G. Thrall	Hartwick
1836	E. G. Almy	Hartwick(Toddsville)
1840	Jesse Patterson	Hartwick
1841	L. B. Skinner	
1859	P. S. Smith	Hartwick
1863	H.A. Almy	Hartwick
1868	S. L. Robinson	Hartwick

Notice in the "Freeman's Journal"
June 23, 1832.

"Hartwick Board of Health

In pursuance of the provisions of an Act for the preservation of the Public Health passed June 22, 1832, the Supervisor, Overseer of the Poor, and the Justice of the Peace of the Town of Hartwick, Resolve that it is expedient to organize a Board of Health in and for the Town of Hartwick Resolved that Isaac Burch be the Pres., and David Kendal, Secry. of said Board. Resolved, that Dr. F. G. Thrall be, and is hereby appointed Health Officer."

The following regulations were adopted by the Board to be observed by each and every inhabitant of the town.

REGULATIONS

1st-Each and every inhabitant of the town hereby strictly required forthwith to remove any nuisance, if impossible and impracticable to remove, to correct it by lime, or the chloride of lime, to remove any nuisance arising from stagnant waters, wheel pits, artificial ponds, cellars, drains, stables, pig-styes and privies, or from any cause whatever.

2nd-Every person is hereby forbidden to throw or suffer to remain any dead animal or offal of any description whatever above ground on their premises.

3rd-Every physician practicing within this town is hereby requested to make from time to time, immediate report to the Board of Health, of every case within his knowledge, of the existence of any malignant or contagious disease within said town.

Isaac Burch
David Kendal
Lemuel Todd
William Tinkum
Henry Baker
Asa Pride
William Fry
Hartwick - July 16, 1832

In some cases we have little information about the physicians who practiced in Hartwick in the distant past. Long before we were born these doctors walked our village streets, made house calls traveling the area in horse and buggy. They were important figures in the community, and their abilities lauded. Now many of their names have been lost to time.

Many old timers have been heard to say, "I wouldn't be here today if it wasn't for old Doc "So and So." Yet often all we know of these learned men is what can be found in the pages of dusty old scrapbooks.

Dr. Freeborn G. Thrall, son of Roger Thrall, was a physician during the years of growth and prosperity in Hartwick. In 1831 his name appears on a deed for the purchase of property in Toddsville. He married Maria S. Almy, daughter of Toddsville doctor, Walter Almy, and it is assumed that Thrall apprenticed to him.

By 1831 he was considered a physician, as he became a member of the Otsego County Medical Society. The Otsego County Medical Society, like other medical societies, was organized to counteract the unscientific practices of eighteenth century physicians. When Freeborn Thrall announced his intention to practice medicine in an advertisement in the Freeman's Journal, he was endorsed by Paris Pray and Theodore Fuller, both members of the Otsego County Medical Soc.

By 1833 Thrall had moved to Hartwick, and bought the medical practice from Dr. Paris Pray. Buying both the large stone house on Hartwick's four corners, and Dr. Pray's practice indicated that Thrall was enjoying some measure of success during this period. As has been mentioned Dr. Thrall had been appointed Health Officer for the Hartwick Board of Health. Thrall's duties were to remove potential health hazards. Malaria and dysentery were two common endemic diseases during this time and their primary cause was lack of proper sanitation facilities.

Between 1839 and 1842 Thrall built a new brick Greek Revival building across the driveway from the stone house.

This house was built in 1833 by Dr. Freeborn Thrall. A brick building next to the house was the doctor's office. Leonard Proctor bought the house, and that family lived there many years. Proctor and a Mr. Avery had a race track where Hartwick Cemetery is now. The doctor's office was moved to the Village Crossroads at the Farmers' Museum.

In the "Otsego Republican" on October 17, 1842 Thrall printed the following notice.

"F. G. Thrall having lately fitted up an anatomical theater lighted by a skylight will give a gratuitous course of lectures on all aspects appertaining to the science of medicine with practical and ocular demonstrations on anatomy commencing the second day of January and will continue sixteen weeks and longer if necessary for the benefit of his and all other medical students who may see fit to attend. Lectures will also be delivered by John R. Davis, A. B. during the course

on natural philosophy and chemistry and the important principles of these sciences will be illustrated by means of the requisite apparatus. Good board can be obtained at the village for $1.50 per week.

Thrall's notice places him in the mainstream of the 19th century medical practice. Public anatomy lectures like the ones given by Thrall were a part of a serious effort to educate the public as to the need for improved medicine. Autopsies and dissections were the primary method of better understanding disease. The anatomical lectures mentioned certainly included dissection.

An interesting aside - there were those who lived in the neighborhood of the Robinson Cemetery south of the village who told of strange activities taking place in the cemetery in the wee small hours of the morning. Lanterns were seen, and the sounds of digging and shovels were heard. This story may have been told to scare small children, but many old timers told it seriously. Disturbing graves to obtain cadavers was not unheard of.

Dr. Thrall sold his house and office in 1845. In 1858 his name appeared on a land transaction in Cleveland, Ohio.

The red brick surgery building was moved to the Farmers Museum in 1951 where it is the Apothecary Shop in the village.

Many, many years later the following prescription was found in the walls of the stone house.

1/2 oz tincture Lobelia
1/2 oz Blood Root
2 oz Syrups Balsom Tarlar
1 oz glicerine
1/2 oz Peppermint Esc

Anson Cook of Hartwick kept an accurate account book for many years, detailing all family expenses. The following are items drawn from his account book that tell us of several doctors that paid house calls for his family.

Dr. Walton Almy
1851 July 2-
        By 1 visit to Bleed Paulina   1.00
1852 Aug.22-
        By 1 visit to Bleed Paulina   1.00
1853 Feb.14-
        By 1 visit to Bleed Paulina   1.00—
        May 27-
Visit to see Paulina and baby 3.00

Anson Cook's records covered a period from 1851 to 1875, in which he details doctors visits for his growing family.

He mentions visits not only from Dr. Walton Almy, but also Dr. Edmund Almy and Dr. Henry Almy, Dr. Leaning and Dr. Smith. All house calls were a dollar.

Dr. Peter S. Smith was born in Delaware Co. on Christmas Day 1812. At the age of 24 he attended lectures in Fairfield College in Herkimer Co. He furthered his education at Woodstock, Vt. where he received his diploma in 1838.

After practicing medicine in Delaware Co. he came to Hartwick in 1848 where he practiced for over 30 years. He had his home and practice in the large house on West Main that we currently remember as The Patterson Funeral Home. Dr. Smith worked closely with Dr. Mary Imogene Bassett. He eventually moved his practice to Cooperstown, where he was affiliated with Dr. Bassett.

Dr. Smith was called "The Philanthropist of Otsego." Highly thought of in Hartwick, a grand festival was held in honor of his 70th birthday on Christmas 1882.

Dr. George Harter was born in Warren, Herkimer County, July 3, 1853, and was educated at Whitestone Seminary. He then apprenticed to his brother-in-law Dr. Getman of Richfield Springs. Later he attended New York Homeopathic College graduating in 1877. He then came to Hartwick village where he practiced his profession for eight years. He then moved to Oneonta where he had a very successful practice visiting his patients until the last few days of his life. He was buried in Richfield Springs.

Dr. S. Robinson was a native of Hartwick and was listed as a member of the Medical Society in 1868. Active in town affairs he served on the Board of supervisors for two years. We have little information about the doctor, but the following interesting news item shows that he still lived in Hartwick in 1880.

"Dr. S. L. Robinson of this town, a few evenings since, administered chloroform to himself and successfully extracted three teeth. He said it was laboring under difficulties to hold light, administer the chloroform and extract teeth from the lower maxillary; one a large eye tooth; and that it requires some practice and close atten-

Dr. and Mrs. Peter S. Smith

tion to business, as there are some nice points in the operation. Having been an invalid for a year, his nerve is gone, and the sight of a dentist with instruments in hand, causes an indescribable sensation he cannot endure. He says that a quarter of a century ago, his old friend, Dr. Byram of Cooperstown, usually operated for him— approaching without words or noise, his countenance lighted up with a genial smile and that peculiar twinkle of his eye, with a soul and heart in him as big as a two bushel basket, would soon remove the offender."

Dr. Robinson moved to his son's home Mt. Vision in 1882 and died there in 1883.

Along with medical treatment by legitimate doctors, people often treated themselves with Patent Medicines.

Traveling medicine shows had long been a part of the American scene, but soon after the Civil War medicine shows descended on every town and village selling their wares. Not doctors, but glib salesmen, they billed themselves as doctors and sold their concoctions to the ailing public. More than willing to provide a cure for any condition of man or beast, these so-called doctors had a cure for every ailment. Their medicines were never actually patented, but salesmen extolled the virtues of their cures. The medicines were usually decoctions, infusions and tinctures made from material gathered from forest, field and stream. No one was regulating these so-called cure alls.

The following are just a few of the concoctions sold as sure cures for what ails you.
Dr. W. H. Gregs Constitution Water
Ebenezer Pearl's Tincture of Life
Roche's Embrocation For The Hooping Cough
Clark Stanley's Snake Oil
Healy & Bigelows Kickapoo Indian Oil
Mrs. Winslows Soothing Syrup (for the little sufferer)

D. S. Barnes Mexican Mustang Liniment
Dr. Kilmers Swamp Root for Kidney and Liver
Lydia Pinkhams Vegetable Compound
Pratts Distemper and Pink Eye Cure
Shiloh's Consumption Cure
Hoods Sarsaparilla
Dr. Pierces Golden Medical Discovery

Dr. Ceylon Ismond was a Homeopathic Physician listed in Hartwick in the 1872-73 Otsego County Directory.

In 1883 a news item proclaimed that Dr. R.A. Walker of Albany, a recent student of Dr. A. Vandermeer of that city and by whom he is highly recommended, has opened an office in the Sergent Block. Dr. Walker is a graduate of Albany Medical College.

This news clipping was found in a scrapbook. "Dr. R.A. Walker extracted a portion of a broken needle from Mrs. Tanners hand, which has caused her great trouble for more than a year, and she not being able to ascertain the difficulty, as she has no remembrance of a needle ever having been broken off in her hand."

Dr. Walker practiced here in the 1880's.

Dr. Daniel Luce advertised in the "Otego Valley News" in Feb. 1899. A member of one of Hartwick's early families, Dr. Luce practiced in the village at the turn of the century.

A new Board of Health was organized in 1903. It was announced that Dr. Luce was to head the Board, and every citizen a member.

Dr. Luce later moved to New York City and had an office and residence at 1723 Madison Avenue.

"Dr." Ira Sweet made newspaper headlines in the Brookfield-Waterville area about 1902. Referred to as the "Bone Setter" he had a natural ability to set broken bones and reduce fractures. His reputation was widespread, and he performed many operations effecting cures where regular practitioners had failed. He did not charge a fixed fee, but accepted whatever a patient saw fit to give him. People came from afar to be treated by "Dr." Sweet.

Not only did the "Bone Setter" have this healing gift, but other members of his family had the ability, particularly his daughter, Matie. At the age of 16, Miss Sweet was successfully treating patients. She had been an ardent student of anatomy since early childhood.

The Otsego County Medical Society brought action against "Dr." Sweet charging him with practicing medicine without a state license. A Grand Jury heard the case, and refused to indict him. Whether he practiced bonesetting after that is uncertain. However his daughter went on to get a medical degree, and practiced in the Hartwick area in the 1920's and early 30's. The Sweet farm was located in Pleasant Valley where the Auriama family lives. This may have been a summer residence, and she may have had a larger practice elsewhere. Some of us recall that older members of our family had great faith in the "Bone Setter" and were treated by "Dr." Ira Sweet, or by his daughter Dr. Sweet.

Dr. John McClellan graduated from Albany Business College. He then graduated from Albany College of Pharmacy, and Albany Medical College in the Class of 1888. He came to Hartwick in 1889 and was a druggist and physician in the village for 11 years. He married Maude Field in 1894.

He was to treat many Hartwick citizens while here, and his name appears in many news items. One interesting item of 1898 tells "Miss Maud Manzer who is engaged in the dining room of Hotel Gardner, met with quite a serious accident one day last week. Mr. Bedford, proprietor of the hotel, was endeavoring to cleanse the sink pipes, and for that purpose lime was introduced into the pipe which was found afterward to be obstructed. Miss Manzer was standing at the sink when an explosion occurred, and a discharge from the pipe struck her full in the face

and eyes. Dr. McClellan fortunately was nearby and came to her relief. She was badly scalded by the hot lime, but it is thought she will not lose her sight. It was a close call.

Another 1898 news clipping – "Dr. McClellan has sold out his practice to a Dr. Schoolcraft, a young physician formerly of Esperance, N. Y. Dr. McClellan, we learn intends to remove to Oneonta in the near future.

C. L. Harrington advertised as a druggist. He sold several products of his own making. Among them were medicines that would fall under the category of Patent Medicines.

From an old scrapbook the following news item was found.

"Mr. C. L. Harrington of this place, refused an offer a few days since of $3000.00 for the exclusive right to manufacture and sell his Golden Cough Syrup, Inhaling Balm, and Mandrake Bitters."

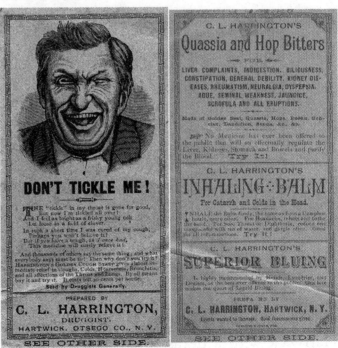

1909 Dr. W.D. Buell had an office in the village. It is believed that he was a chiropodist.

1912 Hartwick had a new physician, Dr. Hafford Pattengill. He was practicing from the Lonsdale place on Main Street. This was the house across from the Methodist Church and had been used previously as a physician's office.

Dr. Wesley Adams graduated from Albany Medical College in 1913. In 1914 he moved to Hartwick where he opened an office in the Lonsdale home on Main Street.

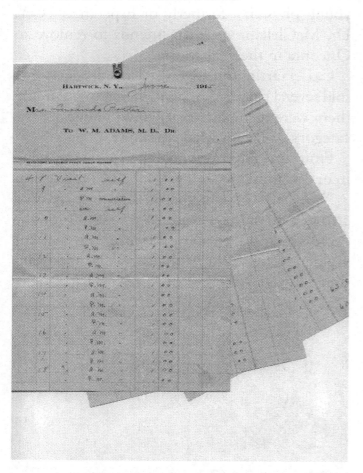

In 1917 he left Hartwick and moved to Schenevus to open a practice. In less than a year he succumbed to the flu in the deadly epidemic of 1917-1918 at the age of 31.

Dr. Charles Taffle opened an office in what is presently Caroline Dickies' home.

The influenza epidemic swept through Hartwick with a devastating effect. The flu quickly turned into pneumonia and took a terrible toll. Among the victims was Town of Hartwick Supervisor Roy Adams, three employees of the Southern New York, Chauncey Beach age 26, Grover Perkins age 28, and Earl Ellsworth age 36. In another case three members of one family including a six year old child were victims, also in other homes two young mothers with families. At one time Hartwick lost 6 citizens in 11 days.

John Mott tells that he was 4 years old in 1917. His parents both had the flu and Dr. Taffle immediately put them to bed. Within minutes they were too weak to lift a hand. Dr. Taffle stayed for several days and cared for them day and night. John said as a little child he helped in small ways such as providing a drink of water, until he finally became ill and was put to bed.

Dr. Taffle was one of the few men in those days that drove a car through all of the seasons. There were no means of clearing snow from the roads; so most people put their cars up on jacks until summer. The Model T Ford such as Doc owned was powered by a magneto system and had to be cranked by hand. Sometimes if you forgot and left the spark lever down the motor would reverse and made a bad kickback. Many arms were fractured in this way. In cold weather the heavy oil that was used would set-up so it was hard to break the pistons loose in the cylinders of the motor. When the cold had set the motor, the Doctor would jack one wheel and revolve the motor by turning the wheel.

After Dr. Taffle, Dr. Barney Phillips also located his practice in the same house on East Main. A Hartwick native, he was the son of Charlie and Fannie Phillips of Scotch Hill. Barney Phillips graduated from Hartwick High School, Class of 1911. He then graduated from Cooperstown High School. He went on to attend Albany Medical College. After graduating from there he went to New York Homeopathic Medical College. He came back to Hartwick and set up practice. After several years here, he moved to Milford in 1927. He was a highly thought of physician in the area, and was still active in his profession when he died suddenly in 1942.

Dr. George Schoolcraft was born in Gallupville NY in 1868. He graduated from Albany Medi-

cal School and before coming to Hartwick, he was a surgeon and physician at St. Peters Hospital in Albany. He bought the practice of Dr. McClellan and came to Hartwick in 1897.

He was to be Hartwick's doctor for over 45 years. In 1921 he bought a house on the four corners of Hartwick which was his home and office for the rest of his life. After Dr. Schoolcraft's death, Walter Block bought the house and tore it down.

Being Hartwick's doctor for so many years, the town's older residents remember him well, and he ushered many of us into the world.

He was rather eccentric. He never married, saying of this state, "of those I would have, they wouldn't have me, and of those who would have me the devil wouldn't take."

As all doctors did in the old days, Doc made house calls. In his later years he grew corpulent, he always wore a gold watch and chain across his chest. He had the habit of humming to himself as part of his bedside manner. He has often been heard to say "Ho Ho Ho Hum—Another day another dollar."

If he dispensed medicine he would frequently taste a pill to be sure it was the right medication.

News item 1912-"Sunday afternoon when Dr. George Schoolcraft was returning from Lena, he met a motorcycle on Hemlock Hill road. His horse became frightened and ran up on the bank and two wheels of the carriage were smashed. The doctor was thrown out, and the horse con-

tinued down the hill, and ran into the barn of Silas Van Auken. Dr. Schoolcraft was not seriously hurt, although severely bruised- neither was the horse harmed."

Dr. Schoolcraft was active in the community. He was a 32nd degree Mason. He was president of Hartwick Bank, president of Hartwick Library Board, served two terms as County Coroner, was Health Officer for many years, and was a Democrat Committeeman.

After two days illness he died of a stroke in 1944.

Dr. Angelo Franco came to Hartwick about 1937. He started his practice on the Brooklyn side of town just across the bridge on the left as you leave the village. In 1940 he bought the beautiful home of John Parr on West Main Street. He designed a fine office, and equipped a modern laboratory. He made the change to the center of the village as he thought it would be more convenient for his patients.

Dr. Franco was a member of the graduating Class of 1935 of the Long Island College of Medicine, following which he spent 2 years in the Bayonne Hospital and Dispensary. The doctor practiced 2 years in Brooklyn before coming to this village.

He was just nicely settling in his new office when he joined the Army Air Force and became Captain Angelo Franco.

He returned to his practice for awhile after World War Two. It is uncertain how long he practiced here after the war, but a news item tells that he sold his Main Street home in 1949.

Dr. Steffi Baker was born in Furth in the Bavarian part of Germany. She studied medicine for three semesters in Munich from 1932-33 and was graduated in 1938, after 5 years of medical study, done in Italian, at the University Of San Marco in Florence, Italy. She later worked in Italian hospitals before leaving for Bolivia, South America in January of 1938.

After working for about a year in a private clinic, learning and speaking Spanish, Dr. Baker accepted a position as a physician employed by the Bolivian government, working to combat tropical and infectious diseases. She worked in this capacity until 1945, traveling by mule and under the most primitive conditions throughout the mountains and jungles of that country.

Dr. Baker and her mother left Bolivia for New York City, arriving on Dec. 23, 1945, joining her brother Hans, who had been there since 1938. She then interned at Bronx Hospital for a year and went to Flushing Hospital for ten months.

She received her license to practice medicine and surgery by the University of the State of New York.

She noticed an ad "Doctors Office For Rent" in the New York State Medical Journal. She found the office to be that of the late Dr. Wahl in Mt. Vision. She bought the office equipment from Mrs. Wahl, and arranged for office space and living quarters in what is now the American Legion Building on Hartwick's Main Street. Dr. Baker had her office there for a couple of years before moving to her permanent office on South Street where she has treated thousands of patients and delivered hundreds of babies.

In 1968 the Hartwick community honored Dr. Baker at a reception held in the American Legion Hall. She was presented with a plaque of appreciation for her twenty years of being doctor and friend to the community. More than 250 people attended this occasion.

She was to continue her work as physician to the community for another ten years. In 1978 she began to look towards retirement. She scaled back her office hours and no longer accepted new patients. The community again honored her. On Sunday October 29, 1978 at the Hartwick No. 1 Fire Hall the Hartwick Business Association sponsored a reception to mark her 30th year of community service. Almost 400 people came to pay her tribute.

She now had more time to enjoy her friends and to follow her favorite pastimes such as photography, riding her bicycle, picking mushrooms, traveling and skiing. She said skiing was her favorite sport, but she had to curtail it due to an accident in 1968.

She married Francis Pullis, businessman and commercial artist on Nov. 24, 1982. Fran was a man of many accomplishments. He was a sportsman, a competition and trick shooter, and avid outdoorsman. Steffi enjoyed her retirement years with Fran, and they pursued their mutual hobbies together.

Dr. Steffi Baker Pullis passed away Feb. 2, 1999. Francis Pullis passed away April 15, 1999.

Dr. Steffi Baker was very generous to her adopted hometown. In her will she made many thoughtful bequests to the community. Among them is the meeting room at the Fire Hall. "The Dr. Steffi Baker Room" is a fine memorial to our small town country doctor.

Dentists

The following ad appeared in 'The Freeman's Journal' on November 19, 1832——Physic and Surgery

"Dr. J. M. Peak would respectfully inform the public that he has taken his residence in the village of South Hartwick, a few rods north of J. Holden's store, where he will be happy to attend to all calls in his profession as Physician, Surgeon and Surgeon Dentist. Those afflicted with diseases of the teeth, inflammation and scurvy of the gums, will find important relief from his immediate means."

It appears that Doctor Peak had a partnership at some point after the above ad, with a Dr. Otis Avery as the following ad appeared in 'The Freeman's Journal' April 12, 1838. "Dr. Peak would inform his friends and the public that the practice of Dental Surgery in all its varieties will still be continued by him at his office at West Hartwick. He manufactures the improved incorruptible porcelain teeth, which for their natural appearance, beauty, and durability are not surpassed by any. Natural teeth will be cleaned and filled with gold in a perfect and serviceable manner, artificial teeth inserted from one to an entire set. Ladies, gentlemen and families attended at their residence if requested by letter or otherwise."

Dr. Avery recommended his former partner and friend Dr. J. M. Peak 'whose integrity and professional skill they may rest assured will be sufficient warrant that all operations entrusted to his care will be performed in a judicious and satisfactory manner. West Hartwick April 12, 1838.

Otis Avery

'Freeman's Journal' Sept. 17, 1838 Notice—
—The Co-Partnership heretofore existing between the subscribers in the practice of Dental Surgery is by mutual consent dissolved.

J. M. Peak
Otis Avery

No other information concerning Dr. Peak and Dr. Avery was forthcoming.

In 1879 F. T. Newell, Dentist placed the following ad.

"Would respectfully announce that he has opened an office in Hartwick for the practice of Dentistry and is prepared to do all kinds of work, at as reasonable rate as any responsible Dentist in the county.

'Crowning and Building Up' the natural teeth with gold, when badly broken, a specialty. Teeth extracted, without pain, by the use of Nitrous Oxide Gas. Office in the Bottsford Building upstairs."

Hartwick—Nov. 3, 1879

Dr. Melvin Jenks was a dentist in Hartwick in the 1870's. He had an office on North Street north of the red brick building that was moved to the museum. Dr. M. E. Jenks learned the dental art from Dr. Siver at Cooperstown. He was a well-liked young professional man in the community. A pneumonia epidemic swept through the village in 1879 and claimed the young doctor. Dr. Jenks died in May 1879 when he was barely 30 years old.

His older brother Dr. James Jenks bought the North Street office from the young widow, and was to practice dentistry from that location for many years.

Dr. James Jenks had two children, Alta, who married Ziba Holbrook, who was at one time Sheriff of Otsego Co. and Ray who was a farmer in South Hartwick.

The Jenks brothers were natives of Otsego County having been born in Burlington. Dr. James Jenks died in 1925, and is buried in Hartwick Village Cemetery. Some of his descendants still reside in Otsego County.

About 1912 Blaine and Benjamin Talbut sons of Mr. & Mrs. Dorrance Talbut of New Lisbon, graduated from Ohio Dental College. The following news item found in a scrapbook tells "Messrs. Blaine and Benjamin Talbut have received their office furniture and equipment, and are busily engaged in fitting up the suite that was vacated by Kinne, Bush Bank for their dental office.

The Talbut Brothers later moved to Ohio to practice their profession there. They retained their ties to the area by owning and visiting the family home in New Lisbon for many years.

Dr. Herman Backus graduated from the University of Buffalo School of Dentistery in 1905. He practiced in Buffalo for 12 years, six of those years on the staff at the School of Dentistry. He opened a dental office in Hartwick in 1917, after eight years of practice here he moved his office to Cooperstown in 1925. He continued to treat some patients of long standing at his Hartwick home.

Dr. Backus retired in 1964 after 39 years of practice. He was a member of many lodges and was a 32nd Degree Mason.

His hobby was horse racing, and over the years he owned several racers and trotters. He purchased his first horse in 1940, and that horse "Inspector" won 9 races during the fall season at Roosevelt Raceway. Dr. Backus, along with his brother Stanley Backus, and George Tingley of Afton, were to own several horses together.

His most successful horse was "Johnsie Lybrook" which he raced for 7 years until it broke a leg at Saratoga Raceway, and had to be destroyed. Dr. Backus retired from racing after the loss of "Johnsie Lybrook."

Veterinarians

Information regarding early veterinarians is scarce. There must have been many of them, but their names do not often appear in the news, nor did they do much advertising of their skills.

In the 1872-73 Otsego County Directory, Dr. Oliver Bishop was listed as Veterinary Surgeon. His father before him had been a veterinary, and it is assumed that Oliver Jr. received much of his training from him. He lived north of the village in the White House, which he owned until his death of tuberculosis. Dr. Bishops name has been notable in the memories of many long gone oldsters.

A serious epidemic of horse distemper swept across the U. S. in 1872-73, and many horses sickened and died. Dr. Oliver Bishop is said to have worked day and night visiting farms. He would often stay up all night trying to save a horse. The epidemic struck down a lot of horses in this area.

The following news items were found in an old scrapbook. —"On Sunday, Sept. 1 J.H. Barney found one of his horses in the pasture with it's leg broken close to the knee joint. Dr. Bishop is making an effort to save the animal as it is a valuable one."

Nearly a month later, on Sept. 27, 1878 we read – "J.H. Barney's horse which broke its leg a few weeks ago is doing well. Hopes are entertained that it will recover from the injury."

Another early veterinarian was Dr. Delos Matteson. Unfortunately we know little of his practice, but because of health problems we know that he practiced in the area for many years. In 1882 the following appeared in "Items from Hartwick," "Dr. Delos Matteson, Veterinary Surgeon has suffered so severely from typhoid fever this past autumn, that he plans to remain in Laurens until spring, when he hopes to be strong enough to continue practice."

In another item dated 1891 again from an old scrapbook "Dr. Delos Matteson came near being killed as he was driving one horse on a lumber wagon. One side of the thills became detached from the axle which caused the horse to spring forward throwing Dr. Matteson out on his head and shoulder seriously injuring him. They think he will recover."

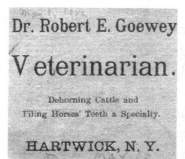

Dr. Robert E. Goewey

Veterinarian.

Dehorning Cattle and Filing Horses' Teeth a Specialty.

HARTWICK, N.Y.

Dr. Robert Gowey had a practice in Hartwick in the early 1900's. A news item tells that he had a very busy and successful practice in his veterinary work for the farmers of the area. Prompt attention to suffering horses and cattle and fair prices have won him good patronage.

Bill Powers remembers a man who lived on Sweet Hill. He was called by neighborhood farmers to treat their sick animals. He didn't take any money but you needed to leave money by the wash basin where he washed up (otherwise he didn't come the next time you called). He got the money, as he was good although he wasn't a veterinarian.

Present day Hartwick is fortunate to have Dr. Francis Fassett practicing in the area. He operates the Heritage Veterinarian Clinic, a modern well-equipped clinic where he treats small animals, as well as traveling around the countryside treating his larger four-footed patients.

By: Nadine Phillips

Bibliography
Dr. Roy Butterfield
Otsego County Biographical Review
Country Store – Dave Rickard
Oneonta Herald Democrat
Corrinne Pollack – Oneonta Star
Hurds History of Otsego County
Hilda Augur – Ads from local newspapers
One for a Man, Two for a Horse — Carson

Home of Oliver Bishop, Veterinarian

Lawyers

Not much is recorded about early lawyers in Hartwick. The town must have been law abiding! Of course, many cases were tried by the Justice of the Peace!

In 1860 we find Marcus Wells practicing law in the building next to the American Legion. He may have built this, as he was a carpenter before studying law with Attorney Scofield here in Hartwick. I found no mention of Attorney Scofield, but he must have been here a few years before 1860. F. Wilcox, Lawyer, 1868, was in the same building as M. Wells.

We find E. Woolsey Lockwood, age 33, Attorney, joined the IOOF in 1982 He & Wm. Davis were listed in the 1872-1873 Gazeteer as attorneys.

Chester Winslow, Jr.

In 1880, it was noted "A teacher turned to the law. The higher department of our school closed Friday. Mr. Cook will now turn his attention to the legal profession."

A M.C. Brady was a lawyer in Hartwick according to the following quote: "Clarence Cook, esq. has rented the Law office lately occupied by M.C.Brady, the latter having moved to Colorado."

The Hartwick Reporter advertised the law office of W.O. Hintermister 1915-1919. He had his office on the second floor of the corner block (Winslow's later). This was mentioned when there was a fire in the building (in the bakery). Mr. Hintermister moved to Cooperstown in the 20's.

In 1922 it appears E Woolsey Lockwood would have been in his early 80's but he is listed in the "Oneonta Daily Star Directory" under Attorney. We can assume he was a lawyer in Hartwick from 1872 to 1922. We have legal documents signed- E. Woolsey Lockwood, Justice of the Peace.

A clipping tells us about a sign that was put in front of the new Fire Dept. building, formerly the James Byard, Jr. Law office, so Mr. Byard, Jr. practiced in Hartwick for a short time anyway. This site was the location of the former Winston Jewelry Store, now torn down.

Chester Winslow came to Hartwick in 1945. His office was on the first floor of the corner building that we still speak of as the Winslow Building. Mr. Winslow practiced here until his death.

By: F. H.
1. Pearl Weeks History of Hartwick pg. 66
2. Clipping Wed. Aug. 28, 1935 Dedication of Home of Marcus Dells
3. Old Potter Scrapbook pg. 18
4. Old Potter Scrapbook pg. 19
5. Obituary

Rte. 205 accident - 1940

Accident involving Dr. Schoolcraft - 1937

Elections

1818 – Otsego Herald – May 11
p 2 – c 1 – Hartwick cast 249 votes in the state election and was about fourth in size, after Otsego, Burlington, and Butternuts.
p 3 – c- 1 – Justices of Peace in Hartwick were Rufus Steere, Asahel Whipple, Eliphalet Dewey, and Henry Baker.

1869 – Oneonta Herald – November 17
Benjamin Cutler of Hartwick was the oldest voter in Otsego County. He was 100 years old on November 9. It was his 78th vote.

1876- Potter Scrapbook
p 2B - The Hayes and Wheeler Club of this place are making preparations to raise a fine pole, from which to float a flag bearing the names of our candidates; notice of time will be given hereafter.

1877 - Potter Scrapbook
p 1- Dr. P.S. Smith has received the nomination for supervisor on the temperance ticket in this town. We hope that all temperance men will support the Doctor, for he is just the right stamp for that position. He'll have no thieves to recommend for any position of profit or trust- a man that people can trust to represent their interests

1877- Potter Scrapbook
p 17-On Christmas day Mr. Samuel Pashly had a family gathering at his house. Of those present who were voters, only one was a Democrat, and he only related by marriage. Uncle Sam, as he is called, is a Christian in every sense of the word, and how could he be anything but a Republican.

Potter Scrapbook
p 18 - The Democratic boys raised a pole here last week Thursday and hung out the names of Hancock and English, and in the evening two of their number made political speeches, followed by Wm. Davis. This is the first introduction of political action in this place, and now that the ball has been set in motion, we expect to see on Friday P.M., of this week, the young Republicans move to the front with a flag-staff bearing the names of Garfield and Arthur.
p 8 -1883- Dr. S. L. Robinson- The citizens of Hartwick, his native town, selected him to represent them in the Board of Supervisors for two terms which he filled with honor to himself and to his constituents.

1878 -Potter Scrapbook
p 32- The election of last Tuesday passed off very quietly in this district. The polls were held open at the hotel of Harrington and Norton. The spirit of rowdyism, usual upon such occasions, was nowhere manifest during the balloting, and right here we would say, "we are proud of the fact, for we believe it was through the de-

termination and pluck of the Murphy boys, that this was accomplished. Success to the boys in blue."

p 41-1879 - Politics seem to be the leading topic of the present time. M. C. Brady and W. H. Bunn held forth at Harrington & Norton's hall, last Saturday night, in what was styled a Robinson club organization. With the friendly aid of Republican drumming, the crowd was called together about eight o'clock, and after listening to the speeches, a club was organized, with W. J. Kellogg, president.

1882 - Potter Scrapbook

p 37- The 'Freemans Journal' had important news from Hartwick last week, the Election of the License Excise Commissioner in said town. In the first place be it known that the town of Hartwick is entirely in the hands of Democratic officials, is run entirely in the interests of free whisky, license being granted by the Excise board, but no record of them or the money received is kept in the town clerks office as the law directs, neither have any such moneys been audited by the town board and no one can ascertain anything in regard to it. The condition of things having become so intolerable, it seemed necessary to the good citizens of this town to make an effort for the election of a no-license Excise Commissioner. In order to attain this important object, a large force of ladies attend at the polls with the worthy motive of assisting in the good work by furnishing a good dinner at the church close by, and trying to persuade voters to give their ballots to no license; this act of the ladies raised the ire of the town board (entirely Democratic) which after consultation manfully concluded that tobacco smoke and indecent language would dislodge the ladies. To effect this the crowd were freely supplied with cigars. The windows were ordered closed (the day being warm) by the gallant board, the two dispensers of justice from Hartwick, (one of them the candidate in future for Assemblymen, and at present the vender of much rot gut,) filled their jaws with tobacco, to the full extent, in order to cover the stove with spittle, while others of the unterrified filled with bad whisky, began to use vulgar and indecent language to-

Registry – Kathryn Lyding, Bernice Fuller Carr, Mrs. Dunnigan, Mrs. Paul Jones, Anita Harrison - in old firehouse

ward the ladies - he of dollar and half hops and turkey fame being foremost. The board furnished information in regard to the friends of license, and teams were quickly dispatched for license voters when the opposition seemed to be gaining ground - certainly a fine precedent for a town board to put on record. To finish our narrative, the license candidate was elected and whisky and indecency ruled the day, while the large pile of license ballots lying on the ballot box table might have been used, ala southern bourbon, without the tissue part. Whiskey triumphed, and Hartwick was saved to whiskey.

Yours, & c., TEMPERANCE DEMOCRAT

1884- Potter Scrapbook

p 38- The Prohibition Co. Convention which convened here last week, made the following nominations to complete the County ticket; Hezekiah Lenardsson for Judge; Edwin B. VanFradinburg for Dist. Att'y; Dr. Peter S. Smith for Coroner.

1895 - Potter Scrapbook

p 26 –Among the different highway wards of this town, the one under the supervision of A. S. Hollister, leading from this village up Phillip's Hill to the east, is the banner road for best condition.

1903 - Potter Scrapbook

p 30 –The Town Com. has called a meeting of the Republicans of this town to meet at the Otego Valley Hotel (Post Office) in this village, Friday, June 19th, at one o'clock p.m., for the purpose of selecting three delegates to attend the county convention to be held in Cooperstown June 26th, 1903, and transact any other business that may come before the primary.

By: Barb Potter

Primary Enrollment

TOWN OF HARTWICK

County of Otsego
State of New York
1953

TOTAL ENROLLMENT OTSEGO CO.

Republican	18,374
Democratic	7,064
Liberal	45
American Labor	21
Total	25,504

ELECTION DISTRICTS

24 Towns	48 Districts
Oneonta City	6 Districts
Total	54 Districts

Entertainment & Amusements

Entering a new century, everyone is busy, working, exercising, trying to keep up with their children's activities, and hoping to find time for entertainment.

When we think back to the people who settled our town, we find them clearing the land, making clothes, shoes, and everything they needed but they found time to enjoy life. What energy they must have had!

When a settler was ready to build a barn, neighbors came from miles for the barn raising. After this hard work, often the men would wrestle until all had participated and there was a winner. The boys also wrestled.[1]

Women had quilting bees with the men coming at night for dinner and sometimes staying for dancing afterwards.

Husking bees were also held. Finding a red ear guaranteed a kiss! Bees were held through the 1930's. After this time farmers raised corn mainly for ensilage. Stuart Ainslie remembers going to a bee at Holdridge's and Don and Stanley Phillips one at Kallans. Dorothy Weeks' father, Charles Manley, had husking bees at his place.

In 1878 a different kind of entertainment was in the village of Hartwick: "Mr. Hurd has just completed a mammoth balloon. An ascension will be displayed, together with other amusements, some time during Oct."[2]

"The balloon ascension spoken of two weeks since, came off last Friday evening in front of the F. H. Robinson store. The inflating and starting off worked very finely but as the balloon rose to the height of about 75 ft. a strong current of air caused it to take fire, which soon put an end to what would have been a fine display, as it was a variety of colors. What a disappointment to all who had gathered there."[2]

Hartwick turned to other kinds of amusements. In 1878, a baseball team was organized as the Red Stockings.[3] Numerous baseball games are mentioned in local papers.

In 1908: "There was an interesting ball game between the office (conductors) and motormen on Monday afternoon at the Hartwick baseball field on South Street. Notwithstanding the rain, the game was played to the finish. The office men winning with a score of 13 to 14. Baseball was played down through the years. In 1930 there was a game almost every Sunday afternoon, either here south of town or at a neighboring town.[4]

The first basketball team (1914) consisted of

Hartwick Basketball Team - 1914: George Porter, Carl Thomas, Chancy Beach, Ben Talbut, Blaine Talbut, H. L. Harrington, Lynn Sill

George Porter, Carl Thomas, Chancy Beach, Ben Talbut, Blaine Talbut, H. L. Harrington, and Lynn Sill. The town seemed to fall in love with basketball! In 1914 it was played in Kimball Hall.[5]

The games were played upstairs in the Otego Valley Hotel (Post Office now) until the E.M.B.A. Hall became available. The sides were lined each night with enthusiastic spectators.

Hartwick had early horse racing with a race-track near the cemetery. Many came to see who had the best horse.

> *Freeman's Journal, October 12, 1871:*
>
> ## Notice
>
> Don't fail to attend the trot at Hartwick, October 18th, as Billy Mix, Sarah, Nellie Brown, Buckskin, Ostrander's black mare, and Hamlet will contend for the prize of $100, and a close and capital race may be expected, as the horses are very closely matched. It is a condition that if all the horses start, the purse will be increased twenty-five percent.

Later in 1897 there was a convention of horsemen held in Hartwick with street races.

By the track was a fairground. Henry Murdock's father told him it was on the east side of the cemetery, the boundary about from Harold Bush's grave, running north and south on the line of maples, out to the hatchery.

My uncle, Sidney Potter remembered an Indian Show coming to the fairground. They sold patent medicines. Perhaps these were the same ones who came back. "W'm Wasterfield, who was here about a year ago with the Kick-a-Poo Indians, was holding forth at Brownell's Hotel last week, selling medicine under the name of Dr. Red Sky." [4]

Churches were an important part of the social life in early Hartwick. Here people got together for picnics, dinners, socials, as well as worship!

1877 – "A group of colored singers held a concert in the Methodist Church in this place on Sat. & Mon. evenings last, under the management of Rev. Mr. Rodgers, pastor of the African M. E. Church of Norwich, NY. The proceeds to be applied to the debt on Mr. Rodgers church. Their singing is of a superior character." [7]

1899 – "Captain P. B. Roys will give a lecture on his experiences at sea while in the whale fisheries and will give illustrations of the different kinds of whales, seals, sea otters, etc. by means of large crayon pictures at the Christian Church Fri. Evening." [8]

1914 – Also in the Baptist Church: "The Patterson's Jubilee & Concert Co. of Buffalo, NY is giving their popular entertainment Tues. evening. They are recommended as being the most versified and unique co. of character songs, plantations, and readings. Tickets on sale at 25¢ & 15¢." [4]

It appears dances have always been held in Hartwick. Often these dances were held at the Otego Valley Hotel. The hotel was often called by the name of whoever was running it at the time: Kimball, Harrington, Harrington, & Norton, are a few of the names.

The hotel on the west side of Hartwick also had a ballroom on the top floor. This was later called the Brooklyn House. The earliest dance I found was held there.

In 1878 – "Independence Party"

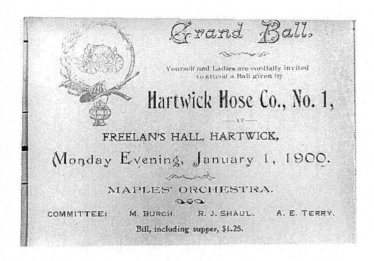

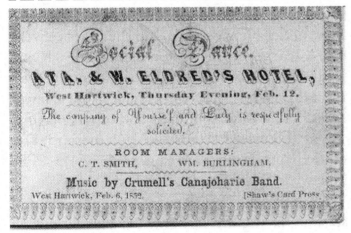

There will be an Independence Party at the hotel of Harrington & Norton, Hartwick, NY, Wed. evening, July 3rd, 1878. Music by the Laurens Full Band. The public is invited. Bill $2.00"[20]

The Cottage Hotel was across from the Otego Valley Hotel. It was three stories. In an inter-view in 1994 with Ford Risley, he told us his parents, William and Ethel Risley, went to dances upstairs there "as did almost everyone else." They were held almost every Saturday night. The square dance or a similar dance called a Lancier (listed as a waltz on an early dance program) was a favorite.

The firemen and other organizations had an-nual dances. Many neighborhood dances were held in homes, even up through the 1930's and 40's. These were square dances.

In 1939 dances were also held in "Burch's Hall" in back of Burch's store (this building fell down in 1991).

Dramas of all kinds were put on or sponsored by the many organizations.

1876 – "The popular drama entitled 'Ten Nights in a Bar Room,' interspersed with a beau-tiful tableaux, illuminated with colored fire, will be played in Harrington & Norton hall by the Temperance Dramatic Association of Cooperstown."[21]

Hartwick had a couple of dramatic groups organized in the early 1900's.

1902 – "The Hartwick Dramatic Asso-ciation having had many earnest requests to re-peat the entertainment they gave Mar. 5th & 6th at Freemans Hall, have decided to comply & will on Thurs. evening repeat the play 'Tony the Convict.' There will be excellent music on the occasion."[22]

I don't know what happened to this Dra-matic Association but another one was formed in 1914.

"A recently organized 'Mansfield Dra-matic Society' will present 'Uncle Rube' – se-quel to 'Down East.'

Uncle Rube' was given last Thurs. & Fri. in Kimball's Hall by the Mansfield Dramatic Society. It was a decided success. New chairs had been purchased for the comfort of the specta-tors while the curtains and the stage settings were designed and painted by Mrs. Clark Beach. The curtains especially, a scene taken from the bridge on North Street, it showing the country side lying north, was an excellent reproduction of artistic skill. The Hall was filled both nights but Saturday's was called off on account of the streets & roads being impassable with snow. Music by our Orchestra consisting of Mr. & Mrs. W'm. Risley, E. R. Card was also worthy of commendation. The cast included: J. A. Andrus, C. T. Beach, L. Brezie, Walter Andrus, Mrs. W'm. Stillwell, & Mrs. J. A. Andrus. [4]

Plays were given later in the E. M. B. A. Hall (Community). While the High School was here, school plays were enjoyed. Even 4H clubs joined in giving this kind of entertainment.

Band concerts were another activity the people of Hartwick could enjoy.

Several different bands played at different time periods. I found mentions of early bands but no information about who played in them.

1875 - "Ice Cream Raspberry Festival for the benefit of the Hartwick Cornet Band, will be given at Harrington & Norton, Aug. 18,1875. Supper served at 8:30 PM   Roast Pig Etc.

R. R. Luce & P. G. Williams managers" [4]

"The citizens of Hartwick and vicinity will hold a festival at this place on Fri. evening, May 17th, for the benefit of the Hartwick Cornet Band. The boys have had a hard struggle to get started and have some expense for instruments and music. The boys do their best to entertain you." [6] There is mention in the clipping of a Decoration Day parade that was led by the Hartwick Cornet Band.

These bands and orchestras, I'm sure provided very good entertainment for the people of Hartwick, as did the ones that followed.

Stuart Ainslie remembers playing in a band that practiced over the Post office when it was in the corner building (Winslow's). Apparently Dr.

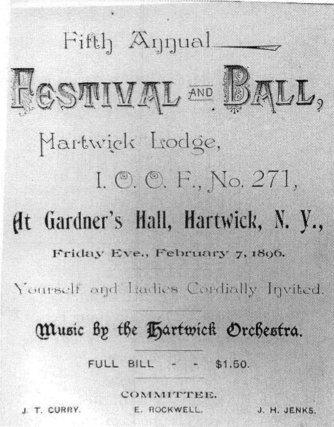

Schoolcraft didn't appreciate their music. He lived right across the street (the house is torn down now). The Doctor hired some boys to throw firecrackers in the open window. One went right under Henry's chair, but the practice went on! A teacher from Walton came to teach and lead them. Mr. Ainslie remembers Henry Hoose, Donald Holdridge, Stanley Jensen, Henry Murdock, as well as himself and others playing.

The following are Ford Risley's memories recorded in Gladys Harrison's notebook: "The Hartwick Town Band as I remember it."

After World War I we started the band. I started playing the cornet when I was about 12 years old. We rehearsed in the old trolley railroad car barns because they were warm and out of bad weather. We played at parades such as Memorial Day, picnics at Arnold and Gilberts Lake, also concerts at the Hartwick Post Office, Ferrara Gas Station, etc., also at church socials and ice cream socials. They usually took up collections so we could buy new music. Most of the members had their own instruments; the band owned only a few. We usually wore white shirts and had band caps to wear. We played up to World War II and a few years after and then disbanded.

Here is a list of the old band members I can remember:

Silas Robinson-Leader	Fred Brown
Bert Robinson	David Ward
Seymour Robinson	Ed Risley
Oscar Angela	Will Risley
Worthy Clark	Ford Risley
Harry Clark	Harley Cummings
Barb Clark	Elmer Talbot
Harold Clark	Vaughn Hollister
Howard Murdock	Henry Murdock
Linn Augur	Harold Salisbury
J. Paul Jones	Mary Jones Hoose
2 Harrison boys	

In later years:

Lewis Sheldon	Russel Aunger
Ken Eaton	Clarence Knapp
Ernest Ward	

The Hartwick Band was a lot of fun and we all enjoyed it."

Glenn Harrison remembers more of those who played in the Hartwick band under the leadership of Silas Robinson.

Puff Brown - Drums
Henry Murdock - Alto
George Ainslie - Trombone
Howard Murdock - Alto
Archie Ainslie – Trumpet
Ford Risley - Trumpet
Glenn Harrison - Tombone
Oscar Angell - Trumpet
Ford Harrison – Cornet
Charles Stevenson - Flute

The band practiced in the E.M.B.A. Hall once a week. "We played outdoors in the summer. Concerts were held in front of the Otego Valley

E.M.B.A. Hall

Hotel (P.O.), across the bridge by the gas station (Brooklyn side), at Glen Tilley's store in Mt. Vision and the school in Laurens. A large crowd would turn out. After practicing Silas, the director, would leave Hartwick in the dark, with his wife in a horse drawn buggy with a kerosene lantern tied in the back, down 205 headed for Pleasant Valley where he lived."

Another place they played was on the bank's steps. The cars would line up and down the street to hear them play. Then some one would pass the hat.[11]

About the last time the band led by Silas Robinson played was at the Rod and Gun Picnic held at Alex Forster's.[11]

Bill Powers had a Square Dance Band. It consisted of Charles Millard, pianist, Tony Feola, caller, and Bill on the fiddle. They played at Grange Halls and twice a month at the Middlefield schoolhouse for a couple of years. They also played at Meyers store in South Hartwick. This group got $2.00 a piece for playing one night![11]

There was another group with Fred Gill on the drums, Ralph Leach, and others. They played at the Morris Fair at least once.[12]

Over the years Hartwick made music! The last band I heard of was a group of high school musicians and others that Rev. Holmes got together to practice and play. They may have led one of the Hartwick Day's parades. They didn't play together long.

One of the exciting groups that came to Hartwick was the Chautuaqua Shows. Eleven different kinds of entertainment made up their show. These were held back of Woleben's (Varney's 2001) afternoons and evenings. Howard Marlette, John Mott, and many others remember "the rattling good shows."

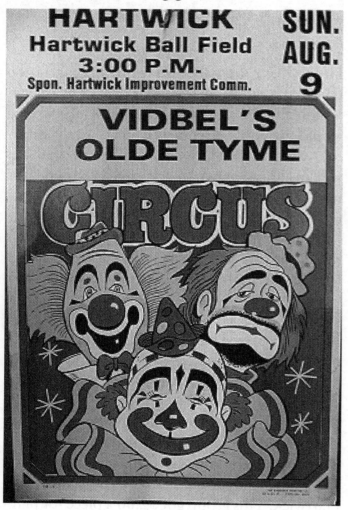

We can't leave the circuses out for they also came to Hartwick. In about 1897 a clipping we read:

"The 'Sautrelle Circus Company' gave the people a very good show; the best entertainment of the kind this town has had in a long time. They have a fine band, and their horses, the bareback rider and slack-wire performer are hard to beat." The circus was usually held up by the hatchery. [13]

Many socials were held during these years. There were box socials, Ice Cream Socials, Carpet Rag Socials, and there is a clipping of 'News paper Social."

"Class of 1914 of Hartwick Union School will hold a Box Social Fri. night at the home of Charles Wright. Everyone invited & teams will be at the Christian Church to carry any who wish to go." [4]

Each girl would make her best lunch; men bid on the box, then eat the lunch with the one who prepared it. Some boxes brought many bids!

The Ice Cream Socials were very popular (those held at the Methodist Church during recent 'Hartwick Days' have been also). In earlier days the ice cream was made in a large 5 gal. freezer. First the custard was cooked with fresh eggs, milk, plenty of cream, sugar, and flavoring or some times canned fruit. Then when cooled, it was put in a canister that had a removable dasher, which turned around inside when the handle outside was turned. The canister was packed around the outside with chopped up ice. A little salt was added to start the melting of the ice that in turn started the freezing of the custard. Then it was the men's turn to take over the turning of the freezer. It had to be turned and turned and turned. Then came the reward. The dasher was removed and all the kids took spoons to eat the ice cream that stuck on the dasher! The canister was repacked with ice and left to be dished up at the social.

Maple syrup and sugar have always been produced in Hartwick. After the end of the season (maybe before if people couldn't wait) syrup was boiled down, neighbors invited in, containers packed with snow were brought in, and the boiled down maple syrup drizzled on the snow and there you are -Jack Wax - eaten off the snow with a fork, delicious. Sometimes pickles were served with the jack wax.

The class of 1915 held yet another kind of social: "The class of 1915 of the Union School will hold a Carpet Rag Social at the home of the president, Thomas Kirkpatrick, on East Hill. All wishing to go please meet at Rainey's Store to go at 6:30. Girls bring a ball of carpet rags with their name wound in the center. These are to be sold to the highest bidder by Walter Andrus, auctioneer." [4]

Radios came along in the 1920's. What excitement! Voices coming through the air from far away! Pittsburgh's KDKA came in best in our area. Neighbors gathered at the home of the lucky owner, who had the first radio here.

Freeman's Journal – Feb. 20,1924

"Hartwick – radio is first, last, and all the time, in our little village at the present time. Some get so interested they almost forget to go to bed. Later kids hurried home to hear "Jack Armstrong, The All American Boy" and families huddled around the radio listening to 'Amos and Andy!' It's a problem to figure out what will come next." [4]

About twenty years later, pictures were added to the voice and here was television. Now there are not only one in every home, but many in bedrooms and kitchens too.

In the 1940's some public-spirited sponsors of Hartwick and the community (may have been the Businessmen's Association) brought a series of the Collin's Entertainment festival to Hartwick. Irene Matteson remembers they had different kinds of programs, dramas, and musicals. Carleton Roberts was the M.C.

In the October 29,1941, Hartwick reporter: "The program for Nov. 5th was the Ritz Trumpeteers, comprised of 4 men and instrumental ensemble and after telling of their education and experiences, concluded. This program has been called a 'Fanfare of Instrumentals' and is a soul-stirring, foot-tapping adventure with

captivating rhythm and sweet melodies as 'The Band Played On.'" [14]

Hartwick had movies. One item told of a moving picture being shown in Kimball Hall. Then in a 1917 clipping: "First moving picture attraction was given in the village theater Saturday night 'Around the World in 80 Days.'"

1929 Advertisement:
'A Little Girl in a Big City'
Special added attraction
Charlie Chaplin in 'A Pawn Shop'
No advance in Price
Doors open 7:15   Starts 8:15
Adults 25¢   Little Children 15¢

Smalley's, owner of the Cooperstown Theater, gave movies in the E.M.B.A. Hall. There were stairs, as you came through the front doors, to the projection room that was built out above the doors. [15]

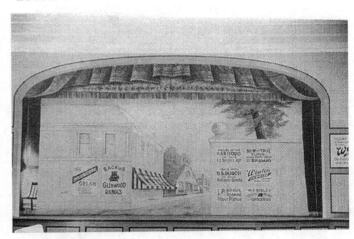

E.M.B.A. Stage

The movies were silent and were shown once a week. Twice in 1923 they were canceled as once the film did not arrive and the other time the machine broke. The admission cost was 25¢ for adults and 10¢ children. When 'Robin Hood' was shown it was raised to 50¢ for adults and

22¢ for children, but the film cost $34.72 and most films seemed to be $2.00 to $8.00. Other expenditures were: rent - $10.00, Ticket seller - 75¢, Operator and Orchestra - $1.50 each. There was also a War Tax of $2.59.

Later the music that accompanied the film was a piano and Thelma Perkins Lally was one of the pianists.

A few other films shown in 1923 were 'Prince and Pauper', 'Dawn of the East', and a series of 'Buffalo Bill' films."

There has also been Dance Classes in town. In 1890 there is this invitation:

Finale

Yourself and Ladies are Cordially Invited to Attend the Final Reception to be given by

Prof. C. W. Mathewson's Dancing Class,

At BROWNELL'S HALL, HARTWICK, N. Y.,

Friday Evening, Feb. 21st, 1890.

MUSIC BY MATHEWSON'S ORCHESTRA.

Dancing Bill 75 Cents.   .   .   Supper to Order.
Grand March at 8 P. M.

There was one given in 1889 so at least two years there was a dance class.[16]

Dance Recital

A later one was in 1955: "Conte Dance Pupils Presents Hartwick Revue."

Stars on Parade

"Hartwick's Stars on Parade shone brilliantly Friday night when the dance pupils of Mrs. L. R. Conte presented their dance revue in the Hartwick gym to a capacity crowd.

The show opened with the audience singing the Star Spangled Banner and the following program was presented. Arranged to represent a Fifth Avenue toyshop the first number was a doll dance by the little tots. Other numbers in order were: Military Dance by the Junior group; song by

Barbara Gill and Carol Burch

Barbara Gill, assisted by Larry Santos in costume; Cowboy Dance by the Little Tots, short act by the Master of Ceremonies; song by Tonya Slater;

Tonya Slater, Jean and Evelina Fuller

Waltz Clog by the Junior Group; song by Evelina & Jean Fuller; Rhumba Tap, by the teenage Group; Good Ship Lollipop, by the Little Tots; Chinese Dance, by the Junior Group; Recitation by Carol Kohinke; Rhythm Tap, by the Teenage Group; song by Bonnie & Suzanne Jensen; Tap Dance by Carole Burch; guest act by Larry Santos, who played and sang "Unchained Melody" and sang without accompaniment, "Hold My Hand." The Teenage Group then gave the Alice Blue Gown Dance, assisted by Mr. Santos. A Can-Can Dance by the Junior Group, A Gypsy Dance by Carole Burch, and a Hawaiian Dance by the Little Tots concluded the dancing numbers. The final Entertainment's & Amusements number was a guest act, Bathing Beauties On Parade, put on by the boys of the High School, in which Miss Oneonta was represented by James McGrath, Miss Laurens by Herb Schweitzer, Miss Edmeston by William Burgess Jr., Miss Cooperstown by Stephen Raimo, and Miss Hartwick by Robin Dibble. It proved to be a hilarious finale. The entire cast took a bow.

Personnel of the various groups: Little Tots: Tonya Slater, Evalina Fuller, Jean Fuller, Gail Risley, and Marcia Lisiesky. Junior Group: Sondra Ainslie, Mary Lynn Marlette, Cheryl Marlette, Mary Marlette, Carol Kohinke, Bonnie Jenson and Linda Bresee. Teenage Group: Carole Burch, Sylvia Briscoe, Kathy Kohinke and Barbara Gill.

The dances presented were arranged and directed by Mrs. L. R. Conte, costumes by Mr. Conte, Mrs. Henry Fuller served as business manager for the project, Charles Smith was Master of Ceremonies and Miss Norma Gavlin was pianist." [23]

In 1952 Hartwick went all out in celebrating the 150th anniversary of the founding of their town. Many people worked on the planning. The following tells of the highlights.
Oneonta Star   Oct. 13, 1952

"Hartwick's 150th Birthday"

"Colonial day treasures, plentiful in homes of Hartwick Township, came out of seclusion during the past three days to bask in Twentieth Century limelight as the town celebrated its 150th birthday.

The dining room of the Baptist Church became a rich colonial museum, graced by the largest and most interesting grouping of early Americana ever displayed on a temporary basis in this section.

Documents, costumes, Revolutionary smooth bores and flintlocks, hand flute irons, furniture from pioneer cabinet shops, wooden plows with iron points. These and many more drew steady streams of visitors."

The judges at the parade on Saturday were Moses E. Lippitt, Lynn H. Bresee, and G. Reed Sill made awards in two divisions, as follows:

Historical Floats:

First Prize, Hartwick 4H Club-Cradle and Combine

Second Prize, Hartwick Boy Scouts, for their Indian Scene

Third Prize, Hartwick Baptist Church, float showing old melodeon and choir singing Marcus Well's "Holy Spirit Faithful Guide"

Fourth, Hartwick Seminary's Home Bureau, an early household scene.

Costumes of early days:

First, Stanley Fish of Hartwick and family in horse and buggy, dressed up for Sunday Meetings

Second, Arthur Telfer, 98, driving his 1917 Ford (his photo studio was in Hartwick until 1878)

Arthur Telfer "Putt"

Third, Mrs. Grace Augur, 95, dressed in costume of her youth, marching on foot.

In keeping with the spirit of the day, Hartwick football team beat Gilbertsville.

A second bus was required to take visitors to historic points and the sesquicentennial dance was held in the High School.

At the closing event in the Hartwick Seminary Lutheran Church, Roy Butterfield, chairman of the Sesquicentennial Committee and President of Hartwick College, Henry J. A. Arnold spoke. This concluded the 150th Birthday celebration of the Town of Hartwick.

Then we had the 200th anniversary of the forming of our country, 1776-1976. There were sales, display booths, and a Bicentennial parade on July 3rd, 1976. A smorgasbord at the Fire hall followed this. The dedication of Memorial Park (on the old Union School lot), an Ice Cream Social, and a street dance at the school grounds. On Sunday, July 4th sale and display booths opened and the Union Church Service was held on the school grounds, followed by a family picnic. Games, relays and races filled the afternoon. Open House was held all day at the firehouse. The weekend closed at 8 PM with a film "In God We Trust" at the gym. [17]

Everyone had enjoyed the Bicentennial activities, so the Hartwick Historical Society voted to sponsor "Hartwick Home Days" in 1978, and to make it an annual event.

Bruce Phillips won the footrace. Betsy and Doug Sargent won first prize for their portrayal of a farm family in the parade. Even son Chad was in costume in the stroller with a fishing pole, a serious fisherman. Lori Holmes and Heather Drake were also part of the family.

Riders of decorated bicycles were Richard Smith, Samantha Phillips, Patrick McGregor, and Jeremiah Crossman.

Tim and Mara Neski had a pottery demonstration. Andy Wallace played, sang, and showed how guitars and banjos are constructed.

A Costume Ball was held at night. Mr. and Mrs. Bill Powers were judged 'Most Distinguished Couple' with Mr. and Mrs. Al Crossman 2nd.

A community church service was held Sunday morning on the school grounds, followed by a picnic with games and music in the afternoon.

A reception was held at the Library in honor of Mrs. Augusta Hollenbeck, retiring librarian and to welcome Emily Potter, the new librarian.[18]

Mr. Holmes chaired the 1979 'Hartwick Days.' This was the opening of the Historical Society's Museum located on the second floor of the Hartwick Grade Center. This was also the 10th anniversary of the dedication of the fire hall.

Hartwick Tree Committee won first prize for floats, The Cub and Boy Scouts took second, 3rd was won by The American Legion, and 4th by Hartwick Playground.

"Although there were 10 entries in the tractor backing contest, none was held. The weather was just great for haying and that was where all the farmers were – in the hayfields."[18]

In the late 1980's, balloon rides were planned. It was a big disappointment when a strong wind came up and this had to be canceled.

The 1994 'Hartwick Days' started with a covered dish supper in the pavilion behind the American Legion. This year was the 25th anniversary of the Town of Hartwick Historical Society and an open house was held. A craft show was held at the Community Center and a book sale at Kinney Memorial Library. There was also a quilt show, a food stand, and an Ice Cream Social.

Sunday concluded with the craft show continuing, a chicken barbecue, and a lawn tractor pull. [18]

Some years 'Hartwick Days' were not held. The last was in 1999.

Different activities were introduced at times. One in 1991 was a ceremony held at the park on South Street in memory of Steve Raimo, late highway superintendent. On Friday of that same weekend, a spaghetti supper was held at Beaver Valley campground for Dan and Cynthia Powers, dairy farmers who had lost their barn to fire.

This year the community church service was held at the gazebo. Garden tractor pulls and chicken barbecue followed at the town barn. The weekend closed with a picnic at the community center.[18]

Other 'Hartwick Days' activities enjoyed over the years were a gymkhana horse show, which was very popular, pie contests, a hog roast, fishing contests, wagon rides, petting zoo, dog carnival, cloggers, dance contest, even a watermelon contests, and many more.

Horse Gymkhana Participant

Some of the people who have worked very hard with their committees to make 'Hartwick Days' successful are: Reverend Gerald Holmes, Al Crossman and Mrs. Nadine Phillips, Co.-Chairpersons. Also Everett Kane and Orrin Higgins, Co.-Chairmen, Debbie Clegg, Laura Kane, Barb Potter, Laurie Phillips, Michelle Weir, Gwen Dowsey, Joan and Wayne Bush, and Toni Griffith.

Every year Hartwick Days was held a person who had contributed much to our town was designated as "The Citizen of the Year." Some of those honored were: Bill Powers, Orrin Higgins, Nellie Balcom, Gerald Holmes, Bob Phillips, Kay Tarbox (Honorary Citizen of the Year), Emily Potter, John and Jan McGrath, John Hall, Don Phillips, and Laura Kane.

Carol Donahue presents plaque to John and Janet McGrath, Citizens of the Year. Cecil Hoose providing transportation to the honorees.

Back in 1979 and early 1980's there was a Community Center Association that sponsored entertainment at the Community Center.

At the December 16, 1979 program, Corrinne Pollack was Master of Ceremonies. Everyone enjoyed singing Christmas carols and special solos by Richard Pollack, accompanied by Helen Tirrel. A skit 'The Gift of the Magi' was presented by Jan and Jackie Conklin, Claire and Al Crossman and children, Anthony Gage, Dennis Dibble, Kathryne Lyding, Glen Smith, Christy Martindale, Mr. and Mrs. James Coon, The Hartwick Methodist Sunday School, the Hartwick Seminary Sunday School, Reverend Stephen Rosendahl, Mr. and Mrs. Grant Ward, Walter Ashley, Ronald Martindale, Jerry Gage, and two young ladies from Christian Church Youth Group. Refreshments concluded the Christmas program.

In May 1980, the Community Center Association sponsored "Hartwick Harmony Times' featuring the Midstatesman Chorus and quartets. These barbershop quartets were enjoyed by many.[19]

Preparing for a tractor pull

The tractor pulls and barbecues have continued every year. Local organizations have had card parties, dinners, and other community activities.

Now we live in a very exciting time, with games to play on computers and the opportunity to find almost any information we need. Here on the computer we can meet new people and make new friends,

Some need not go out to work. They work at home on their computers.

Our early settlers would not believe the "fast lane" we live in.

We've gained so much but have we lost also?

———

By: Frederica Hornbeck

Bibliography:
1. Butterfield Papers
2. Old Potter scrapbook pg. 3
3. Pearl Weeks "History of Hartwick"
4. Clipping from Elisabeth Curry's Scrapbook owned by Linda Foody
5. Photo in Hartwick Historical Collection
6. Old Potter Scrapbook
7. Old Potter Scrapbook pg. 17
8. Old Potter Scrapbook pg. 23
9. Program Donated to Hartwick Historical Society by Mrs. Denmeade
10 Advertisement in Hartwick Reporter
11. Bill Powers
12. Beatrice Griffith
13. Henry Murdock
14. Hartwick Reporter October 29, 1947
15. Ken Harrington
16. 1923 Smalley Theater Records in NYSSA Library
17. Program for Bicentennial
18. Clippings and Program in Historical Society 'Hartwick Days' Folder
19. Programs
20. Scrapbook
21. Clipping
22. Clipping
23. Clipping

4th of July and Memorial Day

The following news item from the Otsego Herald of July 6, 1811 shows how the 4th of July was celebrated in former years.

"Celebration of Independence at Hartwick."

"An assemblage of twelve hundred republicans at 10:00 o'clock a.m. took place at the house of Philo West, in the town of Hartwick, and a procession formed by Cap. Calvin Comstock, officer of the day, which marched to the meeting house, escorted by Capt. Bowen's companies of militia, in the following order: Officer of the Day, Clergy, Orator, Civil Authority, and Militia Officers.

The Declaration of Independence was read, and a sermon appropriate to the occasion was delivered by Elder Bostwick and Oration by Dr. Comstock. The procession then returned in the same order to Mr. West's, where they sat down to an excellent dinner prepared for the occasion. After dinner they moved to the meeting house, where the young people performed a number of dialogues, etc. to the great satisfaction of all present, after which they returned to their homes. Not a jarring sound was heard during the day, nor was anyone known to be intoxicated."

Independence Day at Hartwick – 1878 - from the Hartwick Historical Letter, June 1980:

"The citizens of Hartwick and vicinity were awakened early on the morning of the fourth by the national salute of thirteen guns, though the writer would not vouch for the exact number as the cannon went off on a "bust" very early.

At 9:30, a procession of worthies marched through the streets, provoking an abundance of laughter from the crowd.

At the appointed time the band led the people to a pleasant grove at the edge of the village and the exercises begun at once. An appropriate prayer was offered by Rev. J.W. Ainsworth. The Declaration of Independence was read by Dr. S. L. Robinson. The orator of the day was Dr. Richard Fry of Cleveland, Ohio. Dr. Fry was born in Hartwick and made it his home for his first twenty-five years. He is now seventy-five. (Dr. Fry had addressed the celebration in 1826.)

From these recollections of the sad changes a half-century had made among his early associates, Mr. Fry passed to a very interesting review of the progress that had been made in arts and sciences. In mentioning the invention of the lucifer match 40 years ago, he gave this reminiscence of his boyhood:

"Then a boy, our fire not having kept overnight, I went across the woods, some half mile, to Asa Irons, to get some. His had not kept. He took down his old firelock, put priming in the pan, holding some to be ignited by the flash, and at the second or third trial, succeeded in getting a flame. I waited till he got some wood on the fire, and started homeward with a burning brand, when a shower of rain came and quenched the fire. I returned, got another, and in due time got it safely home. It was rather late when the warm journey cake came upon the table that morning."

Dr. Fry spoke of other inventions of the past 50 years; the railroad, the telegraph, daguerre, the mower and reaper, the sewing machine and the phonograph. He also told of the progress in the political conditions of the world.

He concluded his speech describing the freedoms we have of free speech, the pulpit and press and a "very impressive apostrophe to our national flag."

Immediately after the address, a grand public dinner was served underneath a tent, just at the edge of the grove."

Rev. A.W. Clark, pastor of the Baptist church presided and proposed a number of toasts which were responded to by Dr. Fry, Rev. F.J. Parry, Mr. I. K. William, Mr. R. H. Potter, Hon. Harvey Keyes, Cpt. Andrew Davidson, Dr. L.H. Hills, and Mr. Wm. Thorp.

"Other entertainment of the day were the foot race, egg race and the greased pig which afforded an abundance of fun. In the evening the concert given for the benefit of the Baptist Church was the chief feature. The only drawback was that so many could not obtain entrance to the hall, it being crowded at an early hour."

After the concert, the balloon ascension made a fitting close for a day which is universally conceded to have been one of the pleasantest Hartwick ever enjoyed. All honor is due the committee and all who assisted. Not withstanding the crowd present during the whole day, no accidents occurred and no signs of those disturbances which sometimes mar such occasions, were visible. May the National Anniversary always be as becomingly celebrated, and as richly enjoyed as the Fourth of July, 1878."

1896 - "The Fourth of July passed very quietly. In the forenoon a game of baseball was played between the Second Nine and the Wileytown boys, the score resulting in favor of the former. In the afternoon, the Schuyler Lake club crossed bats with the Hartwick team. After four innings a storm set in so strongly they were forced to throw up the game. The score 8 – 0 in favor of the home team.

In the evening the Baptist Church held a festival which was interfered with by rain, but was quite a success as they took in $50. Two notable features of the evening were the patriotic address delivered on horseback by E.N. Higbie and a fancy drill by eight young ladies. Quite a display of fireworks took place in the evening in front of W.C. Parr's store." [1]

1902 - One hundred years ago, the celebration started early! "The Centennial."

12 a.m. Steam Whistles, Ringing of Bells.

1 a.m. Grand Conflagration and filibustering operations in all parts of the town, until daybreak.

Sunrise, Centennial Salute of 100 guns

8 to 10 a.m. Reception of guests

10 a.m. Grand Fusilier Parade

Head of column near depot, Order of Parade: Marshall and side Officers of the day, guests, Prominent Citizens, Band, Company G., First Regt., N.G., N.Y., Clark Hose Company of Cooperstown, G.A.R., Mechanic Hook and Ladder Company of Cooperstown, Fraternal Orders, Steamer Company of Oneonta, Business and other floats and Rough Riders

Order of March - Through Main to West side, counter march to Speakers stand,

Northeast corner Main and North Street.

PROGRAMS:

BALL GAMES   Hartwick vs. Morris in the forenoon; Hartwick Maccabees vs. Oneonta Maccabees, in the afternoon

Great Exhibitions

Worlds most daring High Wire Performer

This wonderful performer walks, dances, rides a bicycle, wheels a wheelbarrow and other things on a wire 50 feet above ground.

Cake walk, Main Street

8 p.m.   Band Concert

9p.m. to 12 p.m. Grand illuminations and fireworks

OFFICERS OF THE DAY

President of the day   Dr. Daniel Luce

Secretary Glenn Jackson

Treasurer Dorr Gardner

Chaplin   Rev. A .D. Finch

Orator   Robert L. Luce, esq. New York City

Reader   Rev. H.G. Hardway

Master of Ceremonies Rev. H. E. Martin

Marshall   E.N. Higbie

Remarks - Rev. Wellesley, W. Bowdish, D.D. of Brooklyn, New York Committee on Events

General - E.L. Sergent, E.C. Reynolds, Dr. Daniel Luce, H.E. Martin, Dorr Gardner, B.R. Williams, Glenn Jackson

Entertainment - Rev. A.D. Finch, Rev. H.G. Hardway, Robt. Gardner, E.L. Sergent, Monroe Burch, H.S.Bradley, G.M. Augur

Horse Race - Jacob Bush, Channing Naylor, Norman Purple, Solomon Spraker

Fireworks & Decoration - J.I. Mange, John Parr, H.E. Martin

Parade - C.T. Beach, V.C. Porter, F.B. Sheldon, Bart Elliott, Jacob Bush."

At 12 PM. The Centennial Ceremonies with orations, music, reading of the Declaration of Independence and remarks by descendants were held.

From 2 to 5 automobile, horse and even bicycle races were held on South Street with an entry fee for the horse. Prizes of 1st - $10: 2nd - $5; 3rd - $2. Auto had 1st and 2nd Prizes, Bicycle – 1st - $3; 2nd - $2. Also a 100 yard; 1st - $2; 2nd - $1. On Main Street, from 3 to 4 p.m. were held sack races with 1st - $1.50; 2nd - $.75 and the same for the Wheelbarrow race. There were also prizes for the fat man's race (200 pounds or over), three-legged race and a potato race.

South and Main Street must have been crowded.

Centennial Celebration July 4, 1902, Hartwick, NY

A Tug of War, between Oneonta and Cooperstown was held. LOUIS STANTON TRICK BICYCLIST gave exhibitions, both forenoon and afternoon on Main Street.

What a celebration for Hartwick's 100th year birthday. [2]

1916 - An interesting Fourth of July celebration was held in 1916.

"First event was a trap shoot between Edmeston & Hartwick; Edmeston winning by 5 birds after close competition.

Lewis Rose of Hartwick & Truman Smith of Hartwick Seminary won first & second prize in that order, in the bicycle race.

The horse race brought out three entries, which finished in the following order: Morgan, rider Willis Morgan, Snowdon, rider George Hecox, and Jolly Jack, rider Lewis Rose.

The hundred yard dash for boys won by Clyde Mills, 1st, William Feeney, 2nd.

The relay race was won by a team of Clyde Mills, Truman Barton, Clifford Stoller & Lewis Rose.

Sack races for boys won by Verne Deforest, second William Feeney. (Where were the girls?)

Potato race - Myron Harrington, first, William Decker, second.

At one thirty p.m. the parade started at the trolley station & marched the entire length of Main Street and counter marched to South and then to the Athletic grounds.

It was led by the Burlington Flats Band, followed by a number of vehicles and autos in attractive decorations.

The Hartwick Military Band came next leading the fusiliers. There was a large number in this part of the parade.

Miss Ruth Johnson was awarded first prize for the best decorated vehicle, second prize going to the float entered by the Rod & Gun Club. The fusiliers attracted no end of attention and the first prize went to Paul Robinson and Don Rose, second to B.H. Talbut in a single cylinder Brush runabout.

Miss Lavina Cook appeared leading a goat drawing a two-wheeled cart nicely trimmed with flowers. Roderick Cook occupied the seat in the cart. She was given a special prize. Others deserving mention were the auto of James Feeney, decorated in yellow and white and the single rig of Miss Ora Weeks, trimmed in pink & green.

The baseball game in the afternoon was easy for Edmeston. Costly errors lost the game for Hartwick, while Cushman and Mathewson... gave a good account of themselves. Final score 13 to 2."

Independence Day has been celebrated since the signing of the Declaration of Independence, July 4th, 1776. In contrast, Memorial Day (Decoration Day) was established after the Civil War to honor the fallen soldiers.

In the late 1890's the following appeared in the newspaper:

"Thurs. May 30th proved to be a red letter day for Hartwick. The Decoration services were largely attended. The following was the general order observed. At 12 o'clock dinner was served

on the Baptist church lawn; at one o' clock the G.A.R. men formed in line at the Post rooms and were led by the Hartwick Cornet Band preceded by E.H.Higbie, marshal of the day, to the Baptist church ground where the general line of march was taken up. The Grand Army men were followed by the school, after which the citizens made up the balance of the column, and with appropriate music by the band, marched to the cemetery where the decoration services were led by L.W. Murdock, Post Commander. These duties performed the column marched back to the church, where the Rev. H.H. Fisher made an excellent address to a large and appreciative audience. He was assisted in the service by Rev. Griffing. Although the day was oppressively warm, everybody seemed to take a deep interest in all that transpired."

The Memorial Day committee needed support at times.

1914 clipping; "Our town board is one of the few in the State that doesn't appropriate even a small sum to help dispel the expense of Memorial Day. Were it not for the faculty and children of our High School and the Boy Scouts the decorations would have been a slim affair! Where is your patriotism?" (It's apparent that criticizing the town board isn't just a 2001 occupation.)

May 1929 clipping: "Union Memorial Services were held in the Baptist Church Sunday morning at 10:30. After the service at the church, a line of march was formed and proceeded to the cemetery where appropriate exercises were conducted by Rev. George Youngs of the Methodist Church, who offered prayer and Rev. Trever delivered a short address. The decorating of soldier's graves followed."

1937 clipping: "Memorial Day observances opened with the union service in the Congregational Christian Church last Sunday. The Memorial sermon was delivered by Rev. R.E. Austin, pastor of the M.E. Church."

The Memorial Day exercises on Monday were under the direction of Prin. John B. Weinhauer. The parade which left the school house at 9:30 was made up of school children, Brownies, Girl Scouts, Members of the W.C.T.U., horses ridden by Jay Davis and Buster Jensen; a bicycle brigade consisting of Archie Ainslie, Charles Armstrong, Norman Bowmaker, Douglas Wayman, Ralph Leach, Walter Lyding, Gordon Edgett, Junior Roberts, Arnold Staffin and several cars.

Upon their arrival at the cemetery, the program was opened with the singing of "America" led by Rev. R. C. Updyke. Rev. R. E. Austin gave a prayer. The march "Onward Christian Soldiers" was played by the High School Instrumentalists, led by Miss Eleanor Forristel and Rev. Updyke led the song "America the Beautiful." Rev. L. L. MacLain then delivered the Memorial address. This was followed by a medley of patriotic songs by the High School instrumentalists. After the medley the flag was saluted and school children under the direction of Mr. Revo Ward decorated the graves. Howard Ainslie played "Taps" to end the day.

Spirit of 1776 was re-enacted in the Memorial Day Parade in Hartwick. Left to right, Front: Gary Roberts and Jayson Campbell, drummers; and John Van De Weghe, fifer. Back: Archie Ainslie, color bearer, James Hamilton, musketeer, and far back George W. Monsell, straggler. Dying at the cannon wheel, Hobart Cornell. Memorial Day, 1976.

There does not seem to have been a 4th of July celebration in Hartwick in the late 1900's. The exception was the National Bicentennial and as part of Hartwick Days. It appears Memorial Days have been celebrated with parades, speeches, etc.

May 1949 – Freeman's Journal
"There will be a union Memorial Day service in the Congregational Christian Church."

May 27, 1964 - Freeman's Journal
Memorial day parade will form in Hartwick at 9 AM Saturday at the gas station owned by Floyd Bresee and the line of march will be on Main Street to the G. L. F. store, returning to the Memorial monument on the four corners for the memorial service. Attorney Chester Winslow, Jr. will be the guest speaker and the Cooperstown School band will furnish the music."

Some of the other speakers at the Memorial Observance were: Sam Sratton, Dean Winsor, George Kepner, Jim McGrath, Frank Nowicki, Armed Forces Recruiters from Oneonta, Carole Donahue, Mary Balcom, Anita Harrison, Carol Niedzialkowski, and Dick Thompson.[3]

The American Legion has been responsible for Hartwick having a Memorial Day parade and program at the monument. The Cooperstown Central School Band has furnished music and 'Taps' have been played each year. The Legion provides the Honor Guard. Bob Croft (Redbeard) has been Master of ceremony for several years with a good attendance whether rain or shine.

By: F.H.

Bibliography:

1.   Elizabeth Curry Scrapbook – Clippings
2.   "Centennial Souvenir" printed by Hartwick Review
3.   Interviews with area residents

Crimes

1818 – Otsego herald – December 7
p3, c1 – Absconded from the service of the subscriber, on the 3rd inst., an apprentice girl named Polly Cole about 12 years of age....one cent reward...Eleazer Bliss, Hartwick

1820 – Otsego Herald – June 12
p3, c4 – One cent reward. Ran away from the service of the subscriber, on the 28th inst., an Indented Apprentice boy named Alexander H. Hopkins, aged 15 years. All persons are forbid harboring or trusting him and runaway on my account, as I will pay no debts of his contracting. John Butterfield – Hartwick, May 29, 1820. (note ran 2 weeks)

"They have Disappeared."
Samuel White, of Hartwick has decamped for parts unknown; he and Mrs. White having rather abruptly left the town. Mr. White commenced business as a jeweler in a front corner of O. S. Burch's general store at Hartwick, about two years ago, continuing until the last of April or first of May last, when he succeeded to the mercantile trade conducted by E. O. Rogers on the west side of the creek in that place having quite a good patronage from that part of the town. In August he had the misfortune to lose nearly all his household effects and $40 in cash by the burning of the dwelling in which he resided. The good people of Hartwick were stirred with sympathy for the unfortunate family (which included the mother of Mrs. White, Mrs. James Goodenough, formerly of Cooperstown).

"They have reappeared."
Mr. and Mrs. S. D. White beg to inform the good people of Hartwick that they have returned and would like to know how long it is since the Law went in force as to be obliged to inform all the gossips of the town what you were going to do, where you went, and when you were coming back. I wish to say as I do not know as we have broken any laws in not informing the public when we were going. We certainly did not steal away in the night but went in broad daylight and as I have always been in the habit of doing as I was a mind to, I would like to know if it was any of the man's business that inserted the article entitled "They have disappeared," and would like to have him keep his nose out of my business and if he attends to his own business and lets other people alone he will have all he can do.

1893 "Hobos make Havoc."
An unusually large number of hobos have been in the vicinity drinking firewater. Saturday 2 went against each other and 1 got a badly lacerated eye. Monday morning, Mrs. Lewis Giles went out to feed her fowls. She found only the heads of them left, very unfortunate, she being a widow of small means.

1895 Our Hartwick corespondent under date of the 15th inst. says:

Mrs. D. C. Field found one of her cows dead in the stable last Thursday morning with eight others very sick. Dr. Matteson was immediately called and having made an examination, pronounced it the result of strychnine, which is thought to have been fed to the cows during the night, as they were well and some quite playful when they were put in the stable. At this writing two are dead; it is thought the others may possibly be saved. It will prove a great loss to Mrs. Field as it will nearly spoil her dairy for the summer. The wretch who performed this dastardly act ought not to be suffered to live, much less to be at large.

Taken from the Potter Scrapbook 1876-1900's

Last Sat. night the store of L. R. Sergent's in this village was entered by thieves, who confiscated 2 or 3 suits of clothes, 3 or 4 pairs of boots and shoes and other things of value. They effected an entrance to the cellar by cutting and removing glass. - No clues.

1878 p2- Tramps are getting quite numerous in and around this village and in some instants are becoming very impenitent, and if we are not mistaken some of them may by and by get into the wrong pew.

1878 - p2 - Mrs. A. G. Drake had the steps in front of his store torn up and demolished one night last week and we understand he has commenced legal proceedings against 3 young men.

1884 – p40 - Leverett Robinson was arrested here last week Monday evening, charged with opening a letter directed to his sister-in-law. He had been drinking excessively for several days, and had greatly annoyed his sick wife, who at the present writing is very low with that dreadful disease, cancer of the breast. He was arrested as a means of procuring quiet for his sick wife.

He was taken to Cooperstown by Deputy Sheriff Gardner, and the next morning was found dead in his cell, and is supposed to have taken too much morphine. Friday previous to his arrest he had taken into his possession a sum of money, which his wife had laid by as a result of her own labor, with which to defray the expenses of her last sickness. On Sunday following he claimed that the money had been stolen from him while he was asleep. His wife however, had strong suspicions that he had the money somewhere and had forgotten it, consequently on Thursday last two neighbors were called to search the premises, and after four hours diligent searching Mr. Thompson, one of the searchers, found the identical money secreted in an old boot among some rubbish in the woodhouse. With this money, consisting of six twenty-dollar gold pieces, there was also 27 dollars, which Robinson had gathered together during the forepart of winter as a matter of speculation. Unfortunately for the poor man, he was not possessed of an amiable disposition, hence it was not improved by drink; yet while we hear him denounced on all sides, we can but think that there are those who are somewhat responsible for his sudden demise, having catered to his appetite for drink, so long as he paid well for it. He was buried here on Friday last, from the house of his sister, Mrs. J. H. Shaul, living north of this village, on the edge of Otsego. He leaves one child, a boy in his teens, who is much respected, and who has the sympathy of the whole community.

1890 - p31 Burglars entered the house of Samuel Ward about a mile below this village one night last week and took $150 from his pants pocket. Mr. Ward said they affected an entrance by cutting a window light and removing the fastening. They made their escape at 3 am in the morning. No trace of the parties have been obtained.

1893 – p10 - The village chicken thief has made his first raid on our R. B. Brownells Hennery. He has become chicken hungry earlier than usual- (they know who and should stop such thievery).

1900 - p9 - A tramp who had been helping William Weeks since last fall, getting his board and compensation absconded with Mr. Weeks overcoat and Mrs. Weeks pocketbook containing 90 cents in cash and a check for two tubs of butter- so much for harboring tramps.

1902 "Excitement ran high in Hartwick on Saturday night when it was learned that 2 State excise officers spent the 4th here and received samples of liquors over new bars established for the day. Harry Yager was arrested for selling liquor in violation of the law. He waved examination and gave bail —— W. J. Hall, S. V. Holbrook, and H. E. Freeland also were arrested."

Widow and children of murdered man. Mrs. Ned Austin who, with four babies, is left destitute.

May 23, 1911

Austin murdered at Hartwick, Saturday.

An old grudge, some liquor, a fight, a man shot dead; these to have been the successive states of a tragedy which was enacted in the usually quiet village. Ned Austin was shot and killed by Stephen Brown, in the latters saloon, about 5 O'clock in the afternoon. Brown is now in the county jail at Cooperstown with a

Saloon where the shooting occurred. The corner door gives entrance to the pool room.

Where Ned Austin met his death. The fatal shot was fired through the crack in the doorway which opens to the rear of the bar.

charge of murder in the first degree.

At 5:10 Saturday afternoon word was received over the telephone by Sheriff Orlo Brown at Cooperstown that there had been a killing at Hartwick. The sheriff lost no time but took the 5:13 trolley car for Hartwick.

Commendable though his promptness was, it happened in this instance that there was no need of haste to get the trail of a murderer, for Brown made no effort to get away. On the contrary, directly after the shooting, he went to the office of Justice Ziba Holbrook and announced that he was ready to give himself up. Then he returned home and engaged in caring for a trotting horse, which he owned, and he was so occupied when the sheriff arrived and placed him under arrest.

When he was placed in jail at 11:15 Saturday night, Brown had a bad bruise over his right eye, which he claimed was inflicted by Austin's fist. His line of defense will be that he shot Austin to save his own life.

"Steve Brown" is well known throughout this region. He has been the proprietor of hotels at Mt. Vision and at West Oneonta, and has been arrested for keeping a disorderly house and for violating the liquor laws. He has the reputation of being quarrelsome and reckless in his regard for the law. His age is about 63 years.

The victim, Austin, was known as a town "bruiser." He was a habitual drinker and was usually ugly when drunk. It is said that he and Brown had had many differences. Austin was about 35 years old. He leaves a widow and four children.

1913

Monday afternoon one of the largest bands of gypsies seen in the vicinity in many years visited the town. There were about 6 caravans, each one accommodating several people – as soon as the wagons reached the village, these people tried to enter the stores and other public places and secure whatever was easy to access. It was a difficult matter to wait upon them and several small thefts were reported in local stores. At one home they entered while the mistress was in the cellar and when she returned bringing a can of fruit they relieved her of it and left at once. One flock of hens was attacked enroute from Mt. Vision.

February 9, 1915

"Seven years ago a valuable fur coat was hung outside the door of the store conducted at that time by Dorr Gardner. When Dorr Gardner went outside to bring the coat into the store, the fur coat was missing. No clue to the person who had committed the theft was ever found. Tuesday while M. J. Boer was digging underneath his barn on South Street, he discovered a bag and upon opening pulling it out into the daylight and opening the same it revealed the stolen coat! The tags were on it and it was well preserved."

1917 - "Hartwick Store Burglarized."

Burglars entered the feed store of Burch Bros. and Talbot in this village last night, while they secured only $18.15 in money, they carried away the McCasky account register and the day book in which accounts of the firm were kept and the loss seriously handicaps any effort to collect from their customers at this period, when the dairymen and others have stocked heavily to avoid hauling feed during the times the highways are heavy and before the monthly milk checks have been received. The firm has a large amount on their books, said to reach into the thousands. The members of the firm refuse to make any statement as to the amounts of the accounts, which were lost.

The discovery of the burglary was made by Arthur Andrus, when he went in to open the store about 7 o'clock. He summoned Mr. Talbot and they made an investigation. It was found that the burglars had entered through a basement window at the rear of the building into the office. It is believed after securing the contents of the safe – door shut and knob was broken and hinges mutilated.

Officers were summoned and Sheriff Brown, under Sheriff T. W. Snyder, Deputy Sheriff Dan Chapman and District Attorney Van Horn visited the store and made a thorough investigation. No Clue – believed it was someone who had a motive to carry off the accounts. Expected the crime will be shifted to ——Chester Burch.

January 7, 1922 - Hartwick Hotel Raided
On Saturday night Deputy Sheriff C. L. Williams of Otsego County, assisted by other officers visited the Commercial Hotel, conducted by John Chase at Hartwick, and after searching the premises and finding intoxicants on the premises, placed the proprietor, John Chase under arrest, charged with violating the law relative to the sale of intoxicants. He was held in $1,000 bail for the next grand jury. Bail not being furnished he is now detained in the Otsego county jail at Cooperstown.

January 1923
One of the most despicable and unfortunate criminal cases in the county annals surrounded the death of John Chase which occurred on the night of January 8 at the home of Ira Green on Christian Hill near Hartwick.

A drunken debauch in which at least five men had participated and which had followed nights and days of continous imbibing of bad moonshine culminated in the events which caused the death of Chase, himself in an intoxicated condition.

According to the evidence which has been drawn from the survivors of the debauch, and which by the way has been obtained by county officials with the aid of Corporal Montgomery of the state troopers and four of his assistants only after painstaking efforts and frequent visits to the scene of the crime at all hours of the day and night, the home of Ira Green has been a gathering place for men who had a preference for drink and a grudging willingness to do a little work in return for satisfying their thirst. And so four or five of Green's cronies had been living and drinking at his farm, doing a little work on the side.

On the days following Christmas and following the importation of a five gallon keg of moonshine from a still about three miles distant, it is alleged that George Hecox, Cecil Green, a nephew of Ira, Warren (Bill) Dingman, and John (Jack) Chase had been spending most of their time drinking. On January 6th their supply of liquor running short an expedition was made to their moonshine friend and another five gallons cask was brought in.

January 7th and 8th were spent in consuming a portion of the new supply and in fact it was apparent to the authorities that on the day of the crime little else had been done, except to feed the stock. That evening, the 8th, the drinking progressed and it is stated that Chase, not feeling particularly well had gone up bed. Some time later in the evening it is testified, Cecil Green went upstairs and brought Chase down, who was at that time clad in his shirt and underwear, and after giving Chase a few more drinks, Cecil decided that he needed a bath, and in his own words said, "I am going to give you one." With that he put Chase on his shoulder and took him out through the kitchen and wood shed and threw him into a tub of ice cold water, where it is testified he left Chase to his own resources and went back into the house.

Later, Chase failing to appear, Cecil returned to the tub and found Chase still in the water.

Realizing that this was not as it should be, he took Chase by the collar and dragged him back into the kitchen, laying him on the floor before the fire. After the lapse of some time the other members of party discovered that Chase was cold and apparently stiff, and it was also stated that he did not move. When this was suggested to Cecil he took a teakettle of hot water from the stove and poured it over the prostrate body, as he said, "to warm him up."

This failed to have any effect on the unfortunate victim and so Cecil again took him upstairs and rolled him into a bed where Dingman had been sleeping. Shortly after this Dingman discovered the plight of his bedfellow and went downstairs, reporting that there was a dead man in his bed. Somewhat sobered by this statement and gathering together what intelligence was left in the other members, it was decided that a doctor should be called.

At this juncture it was apparent that Cecil Green was the only one really sober to go to the neighbor's phone to summon Dr. Schoolcraft of Hartwick. When he reached Green's and discovering the condition of Chase immediately notified Coroner Norman W. Getman of Oneonta. Sheriff Williams was notified of the trouble. He with Under-sheriff Robert Converse and District Attorney Adrian A. Pierson went to Greens and began an investigation of the case.

It was apparent the men had to be sobered before they were questioned. Ira and Cecil Green, Dingman, and Hecox were brought to Cooperstown where they were lodged in jail and held on an order from the coroner as material witnesses.

The following day the coroner proceeded with the investigation of the crime, the verdict was rendered to, John Chase had died at the home of Ira Green in the Town of Hartwick on January 8 or 9, 1923, as the result of exposure caused by the negligent, culpable, and criminal acts of one Cecil Green. Orders were then issued that Cecil Green be held to await the action of the Grand Jury on the charge of manslaughter.

From investigation that it was a matter of criminal negligence due to the condition in which the members of the party were from the over use of liquor.

On February 28, 1923 the Grand jury handed in an indictment for manslaughter in the second degree.

Also Anthony Martinus, who is alleged to have sold the liquor consumed at the affair on Christian Hill, received two indictments. His still supplied a five-gallon keg of moonshine. He was only three miles away so when they ran out they'd walk to get more.

August 6, 1924
Safe Cracked in Hartwick Store

Burglars entered the hardware store of S. S. Backus at Hartwick at about 4 o'clock Saturday morning, cracked the safe and carried away about $300 worth of merchandise, including two rifles, an electric sewing machine, electric flat iron, Kodaks, razors, etc.

The job is thought to have been done by professionals. Entrance was made through a rear window and the safe drilled and lock blown, although it had not been locked in five years. Nothing of value was found therein, however, and the burglars had to be content with goods from the store. The proprietor believes that he heard the cracksmen drive away in a high-powered car after they had completed the work. Sheriff Converse and State Troopers made an investigation and have several clues but no arrests have been made as yet.

December 9, 1958

Three fires that went off in firecracker order in Mt. Vision, Hartwick, and Cooperstown led firemen and state police on the trail of arson. Losses might run as high as $15,500.

November 1967

Lone gunman grabs $25,000 in Hartwick bank robbery. The bandit was admitted to

Hartwick Branch: National Commercial Bank & Trust Co. Arrow shows door where bandit entered.

the National Commercial Bank & Trust Co. when he knocked on a glass door while the Hartwick branch was closing at 3 PM.

Fewer than 5 minutes later, according to reports, he escaped after warning bank personnel and two customers to remain silent or he would shoot two children who were inside. He carried the money away in a brown paper bag. The gunman was believed to have sped away in a green 1965 Chevrolet station wagon which was stolen from a parking lot in Oneonta.

The tellers were Lillie Mae Wright and Mrs. Lolita Clark. Standing near the counters was Howard Marlette of Mt. Vision, a director of the bank and George Ashley, 70 of Hartwick, a customer.

Policemen and dozens of FBI agents were called in. Later in the month Eugene Carl Stroesser, 26, of East Branch in Delaware County, was returned by the New York state Police with the cooperation the U. S. Govern-

ment and Otsego County law officials. He was being held in Otsego County jail to face charges of assault and bank robbery.

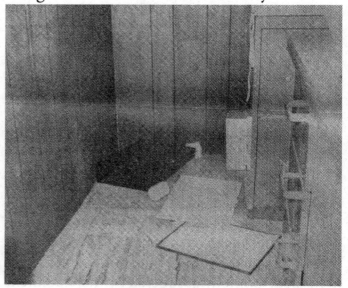

This is where it belonged — The thief or thieves took the Sentinel Safe from this corner in the office of the Hartwick Supermarket and carried it into the woods.

December 1967

Hartwick Supermarket safe torn open in weekend burglary, $2,500 in cash was stolen. The storeowner Carter H. Harrison said the Sentinel safe was taken. The investigator said the safe was pounded open and dumped in the woods in back of the store.

We have had some recent murders, robberies, fires, burglaries, and odd crimes but due to names of some maybe in a book down the road we will write about them.

———

By: Barb Potter

Bibliography
Ramon Chase
Old Potter Scrapbook
Hartwick Visitor
Elizabeth Curry Scrapbook
Hobart Herald Times
Freeman's Journal
The Oneonta Star

4H

4H has been an active part in the lives of many Hartwick young people, teaching them many skills in many fields. In the beginning the projects were agriculture and homemaking related, now in 2002 there are projects for all interests.

4H has been in Otsego County since 1920. At first members were independent.

John Mott was an early leader in Hartwick. In the late 1920's he organized the Whitehouse 4H Club. In 1929 the club won first prize on their float at the Cooperstown fair.

In 1931 the Whitehouse 4H Club conducted a meeting broadcasted over WGY radio station in Schenectady.

Among many activities the club had the opportunity in 1935 of putting on a program for the Mt. Vision Grange. Participants were Catherine and Robert Jones, Alfred Schneider, Deforest Whitney, Donald Morehouse, and Geraldine Curry. A skit was presented with Donald Holdridge, Leona Beckley, Margaret Schneider, Elva Palmer and Stanley Petkewec.

Many things were learned beyond the projects completed. Geraldine Curry became leader when John Mott went to Cornell.

Two other clubs were mentioned in the 4H News in 1932 recognizing the Otsego Clubs who had completed all their projects. These included the Hartwick 4H Club with leaders, Mr. Stuart Chamberlin and Mr. Roderick Cook, with 32 members. The Busy Club with 5 members and Mrs. Anna Wells as leader as well as the Whitehouse Club with John Mott leader and 16 members.

In 1934 Mrs. Jessie Woleben was the leader of the Home Sweet Home 4H Club. Several girls attended 4H camp and as a fund-raiser put on a play at the EMBA Hall.

On Scotch Hill the Hill Billy Club was active about 1935 – 40. Donald Phillips was leader in 1939-40.

Christian Hill had a 4H Club, The Trailblazers, with Ramon Chase, leader; Clifford and Carol Brunner and Donald Chase were three of their members.

Another early leader in Hartwick was Mrs. Agatha Harrington. She was a pioneer in the 4H. Before 4H was in Otsego County, Mrs. Harrington worked with Junior Projects beginning in 1910 in the Burlington rural schools. In 1920 she started a 4H club in Lena School which she led for 25 years.

She came to Hartwick to teach in the elementary school in 1945 and immediately started a 4H club, The Hartwick Hustlers. The club was active from its origin and very successful.

Clipping 3/28/47
"Louise Bunn, 8 year old daughter of Mr. and Mrs. Kenneth Bunn, South Hartwick was selected as the outstanding food preparation demonstrator at a meeting held at the Oneonta High School. She is a junior member of the Hartwick Hustlers 4H Club of Hartwick."

HOMEMAKER: *Nadine Murdock, aged 17, Hartwick, receives a scholarship check for $300 from Herbert F. Murphy, midwestern territory vice president of Sears, Roebuck and Company during 34th National 4-H Club Congress in Chicago last week. Nadine was one of eight national winners in the 1955 National 4-H Home Improvement Awards Program to receive a $300 scholarship and an all-expense trip to the Congress from the Sears-Roebuck Foundation.*

SOIL EXPERT: *John Mott, national soil and water contest winner from Hartwick, explains the soil holding characteristics of a managed forest, terraces and contour farming on a hill-side mockup section of a farm field to Raymond C. Firestone, executive vice-president of the Firestone Tire and Rubber Company (left) and James Cagney, famed motion picture star and authority on soil conservation (right). John was one of eight national winners honored last week at a breakfast given by the Firestone company for more than 1,900 4-H Club delegates, leaders, state and federal extension representatives and friends at the Conrad Hilton Hotel in Chicago. In addition to his all-expense trip to the National 4-H Club Congress, John was awarded a $300 scholarship to the college of his choice. The breakfast marked the 12th consecutive year that soil and water conservation had been sponsored as a 4-H Club project by Firestone.*

From a December 7, 1955 clipping:

Many rewards were received at the Morris fair. Some of the clothing blue ribbon winners in 1956 were Cheryl and Mary Marlette, Helen Bunn, Sondra Ainslie, Marie Weeks, Bonnie Jensen, Janet Potter, Judith Sullivan, Shirley Powers, Nadine Murdock, Sharon Matteson, and Carol Mott.

In a July 31, 1958 article from the Oneonta Star we find that several girls from Hartwick won blue ribbons in the Annual County Dress Revue held on the Farmer's Museum grounds. These included Edith, Gail and Sondra Ainslie, Linda Bresee, Kathy Hovick, Barbara Lee, Sharon Matteson, Carol Mott, Janet Potter, and Nora Roberts. These girls will be rewarded with a trip to the State Fair.

The Hartwick Hustlers had 49 members in

1959. Besides completing many projects such as "Time for Lunch," learning to sew, and ABC's of Cooking, the Hustler's 1959 activities show what a typical year was like. The club members made Thanksgiving favors for the nursing home (probably the Rosie Leone's Nursing home here in Hartwick). They participated in Demonstration day and this year a county poster contest. Participants from

At Demonstration Day in Oneonta, Mary Chamberlin of Hartwick Hustlers 4-H Club demonstrated the techniques of "pounding in" textile paints to insure they work into and between the fibres.

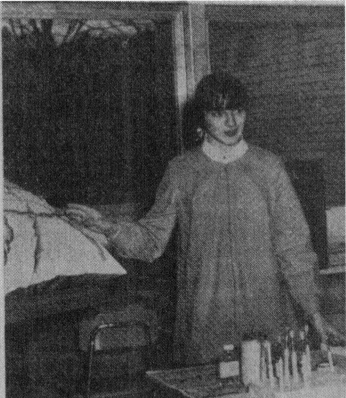

Last year, Mary showed how to paint textiles in designs using stencils. This year she has advanced to making abstracts, and this painted pillow simulates roses to harmonize with the decor of her room

OFFICERS INSTALLED: New officers for the Hartwick Hustlers 4-H Club were recently installed. Shown here, left to right, are, back row, Jeanne Marlette, secretary; Linda Ainslie, treasurer; Linda Barown, Council representative, and Mary Chamberlin, president. Front row, Jean Powers, vice-president; Marcia Chamberlin, news reporter, and Marjorie Matteson, song leader.

clubs sponsored a covered dish dinner at the Methodist Church. The clubs were Uncle Sam's helpers, Eva and Henry Murdock leaders, The Glory Bee's (a horse club) Anna Risley, leader with Russ Vermillion assisting, The Hartwick Dairy Club, Bill Kimmey and Everett Kane leaders, and The Hartwick Hustlers.

Hartwick were Jean and Joann Fish, Cheryl and Mary Marlette, Evalina and Jean Fuller.

To celebrate National 4H week in 1963 four

Nadine Murdock Randall and Agatha Harrington

Mrs. Agatha Harrington was honored for her many years as a 4H leader. Nadine Randall, formerly Nadine Murdock, and a former member of the Hartwick Hustlers presented her a cake. A corsage and memory book were presented by Mr. John Mott and Mrs. Howard Marlette.

Some of the members of the Dairy Club were Gail, Linda, and Larry Ainslie, Robert and Ronald Kane, Robert and Carol Kimmey, Mary and Jeanne Marlette, Jean and Billy Powers, Keith Skubitz, Billy Balcom, Marjory

Mon., March 30, 1964   Oneonta Star

Larry Ainslie demonstrating "4H Calf and Heifer Record" for which he won a blue ribbon at the county demonstration day.

Balcom, Linda Barown, and Bart Barown.

There had been a Hartwick Dairy Club in the early 1950's with Jim Renwick leader. Some members were John Polulech, Jim, John and Sue Renwick, John, Robert, and Carol Mott, Harry (Skip) Lyons, and Peggy Lyons.

In a December 4, 1958 newspaper we read that Robert Mott was one of six in the nation to be cited for his outstanding 4H work in Field Crops. He was awarded a $400 scholarship at the National 4H Club Congress in Chicago.

Uncle Sam's Helpers emphasized community service and demonstrations. In 1959, they received a blue ribbon award from the Oneonta Star for their window display in town.

Also in 1967 Wayne E. Willis, Otsego County 4H agent, reported that Uncle Sam's Helpers won a blue ribbon on their insect collection at the State Fair.

Some of the members of Uncle Sam's Helpers were David and Orlo Burch, Bob and Bill Murdock, Dennis and John Tuller, Daryl Risley, Robert and Ed Rood, James Fiel, John Tedesco, Thomas Mottram, Allen Wright, William Fort, Ronald Hurtibise, Kenneth Tabor, Don Phillips, Robert and Richard Hall, Marie Winslow, and Mary Ward.

In a statewide contest in February 1964 Hartwick Dairy Club, leader William Kimmey, was one of the three clubs receiving the maximum award. Uncle Sam's Helpers and the Glory Bee's ranked high in the statewide contest between one hundred seventy clubs.

In October 1963 the Junior Hartwick Hustlers was organized with 30 members and Cheryl Marlette leader, Agatha Harrington, advisor. This club completed many projects. At Thanksgiving time they made apple-raisin turkeys for residents of the nursing home and at Christmas sang Christmas carols and delivered Christmas packages to the nursing home and shut-ins.

Members also brought items to fill a basket for a needy person.

4H members in Hartwick had a square dance team for several years. Some of the participants were Robert Mott, Richard Mott, Shirley Powers, Billy Powers, Linda, Gail and Larry Ainslie, Cheryl, Mary, and Jeanne Marlette, Bill Murdock, Joe Powers, Donna and Sondra Ainslie, and others.

These clubs had many project leaders including Mrs. John Mott, Mrs. Leonard Wright, Mr. and Mrs. Howard Ainslie, Mr. and Mrs. Howard Marlette, Mrs. Earl Beers, Mrs. Stanley Clark, Mr. and Mrs. Clyde Tuller, Mr. and

Mrs. Bill Powers, Mrs. William Harrison, Cheryl Marlette, Mary Marlette, Shirley Powers, Carol Mott, and Mrs. Betty Bunn.

Robert Murdock

Robert Murdock, who in 1962 won a $400 scholarship, as well as an expense paid trip to the 41st 4H Club Congress in Chicago for entomology, later taught it to local clubs and also others outside of Hartwick.

Some junior project leaders were Sharon and Sandra Matteson, Jeanne Marlette, Jean Powers, and Dawn Hornbeck.

Hartwick had several active clubs in the 1990's. Mrs. Nancy Adikes led the Hemlock Hill

Otsego Group at 4H Club Congress at Cornell

4th Row: ?, Robert Kimmey, ? Green, Jeff Samson, Jay Seeley, ? Adee
3rd row: Fred ?, Russell Martin, Darrell Risley, Robert Murdock, Bill Murdock, Rick Brockway
2nd Row: Wayne Willis, ?, Cheryl Marlette, Linda Bresee, Judy Pernat, ? Barlow
Front Row: Shirley Keane, ?, Rita McLaughlin, Shirley Powers, ?, ?, ?, Agatha Harrington

Cloverbuds. Some of their members were Rebecca Adikes, Sasha Bowlay, Lucius Niedzialkowski, Tommy Potter, and Traci Webb. This club did very interesting crafts and exhibited at the Morris Fair.

Hemlock Hill had another club, a horse club, The Hemlock Hill Horseowner's Club with Mrs. Jane Sheldon and Mrs. Carol Niedzialkowski leaders. They were members of the County Mounted Drill Team. Caitlin Niedzialkowski in 2002 is a member of a neighboring County Drill Team.

Another horse club was the Okee Dokes 4H Club that met at the South Hartwick schoolhouse. Leader was Gloria Waro with members Amy Kane, Cody and Mackensie Waro, Allie Richardson, and Amanda Jones. This club did interesting community service projects and also belonged to the county Mounted drill Team.

Both horse clubs were prominent in all the meets.

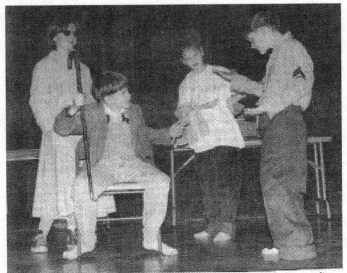

Hartwick Hoppers 4-H Club members Joel Griffith (seated) and, from left, Erin Allison, Katie Allison, and Tommy Potter rehearse their roles in the play the club will present this Saturday at 1 p.m. in the Hartwick Community Center.

From South Hartwick and Hemlock Hill to Scotch Hill where Mrs. Barbara Potter was leader of the Scotch Hill Hartwick Hoppers.

One interesting project they completed was a first aid kit for their pets. Each kit was tailored to their particular pet, which included a bird, cat, dog, horse, turtle, and even a chicken. Dr. Fassett supplied two-thirds of the contents of the kits. They were exhibited at the state Fair.

For a community service they wrote a play and put it on at the community center with the proceeds going to Chris Phillips, a cancer patient.

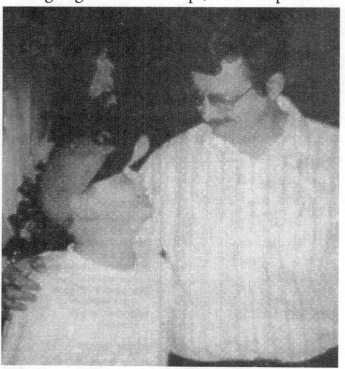

Christopher Phillips and his father Michael.

Some of the members were Kimberly and Brian Wellman, Joel Griffith, Katie and Erin Allison, Tommy and Joey Potter, William Carius, and Tom West.

Mrs. Jackie Manley also had a club for a short time.

4H members from Hartwick have won many prizes at the Morris and State Fairs.

Hundreds of demonstrations have been done at the fairs, district meets, and fruit shows.

Hartwick was often represented at the 4H Club Congress at Cornell as delegates and also winners of Talent Contests.

Marjory Balcom VanDuesen won the cup at the Farmer's Museum Show.

Several Hartwick young people even won a trip to National 4H Club Congress in Chicago including Nadine, Bob, and Bill Murdock, Jeanne Powers, and Robert, John, and Carol Mott.

Several from Hartwick have been chosen to go to Capital Day to meet the Governor and see state government in action.

Cheryl Marlette and Bob Kimmey went to Michigan in a 4H-exchange program. Carol Mott went to Illinois in the same program another year.

An unusual award was won by Jackie Conklin, 15. She was an individual member and had completed First Aid, Guiding Eyes Dog program, a rabbit project, and had gone to a horse camp. Because of her interest in animals and her 4H projects she was awarded a Welsh pony given by Mrs. Raymond Backus of West Winfield.

Hartwick had many 4H clubs, leaders, and members not mentioned here, who have benefited from the program and contributed greatly to the community.

Today Hartwick 4H members are either independent or belong to a club nearby.

There are no 4H clubs in Hartwick in 2002.

By: F.H.

Information from:
Extension Office
John Mott
Oneonta Star
Betty Bunn
Doris Powers
Katherine Kimmey
Laura Kane
Cheryl Christensen
Eva Murdock
Michigan Paper
Binghamton Newspaper
Mrs. Adike
Mrs. Sheldon
Mrs. Waro
Mrs. Potter
Diana Marlette

Tom West, Patrick West, Jay Nieldzialkowski

Travis Manley, Tom West, Patrick West, Tommy Potter, Brian Wellman, Jay Niedzialkowski

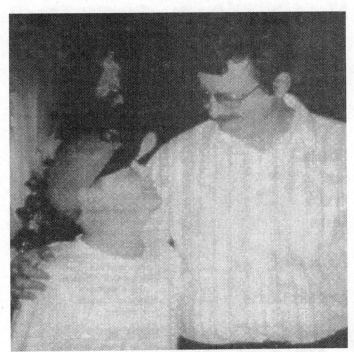

Joey Potter, Tommy Potter, Pat West, Jay Niedzialkowski, Brian Wellman

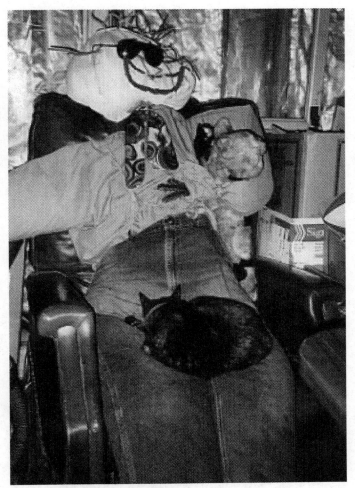

Farmer Fall Apart & Patches

EXTRAEXTRA***EXTRA***

SCARE CROW CONTEST

SATURDAY, OCTOBER 7, 10 A.M.

PIONEER PARK, COOPERSTOWN

The Cooperstown Crier will be sponsoring a Scare Crow Contest in Cooperstown's Pioneer Park on Saturday, October 7. Scarecrows will be in place by 10 A.M.. Prizes will be awarded.

After judging, local businesses will adopt the scarecrows, placing them on display until Halloween. The business that adopts your scarecrow will provide a special reward.

If you are interested in taking part, or if you need more information, please contact Mary-Ellen at the Cornell Cooperative Extension Office.

This can be part of your 4-H week display.
Let's have 4-H well represented!!

P.S. We know this is the same day as the 4-H Member Recognition Event at Holiday Inn, Oneonta. If you would like to take part, please talk to us and arrangements can be made so that you can do both.

Tommy Potter, Brian Wellman, Joey Potter-Farmer Fall Apart

Cookie Sale at Hartwick Key Bank

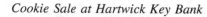

Tommy Potter, Joey Potter, Brian Wellman- Farmer Fall Apart   *Joey Potter, Brian Wellman, Tom West, Tommy Potter, Pat West*

Boy Scouts

B. S. A. Troop 72 Hartwick

It was awards night for these 11 Boy Scouts in Troop 72 from Hartwick Monday night. (First Row, l-r), Mark McKenzie, Gerald Gage, William Eckler and Shawn McGrath; (Second Row), Andrew Sorbera, Brian Jeffers, Daniel Shute, Donald Kelsey and James Croft. (Third Row), Donald Mulberry, Representative from Scout Headquarters; John McGrath, Assistant Scout Master; Gordon Gillingham, Peter Mateunas, Gordon Curry, new Assistant Scout Master; and Richard A Conklin, Scout Master.

Scouting, as close as we can figure, started in Hartwick back in 1948 with scout leader Reverend Kirk from the Christian Church. They had approximately ten boys.

Some leaders through out the years were Cliff Hull, John Hall, Bill Burgess, John Staffin, Russ Griffith, Dick Conklin, John McGrath, Bart Barown, John Bush, and Wayne Phillips.

Scouting has and is sponsored by the Hartwick Fire Department and the Emergency Squad.

Through out the years, Troop 72 has attended Boy Scout Camp at Crumhorn Mountain, which later became known as Henderson Scout Reservation. The troop attended the second year it was opened, 1949, The scout troop still attends, learning Scout skills and character building.

Mr. And Mrs. Robert Walrath with son John, recipient of God and Country Award on Sunday, February 11th, at Hartwick Christian Church.

Mr. and Mrs. Dewayne Block are proud parents of son Terry, recipient of God and Country Award at Hartwick Christian Church Morning Service on February 11th.

Russel and Pauline Griffith with son Doug, who added God and Country Award to a growing list of achievements at Hartwick Christian Church Service, February 11th.

In later years the Canadian Brotherhood Camporee was a yearly experience for many Scouts. They all got to meet many other Scouts from different states and countries.

God and Country -- Alan L. Wright, member of Hartwick Boy Scout Troop 72, has been presented the God and Country Award in Scouting. L-R, Arnold Staffin, Scoutmaster, the Rev. Paul W. Gere, pastor of the Hartwick Methodist Church; Alan, with Mr. And Mrs. Leonard C. Wright, his parents.

Troop 72 participated in the yearly 1ˢᵗ Aid meet Competition in Oneonta. They were instructed by members of Hartwick Emergency Squad. They held 1ˢᵗ place for many years and received many awards with their first aid skills.

As of this year Hartwick still has a troop 72 with the help of willing adults and support of their town.

Eagle Ceremony – 1987 Brian Flack – Eagle with parents

Matthew Blaske – 1985 "Scouting is for everyone."

Crumhorn Scout Camp "Lunch Line"

OTEGO CAMPOREE - 1984

Order of the Arrow Ceremony – L-R: Bart Barown, John McGrath, scoutmaster, Chris McPhail

Otego Camporee - 1984

Scouting Family - L-R: Patricia, Bart III, and Bart Barown, Jr., scoutmaster

Something went wrong.

Canadian Trip 1983: Bottom Row: Nate Lewin, Mike Barown, ?, ?; 2nd Row: Robbie McGrath, Mike Brown, John Morales, ?, David Proctor, Brian Flack, Bart Barown III, Chris McPhail, Mark Simmons, Al Thomas; Back Row: John McGrath, Ken McPhail, ?, Shawn McGrath, ?, Mimi Alba, Bart Barown, Hans Albanese, Jan McGrath, Sandy Ainslie.

Scouts travel on their stomach. L-R: David Sellick, Jeff Vesely, Bart Barown III, Al Thomas, Robbie McGrath, Mike Barown, David Proctor, Jim Mateunas

OTEGO CAMPOREE - 1984

Otego Campsite

Home Cooking

Breaking Camp

Breaking Camp

BROTHERHOOD WEEKEND – 1985 KINGSTON, ONTARIO, CANADA

Opening Ceremonies

Setting up camp

Setting up camp. L-R: Don Phillips and David Sellick

Ina Phillips and David Sellick on Tour in Ontario, Canada.

Ontario, Canada

Taking in a demonstration. L-R: Bart Barown, Jr., scoutmaster, Ken McPhail, Hon. George Kepner, Pete Mateunas, assistant scoutmaster, Al Thomas

L-R: Bart Barown III, Chris McPhail, Mike Barown, Chris Barown, Nate Lewin, Robbie McGrath, David Proctor, Bill Carentz, Jim Mateunas

ADIRONDACK HIGH PEAKS FOUR DAY HIKE - 1986

Hiking the trail

First Nights Camp

L-R: Pete Mateunas, assistant scoutmaster, Al Thomas, Mike Barown, Bart Barown III, Robbie McGrath

On top of Mt. Marcy – highest peak in New York State.

L-R: Bart Barown, Jr., scoutmaster, Mike Barown, Robbie McGrath, Al Thomas, Bart Barown III.

Cub Scouting Pack 72 Hartwick

Cub Scout Pack 72 started in Hartwick as a small group of 5 boys and parents and expanded within two years to Tiger Cubs, Cub Scouts, and Webelo Scouts, a total group of over 40 boys.

Pack 72 was sponsored by the Hartwick Emergency Squad.

Some of its leaders through the years were Donna Miller, Lori Butler, Kari Phillips, Janet McGrath, Ron Kane, Wayne Griffith, Tim Williammee, and Bob Burgin.

Boys attended Day Camp at Henderson Scout Reservation in the summer and Cub Day activities during the rest of the year.

February is Scout Anniversary Week and Cub Scouts hold a Blue and Gold Dinner in the Hartwick Community Center. Family and friends attend to watch scouts receive recognition and advancements for the work they had accomplished.

Cub Scout Pack activities included Pine Wood Derby which was held yearly, helping with the Emergency Squad's Chicken and Biscuit dinner, setting up for the senior citizens dinners, a Christmas program for the community, and various other activities.

Marching in a Memorial Day Parade

Cub Scouts; Nathan Saxer, Lenny Armstrong, Billy Proctor, Nate Phillips, Janet McGrath, Steve Mateunas, Jimmy Goodspeed, Mike Gage, Donna Miller, Brian Butler, Jeremy Willamee, ?, Mr. Miller, ?,?

Cub Scouts: Mrs. Henningsen, Den mother, Roger Hull, John Henningsen, Lynn Larsen, Dick Conklin, Edwin Carvin, John McGrath, scout

Webelos

G. A. R.

"The Grand Army of The Republic" was a society of veterans who fought for the North in the Civil War (1861-65). The G.A.R. was founded by Benjamin Stephenson in Decatur, Ill., on April 6, 1866. The society was formed to strengthen fellowship among the men who fought in the Civil War, to honor those killed, provide care for their dependents and to uphold the Constitution. Membership was open to honorably discharged soldiers, sailors or Marines. The Grand Army was an important political force in the north. The last member died in 1956- and the organization was discontinued."[1]

The Post in Hartwick was organized through the personal efforts of L.W. Murdock; its charter was received Nov. 14, 1891.

From the book "Grand Army Of the Republic" published 1892 by D.A . Ellis:

"This volume contains a short History of the G.A.R. posts in Otsego County complete with membership lists and some biographical material." According to the volume most of the men in the Hartwick area served in the 9th Heavy Artillery, stationed at Fort Fisher, Petersburg and were charged with the defense of Washington D.C. and the 121st or 152nd N.Y. Volunteers (infantry). The building which housed the Post during its charter was donated by H.K. Marsh and was on the site of the house now occupied by Laurie & Dave Butler and their family.

"The Post was named in honor of Horatio N. Duro, a brave soldier, who was killed while charging the rebel pickets in front of Fort Fisher, Mar. 26, 1864. He was shot through the head and fell by the side of L.W. Murdock. The same night his remains were brought into the Union lines and sent to New Lisbon, N.Y where he was buried, his funeral being largely attended by friends & relatives."

"At the first meeting of the Post, Lester W. Murdock was elected commander. He was born in Hartwick, NY, February, 18, 1857, where he was educated, and enlisted Aug. 1, 1862, as a private in Co. E, 121st Regiment, N.Y. V., was at Crampton Pass, Sept. 14, 1862, was struck by a fragment of a shell which sent him tumbling down a steep bank." Mr. Murdock was wounded several more times during the war, including once at the Battle of the Wilderness, May 6, 1864.

Was taken prisoner: in an effort to escape he was shot in the neck by an officer with a revolver; on the tenth of the same month he took his place in the ranks, and participated in the memorable bayonet charge at Spotsylvania. He remained with his regiment to Gettysburg, and through the campaign near Charlestown, Va. August 21, 1864, while skirmishing, was struck in the right side by a spent ball, fracturing his ribs — March 25, 1865 was again wounded in the left leg— discharged at Albany, June 25, 1865 and returned to Hartwick."

"Emmet M. Irons, a brave soldier, enlisting in Co. K 121st N.Y. Vol; always on duty and engaging in the battles of the famous regiment; wounded at Salem Heights, May 3, 1863, in the left temple by a musket ball; April 2, 1865 in front of Petersburg, struck by a spent ball between the shoulders, and wounded in the face and neck by the concussion of the shell, April 6, 1865 but remained with the regiment, fighting to the last.—"

"William Holdridge was born in Monroe County, in 1849; enlisted August 25, 1864, in Co. B, 9th Heavy Artillery, was wounded in front of Fort Fisher, March 25,1865, by a gun shot in the left thigh. He was a faithful soldier and- a charter member of Duro Post." "A little background on William if you will bear with me — He was only 16 at the time he was wounded. He had joined as a substitute for someone else and received a bounty, this money was used to buy the farm in Burlington, the farm his grandson, Donald Holdridge inherited. He may have chosen Otsego County to settle because of Otsego friends he made at Petersburg."

"James Simmons, born Feb. 22, 1845, and enlisted Jan. 3, 1861 as a private in Co. I 89th N.Y. Vol. After the battle of Chapins farm he was detached from the regiment and placed on duty as a sharpshooter, where he remained until discharged. He participated in the battles of Kingston, Whitehall, Goldsboro, seige of Washington D.C. seige of Suffolk, Quaker Bridge, Great Swamp, Bachelor Creek, Drewerys Bluff, Bermuda Hundred, Cold Harbor, Petersburg. June 15 Mine Explosion, Petersburg trenched, Chapins Farms, Fair Oaks, and the Fall of Richmond. No mention of his being wounded at any time which with his record of battles is extraordinary." [2]

"Thomas Jenks was born at Burlington, N.Y., in 1812; enlisted Sept. 6, 1862 in Co. H. 152d Regt. N.Y. Vol.; is an honored citizen of Hartwick and a worthy member of Duro Post. Although advanced in years he takes a lively interest in the G. A. R. He did good service for the right, and recalls with pleasure the many scenes and incidents of camp life during his service."

"William Blanchard, charter member of Post, was born in Franklin, Delaware County, in 1845; educated at the common schools; enlisted in June, 1862; and mustered in at Norwich, Sept.21, 1862, as private in Co. K, 114th N.Y. Vol.; went by canal to Binghamton, and thence to Elmira and to Baltimore, where he was one of ten selected from each company to do police duty; remained there until charter election; Dec. 15. 1862, went aboard steamer Thames under General Banks, for Fortress Monroe; thence to Cape Henry and from Cape Henry, with fifteen vessels, for Cape Hatteras, experiencing a rough voyage; ran up a signal of distress and was towed into Hilton Head by the Erricson. The storm was so severe that the life boats were of no avail; the two boats were tied together; the water being three feet in the boat, and with no food or water to drink they lay in the water for 56 hours; remained at Hilton Head 12 days, and went aboard another boat, Jan. 9th, to Carlton; contracted fever, went to New Orleans, and was sent to regimental hospital; thence to Brazo City, May10, 1865; was in a skirmish at Irish Bend, May 10, 1865. He had a relapse, and was sent back to New Orleans, and discharged from the service in July 1865. Returned to Hartwick, where he is now residing with his wife and daughter, aged 21; He is at present time Senior Vice Commander of the Post."

Samuel Drew, born in Chenango County in 1836; educated in Otsego County and enlisted, Oct. 10, in Co. E, 6th N.Y. Cavalry; mustered in at Staten Island, Oct. 10, 1861. He did splendid service with his regiment; was wounded near Barryville during Sheridan's retreat in the Shenandoah, Sept. 17, 1864; sent to hospital at Arlington Heights, thence to Baltimore, Philadelphia and Albany, and in February transferred to the Third Veteran Reserve Corps; participating in the battles of Antietam, Gettysburg and Chancellorsville. Discharged, Sept. 12, 1865. Located at Hartwick in 1877. He joined the Duro Post as a charter member, and at the present time is Junior Vice Commander. He is now residing at Hartwick with his family, wife and daughter aged 16." [4]

There are other records just as honorable. Please remember also the many brave men who came home from war and had no desire to ever hear a word about its horrors again, such as Augustus Bush, another ancestor of Donald Holdridge who did not want to talk about the war and wouldn't join the G.A.R. Post that gave his son in law William such pleasure. Then there were those who didn't make it home, such as William Richards ancestor, Philander Richards, who fell at Spotsylvania and may or may not, be buried under the monument in the Robinson cemetery that bears his name." [3]

Regular meetings of the H.N. Duro Post were held the first and third Saturday evenings of each month.

1892 officers:

Lester Murdock	Commander
William Blanchard	Sr. Vice Commander
Samuel Drew	Jr. Vice Commander
W.A. Johnson	Chaplain
Emmet M. Irons	Officer of the Day
James Simmons	Adjutant of the Post
Ansel McTice	Surgeon of the Post
Allen Colton	Quarter Master Sargent
Cornelius Bird	Sargent Major[4]

Information from the newspaper:

1890— "Several Grand Army Boys go to the battlefield of Gettysville this week on free passes issued by the State to all soldiers who participated in that memorable battle of the War"

1895 "Several of our Grand Army boys attended the State G.A.R. encampment at Saratoga Springs."

1895 "Several G.A.R. members attended the Soldier's gathering in Oneonta last week." [2]

1901 "Union Memorial services for President McKinley—The Grand Army, Macabees and the Odd Fellows attended in a body."

FROM THE. G.A.R. RECORD, PACKAGE 34. H.N. DURO POST 653, DESCRIPTIVE BOOK. P3

"At a regular meeting Sept. 2nd, 1911 only five members were present when it was unanimously agreed by a vote, to surrender the Post's Charter, on account of the decreased membership and being almost impossible to get a quorum together. James H. Parks." [6]

In good standing when surrendering charter: Jacob Nickle, Cornelius Bird, George Tanner, James H. Parks, Lewis Briggs, Charles Nelson Markel, Edwin D. Lake, Emmett M. Irons.

Members of the H. N. Duro Post 653:

Blanchard, William	K,114 N.Y. V.
Bird, Cornelius	H 20 Regular
Colton, Allen	K, 10 N.Y. H A.
Card, Tabor	A, 1 N.Y. LA.
Drew, Samuel	E, 6 N.Y. C.
Gilbert, Addison	E, 2 N.Y. H.A
Holdridge, William	B 9th H.A
Irons, Emmet	E 121 N.Y. V.
Jenks, Thomas	H.152 N.Y. V.
Johnson, William	F, 121 N.Y. V.
Murdock, Lester	E, 121 N.Y. V.
McTice, Ansel	14 N.Y. H A.
Murdock, G. W.	G, 17 N.Y. V.
Simmons, James	I, 89 N.Y.V.
Wrigley, Abel	Ind. Co. Penn. Inf.

Other Members—Some from outside town-Copied from "G.A.R. Records, Package 5 H. N. Duro Post. No.65:

Geo. Tanner	Co. 6 Sharpshooter

J. E. Bisimer   Co. B 5 Regiment
John Moran (Burlington) 152 N.Y. V.
James VanAuken
Jacob Urkle(?)   Co.7 4 N.Y. ?
William Hughes   Co. E N.Y.
Jacob Micle   Co. E. N.Y. Cav.
Hiram E. Freelan   Co. D 2nd Reg.
Aaron Hearn (?)   Co H 152 N.Y.V.
Edgar B. Church

Other members of the H.N. Duro Post:
James H. Parker   U.S. Army
Uri (?) B. Shumway (New Lisbon)
     Co. K 86 Infantry
Allen Dickinson   Co. E. Heavy
     artillary
Stephen Ramsey (Laurens)
     Co. A 144 N.Y. V.
James Vosburg (Laurens)
C.G. Shaw
Warren Dunham
Lewis Briggs   Co. D 3 N.Y.
Charles N. Markel   Co. H 121st.

Edwin D. Lake
James Norris   Co. E. 2 N.Y. Cav.
John Newell(Laurens)   Co. H. 76th.
Cortland Tilley (Laurens)
Hiram J. Persons   "
Andrew Blakley   "   Co. K 4 N.Y.
Peter Neye(?)
Millen P. Voast(?)   Co. K 2nd H.A.
John J. Clifford   Co. 13 N.Y. H. A.
Henry Freelan   H.   152 N.Y.

Graves Decorated by Duro Post:
Alger, Chester   E, 12 N.Y. V
Clark
Higbie, Milton   Bates Battery
Luce, Harvey
Pickins, Edwin   H, 152 N.Y. V.
Rinders, Geo.   121 N.Y. V.
Wicks, James
Westcott,
Walker, Ripley   War of 1812

———

By: F.H.

Bibliography:

1. World Book Encyclopedia
2. Peggy MacGregor Letter, Historical Society, Hartwick
3. Peggy MacGregor Letter, Historical Society, Hartwick
4 Ellis, D.A. Published 1892 "Grand Army of the Republic"
5. GAR record, Package 3, H.N. Duro Post #653, Description Book p. 3
6. Ellis, D.A. Published 1892 "Grand Army of the Republic"

Independent Order of the Good Templar

The Templar Order, itself, was established about 1118 for the protection of pilgrims & the Holy Sepulcher. The Order of Good Templars was an Order among temperance men styled "Good Templars".[1]

One of the early societies in Hartwick was the Independent Order of the Good Templars. According to the Hurd's History of Otsego County, N.Y., between 1848 to 1878, lodges had been started in Hartwick Seminary, Hyde Part, South Hartwick, Toddsville, Hartwick village, Clintonville, and one in Hinman Hollow. Hartwick Seminary and Toddsville were inactive by 1878.[2]

"The Otego Valley Lodge # 733 IOGT was instituted Aug.7, 1874. The first officers were:

John M. Eldred	W.C.T.
Ellen M. Fields	W.V.T.
Rev. J. V. Newell	W.C.
Henry Walden	W.S.
Carrie Fields	W.T.

The present officers are. (1878)

Geo. Fields	W.C.T.
Miss Carrie Barney	W.S.
James Barney	W.C.
Present membership	25 [3]

Mr. Butterfield could not find where this lodge was located but it is listed under Hartwick in Hurd's History.

In 1878 " The county Lodge of the Good Templar was held here, Oct. 15 & 16. The public session was largely attended. Mr. Bruce from Madison had the principle address on Tues. Rev. A.J. Cook delivered the address of welcome which was responded to by B.R. Douglas of the State On Wed. several addressed the group." [4] The scrapbook clipping did not mention where it was held.

The only other mention of the I.O.G.T. was: " The Good Templars of this village will hold a peach Festival next Thursday." [5]

What started out as 7 lodges in the Township, apparently faded away.

———

By: F. H.

Bibliography

1. New International Dictionary
2. Hurd's History of Otsego County pg. 37
3. Hurd's History of Otsego County pg. 164
4. Old Scrapbook
5. Old Potter Scrapbook

The Rebekahs

The background of the ritual & founding of the Rebekahs is based on the Biblical character, Rebekah. It was organized in 1851 as an auxiliary of the Independent Order of the Odd Fellows. The Rebekahs helped to look after the needy.

Several from Hartwick had joined the Golden Light Rebekah Lodge in Fly Creek. By 1911, there were more wishing to join so the members from Hartwick started the Otego Valley Lodge #460 in this town.

Some of the charter members were Mrs. Ella

Hartwick Rebekah Lodge, 1950; Back Row: Francis Weaver, Rose Shepard, Martha Carr, Myrtle Gill, Henrietta Hetzler; Middle Row: Gertrude Morse, Catherine Garvin, Thelma Bunn, Diana Marlette, Lolita Clark, Mildred Tubbs; Front Row: Elenor Jones, Bernice Fuller, Agatha Harrington, Alice Shafer, Susie Potter

Sill, Mrs. Elinor Jones, Mrs. Carrie Robinson, Mrs. Martha Fuller, Mrs. Eva Pattingill, and Ralph & Susie Potter,

Officers installed Jan. 2, 1912:

Susie Potter   Noble Grand
Elinor Jones   Vice Grand
Ella Sill   Secretary

Carrie Robinson was the delegate to the State Assembly in Binghamton. Her expense was $10.00.

Jan. 2, was the 16th meeting of the lodge. They had initiation nearly every meeting as so many were joining.

In 1912 they had a float in the Fourth of July Parade. They took part in parades and community events in the following years.

Thelma Bunn joined in 1928 when she was 18. She remembers there were over 100 members. There were two rows of members sitting around the hall. Thelma was a member for 70 years & Noble Grand for over 30 years.

The members didn't want to miss a meeting! Before she had a car, Agatha Harrington walked from the foot of Hemlock Hill where she lived to the Lodge rooms on 205. Before this, she lived up on what is now Weeks Road, and walked from there. One night she wore a new coat. Going home she met a skunk! Her new coat had to be thrown out. Others also walked to the Rebekah Meetings.

Like other groups, the Rebebahs had parties. At Christmas they had dinner, a program & then a Christmas Tree. They also had public dinners & bake sales.

They were active in Hartwick and also in the District. After the Odd Fellows sold the hall, they met in member's homes. In 1999 they consolidated with the Oneonta Lodge.

———

By: F. H.

Maccabees

"**K**nights of the Maccabees—A large secret beneficiary society formed in Ontario, in 1878 and introduced into the United States in 1881, having a ritual based on the characteristics of the ancient Maccabean family."[1]

About 1901 the Maccabees were organized in Hartwick by the efforts of Misses McElhenny & Eldred of Cooperstown. They rented the Odd Fellow hall for their lodge meetings (upstairs in the Sergent Block). "Both orders will occupy the same room, having different nights of meetings." [2] The Maccabees are progressing nicely and bid fair to number 50 in short time. [3]

I was told by Mr. John Mott that the Maccabees had a very good insurance policy. Many joined to obtain the insurance.

They were also active socially. They held ice cream socials, suppers, and picnics. In 1912, they held their annual picnic at Walnut Grove. "Half fare tickets will be sold by members – Games, Sports and races will be held." [5]

1912 "The Maccabees have received a consignment of furniture for their new quarters over Gardners store, formerly occupied by the I.O.O.F. The rooms are being papered & painted & otherwise beautified. All the furnishings are to be in Mission finish." [6]

In 1902, "The K.O.T.M. are agitating the subject of erecting a hall on South Street on the north side of the school lot. I don't know what happened, but it was on that lot the I.O.O.F. built their hall in 1912. [7]

Undated and Unidentified

Certificate:

Maccabees Home and Relief Association

This certificate that Sir Knight G.O. Mayne of tent #641 is a member of Maccabees— Home Relief Association and entitled to full participation of all Benefits.

Dated   April 21, 1921 D.F. Morkey, Pres. [8]

From this certificate we know the Maccabees were still in Hartwick in 1921.

By: F. H.

1.   Websters Dictionary
2.   Old Potter Scrapbook
3.   Old Potter Scrapbook
4.   Eva Murdock
5.   Elisabeth Lough Curry Scrapbook
6.   Elisabeth Lough Curry Scrapbook
7.   Old Potter Scrapbook
8.   Henry Murdock

Women's Village Improvement Society

The Hartwick Historical Society is fortunate to have an original manuscript of a speech given at the 7th annual meeting of the Women's Village Improvement Society in 1896 which gives a history of their accomplishments till that date. It gives us some insight into village life before the turn of the century.

We have assembled this evening for two objects, 1st to procure funds for advancing our work, 2nd to celebrate the 7th anniversary of the Women's Village Improvement Society. Thinking it would be of interest to the public, the Society requested that a history in a condensed form be presented to you this evening.

The origin of the W.V.I. Society is as follows. Dec., 1889 two friends attempted to reach the Post Office but the deplorable condition of the side walks made progress almost impossible. It was then and there decided that the ladies make a move towards the improvement of our village. Hence, after many meetings it was decided we have an entertainment Feb. 6 where the entire village could be represented and permanent organization formed.

The interest manifested on that occasion can be ascertained from the fact that $51.67 was the net proceeds of the meeting. A constitution framed and written by Robert L. Luce was read and adopted on that evening and with the exception of three amendments it remains entire. Doubtless many present recall the purport of the document

On that occasion officers for the ensuing year were elected. Namely President, Vice President, Sec'y and Treasurer. The executive committee being appointed by the President. Our meetings to be held the first Tuesday in

While talking about the new sidewalks, I became curious about the first ones that were laid in Hartwick. They were laid in 1908. What is now Chester Winslow's Law Office was then a general store. As near as I can tell, it was run by Dorr Gardener. Half of the store was a general clothing store and the other side was a grocery store. What was not too long ago the old Victory Store run by Joe Fields was then the Cottage Hotel — C. Dudley. As you can see, the work was all done by hand with the help of buckets of water and horse-drawn wagons to haul supplies. You will note that the sidewalk was laid right across what is now Route 205 to afford safety to those walking on foot across the then dirt highway. Note that the trees were then old trees. There was a barber shop in the building in the foreground, and it was run by Chapman. I am told this gentleman was the great grandfather to John Chapman of West St., Hartwick and Don Chapman of Oneonta. Thought you'd like this item. Photo reproduced through courtesy of New York Historical Association, Cooperstown, New York.

each month and on March 4th, it was voted to purchase a lamp for the bridge in the centre of the village. In April a number of gentlemen were invited to meet with the Executive committee to decide the best methods of improving our sidewalks. It was concluded to use gravel and twenty eight days work was volunteered for that purpose. They worked several days and improved the walks materially.

At the May meeting, $50.00 was voted for the repairing of the same. As many were opposed to gravel and objected to having it used on their lots the work was abandoned.

It was then decided to purchase street lamps which cost about $7.00. Sept. 17th the Executive Committee met to consider the feasibility of laying cross walks. J. H. Barney would furnish stone for 6¢ per sq. ft. M. H. Field was appointed to see that the stone was gotten and delivered in a proper manner, also to select lamp posts and see to the setting of the same. John Burlingham being hired to assist.

Our finances were never so low as the present year. We have usually had our entertainment earlier in the season. This has been a year of unusual depression as we are all aware and it was deemed wise not to bring our wants to the public more than was really necessary. Seven years ago it was much easier to raise $50.00 than today. The call for ladies work and funds have multiplied surprisingly. I knew of only five officered societies in the village, if I mistake not, there are fifteen at the present time that sustain life by entertainments, socials etc. Few towns can boast of more enterprising people than Hartwick. Aside from the above each church has Bible Day, Children's Day, also Christmas, Decoration and Independence Day. All call for funds and labor. Our expenses have increased materially the past four years notwithstanding we are desirous of procuring more lamps as they are needed in many places. We shall make an effort in that direction as soon as possible.

We have had sixty two names on our roll and with scarcely an exception they have been workers. The public have responded nobly to each and every call and on behalf of the Society, I thank you for the past, and as far as is convenient and agreeable all future contributions will be fully appreciated. Wishing success to all public enterprises, and in the future as in the past, we are ready to assist in every laudable enterprise.

To give an itemized account of all money received and expended would be long and tedious but I will read a statement of each year. The treasurer's book is open for inspection and will show that each penny has been accounted for.

Treasurers statement for:

1890	Cr.	$135.06	1894	Cr.	102.37
	Dr.	111.11		Dr.	83.72
	Bal.	23. 95		Bal.	59.23
1891	Cr.	56.15	1895	Cr.	73.58
	Dr.	35.02		Dr.	83.11
	Bal.	39.64		Bal.	49.70
1892	Cr.	73.80	1896	Cr.	29.99
	Dr.	44.03		Dr.	73.61
	Bal.	74.85		Bal.	6.08
1893	Cr.	73.55			
	Dr.	107.82			
	Bal.	40.58			

Therefore the entire amount raised by the society in past seven year is $544.50 all of which with the exception of $6.08 now in the treasury has been expended for the improvement of our village.

Footnote: A mention of the Society was found in the Hartwick Review and Visitor, Nov. 6, 1902. "Ladies Village Improvement Society meets the first Tuesday of each month. President, Mrs. May Sliter, Vice president, Mrs. J.M. Bush, Secretary, Mrs. Carrie Williams, Treasurer, Mrs. Ida Burch. Their aim was to make a decaying village converted into beautiful resorts."

By: A. Harrison

W.C.T.U

The Women's Christian Temperance Union (W.C.T.U.) is a non-profit organization that works to lessen social problems. The first Union was organized in Cleveland, Ohio in 1874.[1] The chief aim of the WCTU is to educate people, especially youth, on the harmful effects of alcohol, other narcotic drugs and tobacco. The WCTU has helped enact State laws

Packing gifts for the County Home kept members of the Hartwick WCTU busy the other day. Part of the membership is shown here with an array of gifts to make a merrier hiloday. Left to right: Mrs. Florence M. Groff, Mrs. Gertrude Turney, Mrs. Gertrude Elmer, Mrs. Susie Potter, Mrs. Edith Cronkite, Mrs. Grace Morehouse, Mrs. Grace Whitney, Mrs. Rose Shepherd. Newspaper photo 1941.

requiring schools to teach about such effects. WCTU programs also promote good citizenship, child welfare, world affairs and humanitarian concerns. The WCTU developed out of the Women's Temperance Crusades of 1873. During this campaign, women church members, went into saloons, sang hymns, prayed and asked the saloon keepers to stop selling liqueur."[2] We find the Hartwick W.C.T.U. tried to carry out the aims of the National Union. Through the work of the second president, Frances Willard (1879-1898), the organization became a strong Union.

"The organization of the W.C.T.U. worked through the churches to spread their Union.

Amelie U. Burgess spoke in the Methodist Episcopal Church to encourage the women to unite to help solve the alcohol problem. Hartwick, as well as through out Otsego County, had many disturbances and crimes committed because of drunkeness and also many abused spouses."[3]

This meeting was followed by the organizing of the local W.C.T.U. in 1903. We see by the number who joined that the women (and some men) realized there was a problem and wanted to help solve it. In 1907 there were 52 members. Half of the member's husbands were either farmers or employed by the Otsego and Mohawk Railroad. The rest were made up of the wives of three clergymen, wives of two principals, wives of a Doctor, merchants, butchers, a tin peddlar, clerks, carpenters and three unskilled laborers. This was an unusual group as most membership were made up of mainly the wives of businessmen and professionals. [4]

Of the 52 members, 41 were affilliated with one of the churches so they were familiar with conducting meetings and serving on committees. Because of these affilliations, churches were influenced to start regular temperance programs. [5]

In 1908, The Otsego Farmer reported that the Christian Church did more then just present lessons. "The Sunday School of the Christian Church was made more interesting on Sunday last, by the singing and recitations by several boys of the primary class, all appropriate to the temperance lesson which was of special interest." (When I was growing up in the 20's and 30's, Mrs. Lula M. Morse gave a temperance lesson every quarter in Sunday School.) The other two churches also had special programs.

Besides encouraging children and adults in the churches and the Sunday Schools to abstain from drinking alcohol, the WCTU worked in schools where they could reach all the children. They subscribed to the "Crusade Monthly" (The WCTU's children's magazine) for the school and gave the book "The Life of Frances Willard" and also her picture. [6]

Another way the WCTU reached children was through the Loyal Temperance League (LTL). Hartwick also had an active LTL. There were games, marching, lively songs such as "Saloons Must Go" by Frances Willard. The members participated in rallies and competed in oratorical and musical contests. The LTL encouraged the boys to vote for prohibition when old enough to vote and the girls to join the Young Womens Christian Temperance Union when they were of age. [7]

Not only was the LTL active early in 1900s but was still active, in theory at least, through the 30's. In an item in the Hartwick Reporter it seems that most, if not all the members held office: "President-Miranda Wilson, second President-Howard A. Ainslie, First Vice President-Rowena Mead; Second Vice President-Marie Turner; 3rd Vice President-Richard Kelsey; 4th Vice President- Diana Harrington; Secretaries-George Ainslie, Archie Ainslie, Melrose

Harrington; Treasurer-Marjorie Wilson; helpers- George Ainslie, Donald Bush; Drill Master-Loleta Mead, Assistants- Norma Oldfield, Irene Tuller; Librarians- Frances Murphy, Ruth Bush; Song Leaders- Ruth Bush, Alice Ainslie, George Ainslie, Martin Bush, Donald Bush; Visiting Comm.- Smith Shepard, Assistant-Howard Ainslie; Minute Men Leaders- Jeanette Murphy, Ella Kelsey, Alice Ainslie, Betty Jean Francis; Play Superintendents Frederica Potter, Martin Bush, Melrose Harrington and Letha Balcom. LTL leader is Miss Lina Potter." [8] Just as the LTL combined merrymaking with temperance instruction, so did the Young Womens Christian Temperance Union. In 1907 the YWCTU held a picnic for themselves and their invited guests at Rainbow Falls, just north of the village. "Good weather, went wading, several fell in for fun, all very happy." Unlike the LTL, the YWCTU members took a more active part in the WCTU. In 1908 the Y's elected Kate Bush to serve as delegate to the annual WCTU County convention in Unadilla and present a paper "What are the needs of the Y's?"

The WCTU had a department for the "Supression of Impure Literature." They devoted one meeting to this but the minutes do not tell if they followed up by inspecting schoolbooks and textbooks or if they only examined those in their homes. [9]

At the same time, a Medical Temperance Department was formed. One thing they worked against was the popular Patent Medicines (which were made mostly of alcohol). [10]

A large number of the population of Hartwick worked for the Railroad so the WCTU organized a Department to work with these men. Grace Sheldon, wife of a motorman, was made the superintendent. Free literature was put in the depot. [11]

Besides working for temperance, the local was

against gambling. In 1908, the members ordered anti-gambling literature from Albany, presumably to distribute to Hartwick residents. They wrote a letter to the State Senate and the Assembly urging them to support a bill which would restrict gambling as well as indecent shows. (The fairs were important to them and there was much gambling on the horse races.) The Senate did later outlaw the games that relied purely on chance such as dice, slot machines or "Drawing the paddles - with sealed prizes." (but not the betting!) [12]

They were also against Sunday Baseball. They sent a letter to Assemblyman Lavern B. Butts against it. [13]

In 1908, they educated themselves with a lecture by Mrs. Ella Stewart on women suffarage. [14]

From the beginning this group worked to help the poor, the sickly, and their neighbors. They established a reading room for the community and even a place in it where an impoverished member could lodge. For a time their meetings were held there. [15]

One of the departments that sometimes required two to head it was the Flower Mission. It had four in 1908. This department took flowers and gifts to the ill, shut-ins, grieving members and the needy. "By November 1907, the department had distributed 65 bouquets, 30 texts, one can pickles, apples, squash, 15 dinners, 6 bushels potatoes and made 50 visits." [16] Some meetings were given over to sewing. Later the WCTU packed Christmas boxes of goodies. These were distributed to the people in the County Farm (The Meadows).

The Local Union had dues of 50¢ a year. They also served suppers, 15¢ a dinner, later 25¢, and took a collection at meeting. Collections were never over 65¢ between 1907-1909. Some years they sold items and filled coin cards to raise money for their causes. [17]

The treasurer's record shows how the WCTU helped people locally and across the country. A few of the entries:

—1908 $6.00 sent to the county Chairman for prohibition

—$5.00 Paid Mrs. Lula Walker for her Sunday address

—1909 10¢ for twins to wrap a box of flowers for the Utica Hospital

—1910 $7.00 to Edward Risley treasurer of the Hartwick Band

—1911 $5.00 sent to Helen Bullock Training School

—$2.50 freight on box of clothes for Live Oak School

Helped flood victims

—1912 $5.00 Mrs. Ella Stewart for sufferage literature.

$3.00 supplies for colored school

10¢ Good cheer box for Mrs. Sheldon

—1912 40¢ 2 books "Story of Frances Willard"

7¢ Red Turkey calico

20¢ 2 yds. cotton cloth

—1913 $4.00 given to women's shelter in Chicago

—1915 $3.00 Supplies to colored School.

$25.00 to Live Oak School

—15¢ wire netting and tacks for Mrs.—window.

—1916 $1.49 "Milford Tidings" for No Licence paper

Even though the local Union was busy sewing for the needy, helping the causes of the National Union and caring for the needs of their members, they never forgot that their primary purpose was to work for prohibition and educate.

The local Union members read the "National Union Leader" and the Hartwick WCTU responded to requests made by the National organization regardless of their relevance to Hartwick. For example, in 1903, it authorized the secretary to write in support of the Hansborough Anti-polygamy amendment to the Constitution. In

1905, it had funded evangelistic work in Utah. It is highly doubtful that polygamy was a problem in Hartwick! The National Union had alerted the Hartwick WCTU to the importance of the pending bill and the local members had lent their assistance....despite the fact it had no bearing on their lives. [18]

In 1915 there was a temperance lecture in town; Hartwick, N.Y. May 11, "Last Friday evening a large audience was present to listen to a message delivered by Charles Howard, an ex-convict from Dannemora prison. The address was very powerful and was appreciated by the congregation. He laid bare his own life in spite of its humiliations, in order that by so doing, he might create a sentiment among thinking people, that would arouse them to a more conscientious vote. After the meeting proper, a conference was held and a large number of signatures were secured to work for prohibition."

The WCTU was willing to use a form of blackmail to influence the local merchants;

1913 or 1915 "at the recent town election some of the business men maintained that if the town should vote for license, it would be greatly to the advantage of the business interests. The members of the WCTU and a number of others have decided to let the businessmen test their Theory for the next two years for themselves and have voted to transfer their patronage to other businessmen who do not hold this theory but believes that no license would be better for the businesses of the town." [20]

Another time that the WCTU participated in local politics was back in 1909. At that time the Hartwick Union actively campaigned for a town ordinance that would have prohibited licensing tavern owners, store keepers, physicians and hotel keepers to serve or prescribe alcohol. Between 1908—1909 almost all the townships in Otsego County voted on the question. It is apparent, however, that the Hartwick women actively sup-ported the referendum by distributing literature among the voters and tried to convince male relatives to vote against licensing. Despite their work, the referendum was defeated in Hartwick. [21]

The Local Option Law gave communities the right to decide if their town would sell alcohol or vote "No License."

1917 "The license people have circulated a petition and filed it. The question will come before the voters at the coming election. The town went 'No License' two years ago by the majority of 77." [22]

In 1918 the 18th ammendment was passed and went into effect in 1919. Even though this prohibited the sale of alcohol, the WCTU still had their work to do. Like all communities, Hartwick had their stills that supplied the people their liquor. There was one on East Hill. It was raided almost every week, but it seems there was never an arrest. There was one over in Burlington. She too, never was arrested. When she was told of an upcoming raid, she would push her old model-T Ford over the well where she kept her liquor. Probably a half dozen cider mills were in the township so there was always a supply of hard cider. [23]

After the repeal of the 18th Amendment, the three hotels were back in business and a new bar room opened. The WCTU worked hard to have the sale of alcohol outlawed.

The Local Option was used and often the question -Giving a license to sell liqueor in Hotels and Boarding Houses-was defeated but a package license to sell beer and wines in stores was usually passed.

January 1954   "The first beer to be sold legally in the town of Hartwick since before the days of national prohibition has gone on sale.

The Otsego County Alcoholic Beverage Control Board has granted a license for the sale of beer for off premise consumption to O. S. Burch and Son, a Hartwick grocery store which has been in operation by the same family since 1879."

Membership declined over the years but the WCTU remained active. In a 1935 meeting, we find members reading letters and articles on prohibition. The collection was 75¢... Flowers were brought by different members..also a large basket of gladiolus by Mrs. Lynn Sill. Refreshments were served. The flowers were carried to shut-ins and "as voted at a former meeting, a bouquet was to be placed on the grave of Mrs. Lucina Potter, our local president, from the time the Union was formed until her death; a period of over 25 years." A bouquet was placed on the grave of Mrs. Eva Edmunds who the Union lost by death last year. There were 9 members and 6 visitors present. [24]

The 40's & 50's continued to have about the same number of members attending meetings.

Hartwick Reporter   Dec. 28, 1945

"At the W.C.T.U. all day meeting with Mrs. Lizzie Talbot, to pack basket for the County Home and the aged people of this community, A delicious dinner was served at noon. There were ten present and over 150 baskets were filled. The W.C.T.U. wishes to thank all who contributed and helped."

Not only were the faithful members growing older but death was claiming them one by one.

On October 9th, 1960, Grace Whitney's death occurred and the last meeting was held October 14, 1960. The treasurer reported flowers sent to Mrs. Whitney's funeral and there was "no balance" on hand. That was the last meeting recorded in the treasurer's book. [25]

The W.C.T.U. had a great influence on the quality of life in the village of Hartwick.

By: Frederica Hornbeck

1. Encyclopedia
2. World Book Encyclopedia 1996
3. Adams, Gretchen, "To Make The World More Homelike, The Women Christian Temperance Union"(1907—1909) Pg.8 Coop. Graduate Prog.
4. Adams, Gretchen, "To Make The World More Homelike, The Women Christian Temperance Union"(1907—1909) Pg.6 Coop. Graduate Prog.
5. Adams, Gretchen, "To Make The World More Homelike, The Women Christian Temperance Union"(1907—1909) Pg.19 Coop. Graduate Prog
6. W.C.T.U. TREASURER Book
7. Adams, Gretchen, "To Make The World More Homelike, The Women Christian Temperance Union"(1907—1909) Pg.21 Coop. Graduate Prog
8. Clipping, The Hartwick Reporter"
9. Adams, Gretchen, "To Make The World More Homelike, The Women Christian Temperance Union"(1907—1909) Coop. Graduate Prog
10. Adams, Gretchen, "To Make The World More Homelike, The Women Christian Temperance Union"(1907—1909) Pg.27 Coop. Graduate Prog
11. Adams, Gretchen, "To Make The World More Homelike, The Women Christian Temperance Union"(1907—1909) Coop. Graduate Prog
12. Adams, Gretchen, "To Make The World More Homelike, The Women Christian Temperance Union"(1907—1909) Pg.29 Coop. Graduate Prog
13. Adams, Gretchen, "To Make The World More Homelike, The Women Christian Temperance Union"(1907—1909) Coop. Graduate Prog
14. Adams, Gretchen, "To Make The World More Homelike, The Women Christian Temperance Union"(1907—1909) Coop. Graduate Prog
15. Adams, Gretchen, "To Make The World More Homelike, The Women Christian Temperance Union"(1907—1909) Coop. Graduate Prog
16. Adams, Gretchen, "To Make The World More Homelike, The Women Christian Temperance Union"(1907—1909) Coop. Graduate Prog
17. Adams, Gretchen, "To Make The World More Homelike, The Women Christian Temperance Union"(1907—1909) Coop. Graduate Prog and Treasurers Record
18. Adams, Gretchen, "To Make The World More Homelike, The Women Christian Temperance Union"(1907—1909) Coop. Graduate Prog
19. Elis. Lough Curry's scrapbook
20. Old Potter scrapbook
21. Adams, Gretchen, "To Make The World More Homelike, The Women Christian Temperance Union"(1907—1909) Pg.29 Coop. Graduate Prog
22. Elis. Lough Curry's scrapbook
23. Interview with Henry Murdock
24. W.C.T.U. Minutes
25. Treasurers Book

Independent Order of the Odd Fellows

In 1815, at a convention in Manchester, England, the Independent Order of Odd Fellows, Manchester Unity was formed. The I.O.O.F. was introduced into the U.S. in 1819. They organized to help those in need. [1]

The annual State Convention was held in Oneonta in 1953. A reporter asked a 37-year member from Binghamton about the origin of the I.O.O.F. He said it was called "Odd Fellows" because there were 5 (odd number) original members (fellows). Another one said it received its name from the fact the order was established in England to provide care for the aged and orphans. Before this only the Government had done this - so they were thought "Odd Fellows."[2]

The first recorded meeting of the Hartwick I.O.O.F #585 was held Sept. 25, 1848.

They had 70 members in 1858. For some unstated reason, perhaps membership declined due to the Civil War, the Lodge was reinstated in 1871 as no. 271. [3]

From a clipping in an old scrapbook (1879-1880);

"Odd Fellows.- At the public meeting of Hartwick Lodge, I.O.O.F., held at the Harrington & Norton's Hall last Saturday evening, the following persons were installed as the officers for the ensuing term, by District Deputy M.L. Halbert: E. Robinson N.G.; A.S. Hollister, V.G.; H.A. Hurd R.S.; H.S. Bradley, P.S.; J.H. Jenks, treas.; A.A. Avery, Warden; E.L. Sergent, Con.; M. Aldrich, R.S.N.G.; S. Harrington, L.S.N.G.; G.D. Harter, R.S.V.G.; Daniel Wheeler, L.S.V.G.; C. Kellogg, R.S.S.; A. Kenyon, L.S.S.; H.J. Luceo, G.; Q. Murdock.G. After the installation services, Rev. S.M. Cook made a few appropriate remarks, after which the company marched to the dining room, where, between fifty and sixty persons were served an excellent oyster supper, furnished by Messrs. Harrington and Norton. They very courteously complied with the rules of the Order in closing their bar for the evening, and everything passed off quietly. All seemed to enjoy the occasion very much, and many who were present became convinced that "Odd Fellowship" did not approve of anything so immoral as some would make it appear."

The Odd Fellows started having an annual dance in 1891 as we can see from the program in 1895:

Fourth Annual Festival and Ball
Hartwick Lodge, I.O.O.F. No. 271
At Irish Hall, Feb. 7th, 1895
Music by Prof. Maples Orchestra
Bill $1.50   No extras
Committee
H.O. Branch   J.T. Curry   E. Rockwell

The fifth Annual Festival & Ball was held at Gardners Hall, Feb 7, 1896 with music by the Hartwick Orchestra; Full bill, $1.50. The committee was J.T. Curry, L. Rockwell and J.H. Jenks. [4]

Another newspaper clipping, no date, "about 200 people attended the I.O.O.F. dance held last Friday evening at the Otego Valley Hotel-music furnished by Walcott's Orchestra of Oneonta. They delighted the dancers and also those who went as spectators to listen to the concert."

The last dance I found advertised in the 'Hartwick Reporter' was at the Community Hall in 1942. Gents 55¢, Ladies free, Lunch Extra. There were probably more held!

The Brotherhood was loyal. If a member was in need, he was helped. If a member's family was in need, they were helped. Members would walk off the hills to attend meetings, after working all day.

They rented a meeting room upstairs in the Sergent Block. This room was shared by other organizations. In 1912, they wanted a place of their own and also a place for their sister organization, the Rebekahs, to meet. They hired David Willsey, contractor, to build their meeting hall, just north of the old Union School. (Their meetinghouse is now an apartment building).

The I.O.O.F. marched in parades, conducted services for departed brothers, attended local and State Conventions, held public initiations, held card parties and many dinners. They had wonderful oyster stew dinners. (Elmer Talbot was an expert at this). They were an active group.

Slowly membership decreased with the coming of outside interests. About 1979-80, t h e y sold their Lodge Hall to the Eastern Stars. The few remaining members met in homes, but soon felt the need for fellowship with other Odd Fellows, so they took their membership to the "Centennial Odd Fellows Lodge" in Oneonta. This Lodge is alive and active at this time.

By: F. H.

(1)   Encyclopedia Britannia
(2)   Clipping Oneonta Star 1953
(3)   I.O.O.F. Record Book
(4)   "Program" of dance (scrapbook)
(5)   Elisabeth Lough's scrap book (Linda Foody's)

Caption: Hartwick I.O.O.F—Back Row: Jasper C. Potter, Arnold Kolicker, Fred Gill, Ralph Weeks; Front Row: Ralph Potter, Clarence Bunn, Byron Fuller, J. Paul Jones

The Order of the Eastern Star

1961 Installation of Officers Hartwick Chapter, Order of the Eastern Star. Front: Mary Hoose, Geraldine Croft, Mildred Gregory. Back: Anita Harrison, David Skellie, Wilma Skellie Dodge

The Order of the Eastern Star originated as a social and benevolent organization composed of blood relatives of Master Masons. Many men and women in Hartwick belonged to Fly Creek Chapter #201 which organized in 1900 and regularly journeyed there for meetings.

In 1918 the decision was made to form a local chapter in Hartwick and thirty-six members demitted from Fly Creek to constitute Hartwick Chapter #617 with Sarah G. Smith as matron and Frederick Sheldon as patron.

Organizing members were Mary Branch Dickinson, Mary Burpee Backus, Stanley S. Backus, Sarah J. Smith, Josephine Knoch, Elizabeth Branch, Henrietta M. Hintermister, Diana Talbut, Kay Gardner, Grace Sheldon, Adelaide Lonsdale, Dr. B. H. Talbut, F. B. Sheldon, O. Alonzo Smith, Elizabeth Augur, Mary J. Ellsworth, Julia E. Ward, Daisy Shellman, Osie

A. Joslyn, Abbie P. R. Baumes, Martha S. Baumes Carr, Jessie M. Baumes Harrington, Lulu J. Adams Morse, Emma J. Burk, Bertha M. DeMett, Bessie L. Matthewson, Chester A. Matheson, Lewis A. Shellman, Herbert O. Branch, Etta A. Winton, Myrtle H. Brownell, Dorr Gardner, May M. Sliter, Ella Curry, Carrie L. Rainey Sill, Susan Chittenden, and Theresa Ingalls.

In addition to providing for local sisters in need, the activities of the chapter members often mirrored the conditions of the world around them. World War I saw them contributing to the Red Cross War Emergency Fund and attending Home Defense meetings. During the Depression winter clothing was collected f or the needy. Hartwick Chapter started a Christmas Fund for children within a radius of six miles from the chapter, which would have included the entire town of Hartwick.

During World War II the members knitted sweaters for service men and women and old phonograph records were collected for distribution to service centers. After the war the knitting continued with orphaned and refugee children being the recipients.

Today's efforts continue to be directed to assisting needy members, to providing scholarships to Eastern Star related students, knitting for veterans hospitals and supporting the Home in Oriskany, a beautiful and well run home for aged sisters and brothers.

Hartwick Chapter met in various rooms in the village finally settling in the Odd Fellows Hall on South Street. They bought and repaired this building when the Odd Fellows were unable to keep it going. They were active in Hartwick until 1983 when they consolidated with Otsego Chapter #201, the original Fly Creek Chapter that charter members had demitted from sixty-five years before, now to become Otsego-Hartwick Chapter #201. Over the years membership requirements have changed to include any woman, 18 or older, needing only a Masonic sponsor.

By: A. Harrison

Back:: William Harrison, David Skellie
Front: Mary J. Hoose, Anita Harrison (1965?)

Hartwick Rod and Gun Club

Henry said he belonged to the Rod and Gun Club in the thirties and for sixty-five years to 1997 and has a life membership now at 86 years of age (2001). He is the oldest living member. The first he knew where it was held was in garage that Doctor Steffie Baker had on South Street. It was the firehouse at that time. When Henry first joined in 1931 the meetings were held in Winslows office upstairs. Then moved to Winton's jewelry store when it was the firehouse at that time. Some of the members

Early members: M. D. Beckley, Karl Thomas, Claude Tilley, Byron Fuller, Fred Brown, Alex Foster

were Floyd Mead, Art Mead, Jack Potter, Waldo Potter, John Pan, Willard (Barb) Clark, Harold Clark, Lynn Green, Carlton Roberts, Fred Brown, H. L. Harrington, Ralph Weeks and Lyle Jones. These are ones he remembers the most. The Rod and Gun purchased the Power House property in the 1940's. Members built the clubhouse in 1960 and built up the dam. They sold bonds to raise money for the purchase. They only had 50¢ in the treasury to begin with. Some of the bonds

are still out. Henry was president for fifteen years. The club dammed up the pond to make a great place for fishing.

They send 2 or 3 boys to Conservation Camp every year. Frank Stewart was president after

Henry and served many years. They have more than three hundred members in 1999. They hold turkey shoots and trap shoots once a week. Members are from all over the United States. They meet the last Tuesday of every month. Henry and Conrad Lipicier cut wood for fuel for the club a few years. All members furnished wood and all participated in keeping it in repair. They held dances, picnics, barbecues and coon chases for members. Picture of club member's picnic is at the Rod and Gun Club building. It was held at Alex Forresters. Families were invited to attend and enjoyed themselves. A picture is at the Historical Society rooms donated by Donald Bush.

As told by Henry Murdock (1999)

History of Kinney Memorial Library & Hartwick Historical Center

On December 28, 1940 a group of Hartwick citizens filed a petition to the Town Board of Hartwick, New York to appropriate the sum of one hundred dollars per year to be used by the Hartwick Free Library for purchasing books and maintaining a library. The group then applied for a charter. On November 13, 1940 Frank L. Tolman of the Division of Adult Education and Library Extension wrote a letter explaining that in order to charter a library there must be evidence of tangible support of the town or school district. Mr. Tolman advised the Board to organize its materials and operate as an informal, unincorporated library until such time as more adequate financial support could be obtained.

The dream of many Hartwick residents became a reality with the opening of the Hartwick Free Library on May 23, 1943. It was the first genuine public library the village had ever had. Many book lovers and public-spirited residents visited it.

The room was attractively decorated by volunteers and a sign bearing the words "Hartwick Free Library" painted. There were about 700 books ready to loan and more new ones to be ordered in the near future. Use of the books was free to residents of the vicinity. Volunteer librarians were in charge Tuesday and Thursday afternoons and Saturday evenings.

Mrs. James Hamilton was instrumental in keeping the Hartwick Free Library going with only 1,000 books on the shelves. Unfortunately the time came when they needed a new fire hall and this building was torn down to accommodate the present Hartwick Fire Dept.

Robert A. Flores, a public Library consultant of the New York State Education Department, talked shop at a meeting of the Hartwick Town Board this week. L-R, Mr. Flores, Roy L. Butterfield, President of the Board of Trustees of the Hartwick Free Library, and J. P. Kinney, the donor. Standing is William Powers, Town of Hartwick Supervisor.

The old Hamilton House where the original Library was located.

At a special meeting of the Board of Trustees of the Hartwick Free Library on June 29, 1961 a proposal was presented from Arthur R. Kinney and J. P. Kinney to provide free of charge to the Town of Hartwick a suitable building for the housing of a public library provided that the maintenance and management of the library were assumed by the Town of Hartwick. The Trustees of the Hartwick Free Library adopted a resolution expressing willingness to turn over all publications and equipment of the existing library to the proposed Kinney Memorial Library and requesting the Town Board of Hartwick to accept the offered building and assume the obligations of supporting and maintaining the library under the conditions stated in the communication from the prospective donors of the residential property on Main Street. The property on East Main Street was owned by David M. Carr. The Town Board voted to accept the gift of the Kinney brothers and to assume the necessary obligations. The supervisor Mr. William Powers stated that under section 255 of the Education Law of the State the town is authorized to establish a public library, to acquire real or personal property for this purpose by purchase or gift and to appropriate funds thereafter. Thereupon Warren Lyon moved, Clark Miller seconded, that the Board accept a gift deed for the property offered to establish a town public library. Motion carried. The board was then required to raise $1,500 per year of the tax payers money to maintain and run the library.

The library building was given as a memorial to Joseph and Isabel (Stanhouse) Kinney, parents of the donors.

The first Board of trustees were Mrs. Porter Backus, Mrs. Waldo Potter, Roy L. Butterfield, Harry D. Bilderbeck and J. Donald Patterson. As many of the one thousand books from the previous library as could be used were placed on the new shelving in the pleasant new home of the Kinney Memorial Library. Mrs. Augusta Hollenbeck was hired as librarian and moved into the living quarters on the second floor of the library building. Kinney Memorial Library was officially dedicated November 18, 1961.

At the dedication Dr. H. Claude Hardy, Curator of the Yager Museum in Oneonta, and professor of Sociology at Hartwick College said "books are keys to wisdom's treasure, gates to lands of pleasure, paths that upward lead. Books are friends... come let us read."

At Dedication- Prominent at dedication ceremonies Saturday for the new Kinney Memorial Library were: seated from left to right, Harry D. Bilderbeck, Trustee; Dr. H. Claude Hardy; Mrs. Augusta Hollenbeck, Librarian; and Dr. Roy Butterfield, Chairman of the Library Board of Trustees. Standing, (l-r) Mrs. Waldo Potter, J. Donald Patterson, and Mrs. Porter Backus, Trustees.

In July 1978 Mrs. Augusta Hollenbeck decided to retire after 17 years of service. Known as Gussie to many of her friends, Mrs. Hollenbeck graduated from the former Hartwick Seminary and also from the New York State College of Agriculture in 1927.

"I enjoyed serving the community and want to say thanks for 17 years well spent" she concluded.

While Mrs. Hollenbeck was librarian, in March of 1962 the Kinney Memorial Library joined the Four County System. This meant we were joined through the system to Broome, Chenango, Delaware, and Otsego County libraries.

After ten years of being chartered provisionally the Trustees received word from the State Education Department that the absolute charter had been granted in 1972.

In July 1974 an open house was held marking the formal opening of the refurbished children's room as a memorial to the late Barbara C. Higgins, a library trustee.

On hand for the open house, among many others, was Mrs. Emily Potter who was to assume the duties of Librarian. Mrs. Potter graduated from New York State College for teachers, now known as SUNY Albany, in 1939 with a degree in Library Science. She then went to work at the Ilion Public Library as librarian. She moved to Hartwick and served as Director of the Sidney Public Library. Mrs. Potter then worked as librarian at the Cooperstown Senior and Junior High School until she retired and became librarian at the Kinney Memorial Library.

In June of 1999, Emily Potter passed away suddenly from a heart attack. Barbara Potter, who was a substitute, was asked to open the library and was appointed to run the library. The present board consists of Diane Domion, President; Joanne Telfer, Secretary; Barbara Dorsey, Treasurer; and Betty Derr, Anita Harrison, Lawrence Nelson, Martha Henaghen, trustees.

The library has been growing in circulation. We have members from Laurens, Milford, Coopertown, Schuyler Lake, Richfield Springs, and Mt. Vision.

The library is keeping up with the times with a total of 3 computers for the public to use. We also now have a webpage www.hartwickny.org for people to find hours and special events.

The collection has grown tremendously because of the great donations of books, tapes, and magazines and the continued support of the town. We have had numerous functions held at the library, including book readings, story times, book signings, sleepover, writing workshops, and grant workshops.

Town of Hartwick Historical Society

While Louis Jones directed growth of the New York State Historical Association he promoted history on the local level in Otsego County and invited the various towns to provide a presentation of their history. Our county Historian and our own Pearl Weeks selected a panel for a Hartwick night at Fenimore House in Cooperstown with Mr. and Mrs. Harry Bilderbeck to represent the village, Mrs. Porter Backus, Hartwick Seminary, Mrs. Martha Hollister, Toddsville; Kenneth Auger, Hinman Hollow; Ramon Chase, Chase; John A. Mott, White House; and Mrs. Menzo Balcom, South Hartwick. Dr. Roy Butterfield acted as moderator.

They know more about the Town of Hartwick than they had time to tell in three hours. Panelists who appeared in "Hartwick" session of local History Enthusiasts at Fenimore House were (L-R)
(Seated) Mrs. Harry Bilderbeck, Mrs. Porter Backus, Mrs. Martha Hollister, Kenneth Auger, and Miss Pearl Weeks.
(Standing) (L-R) Dr. Roy Butterfield, moderator and Otsego County historian, Ramon Chase, Mr. Harry Bilderbeck, John A. Mott, and Mrs. Menzo Balcom

Photographs were projected by means of an opaque projector along with a narration. The privately owned photos were copied for a slide presentation and prints were made for an archival collection. This was the beginning of our albums, and the original pictures were returned to the owners. The Hartwick Historical Society organized with this group.

The first meeting, as reported by "The Otsego Farmer" on April 24, 1969, read "sixty-two persons gathered at the new firehouse in Hartwick on Saturday evening, April 19, for the formation of a Town of Hartwick Historical Society."

Kenneth Augur of Hartwick was named chairman and he appointed nominating and by-laws committees, who would report at the next public meeting to be held on Saturday, May 3.

Sixty-two people signed up as charter members. The following officers were elected: President, Kenneth Augur; vice-president, Glenn Shepard; Secretary, Emma Chase; Treasurer, William Field. The secretary and treasurer each completed twenty years of service, retiring in 1989.

On Dec. 3, 1969 incorporation papers were completed by Chester Winslow and signed by the Board of Directors. By-laws were approved in Feb. 1970.

From the beginning one of the main concerns was the search for a permanent home. In 1972 plans were drawn up for an addition to the Kinney Memorial Library for the use of the historical society. A building fund was started. Members contributed $5 each to the fund. Many fund-raisers were held to raise money.

In 1973 an attempt was made to begin construction but these plans were not to be completed. The building funds were placed in a high interest account to await further developments.

In 1974 the fire hall became unavailable on the Society's meeting nights. From that time on the meetings were held in the Hartwick Grade Center, Hinman Hollow Grange, Christian Church, Christian Hill Grange, Hyde Park Fire Hall, Hub Restaurant, and Hartwick Community Center, as well as other places.

By 1986 the Revenue Sharing Funds had almost doubled. These combined with the society's own building fund seemed a starting point to reactivate plans for an addition to the library for the combined use of the Historical Society and library.

William Powers and Anita Harrison were appointed to approach the library board and in May 1987 they were reported to be in favor of going ahead with the building plans.

In July local fund raising had begun. Mrs. Anita Harrison wrote applications for grants, which brought in $5,000 from the O'Conner Foundation and $20,000 from the Nourse Foundation. Under her direction a fund raising letter was sent to all property owners in the township as well as to local organizations and businesses. This campaign brought in over $5,515. Mrs. Elizabeth Derr, Trustee made an application for a grant from New York State. With the help of Senator James Seward and Assemblyman John McCann a grant for $10,000 was awarded. The old barn on the property was sold and torn down. Henry Loeffler drew up plans for the addition.

John A. Croft, a local contractor, submitted the low bid and his company was soon at work. After he was finished, Marvin Zachow also did some work on the second floor.

In the fall of 1988 construction was begun

Attending the groundbreaking were: Francis Weaver, Gladys Harrison, Betty Derr, Deane Winsor, Frederica Hornbeck, Eva Chamberlian, Anita Harrison, Orlo Burch, Bill Powers, Reverend Denbleyker, Reverend Saxer.

and in January 1989, the society's regular meeting was held in the library and featured a tour of the new addition. The building was far enough along to allow for an open house during Hartwick Day's in 1989. The original library was carpeted and redecorated. The children's room was moved to the front of the building and the adult non-fiction was put in its new place. Adult fiction was put on the moveable shelving in the new building leaving the right side of the spacious room for the local history and the museum area. Much is due to Mr. and Mrs. William Harrison who donated their services to rearrange the shelving, do the necessary carpentry and the papering. The new building contains a climate-controlled room, a small stage, a kitchen area and ample space for meetings and programs. A ramp and one of the two restrooms provide for the needs of the handicapped. The upstairs area is used for storage.

The collection was moved out of the third floor of the school where Orrin Higgins had allowed the society space. The collections today are in the process of being catalogued, displayed and are continually growing. They include an extensive collection of photos donated by John Mott, many maps donated by the Augurs, and numerous items from many sources relating to Hartwick families, businesses and community affairs.

The society's continuing projects are cataloguing artifacts and papers, recording oral histories, and collecting files on town activities and families.

Currently our president is Anita Harrison; vice-president, David Petri; Secretary, Barbara Potter; Treasurer, Nadine Phillips; Assistant Treasurer, Janice Utter; and Assistant to the President, Brayden Dorsey. We meet January, March, May, July, September, and November on the third Thursday of the month at 7PM.

We welcome new members to sign up; we need the young and the young at heart. The ideas and people of today are what will make our historical society successful in the future.

By: Barb Potter

Information for this article from:

Nadine Phillips Scrapbook
Emily Potter
Bill Powers
John Mott
Historical Scrapbook

The Oneonta Star

Textile exhibit – 25th anniversary of Hartwick Historical Society – 1994

Other Organizations

Y. M. C. A.

1896—"There will be a purity meeting for men and boys at the Y. M. C. A. rooms next Saturday. The topic "A clean tongue": meeting to be led by Dr. Luce."

1896 — "The Y. M. C. A. will hold an entertainment and oyster supper on the evening of Thanksgiving Day. Every one invited to help sustain this grand organization."

1897 — "There will be an open meeting of the Y. M. C. A. at the Christian church on Sunday afternoon March 14, at 3:30. All interested in the work are invited to be present."

Red Cross

During the First World War, the Red Cross had a group in town.

"The regular Red Cross meeting was held Thursday afternoon. The following officers were elected:
Mrs. Clark Beach Chairman of the Auxility
Mrs. Chester Burch Secretary and Treasurer
Mrs. Fred Sheldon, Chairman of the work."

"The 'Auxilary' has moved into the Maccabee's Hall for the winter and the room will he open Thursdays daily during the cold months."

"The work is going on rapidly. Three completed sets have been sent to our boys; sets consisting of a sweater, mitts, scarfs and helmets. The packages have reached their destinations and the recipients have written back letters of 'Thanks'."

Another soldier even wrote the Red Cross ladies before he received his package! Ernest Augur wrote Mrs. Clark Beach to respond to her letter and had heard of the Red Cross package sent to him from her stepson, Clifford Beach, but his unit had been changed and his package had not caught up with him. He said the nights were cold at Camp Wadsworth at Spartenburg SC and he would appreciate the warm articles in the Red Cross package.

Early 1940's — "The Red Cross dance cleared $127, finishing the Hartwick quota of $600, making this branch the 3rd in the County to reach their goal."

The National Protective Legion

Hartwick Visitor - 1902

"A new organ has been placed in the Odd Fellows Hall. Three orders hold their meetings there; Odd Fellows, Maccabees and the new order, The National Protective Legion. An organ will be a valuable addition. It was secured of L. P. Shaul, our musical instrument dealer."

"One of our exchanges say, "Mrs. Jane Baniff has just received a dividend of $88.89 from the National Protective Legion and Mrs. Martha Stranton $30.00 sick benefit from the Protective Legion. The Hartwick National Protective Legion instituted a few weeks ago, have already many new members and applications are underway for more at the regular meeting Friday evening."

"Baked Bean Club"

"The Baked Bean Club of Hartwick has recently reorganized with a total membership of 35. This club is unique. It has no officers, no bylaws, no dues, no fees, and no secrets. It is voted a great success by it's members."

"The second annual picnic of the club has arranged to be held at the Field Grove on Friday the 25th – Wednesday - A portion of the club entertained the Pi Eta society of the Hartwick Union School at the home of Miss Nellie Hall on West Hill."

"On Saturday evening five members, Geo. Proctor, ? Shard, Herman Thomas, Ernest Augur and Byron Clark were guests of John Kirkpatrick, a prominent member on East Hill, in the form of a fishing trip to Goewey Lake, returning with 40 fine bullheads — and much rejoicing."

The Baked Bean Club certainly seemed to have been great fun while it lasted.

———

By: F.H.

Dedication of American Legion Hall Nov. 1958. Congressman Samuel Stratton in center.

Cemeteries

Old Potter Scrapbook   1878
"The cemetery in this village is to be dressed in a new fence in the spring."

Old Potter Scrapbook   Page 28, no date
"Notices are being sent out to the lot owners, as far as possible, of the incorporation of our village cemetery, and it is greatly desired that all those interested in lots in these grounds will see that the grass is removed and said lots put in a respectable condition at an early date."

Same page
"The effort to incorporate the village cemetery has progressed well, so far only two or three of those interested in the old individual association remaining to be transferred. Everyone who is interested seems to be in favor of something being done to establish the fact of it being handled in a more enterprising manner than it has been in past years. If the effort is successful, steps will be taken at once to construct a vault, enlarge the grounds, and care for the lots that have been so long neglected. Last season the grass was not even mowed and if something is not done it will be a disgrace to the village."

Old Potter Scrapbook   Page 39, 1883
"John, George, and Frank Wilson have recently erected a very pretty monument in our village cemetery, to the memory of their parents and two sisters who lost their lives in the burning of their dwelling last April."

Old Potter Scrapbook   Page 58, 1891
"A small yet neat white bronze monument was erected in our cemetery last week to the memory of the late Erastus Benjamin by W. H. Pratt and H. S. Bradley who are agents for the Bridgeport Monumental Company.

Ella May Harrington scrapbook 1894
"A cemetery company was incorporated at this place. It is hoped that the new company will be able to make terms with the Individual Association that has so long controlled our cemetery so that it may be enlarged and kept better."

Old Potter Scrapbook   Page 20, 1895
"The cemetery grounds so long neglected, begin to assume an air of respectability. The association is now having applications for lots."

Old Potter Scrapbook   Page 38,
"Several monuments have recently been erected in our village cemetery, 2 are quincy granite; one by Potter of Fly Creek for Dr. S. L. Robinson and wife; the other by McCabe Bros. of Cooperstown for Perry Barton."

By: Barbara Potter

Hartwick Cemetary

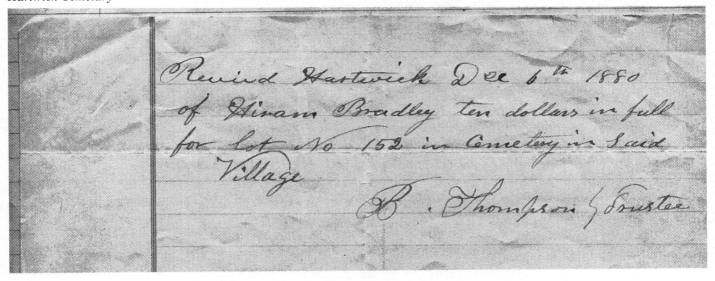

Received Hartwick Dec 6th 1880 of Hiram Bradley ten dollars in full for Lot No 152 in Cemetery in said Village

R. Thompson Trustee

Reurd Hartwick May 25 1885
of Erastus Benjamin ten dollars in full
for lot No 193 in Cemetery in said Village
Commncing at Iron Stak at Northe west Corner
of said lot runing South 24 feet to Corner of
A Bradleys lot thence East 13 feet to F H Bissill
lot thence North 24 feet to Iron Stak thence West
13 feet to place of begining containing 312 feet
of Land mor or less

　　　　　B. Thompson ⎫ Truste
　　　Elisha Robinson ⎭

Hartwick Mar 29/41
Received of Fannie Bradley
$10⁰⁰) Ten Dollars as payment
in full for burial H Bradley
in Hartwick Cemetery.
　　　B G Robinson, Supt
　　　Hartwick Cemetery

Weather

Isaac Bradley, who lived at the foot of Hemlock Hill when he was an old man, recalled that on the 2nd of November 1848, two feet of snow fell. This remained all winter. On the 17th of April, the following spring, Bradley dragged his sap buckets into the woods on a hand sled, not being able to go in with oxen.

Emmett M. Irons Diary Entries

It is said that from 1808 to the middle of the century the weather became colder. 1816 was known as "The Year without a summer." An inch of ice formed on the 10th of June and a foot of snow fell. There were frosts on the 10th of July and the 29th of August. Food and fodder were seriously short and many cattle died.

Emmett M. Irons Diary Entries

Within a week following the 14th of April 1857, there was a snowfall of 5 feet, roofs were crushed, livestock killed, and birds perished in great numbers. In 1859 there was snow on the Fourth of July, thus enhancing the reputation of Phinney's Almanac, which through a printer's error had predicted that very thing.

Emmett M. Irons Diary Entries

Potter Scrapbook

Sixty years ago, that is in the year 1838, we had as rainy a spring as we have had this year. An exchange says that the rainy season ended in a fierce snowstorm. Setting in on the 25th day of May and continuing all that day and night, so that on the morning of the 26th day of May, in some parts of central New York, the snow was from twelve to fifteen inches in depth. For the fun of the thing, several parents took their children to school in sleighs. That year is known as the cold year,

and scarcely any crops were raised. Grain of all kinds was scarce. Wheat was worth $3 a bushel and hard to get.

"The Great Snowstorm" April 14, 1857
Ward's Annals of Richfield

3' of snow fell, and in less than a week 5' of snow covered this entire region.

History of Cooperstwon

Much damage was done to trees and buildings, in April of this year, when snow fell to a depth of twenty to thirty-six inches on the 14th, and about 5 feet in three days. A great many barns, sheds, and a few dwellings were broken down by the weight of the snow.

Harvey Baker, in the Oneonta Herald of April 29, 1897

The big snow of April 1857, large as was the volume of water it contained, melted and flowed off into the Susquehanna doing no marked damage. That storm brought the largest body of snow ever at any one time lying upon the country within Otsego County, within my memory. It covered this entire region with a 7' body of very heavy snow, and it did more damage by crushing buildings, bridges and trees, than has any snow or flood in all the country during my lifetime.

As a result of this storm, much livestock was killed by falling roofs; while many wild pigeons perished from the lack of food. It is furthermore said that the dazzling light from the shining of the sun upon the vast area of snow was blinding.

Oneonta Herald & Democrat – January 6, 1879

Last Tuesday it commenced snowing and blowing, and up to the present time the roads leading to the hills from this village have been completely blocked up. A portion of the time it was impossible for the stage to get from Cooperstown. It has been the worst storm experienced here in years.

Freeman's Journal – November 1900

During the tornado, which swept over the vicinity last week, Wednesday, Mr. and Mrs. Gilbert Murdock had a narrow escape from a severe casualty. At the severest point of the wind they were passing the residence of A. W. Tiffany, where two of the large Balsam trees at the roadside were blown over, one of them striking their horse, knocking it down. The other tree struck the ground just at the rear of the carriage. They could neither go ahead or back up. Help had to be obtained and the trees removed before they could go on their way.

Hartwick Reporter – February 18, 1920
1920 Blizzard

Trolley line is completely paralyzed. No mail reaches Hartwick from Saturday night until about Tuesday noon.

Not a car was moving on Monday on the main line of the Southern New York railway. The company devoted all its efforts to manning the snowplows and breaking through the mountainous snowdrifts, which were piled high by the strong wind. Monday night the line was open between Hartwick and Richfield Springs only.

The first mail since Saturday night arrived from Oneonta about noon Tuesday. The Hartwick rural mail carriers have been unable to make their trips for several days.

Passengers were being cared for by village officials and farmers along the blockaded routes.

Otsego Farmer – October 2, 1927

Severe hail storm – size of walnuts – 6" deep – new 170 ft. hen house, Hartwick Hatchery blown down.

The Oneonta Star – January 1, 1970
Hartwick

The people in Hartwick and vicinity are

gradually getting plowed out so they can get out of their homes through some 3 to 4 feet of snow. Where the snow is piled up from shoveling and plowing our paths look like tunnels.

Many people who have snowmobiles have made very good use of them, some have gone back off the main roads, where they haven't been opened and brought sick people to the main road, where they could be picked up and taken to the hospital. Others took food in to people.

A crew of nine went back on the hills better than a mile and a half to the Goddard farm and carried food as they had not been able to get out. This was Wayne Bush, Mike Corcoran, and Allen Telfer on snowshoes and Clyde Tuller, David Burch, Bob and Dave Sellick, James Renwick, Jr., and Robin Bard on snowmobiles. This is just a few of many who have been helping those out who are snowed in and many of them still are.

DEAD STANDSTILL: *Typifying the condition of many vehicles following last week's snowfall, this Jeep pick-up was finally rescued Saturday by owner Henry Murdock of Hartwick. Murdock bogged down on Route 205; tried to dig himslef out; gave up and stuck up the shovel so he could locate the Jeep if snowdrifts covered it completely.*

The Freeman's Journal – Wednesday, June 23, 1976

Hartwick Hit Hard by Severe Storm

Although what occurred in the town of Hartwick last Wednesday night has not been "officially" termed a tornado, Walter Morrison, Otsego County Disaster and Civil Defense director said he believes it was one.

The severe storm which hit Hartwick about 3:30 PM Wednesday caused an estimated $250,000 worth of damage throughout the town. Two employees of the national weather service out of Albany were sent to Hartwick by Mr. Morrison to survey the debris and file a report.

Trees were lifted right out of the ground, wires and utility poles were downed and telephone lines were also blown to the ground during the severe wind storm. No one was reported injured during the storm or during the clean up operation, which followed.

The storm seemed to direct itself right through the center of town, blowing off the roof of the Hartwick firehall, lifting the garage – sales room at Wright's farm Supply on the North Street off its foundation, in addition to felling trees on a number of houses and two trucks.

A total of 50 trees were reported to have fallen and 24 buildings damaged or destroyed.

Jim Leslie's House

Gladys Harrison:

Everybody talks about the weather but no one does anything about it. However, it is always a good topic for conversation. A few years ago, some people tried seeding the clouds to make it rain. It usually rained, but not always where it was supposed to. It was soon abandoned as too expensive and not very reliable.

On Bowe Hill there is always a slight breeze and very often a harsh wind. I am only going to mention the severe windstorms, which I have first hand knowledge of.

In the early 20's, a severe windstorm blew down the Floyd Tilley barn. Shortly after they sold out and moved to Morris, NY.

In the fall of 1951, a land hurricane went through central New York. There was a heavy rain with it. I don't think I was ever so frightened by a storm before or since. It started blowing hard on Friday morning. We had deer hunters in the woods and they left in early afternoon. It really began in earnest in early evening. One had a feeling the house would explode. We had linoleum on the kitchen floor that raised up and went down when you walked on it. Shingles from the porch kept coming off and hitting the windows. We kept

People were busy all day Thursday in Hartwick trying to undo the damage done during Wednesday Night's severe wind and rain storm. Here, men are shown trying to lift this fallen tree from one of several homes that tress fell on.

the shades pulled but none were broken. It rained so hard that the rain came through the side of the house and came through the downstairs ceiling. I can't remember upstairs leaks except in the kitchen where some sharp strips of roofing were blown off. Merton finished milking and left the barn. We were careful not to open more than one door of the house at a time.

I don't remember trees being blown in our woods but in the Herman Harrison woods, many huge pines were toppled. The wind would take a strip where every tree went down. There was quite a bit blown down in some of the reforested area.

There has been some severe flooding on the hill when the road was washed out. The first with pictures to prove it was sometime between 1910 and 1915. The road in front of the homestead had a deep ditch in the middle. The Bowe Hill road was all dirt until 1937 so the water would have gone down the middle.

The big floods of 1935 also washed out parts of the road from the top of the hill down.

The lower end of the Bowe Hill that is still gravel washes out the sides whenever there is a hard storm. Now the road is not maintained after the Perry residence, however it is still passable with the right vehicle.

There was a severe wind was in June of 1987. A tornado ripped through between a machine shed on Paul Harrison's property and the LaVines's. It took a somewhat diagonal path in front of the LaVines's and into the Paul Harrison pasture. The cows were usually in that area prior to the milking time. Needless to say, it was some time before the cows were all rounded up, but they all survived. The storm took down a two-story heifer barn and sawmill. There was some roofing and debris near the line of fences between the Paul and Merton Harrison fields but most of it landed in a cornfield and meadow to the east side of the road. Some even blew over the pines on top of the hill.

About an hour after the storm a cow was seen behind our house headed back down the hill. She had been seen behind our barn before then. I think the wind must have helped her up the hill, how else could she have gotten so far in such a short time.

We were on our way home from Oneonta when the storm hit and arrived at the scene to see the LaVines out picking up boards, etc. from the road. We wondered what we would see when we got home but the storm hadn't gone up the hill. Some people quite a distance away saw the debris in the air.

The first lightning strike I remember was a heifer pasture on the Floyd Tilley property.

I believe this house has been struck twice, but that was before my time. I do remember seeing a lighting bolt come down on the hill when I was driving up from Laurens. When I arrived home I discovered a tree in the front of the house had been struck. A bird house on the clothes line between the tree and the porch had exploded completely melting the inner core but scattering pieces of plastic string all over the lawn. Merton had been starting for a field below the lawn when he decided the storm was close and started for the house but he was in the driveway when the tree was hit. He had on rubber boots and whether this made any difference or not, he didn't get any shock. The dog who had been with him was never the same again. The thermostat on the electric stove was blown so the oven was on full. A cow in the Pupputti pasture some distance down the hill was found dead near the fence. We wonder if the same strike bad followed the fence down the hill to their pasture.

A few years later I saw out the kitchen window a lighting bolt come down in our pasture where the cows were likely to be after milking. The next morning a dead cow was found there.

In the 1950's the barn on the Cornell farm was struck. A tractor and bull were in the basement and were saved. The upper level was burned but the basement received little damage. A new barn was built on the same foundation.

Winter has always been a challenge to the residents of Bowe Hill. Until the present generation of people to live here the residents were able to cope. There were horses to get you out or you stayed put. The wood fires kept you warm and cooked your meals and the kerosene lamps and lanterns provided light. You drove over the snow and it became thoroughly packed until spring thaw. With the coming of the high line in 1944 things changed although many farms had electric generators for lights and milking machines. The Delco plant had a generator and storage batteries.

Until fairly recent years, the snowplow of Laurens came to the Homestead. The Milford plow went to the Arnold's Lake road and we in the town of Hartwick had to wait to get plowed out hoping that when we could get out Laurens had plowed. In the winter of 1957-58, we were again blocked waiting for the Linn. One or more of these times I remember Merton leaving his car to carry school children at the Homestead and walking back in near zero weather.

In the 1958 winter, I remember a very large drift in the road in front of Raymond Miller's. I was walking on the drift when one leg went down the full length without touching the road. I wondered if I would sink out of sight, but I managed to lie down on the drift and crawl out. Needless to say, I have never walked on deep drifts since.

In the winter of 1970-71, there was a heavy snowfall and wind to make huge drifts. The town of Hartwick brought a bulldozer to open the road at the end of the driveway. I couldn't see out of the window when sitting down.

In the early years, many families had a Model T that they drove until winter and then put it up until spring. Remember, when spring came there was mud and your car could get stuck. I have heard of people driving a lumber wagon to make tracks for the car. Model T's had tires about the same width as the wagons.

If you started with your car, you were lucky if you didn't have to change a tire. The tire had to come off the rim. Probably the tube had to be patched. When all was back together, you had a hand pump to inflate the tire.

If it began to rain, there were side curtains to be fastened. If you drove in cold weather, you kept the side curtains on. In the summer, the top could be put down. If a shower came up it might be over before the top was up and the side curtains on.

My mother learned to drive our first Model T in about 1919 and continued driving cars until her death. Of course, some people thought she was crazy to drive.

I can remember running out of gas on a hill. If you were lucky you could blow in the gas tank and get enough gas to get you to the top.

Model T's sometimes had a mind of their own. I remember once when instead of crossing the railroad tracks the car followed up the track. Luckily no trolleys came along and we got back on the road.

From the crest of the hill, there is a very pleasing view of Otego Valley and hills to the west. It is a place to see very beautiful sunsets. Also it is a good place to watch thunderstorms coming. Sometimes it may be an hour before the storm hits and sometimes they will go north or south and we see very little rain. This was most frustrating in a very dry year when we could see storms going around us.

We would also watch some beautiful sunrises and the full moon over the east hill.

When horses and cutters or babs were the only means of transportation, people didn't stay at home. They bundled up with plush or fur robes and coats. Soapstones were heated on the stoves and then wrapped in paper or cloth and put on the floor to keep their feet warm. I have several soapstones. They make good hot plates to keep casseroles warm.

Lynn, who now lives in Texas, says he wouldn't mind living here in the winter if he didn't have to get out to clean barn and milk cows. It isn't bad when you can sit by a warm fire and watch the snow pile up.

Winter 1993 was a very mild winter until about the middle of January when it changed. We had some snow and then freezing rain that made very thick ice. The ice trough on the garage was filled with snow then ice. One section finally gave up and came crashing down. The ice broke into chunks about the size of bricks.

We next had storms bringing about 3" to 6" at a time, but the temperature was too cold for any melting and then wind put the snow in drifts. In February there were thirteen days when the temperature was below zero in the morning. There were many days when the wind averaged from about 25 to 35 miles per hour. There was one gust at 55 miles per hour.

We would just nicely get things opened when we would have another snowfall followed by high wind. Several days I had to shovel my way out the back door, and the greenhouse door had snow about two feet up the glass. As of March 5th (my birthday) the snow banks have been piled so that only the dog can climb over to get to the barn. Back and front of the house the drifts look like giant whales. I can't get to the meter pole to read the numbers but by standing in front of a garage window, I can read the meter with field glasses. This is due the fifteenth of the month.

It is different now from what it was in the 40's and 50's. The town has big plows and Hartwick does the hill and over the Arnold's Lake road. Perrys live down the hill so the plows go past the house and turn around at their driveway. After they plow and sand, the roads are usually bare, except for drifts, until the next storm.

Two of our biggest storms came out of the east, which piled the snow up in front of the house, and in the driveway. The storms from the west don't hit the front of the house.

Beginning in November of 1995, we began getting snowstorms. The storms kept coming and the temperature stayed below freezing so there was very little melting. Roy ploughed the driveway with his pick-up truck. The piles were very high around the area in front of the garage. Duane finally used my snow blower and a pick and shovel and made an opening in the banks so he could push the snow toward the barn. With lights on at night, I couldn't see on the other side of the banks. It was like the Grand Canyon.

In January, the weather warmed up and the snow began to melt and it started raining. On Tuesday the temperature was zero on Wednesday it was thirty-five, on Thursday 41 and 54 on Friday. On Saturday, the temperature went down and there was ice. Ordinarily my sump pump can take care of water in the cellar but with the snow on the roof, melting on the big piles plus the rain my cellar began to fill. The Mt. Vision firemen came up and pumped it down enough so it didn't get too high again. I think I was about the first to be pumped but soon everyone needed pumping. I wondered how many times the water pumped from my cellar had to be pumped out. The pond overflowed so there were streams of water going down the hill. The town had put in a new tube under the road and had taken out so much dirt that all of the water on this side flowed through under the road. The only washing of the road was from melting snow that plows had piled up on the side of the road. The pond, which was well stocked with large mouth bass before the flood, had almost no fish in 1996.

Everything was so saturated and there was so much rain that planting was delayed. Lynn had tilled my garden patch in the fall so I stood on the grass on the edge and planted my peas in the mud. They did very well.

We seemed to have summer one day at a time without ever having the hot weather.

On The 30th of July, 1996, we were hit with another freak storm. It began as a thundershower and then turned to fine hail, about the size of rock salt. The wind was up to 50 miles and the hail was too thick to see out. It lasted about fifteen or twenty minutes.

Half of the milk house roof rolled up and on the ground. The main part of the basswood tree south and west of the house went down.

The leaves on the tomatoes, cucumbers, and zucchini were stripped and shredded. Any tomatoes not under other foliage were pitted. The leaves were studded and the leaves were stripped off the corn.

One week after Memorial Day weekend in 1998 this area was hit by a tornado. We lost some oaks in the woods. There were stripes of blow downs.

The most damage was to the light lines. The REA line in the Dutch Hill area was blocked by fallen trees. We had no power from Sunday until Tuesday. The barn foundation was moved. The reforested area was hit hard and in 1999 work crews were hauling out the down trees.

_____

By: Barb Potter

Morrell Smith

Morrell Smith House

Morell Smith was a farmer who lived for many years on a farm in South Hartwick that is currently known as the Grigsby farm.

Mr. Smith kept a daily record that spans the years from 1871 until his death in 1914. His writing was brevity itself usually consisting of 4 or 5 lines, or on occasion a single terse word. However, on reading the diaries one can get a picture of the daily life of a local farmer before the advent of the automobile, telephone, radio, etc..

He and wife Asenath (called Senie) were born and raised in the area. Morell was the son of Caleb and Harriet (King) Smith, and Senie was the daughter of Thomas and Armilla (Carr) Clark. Thomas Clark was the builder of the house where the Kennedy family lives. Morell had a sister, Rosaltha, who lived some distance away. Senie had two sisters, Mary who married Thomas Beach and lived in Hartwick and Lydia who married Fenimore Whipple and lived in Pierstown. They visited back and forth the year around. They visited family and friends all over the county traveling by horse and carriage or sleigh, leaving the farm in the care of a hired man. Just as frequently they opened their home to friends and family for two or three day visits.

Morell made almost daily trips by horse drawn conveyance to Hartwick and Jacksonville (Mount Vision), sometimes traveling to both villages in one day.

They rarely stayed home because of weather, but merely remarked about the bitter cold, terrible mud, or stifling heat.

Roads were kept open, if possible, and in repair mostly by the people whose property it bordered.

Sunday was go to meeting day usually at Jacksonville but also to Hartwick, and New Lisbon. Sunday School picnics were often held in Job Card's woods, the Grove at Hartwick, and Three-Mile Point on Cooperstown Lake.

Occasionally church service was held in the South Hartwick schoolhouse. The schoolhouse served not only as the school, but as a meeting-house for community activities.

Uncle and aunt must have been used as a term of respect for elderly people as Morell referred to literally dozens of people as Uncle or Great Uncle or Great Aunt.

Grief was met stoically, just brief entries were noted when Morell's only sister died tragically, or of the untimely death of Lydia and Fen's eighteen year old daughter.

Christmas was usually kept with Fen and Lydia, and Tommy and Mary.

Life followed a pattern, just as the seasons followed a pattern year in and year out.

The following are excerpts from his diaries,

1871

July 8—T. Beach comes along to go afishing go up CatTown get enough for two meals.

Aug. 18—Went over on the commons a berrying Senie and I got 40 quarts of blackberries.

Aug 25— Go to Jacksonville to a ball play at Jacksonville.

Aug. 30—Get a new carriage.

1871

Oct. 5—Finish digging potatoes have 175 bushels in the cellar.

Oct.7—Go to Hartwick to see two horses run.

Oct. 12—Have a husking in the eve husk 42 bushels.

Oct. 20—Done husking have 121 baskets good corn 45 poor.

Oct. 21—Went to Cooperstown attend a circus and menagerie.

1872

Jan. 13—Been no snow in four weeks.

Jan. 18——Been good wheeling for six weeks. Ground froze like a rock.

Feb. 4—Snow a foot deep, first snow of any amount in six weeks.

Feb. 20—Went to Norwich. Go by the Lyon Creek Bridge. A great work of art.

March 14—Scald sap buckets draw them to the woods.

March 27—Hoop some buckets.

March 30—Trim some apple trees in the morn finish tapping sugar bush in afternoon.

APRIL 9—Put up sleighs & get out wagons.

April 20—Boil sap bring down six pails of syrup tired at night.

April 25—Wash and put sap buckets up. warm & pleasant.

June 12—Hoe in garden in morn. Have rain in afternoon & big hailstorm doing a good deal of damage to crops & also window glass. Stones fell that measured 9 in. The oldest inhabitants say they never saw the like.

July 5—Ash corn and potatoes.

Aug. 6—Cradle oats

Aug. 28—Thresh 206 bushel oats

Oct. 2—Husk corn 175 bushels from less than 2 acres.

Nov. 10—Great horse epidemic

Nov. 17—Nearly all horses sick

Nov. 23 —Not much traveling on account horse disease

1874
Oct. 15—Gather apples probably 200 bushel

Oct. 17—Make cider 15½ barrels

Nov. 19—Dig ditch, kill turkey, clean well

1875
March 2—Horse distemper

March 7—Dr.Bishop for horse

March 13— Horse dies

March 14— Bury horse

April 27— Go get horse

July 15—Horse sick

July 16——Dr. Bishop up most of night with horse

July 17 — Horse better

1877
May 14—Hot and dry Pine Hill burning

Sept. 14—Temp 104 in the sun

Dec. 21—Never saw so warm a December

Dec. 27—Continues warm people plowing

1878
Jan. 13—Some go in sleighs, some in wagons

April 22—Put in 150 grafts

April 23—Grub hops 4" high

April 27—Finish grubbing foot high

May 7—Twine hops

May—Tie hops

June 12—Train hops on twine forenoon cultivate hops afternoon

June 26—fertilize hops

June 27, 28, 29—Hoe hops, Hoe corn, hoe potatoes

Aug. 28—Commence hop picking

Aug 29, 30, 31 Picking hops take load to kill

Sept. 2—Finish picking have 93 boxes

Oct. 7 Press hops

Oct. 8 Go to Christian church dedication

Oct.11—Stack hop poles have some to sharpen

Oct. 15—Manure hop yard and burn vines

Nov. 29——Go to Cooperstown and sell hops for 12½¢ per pound have 1449 lbs.

1879
Jan. 3—Do chores and sit by the fire

Jan. 14—Go to Cooperstown get a suit of clothes

April 24——-Have made 800 lbs. of sugar in 2 weeks

June 12 & 13—Work on road

Aug. 4—Mow road and cut brush

Dec. 1—Drawn as juror

Dec. 2, 3,—In court room all day

Dec. 4——Drawn on a jury just at night

Dec. 5—Sit a juror

Dec. 6 —Court ends at noon, Come home on foot roads muddy.

1881
April 7—Go to school house in afternoon to see carpenter about repairing it.

Sept. 19—President Garfield died today.

Oct. 12—Go to Hartwick after paint for schoolhouse.

Nov. 5—Go to Cooperstown for school house desks.

1882
March 31—Attend an oyster supper at the Grand Templars lodge room.

Dec. 27 Work at the water. Get it to running—has not run in the house since last August. Longest drought in years.

Dec. 30—Go rabbit hunting in the owl patch.

1889
Jan. 2—Hartwick people talking about railroad now.

March 28—Attend a railroad meeting at Jacksonville.

Sept. 24—Go to the Cooperstown Fair. Nice day. A man goes up in a balloon comes down in the lake and is drowned.

1900
Dec. 19—A. Carr and I go to Jacksonville to see about Right-of way for the railroad.
1901—Go to Oneonta by rail. The first passenger train from Hartwick.

With the coming of the trolley line through Hartwick and South Hartwick many changes were to take place in the area, and brought great changes in the simple country life of farmers such as Morell Smith. The Smith diaries were to continue until 1914 when he passed away at the age of 70.

———

By: N.P.

The two Buffalo Bills: Bill Mathewson and Bill Cody.
Cut from a Hearst magazine around September 1926.
See Tidbits, *p.405*

Tidbits

The following items were all taken from different newspapers that were in publication at different times. They are of all kinds of things that happened within different time frames. I have picked them randomly just because some are very funny and some are very interesting. This shows just how times have changed in reporting the news.

Otsego Herald, April 13, 1797
FOR SALE

Five valuable lots of land, lying on the Hartwick Patent, three of which consist of one hundred acres each, two of them in a state of nature, the other has two log houses, and thirty-two acres under improvement. The other two contain, one of them seventy, the other eighty acres, one no improvements, the other a log house and four acres cleared. For further particulars, enquire of the subscribers, living on the Otego Valley indisputable title and good chance of payment.

Nijah Griffith
Joseph Mass

Otsego Herald, January 20, 1810
p3, c3- A POCKET BOOK LOST

Lost in or near the village of Otsego, on the 6th inst., containing a set of Surgeon's Pocket-Instruments and a number of notes of hand, payable to subscriber.., generous reward, & c. . .Hartwick, Jan. 16, 1810 Nathaniel Gott

Otsego Herald, July 14, 1810

p3, c1-The season has been much colder than usual in Otsego, but not so much as to cause the farmers to lose sight of his waving crops. Wheat, we understand, will yield but an ordinary crop—the summer crops appear promising and the summer and winter Rye we dare predict a sufficiency for the manufacture of whisky for the county of Otsego, should none of that delicious beverage be exported out of the county. We rejoice to see so many engaged in manufacturing their own cloth; it has a savor of independance, and augers well in our present standing with England and France...

Otsego Herald, September 4, 1817

p3, c1-Note: newly organized Otsego County Agricultural Society has standing committees in each town—In Hartwick it is made up of Stukly Ellsworth, the Democratic political leader, in charge of "Tillage;" Jerome Clark, "Domestic Animals;" William A. Boyde, "Manufactures."

Taken from Historical Scrapbooks-Dated 1832

The old "Fields store", opposite the more westerly tavern site, is said to have been built by the Bostwicks in about 1824; or not far from the same time that James, father of Mott Mead, removed from Oxford to Laurens.

Plain wooden coffins, without cloth or trimmings, were commonly used in central Otsego

County for the burial of its dead, as late as 1835.

Watchtower. November 5, 1827
Whereas my wife Abigail Alger, has from time to time run me in debt without my knowledge or consent. This is to forbid all persons harboring or trusting her hereafter on my account as I will pay no debt by her contracted after this date.
Josiah Alger- Hartwick

Otsego Republican, March 19, 1832
Hartwick Brewery- Sold out

Otsego Republican, March 19, 1832
Brewing Utensils & Co.—The subscriber's lease of the Hartwick Brewery being about to expire on the first day of April next, he offers for sale his Brewing Utensils, consisting of a copper kettle, holding 24 barrels, a Malt Mill worked by horse power, Vats, Tubs, Coolers, and Barrels. Also his horses, wagons, sleighs, and harnesses.

The present affords a highly favorable opportunity for any person desires of embarking his capital in a Brewery; for as the subscriber is declining business (being about to return to England) the purchaser would most probably succeed to his Beer trade which has been for some years the most flourishing in this country. Besides the brewing, any person now embarking in business would owing to the number of distilleries in the county, be able to carry on an extensive trade in Rye, Barley and Malt. Barley and Hops are raised in great abundance in this county and the farmer is seldom paid higher than 50 cents per bu.

The above property, if not disposed of by private contract, will with the subscriber's household furniture, be sold at public auction on Wed. the 29th of March.
Robert Edmenton

Freemans Journal, October 14, 1833
Temperance House
The Subscriber having recently opened a Public House, in Todd's Ville, Hartwick, Otsego County, under the above title, gives notice that he will at all times be happy to accommodate a Temperate Public, with such refreshments for man and beast as the county affords. Those wishing to use other spirits in a temperate and discretionary manner can be accommodated. Good stabling, hay and oats for the beasts, and comfortable fare for the guest, furnished at all times. Public patronage is solicited; and the proprietor pledges himself by unrelenting exertions, to please a generous public.
Nathan Fisk
Todd's Ville, September 9, 1833

Freeman's Journal, November 23, 1835
This will inform the public that I have a few goods on hand, and will sell them as low as they are sold in the place commonly called Cooperstown—and will receive in payment Butter, Cheese, Wheat, Rye, Corn, Oats, Pork, Tallow, Lard and other articles too numerous to mention.

The highest market price in cash will be paid for Flax seed.
L. Harrington West Hartwick, Nov. 11, 1835

Freeman's Journal, August 27, 1838
NEW GOODS! NEW GOODS!
Harrington & Rose
At the old stand of L. Harrington, at West Hartwick, are daily receiving from New York, a new and splendid assortment of Dry Goods, Groceries, Crockery, Hardware, Nails, Glass & etc. all of which they offer for sale at reduced prices. They very respectfully invite the public to call and examine for themselves.
West Hartwick, Aug. 8, 1838

<u>Freeman's Journal, April 12. 1838</u>
Doctor Peck would inform his friends and the public that the practice of Dental Surgery in all its varieties, will still be continued by him at his office, in West Hartwick. He manufactures the improved Incorruptible Porcelain Teeth, which for their natural appearance, Beauty and durability are not surpassed by any. Natural teeth will be cleaned and filled with Gold, in a perfect and serviceable manner. Artificial teeth inserted, from one to entire sets. Ladies, gentlemen and families attended at their residence, if requested by letter or otherwise.

<u>Taken From Scrapbook
in The Historical Society</u>
George M. Sternberg 1838-19 15, Physician bacteriologist, epidemeoinary, born in Hartwick, Hartwick Seminary, College of Physicians and surgeons, NYC 1860; Civil War surgeon. Surgeon general US Army, 1893-1902. Wrote over 150 books reports and articles.

Marvin L. Disley was a miller in Hartwick around 1855.

Chester L. Harrington was a store keeper in his native Hartwick.

Frederick T. Jarvis native of Hartwick and party of eight left Feb. 18, 1850 in a lumber wagon inscribed "Bound for California" and drawn by four horses. They completed the journey in 88 days.

Samuel Wilson helped keep the first store in Hartwick 1792-1807.

<u>Oneonta Herald, November 17, 1869</u>
Benjamin Culter of Hartwick was oldest voter in Otsego County. He was 100 years old on November 9. It was the 78th time he had voted.

<u>The Herald</u>
Old-Time Winters in Hartwick
The Herald's Hartwick correspondent says: Isaac Bradley, who is now 81 years old, says that in 1842 snow came two feet deep the second day of November and remained on the ground all winter. The 17th of the next April he drew the sap buckets into the woods on a hand sled, as he could not get in the woods with a team. Hay that year was $30 per ton. The place where he then lived is about one and one half miles south of the village, and is now owned by E. Rockwell. The farm until recent years had been in the Bradley family for a very long time, Isaac Bradley's father having been born there. I have often heard his father tell of hearing the wild beasts around the log house when he was a boy— more than 100 years ago.

<u>Oneonta Herald, September 8, 1870</u>
There was a notice about hitching horses to trees:
"Horseman, Spare that tree!
'Tis not a hitching post,
Though in its infancy,
it soon would shade a host;
Then spare, oh! spare that tree-
For He who placed it there
Meant not that it should be
By beast of thine knawed bare.

<u>Oneonta Herald, March 7. 1872</u>
A new Jail was built in Hartwick.

<u>Oneonta Herald, April 17, 1872</u>
"A few years ago, a dog collar was picked up in a field on Elisha Field's farm. It was made of brass: 12 1/4 inch long and 1 inch wide; edges turned over a small wire. At one end there were two holes, where there had evidently been an iron staple, long since rusted out or loosened; on

the opposite end were three slots, corresponding in length to the distance between the holes. Engraved on the collar was: "JOHN SLATER, HIS DOG-ALBANY, MARCH 27, 1757."

Oneonta Herald & Democrat, January 3, 1878

Arthur J. Telfer, a student of our school yet in his teens, has a crayon picture of the Rev. Mr. Scott, of Garrettsville, on exhibition at the store of F. H. Robinson in this village, which is really worth the commendation of a critic.

Oneonta Herald & Democrat, January 20, 1879

The Temperance Union of this village has organized a Lyceum. The question, "Should the right of suffrage be extended to women?"

Oneonata Herald & Democrat, January 24, 1879

If the citizens of Cooperstown and Oneonta are unable to agree as to the location of the new courthouse we suggest that they leave it to Hartwick to decide it being the center of the county.

Oneonta Herald & Democrat, October 27, 1879

F.H. Robinson and S. D. Williams are making quite extensive preparations to supply a portion of our village with running water taken from a spring on East Hill, with a fall of nearly two hundred feet. It is said to be of a never failing capacity.

Freeman's Journal, March 5, 1897

Horse Race on Streets of Hartwick

Horse racing on the streets of Hartwick and also Horse trading. Fred Holbrook was thrown from his horse and up against the Sergent Store, he was picked up insensible but recovered with out serious injury. Many voiced their opinion that horse racing on the streets should be stopped.

The Hartwick Visitor, May 22, 1902

Croquet seems to be one of the pastimes of village young ladies and their friends at Brownell park lawn.

We were recently shown two eggs that were brought in one night from a poultryman's hennery. One measured 7 1/2 by 6 1/2 inches and another 7 1/2 by 6 inches.

The Hartwick Visitor, September 5, 1916

Silent Policeman ordered at the four corners.

Freeman's Journal, February 20, 1924

Radio, is first, last and all the time in our little village at the present time. Some get so interested they almost forget to go to bed. It is a problem to figure out what will come next for entertainment.

Freeman's Journal, April 2, 1924

The Hartwick National bank will soon begin the installation of a modern fireproof vault, the door weighing twelve tons and the heavy steel lining weighing 32 tons are the main points of the new vault. A number of deposit boxes will be placed at the service of the public at a small rental. The work will be under the supervision of the Diebol Safe and Lock Company.

Freeman's Journal, April 16, 1924

NEW LAW SAYS EVERY AUTO DRIVER MUST HAVE LICENSE

All person whomsoever operate motor vehicles are required to have licenses. The term "operator" means any person other than a chauffeur who operates or drives a motor vehicle. Such person must secure a license on or before October 1st of the present year.

The Hartwick Visitor, July 5, 1938

Women eligible for jury duty, but may claim exemption.

Freeman's Journal, April 4, 1947
Mrs. Minnie Mead is the proud possessor of a New Deluxe "Nash" car.

From loose Scrapbook—Nadine Phillips
Finish Line To South Hartwick
Residents of South Hartwick, Jones Crossing and Pleasant Valley had the pleasure of turning on electric lights in their homes for the first time Tuesday Evening—Miss Marion Matteson, put away the kerosene lamps in the post office. Mrs. Belle Sherman, former postmistress, who led in asking for the line.

Past Letters from Hartwick Historical Society
South Hartwick—On Thursday of last week about noon the ties and rails were laid to this village. The people began gathering some time before noon with their baskets of provisions for the workmen. About one o'clock the signal was given to quit work and then the feast began. Over one hundred men were fed. They also made away with a 40 gal. can of lemonade. Quite a large supply of provisions was left and this was given to graders in the Conley house.

Otsego Farmer July 7, 1901
"William Mathewson gave William Cody the permission to use his name of "Buffalo Bill." William Mathewson was a first cousin of Mrs. Faith Buechner's grandmother. (Mrs. Buechner is a member of our Historical Society). In 1857, William Mathewson worked as a farm hand for Lyscom Perkins, his cousin's husband. About that time he married one of the daughters of William Clinton, owner of the cotton mill at Clintonville. They had a daughter Jenny and shortly after the old scoundrel pulled up stakes. Eventually 'Bill' arrived out west and hired himself out to one of the railroad construction companies as a meat supplier (buffalo variety). That's how he first became known as "Buffalo Bill." After he had become famous he met up with Bill Cody-an upstart who wanted to form a wild west show with him using the name of Buffalo Bill. William Mathewson was either contemplating remarrying for money or already had, so the proposition held little interest for him, however he gave Cody permission to have all rights to his name if he wanted to go into the show business. Mathewson eventually became a banker in Witchita. A picture of the two Buffalo Bills will be placed in the notebook on Clintonville for the Society.

Samuel Morris and wife recently married, moved into their log cabin on Christian Hill, Hartwick patent in 1793, where Mrs. Morris soon afterwards opened a private school this being one of the first schools in what was later the Town of Hartwick.

FOLK LORE FROM HARTWICK

The Adams family off to Town
Mr. Adams drove a team of lively colts from Pleasant Valley (near South Hartwick) into Cooperstown. When they entered the village he touched the whip to the spirited team. Be it known, that the women folks 'were riding in back on an antique chair-seat. This was similar to a couple of ladder-hack chairs built together. The steeds gave a quick jump and the seat rocked and reeled, both women landed on their backs in the rear end of the wagon.
"Didn't the Adams team cut quite a figure?" boasted the proud driver,
"I don't know about the team, but we women cut quite a figure," said Sylvia as she untangled her feet from the chair legs.

A Fast Walker
Mrs. Phillips was walking from her Hinman Hollow home to Milford, a distant of four or

five miles. A neighbor overtook her and asked if she would like to ride in his wagon. "No" was her reply, "I am in a hurry."

Cleaning the Mixing Bowl

This legend came down from the Maples family. In pioneer days there was a thrifty young man who went out to find a wife. All the young ladies on whom he called were making bread. The first one left lots of dough on the sides of the mixing bowl. So he left immediately and called on another girl in the neighborhood. She also wasted some dough, though not as much as the first lady did. The third young lady mixed bread and cleaned every bit of batter from the pan. She became his wife.

Ham and Eggs

A poor farmer in pioneer days hired a man to cut his grain with a sickle. The farmer could not afford expensive food, so he fed his help on plain corn bread and cornmeal mush. The farm hand just dragged around the field. One day they had ham and eggs for dinner. Then the fussy workman hastened around the field singing "Ham and eggs, ham and eggs, get out the way; or I mow off your legs."

A cure for Decayed Fruit Trees

It is said that Jedediah Ashcraft went to Coopersotwn in 1815 and bought some pears. He planted the seeds. When the trees became old he sought a cure for the decaying trunks. A neighbor told him to pour some whiskey on them. His reply was "I would rather pour some of it down me." These pear trees are still standing on the farm of Fred Field.

Struck by Lightning

Years ago there was a small house near the waterfalls on what is now the Schneider farm (route 205). The ancient well is all that remains to mark the spot. One summer day some women were having a quilting bee in the front room. A severe thunderstorm came up, so they huddled together in great fear.

After the storm abated, they went to the kitchen to see if any damage had been done, They were horrified to see the man of the house sitting by the back door—dead—as he had been struck by lightning.

Several miles across the hills to the east, there is an epitaph on a tombstone which reads:

"Samuel Whaley, here he lies

Called by a mandate from the skies. The messenger was lightning red Electric fluid killed him dead."

(Cemetery on the Gerald Bush farm)

Hartwick, New York
September 1972

Dear Fellow Hartwickians,

I am sure that all of us are aware that 1972 is an election year and as we watch TV we are constantly reminded that this is a year of decision. How true this is, if we are to maintain our great American, heritage which the founders of our country established for us, it is our duty to get out and vote and to urge others to do the same. As we draw nearer to the Bi-Centennial year, I think we realize more and more how much our forefathers sacrificed in creating the greatest form of government that the world has ever known. Let us do our share in keeping our government great by getting out and voting, for whomever we feel best qualified to keep our heritage as we would like it. Surely our privilege to choose our own leaders in our local, county, state and national governments is one of our most treasured heritages we enjoy today. Let us keep it that way by getting out to vote. Through out our history various groups have conducted polls which indicated, quite accurately, the peoples' choice months before the elections. Hartwick had their own poll 140 years ago which was published in the Freeman's Journal of October 29, 1832 and I quote—"A significant Sign: At a squirrel hunt recently had at Toddsville (Hartwick) of which Joseph Robinson, 2nd and Anson Richardson were captains, a vote was taken on the presidential question, which stood 20 for Jackson and 2 for Wirt, counting only qualified voters. The coalition ought to be on the lookout otherwise Hartwick, one of their strongholds, will go on the board. The young men are warmhearted, patriotic, therefore they go for Old Hickory, who saved the "beauty and booty" of New Orleans.

See you October 4th at our next meeting and AUCTION—BRING ALL YOUR FRIENDS.

Kenneth Augur
President

———

By: Barbara Potter

WCTU Picnic

CPSIA information can be obtained
at www.ICGtesting.com
Printed in the USA
LVOW05s1918090717
540744LV00003BA/357/P

9 780970 943309